Legacy of the YOSEMITE MAFIA

THE RANGER IMAGE AND NOBLE CAUSE CORRUPTION IN THE NATIONAL PARK SERVICE

Paul D. Berkowitz

Foreword by J.T. Reynolds

LEGACY OF THE YOSEMITE MAFIA: THE RANGER IMAGE AND NOBLE CAUSE CORRUPTION IN THE NATIONAL PARK SERVICE
COPYRIGHT © 2017 PAUL D. BERKOWITZ

Published by:
Trine Day LLC
PO Box 577
Walterville, OR 97489
1-800-556-2012
www.TrineDay.com
publisher@TrineDay.net

Library of Congress Control Number: 2017936716

Berkowitz, Paul D.
–1st ed.
p. cm.

Epud (ISBN-13) 978-1-63424-127-4
Mobi (ISBN-13) 978-1-63424-128-1
Print (ISBN-13) 978-1-63424-126-7
1. United States. -- National Park Service -- History -- 20th century. 2. Park rangers -- Violence against -- United States. 3. Law enforcement -- Moral and ethical aspects -- United States. 4.United States -- Politics and government. I. Berkowitz, Paul D. II. Title

FIRST EDITION
10 9 8 7 6 5 4 3 2 1

Printed in the USA
Distribution to the Trade by:
Independent Publishers Group (IPG)
814 North Franklin Street
Chicago, Illinois 60610
312.337.0747
www.ipgbook.com

To
Andy Hutchison and Wes Kreis
Unsung heroes
who fought to bring professionalism to the
Rangers of the National Park Service.
I am honored to call them my friends

And to the many extraordinary former rangers and special agents
who left the NPS for opportunities elsewhere.
Your departure was a loss for the National Park Service

TABLE OF CONTENTS

Foreword vii

Acknowledgments x

Prologue 1

Introduction 3

PART ONE

Chapter One: Hidden History (Myth-busting) 11

Chapter Two: Public Lands – Protected Places 19

Chapter Three: A Tale of Transition..36

Chapter Four: Parklands Reclaimed 41

PART TWO

Chapter Five: A Foot in the Door (Indiana Dunes)..61

Chapter Six: Paradise (Yosemite) 74

Chapter Seven: Seeds of a Legacy (The Ranger Image) 83

Chapter Eight: Trouble in Paradise 111

Chapter Nine: Technicalities 120

Chapter Ten: Eavesdropping 127

Chapter Eleven: System Failure 130

Chapter Twelve: Fallout... 143

Chapter Thirteen: Troublemaker.. 146

Chapter Fourteen: The G.A.O. ("Objective, Fair, and Balanced") 160

Chapter Fifteen: A Certifiable Cover-up.. 178

Chapter Sixteen: Outrage and Defiance 180

Chapter Seventeen: Double Cover (The O.I.G. Covers Its Tracks) 187

PART THREE

Chapter Eighteen: Noble Cause Corruption... 205

Chapter Nineteen: Unjust Rewards.. 219

Chapter Twenty: The Price of a Legacy 228

Chapter Twenty-One: Lessons Not Learned (The Legacy Lives On) 236

Chapter Twenty-Two: A New Legacy (A Call to Action) 257

Appendix: Testimony of Paul Berkowitz.. 263

Index... 272

FOREWORD

I spent 38 years working for the National Park Service (NPS). I was one of a group of young men and women recruited in the early 1970s to help the NPS confront the challenges it faced in the wake of changing and turbulent times and the concurrent rise of the environmental movement; an ever-changing and evolving partnership for protecting "Mother Earth." Graduating from the agency's own Introduction to Park Operations training program (predecessor to the Ranger Skills program) and then the Las Vegas Metropolitan Police Academy, I was selected for an assignment at Yosemite National Park, where riots just two years earlier had shaken the agency and the image it tries to project to the public about its rangers. By virtue of the time and place of my assignment and the people I worked with, I became an original member of the group of NPS employees known as the Yosemite Mafia.

I am proud of the uniform I wore and the work that I did in the NPS. Even in retirement, I am actively committed to the cause of national parks and resource protection. Throughout my career I worked with many extraordinary people who I genuinely respect and admire; people who taught me, mentored me, and supported me as I rose through the ranks from patrol ranger, to instructor, to regional chief ranger, and finally superintendent of the largest national park in the lower 48 states. Many of the good people I worked with as supervisors and colleagues – fellow members of the Yosemite Mafia – remain my close friends to this day. But I'm not blind and I'm not naive, and I'm not afraid or too proud to acknowledge the disturbing truth of what retired special agent and award-winning author Paul Berkowitz has written in this book and elsewhere about the NPS and the Yosemite Mafia. His descriptions and his assessments are both spot-on.

I already knew, or at least suspected, many of the things that Berkowitz exposes and talks about in this book. There is no denying that throughout my own career I, too, encountered far too many people and practices that were deeply troubling and should never have been tolerated, much less rewarded and embraced. But while I was a witness to some of the types of things Berkowitz describes, I never fully comprehended the magnitude of the problem and how deeply rooted and tolerated those problems are in the NPS culture. In writing *Legacy of the Yosemite Mafia - The Ranger Image and Noble Cause Corruption in the National Park Service*, Berkowitz has opened even my seasoned eyes, and has helped to shine a light and focus on the historic roots of these problems; demonstrating in graphic terms how these people and practices continue to damage and degrade the NPS and its mission, to this day.

Though I had certainly heard stories about Berkowitz, I did not actually meet him until 1997, when I arrived at the Grand Canyon as that park's new deputy superintendent. Berkowitz had arrived a year or two before me, transferring in from the Washington Office to take charge of criminal investigations and other law enforcement operations in the park. All I "knew" about him was based on his reputation in the NPS as a hard-ass cop and a troublemaker who was somehow responsible for the superintendent in Yosemite getting fired back in the mid-1980s – something to do with an illegal bugging and other criminal activity. The NPS rumors made it sound like Berkowitz was somehow behind the entire affair; a dangerous character, disloyal and not to be trusted; overbearing, and out of control.

It was my practice to have a sit-down, face-to-face meeting with every member of my new staff, to get to know them and size them up for myself. That included Berkowitz. That meeting went on far longer than we had scheduled. There, and in our subsequent interactions, I came to realize that Berkowitz was not the dangerous, hard-ass cop I had been led to believe, but a smart, perceptive, honest, straight-shooting employee who believed passionately in both professional law enforcement and in the national parks; a man of integrity who was deeply committed to somehow improving and professionalizing the NPS law enforcement program. Having seen the sad state of law enforcement in the segregated south where I was raised, and then seeing my own share of misconduct and lack of professionalism in the NPS, those were things we could both agree on. That set the stage for a strong working relationship and friendship that has lasted through the years. While Berkowitz and I never did discuss the disturbing accounts and rumors that had been circulated about him and his time in Yosemite, I came to understand that none of those stories were true. The rumors about Berkowitz and his reputation were B.S., fabricated and circulated by people who were themselves dangerous, who both resented and feared him for his honesty and his courage to speak up and confront corruption and other forms of misconduct when he saw it. In the NPS, that certainly did make him a troublemaker, but he was most assuredly none of the other things that he had been labeled. It took this book to open my eyes and provide me with insights about what was really behind the rumors and what had really happened in Yosemite, as if completing the discussion we had during our first meeting(s) at the Grand Canyon, and explaining many of the things I'd heard over the years.

Six years of my NPS career were spent as an instructor at the (NPS) Albright Training Center, located on the south rim of the Grand Canyon.

Among the many topics that we presented to employees were agency history, law, policy, and philosophy. But our courses barely touched on most of the topics presented in this book. We knew and talked about the 1970 Yosemite Riot, but otherwise we didn't know about most of the amazing history of crime, crime fighting, and other conflicts in national parks that Berkowitz has uncovered and written about. Even if we had known, I'm not sure we would have been allowed to present that material, since much of it does not support the ranger image the agency tries to project and, more significantly, it does not put the NPS in the most flattering light. But now, more than thirty years later, there is simply no excuse for this important information to not be included in the curriculum presented to every NPS employee, and especially the agency's supervisors and managers. They need to know what has gone on in the past if they are to avoid a repetition of the mistakes that others before them have made. For that reason, alone, this book should be required reading for every NPS employee.

Many of my NPS friends and former colleagues will not like this book, and they will not understand or appreciate my endorsement of what Berkowitz has to say. So be it. I stand by my endorsement and urge all of those same friends and colleagues to read this book with an open mind and a willingness to challenge their assumptions.

If you have ever visited a national park, or if you simply care about public lands, government, federal law, law enforcement, conservation, or resource protection, then you, too, should read this book. It is meticulously researched, impeccably documented, and extremely well written. It is a page-turner; a real-life drama about crime, conflict, corruption, and cover-up. This is a great book that covers new ground, delving into aspects about the conservation movement and the NPS that have never before been presented or discussed. Prepare to have your eyes opened.

James "JT" Reynolds
National Park Service Superintendent (retired)
Member of the Yosemite Mafia (also retired)

ACKNOWLEDGMENTS

I am indebted to a number of people who in one way or another - whether they know it or not - contributed to the writing of this book. Some reviewed all or portions of drafts of the manuscript, some participated in interviews, some helped me in answering questions and conducting research, and some helped by simply talking with me, discussing ideas, and stimulating thoughts about issues I've attempted to address. A hearty 'thank you' to all of these people who are listed below in alphabetical order. Sincerest apologies to any others I've failed to mention.

Scott Bales, Frank Buono, Brian Castaldi, R. McGreggor "Greg" Cawley, Dwayne Collier, Colleen Curry, Charles W. Cushman, Chuck Cushman, George Durkee, Ward Eldredge, B.J. Ellis, Reed Engle, Phyllis Faber, Alan Foster, Melissa Fraser, John Freemuth, Kevin Gilmartin, Peter B. Goldman, Chris Hansen, Melanie Haskell, S. Christy Hauff, Ken Hay, Andy Hutchison, Greg Jackson, Kim Kelly, Randall Kendrick, Wes Kreis, Andrea Lankford, Tomie (Patrick) Lee, Rand Lindsly, Kevin Lunny, Bob Marriott, John McDade, Don Miller, Scott Miller, Dave Montalbano, Carol Moses, Kandace Muller, Jeff Ohlfs, Gary Orozco, Barbara Osteika, Beverly Perry, Chuck Pesta, J.T. Reynolds, Steve Rothlein, Alfred Runte, Fermin Salas, Diana Schmidt, Nancy Stone, J.R. Tomasovic, John Townsend, U.S. Park Ranger Lodge of the Fraternal Order of Police, Stephen Verkamp, Ray Waber, Laura Watt, David Weiman, Clark Whitehorn, Dan Wirth, John Wright, Donna Yamagata

PROLOGUE

"This never happened. Don't ever tell anybody about this."

Now *that* was something I wasn't expecting to hear; not from a fellow officer, and certainly not from one of my own supervisors. But those were Connelly's exact words.

Marshall "Scott" Connelly was a federal law enforcement officer, supervisory ranger, and at least two grades my senior. I couldn't stand the guy. A lot of people felt that way for a lot of good reasons. But he had the full support of the park's Chief of Law Enforcement; he did the chief's bidding; and the chief backed him up and even covered for him. Worse yet, he was the local prosecutor; not a lawyer, but authorized by the U.S. Attorney's Office to present and negotiate criminal cases in the local federal court. I can still remember him telling me – ordering me – to keep my mouth shut about what had just happened. I wasn't even sure what *had* just happened, but those were his exact words – the first thing he said to me after he returned to the van.

"This never happened. Don't ever tell anybody about this."

That confirmed that something was very wrong; even worse than I had realized. Connelly had just returned from the headquarters building, where he turned the tapes over to the superintendent. Connelly had directed me to help conduct the surveillance and monitor the wire for what I figured was just another drug buy. He planted the bug under a table in the superintendent's office. Then we secretly monitored and recorded the entire meeting; a conversation between the superintendent and one or two other people about some of the private lands – or "inholdings" – within the park. It wasn't clear what was going on, but it didn't take long to figure out that it wasn't a drug buy, and it sure as hell wasn't just another surveillance or, for that matter, any other kind of legitimate law enforcement operation. That was confirmed when he took the tapes, went into the building, and handed them over to the superintendent. When Connelly returned to the van, his words confirmed for me that what we were doing was illegal, and I had just been unwittingly dragged into the mess.

INTRODUCTION

Legacy: noun leg·a·cy \ 'le-gə-sē
Something that has come from a predecessor or the past.[1]
Something such as a tradition or problem that exists as a result of something that happened in the past.[2]

American author Wallace Stegner is famously credited with the observation that "National Parks are the best idea we ever had. Absolutely American, absolutely democratic, they reflect us at our best rather than our worst."[3]

But another author, humorist and retired NPS historian P.J. Ryan, has respectfully observed that the U.S. Constitution was a pretty good idea in its own right, and must surely rank somewhere at least slightly higher up on the list of "best ideas" to come out of America.[4] After all, were it not for our living Constitution, there would be no government, democracy, or even national parks as we know them; no system of due process and laws to establish, administer, and protect these unique areas, and certainly no concept of special places that are preserved by and for the benefit of *all* the people, and not merely for the privileged few.[5] Mr. Ryan's rebuttal to Stegner's proclamation is a good reminder of the importance of our constitutional legacy and the preeminent place those precepts occupy in our society. Any confusion or disagreement about which of these is the "better idea" – and over the priority these two "good ideas" should receive – is no small matter, and can have serious impacts on how our government and our government agencies function.

That is the primary focus of this book; an examination of what happens when confused values and misplaced priorities come to be embraced as part of an agency culture; the culture of the National Park Service (NPS). It turns out that even when motivated by genuine loyalty and agency pride, the impacts have been self-destructive and corrupting, contributing to the erosion of public trust and, ultimately, diminished support for national parks and the mission of resource protection. Accordingly, our examination includes an exploration of how the NPS seems to have obsessed over the cultivation – and even the fabrication – of its own public image, often at the expense of proper concern for the fulfillment of its statutory mission and other legal standards, for the safety of the public, and even the safety of its own employees. That strategy has long-enabled the NPS to escape legitimate scrutiny and accountability, and to resist the implementation of reforms that might otherwise bring greater integrity to its operations. Ironically, success in promoting and hiding behind its image, in denying harsh realities, and in covering up many of its more serious problems, has also served to constrain the NPS, keeping it from becoming the uniformly virtuous agency that it claims to be – and could really be.

Still, we Americans have certainly benefited from a legacy of conservation resulting from early and largely successful efforts at the federal level to set aside and preserve many of our nation's significant wild, scenic, cultural, and historic places. And nowhere is this more apparent than in our national parks which, as Stegner suggests, are, themselves, an incredible legacy left to the American people.

The agency charged with responsibility for managing our national parks, the NPS, has by most accounts enjoyed a long history of public support, unique in all of federal government. That has been attained, in large part, through development of what is internally referred to as the "ranger image," based on the iconic front-line employees of the agency who are charged with the duty to "protect the parks from the people; protect the people from the parks; and protect the people from the people."[6] Emphasis on that benign image and that noble cause has historically allowed the NPS to benefit from what is generally considered to be unrivaled good will over the one-hundred years of that agency's existence; an enviable legacy in its own right.

But more than most people might realize, and as I have already hinted, there is another aspect to the NPS legacy that derives from a history of contentious relations with various individuals and groups whose lives have been and continue to be impacted by the establishment and the existence of parks. It turns out that away from the public eye (or at least public consciousness), not everybody – including environmentalists – has always been enamored with the agency.

It's true that some of these conflicts are inherent to the notion of conservation and resource protection, including inevitable disputes between public, private, and commercial interests; disputes over permitted land access and land use and other regulation of activities; and even disputes over ideology regarding the proper role of government. Much has already been written in both academic and partisan circles about the politics surrounding environmental laws and policies. Many of those issues are referenced in this book, and I will periodically offer my own opinions about them. But that is *not* what this book is principally about. Rather, I believe there is a case to made that at least some of this controversy, and especially the ill-will directed at the NPS, could have been (and could still be) avoided, and can be directly traced to some of the people, practices, and attitudes that have been widely embraced and even celebrated within the agency for more than half a century. As a result of events, decisions, and ultimately a culture set in motion decades ago, these same people, practices, and attitudes have left their own legacy that has, in a variety of ways that we will explore, proved to be an impediment to lawful and appropriate efforts toward resource protection and to fulfillment of the NPS mission.

The ethical concerns identified in this book can be a challenge for any agency with law enforcement or regulatory authority. After all, the term "noble cause corruption" originated in criminal justice and public administration circles to identify a previously unacknowledged problem. I hope this book will contribute to the literature in those fields. But many cultural, structural, and other factors have come together over time to make the NPS a unique and more vulnerable organization. To understand why that is the case, it will be helpful in the first several chapters to review the incremental steps in our nation's history comprising the conservation movement that led to the establishment of the NPS in the first place, along with other federal land management agencies.

I am neither an academic historian nor an attorney, and while these preliminary discussions reference both academic and popular literature, they are in no way intended to serve as the final word on the topic. For that, readers may want to directly study the many books and other references that are cited, as well as other research materials available through most university libraries and, increasingly, on-line. The introductory materials that I have presented, including explanations of technical legal issues that draw upon court opinions, are intended to merely acquaint readers with notable historical events and basic legal concepts that will help to set the stage for other events that are described later.

Beyond these introductory treatments, the core of this book is based largely upon source material to which I have had unique access, most of which has never before been seen by the public, and none of which has ever appeared or even been cited in either academic or popular literature. Most of this material was acquired through my own independent research, or through unique access to confidential agency reports as well as recorded interviews. Included are first-hand accounts from participants in shootings and shooting reviews, transcriptions of agency suspect and witness interviews, and confidential (secret) agency documents and investigative reports long-withheld from the public. All of these are presented to support a disturbing but well-documented account – a cautionary tale – of corruption and cover-up that serves as the principle case-study in this book. As such, readers will find that many of the accounts I provide and the conclusions I draw about the NPS do not necessarily align with those reflected in most academic or popular literature, and certainly not with those presented in materials distributed by the Park Service. Likewise, as J.T. Reynolds has noted in the foreword to this book, most of this material is still not openly discussed *within* the NPS itself; not even in the classroom. Therein lies a large part of the problem. That is all the more reason why I believe this material will hold the serious reader's interest and stimulate further thought and discussion about our national parks, and how to improve the agency that runs them.

In exploring and discussing, as I do, why some individuals and groups seem to oppose the NPS and its resource protection mission, I am not taking their side or even trying to justify their opposing positions or the tactics they may use. In response to some of my other writing and previous whistleblowing efforts, some have tried to label me as an ideological ally of those who are perceived as enemies or opponents of the NPS. That mistaken view has also been expressed because I have, on occasion, taken the time to listen to and speak with individuals or groups who may, in fact, oppose many of the things the NPS has done or is trying to do. Those who draw such conclusions about me are not only wrong, they are missing a key point. There is value in understanding your opponents. There are risks in drawing unfounded conclusions about the opposition, or in attempting to simplify the debate by characterizing opponents as merely selfish or evil people without a rational perspective or a history of experiences that might explain their feelings and their positions. As I will show through examples, that simplistic approach to the debate over parks and resource preservation has not served the cause of national parks.

Because of my own experiences working for the NPS – a decidedly atypical career that included many opportunities to witness and study these issues "from the other side" and as a criminal investigator – I think I bring another perspective to the conversation, offering unique insights into the behind-the-scenes workings of the NPS and the agency's interactions with both political supporters and opponents. Those experiences have, in turn, spurred me to step back and explore whether the incidents I have witnessed are mere aberrations or are, instead, symptomatic of a more pervasive, deeply rooted problem.

That said, one of the challenges I faced in writing this book was in clearly distinguishing between the acts of a few within the NPS organization, from those of the majority. In exposing and discussing the misconduct and other ethical lapses associated with a segment of the NPS leadership, I am in no way suggesting that all or even most of the agency's employees have or ever would engage in that type of conduct. To the contrary, it's been my experience that most NPS employees are extraordinarily hard-working and honest people, stuck in a love-hate relationship with the agency; committed to a noble cause, while simultaneously frustrated by a culture that tolerates misconduct and incompetence, and lacks consistent oversight and accountability. To them I say, "Take the high ground, and stick to your guns."

Paul Berkowitz

Endnotes

1. *Merriam-Webster's Dictionary and Thesaurus.*

2. *MacMillan (on-line) Dictionary* (http://www.macmillandictionary.com/us/dictionary/american/legacy).

3. National Park Service History E-Library, "Famous Quotes Concerning the National Parks," http://www.nps.gov/history/history/hisnps/NPSThinking/famousquotes.htm.

4. As used in this context, reference to the U.S. Constitution is meant to include the Bill of Rights and subsequent constitutional amendments. *See* U.S. Constitution, Article 5. Impliedly, this also refers to derivative federal statutory law as well as case law, with no editorial intended relating to extrajudicial challenges to contemporary federal law.

5. The term "due process" appears in the 5th amendment to the U.S. Constitution ("No person shall ... be deprived of life, liberty, or property without due process of law") and again in the 14th amendment ("No state shall ... deprive any person of life, liberty, or property, without due process of law."). The term is broadly interpreted to encompass "The conduct of legal proceedings according to established rules and principles for the protection and enforcement of private rights ..." (*Black's Law Dictionary, Seventh Edition*).

6. Uncredited axiom within the NPS.

PART 1

CHAPTER ONE

Hidden History
(Myth-busting)

There are any number of good reasons to study history, not the least of which is the ability to identify significant patterns that might otherwise elude detection. There are patterns in government that are revealed only through a close examination of the historical record. But where the historical record is incomplete – or worse – where the record has been manipulated to conceal important historical events, those patterns may not be revealed or detected. That can have grave consequences, including the acceptance of tactics and even policies that, while appearing successful in the short-term or at the local level, may lead to long-term harm. The lengths to which a government agency will go to conceal that record and to promote those kinds of tactics and policies can, in and of itself, reveal a lot about the culture of that agency.

I became intrigued with this phenomenon in the early 1980s, while researching the history of law enforcement in the National Park Service. Contrary to my own observations and experiences, the NPS maintained that law enforcement did not become a significant problem in parks until the 1970s and 1980s. According to official accounts, rangers did not historically carry or even need firearms and other defensive equipment until then, and had not previously engaged in serious law enforcement activities. As late as 1989, the agency's chief ranger and other officials in Washington, D.C., even claimed that three separate officer-involved shootings that year were "believed to be the first by rangers in the Park Service's seventy-three year history," adding, "it's surprising rangers haven't used deadly force before."[1] Surprising, indeed, because none of it was true.

My own research and that of a colleague, ranger Jeff Ohlfs, supported by dozens of interviews with old-timers as well as hundreds of old newspaper accounts, photographs, and even long-buried reports and agency memorandums, flatly refuted those official accounts.[2] The files in my collection contain documentation on literally dozens of incidents prior to 1989, involving the use of deadly force by – as well as against – park rangers. The numbers beyond that date reveal a continuing pattern of violent crime in parks, including assaults against rangers.

* * *

Yellowstone's first superintendent under the NPS (1919 - 1929), Horace Albright, had proclaimed in a form letter to ranger-applicants that "The Ranger is primarily a policeman," and "The ranger force is the park police force, and is on-duty night and day in the protection of the park."[3]

In 1926, while attending the Park Service's first chief rangers' conference (when the agency was only ten years old), Yellowstone chief ranger Sam Woodring declared "We are the police force of the national parks and are charged with the enforcement of law..."

Notably, Woodring was also strongly opposed to the adoption of what is today the single most iconic symbol of the NPS and its rangers; the Smokey Bear flat hat. Expressing a complaint heard to this day from rangers across the country, he bluntly proclaimed,

> I think the most unsatisfactory part of the present uniform is the hat. From the practical standpoint it is the poorest type that could have been adopted. The stiff brim is an impediment to a ranger while at work as it is always in the way and is continually falling off. Working or riding through the brush it is worse than useless, and it is practically impossible to get in or out of a car without knocking it off.[4]

Yellowstone chief ranger Sam Woodring, 1922. (NPS Photo)

Attending the same conference, Yosemite chief ranger Forest Townsley echoed Woodring's sentiments about the law enforcement duties and challenges his rangers faced, observing that "The greatest problem in Yosemite relates to traffic and police work." Reinforcing this point with surprising candor, while simultaneously foretelling future conditions in the national parks, Townsley explained

> The increase in travel will also complicate an already difficult police problem…
>
> It will bring in many people of a class which is not favorable from a park standpoint, being mostly people who are out to have a good time, and are not in the least interested in the scenic features of the park…
>
> The above are the class of people who are found in any cheap beach resort, and I expect them to cause considerable trouble in the future in Yosemite. The crowded conditions in the valley will no doubt attract criminals …[5]

In addition to statements like these, I discovered a long and continuing pattern of crime in parks going back more than a century, and an equally long record of rangers, both armed and unarmed, attempting to combat that crime, often without the meaningful support of park managers.[6]

Early NPS ranger armed with Colt single-action army revolver. (NPS Photo)

The popular media has long been a willing participant in the perpetuation of the ranger image and the various myths portraying an historical absence of serious crime in parks. My personal video library now contains dozens of recordings of TV documentary and news accounts going back decades – as far back as the 1970s and all the way up to the present – each successively claiming to expose newfound revelations about "crime coming to the parks." Many of these pieces feature the two very parks, Yellowstone and Yosemite, about which chief rangers Woodring and Townsley had spoken in their own 1926 discussions about crime that had *already come* to these same areas, where at least *they* understood that "the ranger force is the park police force." Yet, almost all of these television pieces – year after year and decade after decade – contain misleading statements offered by NPS officials claiming that such trends are a new phenomenon, for the first time (each time!) forcing the agency to arm its rangers and train them to assume an increasingly heavy law enforcement role in the parks.

While the NPS still attempts to downplay the levels of crime and violence that occur in parks and the historic law enforcement role that park rangers have performed, there has been some progress, in many instances the direct result of my own and ranger Ohlfs' efforts to uncover and ex-

Ranger James Carey is now believed to be the first NPS Ranger murdered in the line of duty, in 1927, at Hot Springs National Park, AR. The incident was not acknowledged by the NPS until 1989, when ranger Jeff Ohlfs uncovered newspaper accounts and related records.

Headline of June 24, 1927, *Coconino Sun* (Flagstaff, AZ), reporting apprehension of a fugitive at Grand Canyon National Park by sheriff's officers and NPS rangers. NPS Ranger and deputized "Grand Canyon Constable" Bert Lauzon.

pose this history.[7] But as I will demonstrate with examples throughout this book, that limited progress has not come easily, and the NPS still struggles and pays a very high price in its often-fierce resistance to acknowledging the need for professional law enforcement, not to mention the need for (and the benefits derived from) accurately preserving the unembellished, unfiltered, and sometimes unflattering historical record. And while the focus of my research has been on law enforcement within the NPS, by inference and reference, much of that same research reveals a great deal about the NPS as a whole, and the underlying culture of the agency.

• • •

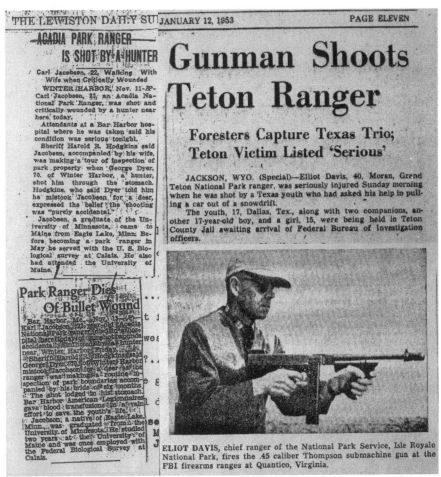

Image on left: Acadia National Park, Nov. 11, 1938 (assailant convicted of manslaughter). (*Lewiston Daily Sun*). Image on right: NPS Ranger Eliot Davis was gravely wounded on January 11, 1953, during a shootout with teenagers who had stolen a car and fled into Grand Teton National Park. He was later among the first NPS rangers to attend the FBI academy at Quantico, VA. (Author's collection, courtesy of Eliot Davis).

15

It's no great leap to move beyond the fiction of historically crime-free parks and unarmed rangers, to the representation of an NPS workforce that is free of misconduct, with agency leaders who are nothing less than wise, benevolent, and free of corruption. But this, too, is a persistent myth that has been embraced and frequently orchestrated by the NPS to help promote the ranger image. During a 1986 television interview, one senior NPS official acknowledged this long-held belief, quoting some of his own predecessors who professed, "Don't they know that I'm a ranger? Therefore I must be good."[8] And by the same reasoning (such as it is) that there is no need for law enforcement or armed rangers where there is no crime, surely there is no need for program oversight and strict accountability where everyone is "good."

These two myths fuel and feed off of each other. A direct relationship can (and will) be shown between the Park Service's dismissive approach to law enforcement and the devaluation of law enforcement personnel and programs, generally, and the perpetuation of an environment where serious misconduct is readily tolerated but seldom acknowledged.

Advances in electronic communications over the past few decades have made recent controversies, political conflicts, and troubles in the

Left: May 14, 1966, Great Smoky Mountains National Park (*Asheville Times*). Upper right: May 30, 1970, Lake Mead National Recreation Area. Bottom right: Sept. 15, 1981, Buffalo National River, AR. (*Harrison Daily Times*, Sep. 16, 1981).

NPS, itself, far more visible than they might have been in the past. Consequently, there has been a tendency to also characterize matters related to agency misconduct and cover-up as only a recent, twenty-first century phenomenon; a departure from a more tranquil and less contentious time, the result of only recent changes in leadership in the NPS.[9] But once again, such conclusions are wrong. This book takes a broader, historical approach, connecting the dots between the past and the present and what may at first seem like disparate topics and events, to reveal how the agency's long-standing approach to not just law enforcement, but agency attitudes and priorities, generally – its culture and its mythology – has compromised professionalism and agency credibility; an unfortunate legacy for which the NPS is increasingly paying a very high price.

At this point, then, it is useful to step back and review some of the conditions and events in our nation's history that first compelled Congress to set aside and protect public lands and resources and, in turn, to designate the first national parks and establish the NPS. That discussion will aid in understanding the political forces at work in the case study presented later, illustrating how "confused values and misplaced priorities" in the NPS have, indeed, "contributed to the erosion of public trust and, ultimately, diminished support for national parks and the mission of resource protection." It will also, I believe, help to demonstrate why, in spite of the many shortcomings we will discuss, agencies like the National Park Service remain an essential part of our government, and why the protection and preservation of our national parks and other public lands remains vital to our national interests.

Endnotes

1. Kit Miniclier, "Park rangers add firepower for violent times," *Denver Post*, July 2, 1989, quoting, respectively, NPS Chief Ranger Walt Dabney, and Association of National Park Rangers president Rick Gale.

2. My research focused specifically on NPS law enforcement and incidents involving the use of deadly force and assaults on NPS personnel, while Ohlfs research more broadly examined all categories of employee fatalities.

3. Horace M. Albright, Superintendent, Yellowstone National Park, to "Dear Mr. [applicant name]," undated form letter (EMA/JJ). See, also, Horace M. Albright, *The Birth of the National Park Service* (Salt Lake City, UT: Howe Brothers, 1985) 144.

4. Sam Woodring, quoted in the *Report of the First Chief Park Rangers Conference*, National Park Service, Department of the Interior, held in Sequoia National Park, Jan. 15-19, 1926, pages 17 and 31. Conference notes prepared by Grand Canyon National Park chief ranger Eivind Scoyen, serving as conference secretary. See, also, Horace M. Albright, *The Birth of the National Park Service* (Salt Lake City, UT: Howe Brothers, 1985) 147.

5. Forest Townsley, as quoted in the *Report of the First Chief Park Rangers Conference*, National Park Service, Department of the Interior, Held in Sequoia National Park, Jan. 15-19, 1926, page 7. Conference notes prepared by Grand Canyon National Park chief ranger Eivind Scoyen,

serving as conference secretary. See, also, Horace M. Albright, *The Birth of the National Park Service* (Salt Lake City, UT: Howe Brothers, 1985) 147.

6. Paul Berkowitz, *U.S. Rangers – The Law of the Land: The History of Law Enforcement in the Federal Land Management Agencies,* (Redding, CA: C.A.T. Publishing, 1989 – 1995).

7. Ranger Lodge of the Fraternal Order of Police website, Sept. 13, 2013, "Misinformed NPS public information officer." http://rangerfop.com/member-forums/?mingleforumaction=view-topic&t=126.

8. Leland Shackelton, in an interview as part of the television documentary, *The Law of Nature: Park Rangers in Yosemite Valley*, Philbin Philms, 1986.

9. *See, for example,* Robert M. Danno, *Worth Fighting For* (Shepherdstown, WV: Honor Code Publishing, LLC, 2012) xvii; *see also,* Bill Wade (commenter), "Not too good," *Parklandwatch* (Googlegroup), Dec. 21, 2013 (0926 a.m.).

CHAPTER TWO

Public Lands – Protected Places

Most Americans take it for granted that we have a national system of special natural and historic places "set apart as ... public park[s] for the benefit and enjoyment of the people." But the development of that system and the growth of a larger national conservation movement was in many ways a reaction to widespread land fraud and abuse that accompanied the expansion and settlement of the American West. Controversy and conflict over the manner in which those special places are managed – and even more so over the manner in which some of those places are acquired – has plagued conservation efforts since the earliest of times. Many of those conflicts have been hard-fought with guns and even fire-bombs, as well as lobbyists and lawyers; from as far back as the 1830s in Arkansas and the 1860s in California, to Pennsylvania in the 1970s, and back to California as recently as 2014.

Most of the great national parks of the American West – the icons, such as Yosemite, Yellowstone, Sequoia, Mount Rainier, Olympic, Grand Canyon, Crater Lake, and others – were in a very real sense carved and created out of public lands "withheld from settlement, occupancy, or sale..." and "set apart as a public park for the benefit and enjoyment of the people."[1] Notwithstanding historic controversies over the manner in which the United States acquired title (a matter beyond the scope of this discussion)[2], the major land base from which these protected sites were established has been in the public domain, owned by the federal government and held in trust for the American people.[3]

In the westward expansion that followed the American Revolution, the United States grew from the original Thirteen Colonies to eventually encompass what we now consider the existing territorial borders spanning from the Atlantic Ocean to the Pacific, Canada to Mexico, and eventually Alaska, Hawaii, and the various territories.

From 1780 to 1802, most of Trans Appalachia – some 233 million acres of land – was ceded to the new federal government by the original (seven of thirteen) states that held claims to lands beyond the Appalachian Mountains extending to the Mississippi River.[4] Those lands were, in turn, divided up into new states according to terms defined in the Ordinance of 1784, the Ordinance of 1785, and the Ordinance of 1787; collectively known as the Northwest Ordinances.[5] Thereafter, pursuant to Article IV, Section 3 (clause 1) of the new U.S. Constitution, through these and various other acts of Congress, the rest of the states we now recognize were carved out of a series of expansions realized through purchases or military domination and treaties with other nations or sovereigns. In most instances, and particularly in the West, those states, through legislation, agreed to "forever disclaim all right and title in or to any unappropriated public lands lying within the boundaries thereof … until the title thereto shall have been extinguished by the United States, [and] the same shall be and remain subject to the disposition of the United States …"[6] As such, the new states recognized the exclusive title of the United States over these lands as "the common property of the nation."[7]

U.S. territorial expansion (USGS map)

The authors of the U.S. Constitution contemplated that the federal government would own property. In Article I, Section 8, they made provisions for a federal district that would serve as the seat of government, authorizing Congress

> To exercise exclusive Legislation in all Cases whatsoever, over such District (not exceeding ten Miles square) as may, by Cession of particular States, and the acceptance of Congress, become the Seat of the Government of the United States, and to exercise like Authority over all Places purchased by the Consent of the Legislature of the State in which the Same shall be, for the Erection of Forts, Magazines, Arsenals, dock-Yards, and other needful Buildings.

The founders also made provisions for the management of that and other federal property in what is referred to as the Property Clause (Article IV, Section 3, clause 2):

> Congress shall have the power to dispose of and make all needful rules and regulations respecting the territory or other property belonging to the United States.[8]

Congressional power to make those *needful rules* "without limitation" or deference to the states, and to set aside and administer lands from the public domain, has been affirmed in several significant Supreme Court cases.

Noteworthy among those cases are two decided in 1911. In *Light v. United States*, the court affirmed Congressional authority to permanently establish and retain federal preserves out of the public domain. In *United States v. Grimaud*, the court affirmed Congressional authority to create federal agencies to administer those preserves and other public lands, with authority to prescribe, through regulations, the types of activities that can and cannot take place, therein.[9]

More recently, in *Kleppe v. New Mexico* (1976), the Supreme Court reaffirmed Congressional authority to retain and assert control over public lands as well as wildlife and other resources, therein, state law notwithstanding, stating

> While Congress can acquire exclusive or partial jurisdiction over lands within a State by the State's consent or cession, the presence or absence of such jurisdiction has nothing to do with Congress's powers under the Property Clause. Absent consent or cession a State undoubtedly retains jurisdiction over federal lands within their territory, but Congress equally surely retains the power to enact legislation respecting those lands pursuant to the Property Clause.... And when Congress so acts, the federal legislation necessarily overrides conflicting state laws under the Supremacy Clause.[10]

Principal responsibility for management of that territory (i.e., public lands) and other federal property initially fell upon the Department of the Treasury. In 1812, that responsibility was vested in a newly created agency within the Treasury Department, called the General Land Office (GLO).[11] The GLO was charged with the duty to "perform all acts and things touching or respecting the public lands of the United States."[12] Among its primary responsibilities was to assess, survey, and then, in an orderly manner dispose of public domain lands in the mid-West and

West. The GLO was later incorporated into the Department of the Interior (DOI) when that new cabinet-level department was created in 1849. Next, with passage of the Taylor Grazing Act of 1934, the U.S. Grazing Service was created to manage the public rangelands. Finally, in 1946, the Grazing Service and the GLO (and their dual missions) were merged together under a new agency, the Bureau of Land Management (BLM), also within the Interior Department. Under management of these various agencies, more than one billion acres of land have been transferred from federal to state and private ownership. But in 1976, Congress passed the Federal Land Policy and Management Act, changing national policy to generally retain the remaining lands in federal ownership.[13]

Settlement and development of the American West was initially encouraged through a series of legislative actions like those cited above. But settlers were not supposed to settle upon or lay claim to land that had not yet been surveyed, and the process of surveying the public lands of the West would take years. Those delays led to large numbers of pioneers squatting on lands that had not yet been opened for settlement. In an effort to address those situations, Congress passed what is known as the Preemption Act of 1841.[14] That law contained provisions for settlers to claim and purchase up to 160 acres of public land for just $1.25 per acre *before* it was otherwise offered for settlement or sale to the public, provided they had already resided on that land for at least 14 months.

The Homestead Act of 1862 accelerated that process in the far West, providing a mechanism designed to allow immigrants and other settlers to legally claim a quarter of a section – 160 acres – of designated (surveyed) public land as their own, for free (not counting registration fees), provided they developed and resided on that land for at least five years.[15] The Timber Culture Act augmented the Homestead Act, allowing settlers to claim an additional quarter-section of land adjacent to their homestead if they planted trees on at least forty acres of that additional land.[16] That was followed by the Enlarged Homestead Act of 1909, authorizing settlers of more marginal lands (especially in the Great Plains) to claim up to 320 acres. Regrettably, these laws also gave rise to rampant land fraud, enabling many speculators, individual as well as corporate, to acquire huge tracts of land in the expanding West.

Concern about this level of fraud had been expressed by Congress as far back as the 1830s. A March 3, 1835, entry into the Congressional Record reflects the following findings and prediction:

> The Committee on Public lands [was instructed by the Senate] to inquire whether any fraudulent practices ... had taken place ...
> It appears by the reports of the commissioners appointed to take depositions in several land districts, that most of the persons

who have been large purchasers of public lands, in connection with combinations or companies of speculators, who were summoned to give testimony concerning frauds practiced by such companies, have either declined or positively refused to appear before the commissioners and testify. ... Many of the speculators were persons filling high offices in the States in which the public lands purchased by them are situated, and others possessing wealth and influence, all of whom naturally united to render this investigation odious among the people; and in this manner influenced numerous witnesses to refuse their testimony to facts within their knowledge ...

In some instances the commissioners were threatened with personal violence, to deter them from the performance of their duties, and all who testified were denounced and put in fear by the powerful combinations whose conduct was the subject of scrutiny ...

Companies of speculators, with an almost unbounded capital, will forthwith employ agents to explore the lands remaining unsold, and every valuable spot will be entered, at the very inadequate price of one dollar and twenty-five cents per acre. The sterile lands alone will remain subject to entry by the emigrating population at the land offices, while all the good lands will be held by companies ... the emigrant is thrown on the mercy of the speculator.[17]

Lands threatened by fraud and abuse of both the Homestead Act and related acts included several sites now treasured as national parks. One infamous land fraud scheme played out at the doorstep to what would eventually become Rocky Mountain National Park in Colorado. An account of that incident appeared in the 1976 edition of *Field and Stream* magazine.

William Thomas Wyndham-Quinn, AKA the Fourth Earl of Dunraven "came to Estes Park [Colorado] in 1872 to hunt..."

In 1874, he decided to stem the tide of three to four American tourists per week that were flooding into Estes Park. He would buy up the entire place (15,000 acres) and preserve it as a hunting park for himself and his friends.

The earl hired miscellaneous drifters in Denver to swear that they had fulfilled the requirements of the Homestead Act and settled on land in Estes Park. In this way, they each gained title to 160 free acres and were allowed to buy more from the federal government for only $1.25 per acre. Dunraven then bought these titles for a small amount.

It was fraud, of course. But it was also standard operating procedure in the West. Westerners even admired men who could pull off such land grabs, unless the grabber happened to be a rich English nobleman. The Americans paid no attention to the earl's titles, land, or otherwise. Tensions, trespasses, confusion, and ill-feeling grew until Dunraven's caretaker, a former squatter in Estes Park, shot and killed Mountain Jim Nugent, another squatter who had refused to sell out to Dunraven.

The shooting drew even more attention to the valley, and the earl saw that the Americans would not allow him to keep Estes Park to himself.[18]

An article appearing in the December 27th, 1871 issue of the *Greeley Tribune* addressed this pattern, observing,

> There is no doubt but lands in America are considered good investments by English capitalists. During the last two years many thousand acres have been repurchased between Denver and Colorado City, mainly with English money, and agents are scouring the country beyond Colorado City, picking up all the choicest pieces of government lands.

Later, on August 26, 1874, that same journal cited a *Denver Tribune* article about Estes Park, that had noted,

> If the few Land Grabbers who have thus technically gobbled up all of these broad acres, are permitted to complete their "airy titles," they will have possession of some 38,000 acres, embracing too, all the smaller and richer parks, canyons, and gulches leading out of or into the park proper....
>
> The question then arises whether the people of Colorado will permit one of the richest and most attractive portions of the Territory to be set apart for the exclusive benefit and behoof of a few English aristocrats, or whether the Government itself shall keep its title to the park, pass stringent laws relative to fish and game, and so have this broad and lovely domain, forever kept as a National "Institution," of a general benefit to the people of Colorado.
>
> Anyway or anyhow the days of Land Grabbing in this Territory are about over.[19]

Accounts like these certainly contributed to tales of the western robber barons, cattle barons, and railroad magnates portrayed in the popular media. This same level of fraud would ultimately lead Congress to change its position regarding the disposition of public lands. It would also, at the beginning of the 20th century, serve as a catalyst for the establishment of what would eventually become the nation's premier law enforcement agency; the Federal Bureau of Investigation (FBI).

Pulitzer Prize winning Author Tim Weiner sheds light on the obscure origins in his book, *Enemies – A History of the FBI*:

> The Republican [president] Roosevelt wanted to fight plutocrats.... Their plunder of oil, coal, minerals, and timber on feder-

al lands appalled him.... Corporate criminals, carving up public property for their private profit, paid bribes to politicians to protect their land rackets. Using thousand dollar bills as weapons, they ransacked millions of acres of the last American frontiers.... In 1905, a federal investigation [conducted by the Secret Service] ... had led to the indictment and conviction of Senator John H. Mitchell and Representative John H. Williamson of Oregon, both Republicans, for their roles in the pillage of the great forests of the Cascade Range...

What happened next is chronicled in a memorandum written by special agent Louis Findlay, who had joined the FBI in 1911:

[When the convictions were overturned] "Roosevelt, in his characteristic dynamic fashion, asserted that the plunderers of the public domain would be prosecuted and brought to justice.... Roosevelt called Attorney General Charles J. Bonaparte to the White House and told him that he desired that the land frauds be prosecuted vigorously, and directed that he obtain the necessary investigative personnel.... President Roosevelt directed Bonaparte to create an investigative service within the Department of Justice subject to no other department or bureau, which would report to no one except the Attorney General." [The president's order] resulted in the formation of the Federal Bureau of Investigation."[20]

• • •

Even as the several states were created from the new territories and as lands were made available (legally and otherwise) for acquisition by private citizens (and corporations such as railroads and timber companies), Congress withheld vast tracts of public land that were to remain in the public domain as the collective property of all the American people. These areas would eventually comprise anywhere from 25% to 75% of the land mass of the various western states, and nearly 30% of the land mass of the entire United States.

Among the first sites specifically reserved for the collective American public (as opposed to Indian, military, and other types of reservations) were lands that both included and surrounded the unique thermal pools located in Hot Springs, Arkansas. That property was acquired by the U.S. in 1803, as part of the Louisiana Purchase. In 1820, the Arkansas Territorial Legislature requested that the springs and surrounding mountains be set aside as a federal reservation. Their request was made, at least in part, in an effort to refute and put a stop to claims being made by a variety of private citizens considered squatters. In 1832, President Andrew Jackson signed legislation that set aside "four sections of land including said [hot] springs reserved for the future disposal of the United States [which] shall not be entered, located, or appropriated, for any other purpose whatsoever." This area was designated the Hot Springs Reservation.[21] Resolution of the old (and even new post-reservation) disputes over citizen claims to those same lands would take nearly forty years of litigation, with a final determination reached in 1875 and then 1877, when the federal courts ruled against all of the would-be private owners, observing that "[this land] never became segregated from the public domain. It never became so appropriated to the claimants as to give them a vested right, and prevent the operation of the act of April 20, 1832, by which [the hot springs and surrounding land] was reserved to the United States" therefore "none of the claimants are entitled to the lands in question."[22] In 1921 the site was re-designated Hot Springs National Park.[23]

Similar motivations were behind the initiative to set aside and preserve the Yosemite Valley and the Mariposa Grove in California, as far back as the 1850s. By that time California was already a state, but Yosemite Valley and the surrounding forests remained in the public (federal) domain. Efforts to prevent logging of the magnificent "big trees" and other private development of the region led to legislation, in 1864, deeding those areas to the State of California through the Yosemite Grant, creating a new park – authorized by Congress, to be administered by the state – for the American public, "for public use, resort, and recreation ... inalienable for all time."[24] The failure of state officials to fulfill that promise eventually led to the retrocession of those same lands back to the federal government in 1906, adding to the establishment of Yosemite National Park.[25]

Not all of the first federal reservations were established out of a pure conservation ethic or desire to conserve the scenery. The Pribilof Islands Reservation in Alaska, including St. Paul, St. George, Walrus, and Otter islands, was established in 1869 (just two years after the Alaska Purchase) in order to protect the breeding grounds of fur seals, which were highly valued as a cash crop all the way up to the 1980s.

> In 1869, the government deployed military and customs agents to protect the [Pribilof] island's Native inhabitants and the fur-seal herds. Congress mandated the islands a "special reservation for Government purposes." In 1870, the government determined to treat the islands as a business monopoly."[26]

Yellowstone National Park – the first federal reservation bestowed with the park moniker – was created by act of Congress in 1872. That vast preserve of more than one million acres was "withdrawn from settlement, occupancy, or sale ... for the benefit and enjoyment of the people" out of what were then the territories of Montana and Wyoming (which respectively secured statehood in 1889 and 1890).

In his classic 1895 book, *The Yellowstone National Park,* author and retired U.S. Army Brigadier-General Hiram Chittenden noted that,

> It was ... clear that the land ... would soon be taken up by private interests, and that the beautiful formations would be carried off for mercenary purposes; in short, that the early history of Niagara would repeat itself in the Yellowstone. To avoid such a misfortune only one course was open, and that was for the government to retain control of the entire region.

Chittenden later added,

> It was a notable act, not only on account of the transcendent importance of the territory it was designed to protect, but because it was a marked innovation in the traditional policy of governments. From time immemorial, privileged classes have been protected by law in the withdrawal, for the exclusive enjoyment, of immense tracts for forests, parks, and game preserves. But never before was a region of such vast extent as the Yellowstone Park set apart for the use of all the people without distinction of rank or wealth.
>
> The example thus set by the United States has been widely followed at home and abroad, but particularly in the western portion of North America, where the obstacle of private occupancy has been largely absent.[27]

Echoing that last key point, historian Merrill Beal, and the NPS itself, astutely observed that the process of creating Yellowstone National Park was simplified by the fact that "As yet, there were no complications of private land ownership to arrest an alert government's purpose. Congress responded with alacrity."[28]

Emphasizing its mandate to preserve the park and keep it under federal jurisdiction, Congress specified that:

> Said park shall be under the exclusive control of the Secretary of the Interior, whose duty it shall be, as soon as practicable, to make and publish such rules and regulations as he may deem necessary or proper for the care and management of the same. Such regulations shall provide for the preservation from injury or spoliation of all timber, mineral deposits, natural curiosities or wonders within the park, and their retention in their natural condition.

Congress added that:

> All persons who shall locate, or settle upon, or occupy the same [land] or any part thereof, except as hereinafter provided, shall be considered trespassers and removed therefrom.[29]

Responsibility for enforcing that mandate was first handed to former Union army soldier and mountain-man Harry Yount, who is widely credited as Yellowstone's first park ranger, or "gamekeeper." He served in that capacity for barely a year – from 1880 to 1881 – before tendering his resignation. Insight into the reasons behind Yount's decision can be found in his final report to the Secretary of the Interior:

> I do not think that any one man appointed by the honorable Secretary, and specifically designated as a gamekeeper, is what is needed or can prove effective for certain necessary purposes, but a small and reliable police force of men, employed when needed, during good behavior, and dischargeable for cause by the superintendent of the park, is what is really the most practicable way of seeing that the game is protected from wanton slaughter, the forests from careless use of fire, and the enforcement of all the other laws, rules, and regulations for the protection and improvement of the park.[30]

Confronted with the continuing failure of Congress to provide adequate funding (and law enforcement authorities) for civilian protection, on August 6, 1886, the Secretary seized upon legislation enacted three years earlier, authorizing the use of military personnel to protect the park. Thereafter and for the next thirty years, troops from the U.S. Cavalry were posted at Yellowstone and elsewhere throughout the West to serve as the police force of the park(s).[31] Additional federal law enforcement authorities within Yellowstone National Park were enacted through the Lacey Act of 1894, which assimilated state crimes into federal law and additionally expanded protection to park wildlife and other resources. Acknowledging these federal law enforcement responsibilities, the Act also called for the appointment of a resident federal "commissioner" (i.e., judge) as well as resident deputy U.S. marshals, and the construction in the park of "a suitable building to be used as a jail…"[32]

Several other national parks were subsequently established by Congress by similar means, setting aside as federal reservations, areas from the public domain that would forever be protected in their natural state for the "benefit and enjoyment of the American people." Among these early national parks were the areas we now know as Sequoia and Kings Canyon (1890), Mount Rainier (1899, the first national park created from a national forest), Crater Lake (1902), Wind Cave (1903), Mesa Verde (1906), Lassen (1907), Olympic (1909), Glacier (1910), Denali (1917, AKA Mt. McKinley), and other treasured national parks.

As for the area around Estes Park in Colorado, author and historian James Pickering summed up the story in *This Blue Hollow: Estes Park, the Early Years, 1859-1915*, noting with a measure of satisfaction,

Though it would take over forty years to establish Rocky Mountain National Park [in 1915], the U.S. government did at length retain title to much of the region, "pass stringent laws relative to the fish and game, and so have this broad and lovely domain forever kept as a National 'Institution,' of a general benefit to the people of Colorado."[33]

* * *

The NPS, itself, as a unifying federal agency within the Department of the Interior responsible for the administration of all the national parks, was not established until more than 80 years after the designation of the Hot Springs Reservation and 44 years after the establishment of Yellowstone National Park. Prior to that, each national park was administered separately, many under the control of the U.S. Cavalry.

The new agency with its "force of rangers" – many former cavalry officers and scouts – took over the role as guardians of those special federal reservations in 1916.[34]

Cavalry troops stationed at Yosemite National Park. (NPS Photo)

The NPS was charged by Congress with the duty to manage all of the parks, monuments, and other areas under its care by such means and measures necessary "to conserve the scenery and the natural and historic objects and the wild life therein and to provide for the enjoyment of the same in such manner and by such means as will leave them unimpaired for the enjoyment of future generations."[36] Today, there are more than 400 sites administered by the NPS, comprising more than 84 million acres. More than 300 million people visit these sites every year. The agency has more

Ranger (and former cavalry trooper) Jack Gaylor in Yosemite, approx. 1919 (NPS Photo). "I remember him very well, patrolling the trails, always on the watch for law violators.... He always carried a .45 Colt revolver and a Winchester Carbine." (John W. Bingaman).[35]

than 20,000 permanent as well as seasonal employees, aided by thousands of volunteers, who provide a wide range of services; from maintenance, fire-fighting, and emergency medical services, to interpretation, resource management, and law enforcement, with designated rangers and even special agents (criminal investigators) authorized to enforce all federal laws and investigate federal crimes that occur in park areas.[37]

The national movement leading to establishment of the first parks was accompanied by growing concerns about the conservation of other natural resources in the public domain. Those concerns focused, in part, on destructive logging occurring throughout the west and resulting destruction of watershed. Much of that destruction had, in turn, resulted from previously cited land fraud that accompanied the homestead movement.

> The General Land Office, itself, estimated that in 1883 fraud accounted for 40% of the 5-year homesteads, 90% of the timber claims, and 100% of the Preemption and commuted Homestead claims. A 1910 survey estimated that 90% of the preemption and homestead land in Wisconsin had actually been acquired for timber. In the 1880s, "the going rate for dummy entrymen ranged from $50 to $125; you could buy a witness for $25."[38]

The government's eventual response to that fraud included passage of the General Land Law Revision Act of 1891, also known as the "Forest Reserve Act," or the "Creative Act."[39] Congress stopped auctioning land

and repealed the Timber Culture and Preemption Acts that had been abused by land speculators to acquire vast holdings. Elsewhere, the Act authorized the president of the United States to "set apart and reserve ... public land bearing forests ... or in part covered by timber or undergrowth, whether of commercial value or not, as public reservations." These "forest reserves" fell under the administration of the Department of the Interior, whose secretary, John Noble, observed that the preserves would also serve to "preserve the fauna, fish, and flora of our country, and become resorts for the people seeking instruction and recreation."[40]

As a consequence of the Forest Reserve Act, numerous mining, agricultural, and other claims were enveloped within the newly established reserves. Those claims accompanied by valid entries into government surveys were allowed to remain in use as among the first private "inholdings" within federal reservations.[41] But settlers on un-surveyed lands and those who had not previously filed proper claims faced loss of their homes and expulsion from the reserves as trespassers. The volatile situation was resolved when the Secretary of the Interior directed the GLO to adopt a posture of "equitable administration of the law," allowing those who had settled "in good faith" and in compliance with other homestead and preemption laws, to make valid entries, post-facto, and remain.[42] This approach was taken for both practical and political reasons. It had the dual benefit of avoiding potentially violent clashes with settlers (not to mention speculators who had already demonstrated violent resistance to government officials charged with enforcing settlement laws), and simultaneously served to diminish public opposition to the designation of more forest preserves throughout the country. It was hoped that this approach would ultimately benefit national conservation efforts, creating public support for the expansion of America's system of protected forests and parks. The 1905 Transfer Act moved administration of the forest reserves from the Department of the Interior to the Department of Agriculture, and thereafter the forest reserves were re-designated "national forests," to be managed by the newly established U.S. Forest Service.[43]

Another conservation milestone occurred in 1903 when, through executive order, President Theodore Roosevelt set aside more than 5,000 acres on Pelican Island in Florida as the first national wildlife refuge. That action was a response to widespread concerns about the loss of critical nesting habitat necessary for the survival of brown pelicans and other native birds. This was the first federal action taken for the express purpose of setting aside land for the protection of a non-marketable form of wildlife. The national wildlife refuge system now consists of more than 540 protected sites, comprising more than 150 million acres throughout the country.

Next, in 1906, concerns over the looting and destruction of "antiquities" located on public lands, mostly prehistoric Indian ruins and artifacts, led to passage of the Antiquities Act.[44] The Act established criminal penalties for the looting and destruction of ruins located on public lands. It also authorized the President of the United States:

> to declare by public proclamation historic landmarks, historic and prehistoric structures, and other objects of historic or scientific interest that are situated upon the lands owned or controlled by the Government of the United States to be national monuments, and may reserve as a part thereof parcels of land, the limits of which in all cases shall be confined to the smallest area compatible with proper care and management of the objects to be protected.

The Antiquities Act has been used over fifty times to set aside and protect, as federal reservations, new national monuments.[45] Among the areas initially protected under this authority was the Grand Canyon in Arizona, declared a national monument in 1908, by President Theodore Roosevelt, for its unique geology and other features of "scientific interest." Just a few years earlier while standing on the rim of the Grand Canyon, he had asked the American public to:

> Leave it as it is. You can not improve on it. The ages have been at work on it, and man can only mar it. What you can do is to keep it for your children, your children's children, and for all who come after you, as one of the great sights which every American if he can travel at all should see.

He added,

> We have gotten past the stage, my fellow citizens, when we are to be pardoned if we treat any part of our country as something to be skinned for two or three years for the use of the present generation, whether it is the forest, the water, the scenery. Whatever it is, handle it so that your children's children will get the benefit of it.[46]

In all, President Roosevelt used various executive authorities to set aside some 230 million acres of public land for preservation.[47]

Though controversial at the time, and opposed by many powerful political and commercial interests, the wisdom of Roosevelt's effort to protect the Grand Canyon from development was rewarded in 1919, when Congress re-designated it a national park, increasing even further the level of protection (and funding) afforded the area.[48] As of this writing, a total of 47 national monuments (including Jackson Hole/Grand Teton, Olympic, Carlsbad Caverns, and Acadia) have, likewise, been re-designated (or incorporated) into national parks, national historic parks, national preserves, or other congressionally authorized units.

Endnotes

1. This and similar language is used in the enabling legislation for several of these parks.

2. *See* Mark David Spence, *Dispossessing the Wilderness: Indian Removal and the Making of the National Parks* (New York, New York: Oxford University Press, 1999) for a discussion of this topic.

3. *See* Charles F. Wilkinson, "The Public Trust Doctrine in Public Land Law," *U.C. Davis Law Review,* University of California, Davis, School of Law, Vol. 14, No. 2, Winter 1980-81. Also, *United States v. Kipp,* 369 F. Supp. 774, 776 (D. Mont. 1974); *Holz v. Lyles,* 280 Ala. 521, 522 (Ala. 1967); *Humboldt County v. United States,* 684 F.2d 1276, 1281 (9th Cir. Nev. 1982); *United States v. Denver,* 656 P.2d 1 (Colo. 1982); 43 USC 1702(e).

4. Paul W. Gates (writing for the Public Land Law Review Commission), *History of Public Land Law Development* (Wash., D.C.: U.S. Government Printing Office, 1968). Of the original thirteen states, only New York, Virginia, Massachusetts, Connecticut, South Carolina, North Carolina, and Georgia claimed holdings to the west. The other states were referred to as "landless states."

5. The Ordinance of 1784 was written by Thomas Jefferson, and called for the new western states to remain part of the United States and be subject to its central government, proclaiming, "First, that they shall forever remain a part of this confederacy of the United States of America." Then, the Ordinance of 1785 provided a mechanism for surveying, and then selling and settling the land. It also established a mechanism for funding public education throughout the West. The Ordinance of 1787 established the basis for the government of the Northwest Territory and for the admission of constituent parts into the Union, assured that slavery would be forever outlawed in these areas. *See, Journals of the Continental Congress,* Vol. 28, p. 375-381. *Also, "Northwest Ordinances, " Encyclopedia Britannica.*

6. This same or nearly identical language (acknowledging federal title to unappropriated lands) appears in the state constitution and/or (enabling) legislation establishing the states of Arizona, California, Colorado, Idaho, Montana, Nevada, North Dakota, Oklahoma, Oregon, South Dakota, Utah, Washington, and Wyoming.

7. Scott Miller, "The Public Interest of Public Lands," *The Deseret News,* May 18, 2014. *See also,* John D. Leshy, *Unraveling the Sagebrush Rebellion: Law, Politics and Federal Lands,* 14 U.C. Davis L. Rev. 317 (1980).

8. "The Congress shall have power to dispose of and make all needful Rules and Regulations respecting the Territory or other Property belonging to the United States; and nothing in this Constitution shall be so construed as to Prejudice any Claims of the United States, or of any particular State."

See, also, James Madison, *The Federalist Papers,* #43; *The Heritage Guide to the Constitution,* "Property Clause," (http://www.heritage.org/constitution/#!/articles/4/essays/126/property-clause); "Law Applicable to National Parks and Other Federal Reservations within a State," Warren H. Pillsbury, California Law Review, Vol. 22, No. 2 (Jan., 1934), 152-168 (http://www.jstor.org/pss/3476613); and *"Understanding American Property Rights, "* "Federal Reservations," http://www.famguardian.org/Publications/Property-Rights/reserve.html)l *Also* Hutchings v. Low (82 U.S. 77, 1872).

9. *Light v. United States,* 220 U.S. 523 (1911); *United States v. Grimaud,* 220 U.S. 506 (1911).

10. *Kleppe v. New Mexico,* 426 U.S. 529, 542-543 (1976). *See, also,* Congressional Research Service Report for Congress, "Federal Land Ownership: Constitutional Authority and the History of Acquisition, Disposal, and Retention," Dec. 3, 2007.

11. Act of April 25, 1812, *An Act for the establishment of a General Land Office in the Department of the Treasury,* "there shall be established in the Department of the Treasury, an office to be denominated as the General Land Office..." and "from and after the passage of this act, the executive duties now prescribed or which may hereinafter be prescribed by law, appertaining to the surveying and sale of the public lands of the United States, or in anywise respecting such public lands ... shall be

subject to the supervision and control of the commissioner of the general land office, under the direction of the president of the United States."

12. Act of April 25, 1812, *An Act for the establishment of a General Land Office in the Department of the Treasury,* "whose duty it shall be, under the direction of the head of the department, to superintend, execute, and perform, all such acts and things, touching or respecting the public lands of the United States, and other lands patented or granted by the United States."

13. PL 94-579, codified at 43 USC 1701, et. seq.

14. 27th Cong., Ch. 16, 5 Stat. 453 (1841), *An Act to appropriate the proceeds of the sales of the public lands, and to grant pre-emption rights.*

15. Act of May 20, 1862 (P.L. 37-64).

16. Act of March 3, 1873.

17. Senate Document #151, 23rd Congress, 2d Session (March 3, 1835), "Mr. Poindexter made the following report."

18. Kent Dannen, *Field and Stream,* "Hiking Into History," June 1976, p. 56.

19. James H. Pickering, *This Blue Hollow: Estes Park, the Early Years, 1859-1915,* (Boulder, CO: University Press of Colorado, 1999), 33-51.

20. Tim Weiner, *Enemies: A History of the FBI* (New York, NY: Random House, 2013), (citing a 1943 memorandum written by retired FBI agent Louis Findlay, recounting events leading to establishment of the FBI) 9-11.

21. Act of April 20, 1832.

22. *Rector v. United States,* 92 US 698 (1875).

23. Sharon Shugart, *The Hot Springs of Arkansas Through the Years: A Chronology of Events* (National Park Service, 2004).

24. U.S. Statutes at Large, Vol. 13, Chap. 184, p. 325. *An Act authorizing a Grant to the State of California of the Yo-Semite Valley, and the Land embracing the Mariposa Big Tree Grove.* [S. 203, Public Act No. 159].

25. A more detailed discussion about Yosemite state and national parks is presented in chapter six (Paradise).

26. National Oceanic and Atmospheric Administration, *Pribilof Islands: A Historical Perspective,* "Preserving the Legacy of the Pribilof Islands," June 20, 2008.

27. Hiram Martin Chittenden, *The Yellowstone National Park: Historical and Descriptive,* (Cincinnati: Stewart & Kidd Company Publishers, 1895, 1903, 1915, 1918), 73, 79.

28. Merrill D. Beal, *The Story of Man in Yellowstone,* (Caldwell, Idaho: The Caxton Printers, Ltd., 1949), 137.

29. Act of March 1, 1872, aka the *Yellowstone National Park Act* (17 State. 32), also at 16 USC 21.

30. Harry Yount (1881), "Report of Gamekeeper", *Message from the President of the United States to the Two Houses of Congress at the Commencement of the First Session of the Forty-Seventh Congress with the Reports of the Heads of Departments and Selections from Accompanying Documents,* Washington, DC: Government Printing Office, pp. 863–864.

31. 47th Congress, 2nd Session, XIV, Part 4; Act of March 3, 1883. *Also,* 16 USC 78. *See also,* Yellowstone.net "Yellowstone History." (The U.S. Cavalry Arrives in Yellowstone National Park. Cavalry troops remained in Yellowstone for thirty-two years, withdrawing in 1918. Troops were dispatched to Yosemite, Sequoia, and General Grant National Parks in 1891, even before the enactment of authorizing legislation. That legislation was included in the sundry civil act approved June 6, 1900. Troops began their withdrawal from those areas in 1914.) *See* H. Duane Hampton, *How the U.S. Cavalry Saved Our National Parks* (Bloomington, IN: Indiana University Press, 1971).

32. The Lacey Act of 1894 (U.S. Statutes at Large, vol. 28, p. 73).

33. James H. Pickering, *This Blue Hollow: Estes Park, the Early Years, 1859-1915,* (Boulder, CO:

University Press of Colorado, 1999), 51.

34. For a more detailed discussion, see Paul Berkowitz, *U.S. Rangers: The Law of the Land*, (Redding, CA: C.A.T. Publishing, 1995).

35. John W. Bingaman, *Guardians of the Yosemite* (Lodi, CA: END-KIAN Publishing Co., 1961) p.86, describing ranger Jack Gaylor.

36. 16 USC 1, AKA The National Park Service Organic Act.

37. National Park Service figures, 2011.

38. George Draffan, *Taking Back Our Land: A History of Land Grant Reform* (essay), (Seattle, WA: Public Information Network, 1998). Fries, 1951, pp. 176-177 and 179; citing *U.S. General Land Office Annual Report*, 1877, p. 35. *Also*, Steen, 1991, p. 24, citing Ise, 1920, pp. 74-75; and *GLO Annual Report*, 1886, pp. 95-200, 213. "Dummy entrymen" were individuals who would apply for homestead lands and then turn them over to timber, mining, real estate, or other corporations.

39. Act of March 3, 1891. Section 24 addresses the Forest Reserves.

40. *Interior Annual Report* (1891), I:XV, p. 523.

41. The term "inholder" (without hyphenation) refers to individuals or entities who own private property that is surrounded by federal lands, including national parks and forests.

42. James Muhn (Bureau of Land Management), *Early Administration of the Forest Reserve Act: Interior Department and General Land Office Policies, 1891-1897*, (The Origins of the National Forests: A Centennial Symposium, The Forest History Society), http://www.foresthistory.org/ Publications/Books/Origins_National_Forests/sec17.htm#28: GLO Commissioner to Secretary of the Interior, 29 January 1892; GLO Commissioner to Register and Receiver, Glenwood Springs Land Office, Colorado, 20 February 1891, GLO, Div. "R", Letters Sent, RG 49, NA; Secretary of the Interior to GLO Commissioner, 2 February 1892, Department of the Interior, Lands and Railroads Division, Letters Sent by the Lands and Railroads Division of the Office of the Secretary of the Interior, Microfilm Publication M620, Record Group 48: Records of the Office of the Secretary of the Interior, NA [Hereafter cited as DOI, L&RR, Letters Sent, RG 48, NA]; GLO Commissioner to Secretary of the Interior, 13 January 1892, GLO, Div. "R", National Forest Files, Bitterroot National Forest, RG 49, NA; and *Battlement Mesa Forest Reserves*, 16 L.D. 190 (25 January 1893).

43. Act of Feb. 1, 1905 (33 Stat. 628; 16 U.S.C. 472, 524, 554).

44. Act of June 8, 1906, *An Act for the Preservation of American Antiquities*. Also found at 16 USC 431-433.

45. An additional 27 national monuments have been designated by Congress, rather than via presidential proclamation through the Antiquities Act. There are more than 100 designated national monuments, 80 administered by the NPS.

46. President Theodore Roosevelt in a speech made while standing at the rim of the Grand Canyon, May 6, 1903. All told, Roosevelt designated or signed legislation establishing 18 national monuments, 5 national parks, and 150 national forests, earning him recognition as the nation's first "environmental president."

47. National Park Service, "Theodore Roosevelt and Conservation," Theodore Roosevelt National Park on-line brochure, http://www.nps.gov/thro/historyculture/theodore-roosevelt-and-conservation.htm

48. *See Cameron v. United States*, 252 U.S. 450 (1920).

CHAPTER THREE

A Tale of Transition

Pre-existing public lands were the principal land base used in the creation of America's national parks (including national monuments) all the way through the first part of the twentieth century. A departure from this practice emerged during the Great Depression in 1926. Responding to political pressure in the East for the creation of preserves that might rival the great parks of the West, and conveniently aligned with the various public works projects of the era, Congress authorized the establishment of Shenandoah National Park in Virginia, Great Smoky Mountains National Park in North Carolina and Tennessee, and Mammoth Cave National Park in Kentucky.[1]

But few if any public domain lands had ever existed in these parts of the country. Much of the land targeted for creation of the new parks had long been held as private property, including homes comprising mountain communities going back centuries, some even before the American Revolution.[2] The rest had been acquired by logging and other business interests. Therefore, the extensive acquisition of long-standing private lands had to occur before the parks could be established and opened for visitor use. Complicating the process, Congress had initially stipulated that legal authorities and funds used to acquire these new park lands had to come from state or private sources.[3] That left much of the contentious land acquisition process to state or other entities who ultimately, in turn, ceded the acquired lands, en masse, to the NPS. The conflicts involved in those land acquisition efforts are legendary, including the forced relocation by state and local officials of entire mountain communities comprised of hundreds of families and thousands of people.[4] That, in turn, left the NPS, as the most conspicuous beneficiary of those efforts, to deal with many of the resulting hard feelings from local residents.

Several years ago, while conducting research for a book on the history of law enforcement in the NPS, I was privileged to correspond with Vernon Wells, who had worked as a ranger during the early days at Mammoth Cave National Park.[5] We spoke on several occasions, and he wrote me a number of detailed letters that are now a treasured part of my research collection. His first-hand accounts of land acquisition practices and related events during the formative years of the park, offer remarkable insights into to the unique political climate and other challenges, including violence, faced by rangers assigned to help in the transition of areas like Mammoth Cave into a national park.

Mammoth Cave National Park had a difficult birth. First, proposed as a national park about 1924, all lands within the proposed boundary were privately owned, including the Mammoth Cave estate, itself. First settled in the late seventeen hundreds, the proposed park area was home to about 600 families. By use of state appropriations and private contributions the Mammoth Cave estate was purchased first, then the profits from operation of the cave and hotel were used to buy additional lands within the boundary.

At the time I appeared ... the area ... was operated by the Kentucky National Park Commission. This was a temporary situation pending acceptance of the area as a part of the national park system. The men employed by the state to purchase the lands within the boundary were local citizens who knew little about national parks. But they did know that life tenancies had been worked out in some cases in the establishment of the Shenandoah and Great Smoky Mountains National Parks. So they told many of the former land owners that they would be allowed to remain in the land throughout their lifetimes. "Gentleman's Agreements" they were called. There was nothing in writing, but the former owners really believed that they had a legitimate claim on the land.

The N.P.S. had other ideas. They weren't about to accept the area for a national park until the lands were vacated. So they loaned one of their employees, Robert Perkins Holland, to the Kentucky National Park Commission to help expedite the establishment of the park. Federal funds were also appropriated to buy the remaining privately owned lands within the boundary.

Bob Holland was a West Point graduate and had served in the horse cavalry before joining the National Park Service. ... Bob Holland's first job as N.P.S. representative was to get the people off the lands already purchased. Joseph M. Ridge and I were hired ... with Bob Holland as our boss, and we entered on duty July 1, 1934. The three of us were lucky to have survived the events that followed.

We had no help from the local authorities in evicting the people. In fact the local elected officials sided with the people, and the county newspaper was very hostile to what we were doing, and the paper's editorials incited the people to violence. But Bob Holland was not about to let things drag on for a long time, so he prepared letters to the people living on the park lands ordering them to move. When some of them refused, the tactics we used were not too gentle. Needless to say, we got to be about as popular as a bad attack of hemorrhoids. We were threatened many times. One time an irate former owner jammed a 12 gauge into my chest and threatened to kill me while I was supervising the demolition of his former home and farm buildings.

We took these incidents rather causally, too casually as it turned out. On October 28, 1935, Bob Holland sent Joe and me to the Turn-hole area of the park to check out an anonymous tip that some hunt-ing was going on in that section. Having no help whatsoever from the local court officials, our efforts to protect the park's wildlife consisted of warning hunters to leave the park lands. On several occasions, we had taken violators to local courts, but got no cooperation. Also, we were not armed, in the belief that no one would shoot an unarmed man. Well, Joe and I walked into a setup. We were to learn long after that a few of the more embittered people had conspired to retaliate by having a ranger shot. It was well known that Joe and I were not allowed to carry firearms, so shooting a ranger was not a risky propo-sition. Unknown to us a killer out of state prison, on parole, a native of the area was waiting for us to arrive. The area where the incident happened was about 2 miles north of Green River which cuts the park in half. We left our truck on the south side of the river and had a local man set us across in a row boat, with instructions to pick us up at about 3 P.M. We heard some shooting and we headed toward it. I went directly toward the area where the firing came from and Joe branched off to approach from a different direction. I got within about 50 yards of the hunters before they saw me. One of the hunters immediately covered me with his 12 gauge shotgun. The other two ran off. The hunter who had me covered ordered me to stop. I didn't know the man or his reputation, and I knew nothing at the time about the conspiracy. So I kept on walking and as I stepped over a small log he pulled the trigger. Stepping over that log probably saved my life because it threw my body out of line just enough that instead of getting the full charge in my chest, I got part of the charge in my left arm and shoulder.

The man later identified as Homer "Dick" Parker, then drew a nickel plated revolver from his pocket, pulled back the hammer, and told me to leave. Being in shock and defenseless, I turned to leave. Parker immediately ran off, leaving me there. Joe heard the shooting and came to me. He assisted me back to the river, about 2 miles away, and because it was noon instead of 3 P.M., Joe had to swim the river to get to the boat. I had lost a lot of blood and couldn't have gotten across to the south side by myself. He got me to a nearby CCC camp, where I received first aid and then I was taken to a hospital for treatment of my wounds, which were painful and serious, but not life threatening. The scars are still there and most of the lead is still embedded against the bones in my left arm and shoulder.

From then on we went heavily armed and took no chances.... We were never again threatened, because the people knew we were well armed and would not hesitate to use our guns....[6]

That incident ... actually ... resulted to be in our favor, because the good people, the decent people, the better class of people in the area were revolted by this attack on an unarmed man, this conspiracy. It was a pretty well-known thing that's what had happened ... But [Parker] was related to quite a few people in the area ... and was pretty well protected by these relatives. Immediately, Mr. Holland armed Joe and me. He got some GI-forty-five revolvers from the army, and a lot of ammunition, so he being an expert shot, he soon had us pretty well trained in the use of handguns.[7] And from that time on, why, things got a little better for us, because we were then able to shoot back if anybody shot at us. ... We went on a hunt for Parker, but we were never able to catch him, because his relatives protected him. And a little later, why, he surrendered voluntarily to the authorities of Brownsville ... he was given some small fine [$300], which didn't amount to anything. He wasn't even sent back to prison for the balance of his term [even though] he was out on parole for murder. So it just showed that the local people had very little regard for ... the park.... But from that time on, we were able to protect ourselves, and things got better for us....[8]

Mammoth Cave became a national park for protection purposes in 1936.... People began to respect the park regulations and the Federal courts. The violence subsided. Neither Joe nor I made the N.P.S. a career.... Mr. Holland became Acting Supt. in 1936 ...

I spent the war years in the Army. I stayed on at Mammoth Cave ... until Feb. 1942. I resigned from the N.P.S. and took a position with the Alcohol Tax Unit of the Treasury Dept., the agency now known as the Bureau of Alcohol, Tobacco, and Firearms. I continued on in that agency until I retired in 1975 after 37 years in the Federal Service.

I have vivid memories of my days at Mammoth Cave and the violent times there when the park was in the making. I remember well my associations with 2 of the finest men I have ever known. Bob Holland was an officer and a gentleman, a born leader, a good friend, a man who never asked me to do anything or to take any risk that he wasn't willing to do himself. I remember Joe as my partner and friend, who got me out of a bad situation. We keep in close touch. We went through times together that cemented a lasting friendship.

The park is a peaceful place now. The forest has reclaimed the farms and villages. The home sites are obliterated and signs of human habitation are few in number. Our old adversaries are in the local graveyards. The man who shot me, an ex-convict who was out of prison on parole when we met, is buried near the park with only a small monument to show he ever lived. I go back occasionally and find quiet places where I can look out over the forested landscape, and think back to those violent times, and thank the good Lord that I survived to be 76 years old, instead of a twenty year old casualty in the struggle to establish Mammoth Cave National Park.[9]

I do appreciate your inclusion of [my] incident in your publication. Oftentimes sacrifices made by old timers are forgotten and disappear into the distant past. Your publication will preserve the true accounts of these difficult, dangerous days.[10]

Ranger Vernon Wells, 1936, Mammoth Cave National Park.
(Author's collection, courtesy of Vernon Wells)

Endnotes

1. 16 USC 403, et. Seq., 16 USC 404, et. Seq.

2. Darwin Lambert, *Administrative History of Shenandoah National Park, 1924 – 1976 (draft)*, National Park Service, p. 220-221.

3. *See* Horace M Albright and Robert Cahn, *The Birth of the National Park Service (The Founding Years, 1913-33)*, (Salt Lake City, UT: Howe Brothers, 1985) 136.

4. *See*: Darwin Lambert, *The Administrative History of Shenandoah National Park, 1924 – 1976 (draft)*, National Park Service; Theodore Catton, *A Gift For All Time, Great Smoky Mountains National Park Administrative History*, Final Report, Oct. 10, 2008 (Gatlinburg, TN: Great Smoky Mountains Association/Great Smoky Mountains National Park, 2008); Durwood Dunn, *Cades Cove - The Life and Death of a Southern Appalachian Community, 1818 – 1937* (Knoxville, TN: University of Tennessee Press, 1988).

5. Paul Berkowitz, *U.S. Rangers – The Law of the Land: The History of Law Enforcement in the Federal Land Management Agencies*, (Redding, CA: C.A.T. Publishing, 1991-1995).

6. Vernon Wells to the author, letter, Jan. 5, 1991.

7. Wells also routinely carried a Colt .380 pistol for back-up (Author's interview with Vernon Wells, Dec. 30, 1990).

8. Western Kentucky University, *Folklife Archives*, Manuscripts &, "Interview with Vernon Wells Regarding CCC (FA81) (1987), *FA Oral Histories*, Paper 4 (55:24).

9. Vernon Wells to the author, letter, Jan. 5, 1991.

10. Vernon Wells to the author, letter, Apr. 30, 1991.

CHAPTER FOUR

Parklands Reclaimed

B y the 1960s and 1970s, a different approach was widely embraced to establish a series of new park areas out of private lands or lands that had left the public domain and transferred into private or state ownership. To help purchase *those* lands, the federal Land and Water Conservation Fund (LWCF) was established in 1964. The fund receives periodic infusions from a portion of receipts generated through off-shore oil and gas leases, as Congress sees fit.[1]

Even before then, citizens and politicians of a number of communities on the outskirts of developing metropolitan areas across the country had initiated efforts to somehow limit the urban sprawl that threatened their own communities and their more rural lifestyles. In *Rethinking Urban Parks: Public Space and Cultural Diversity*, authors Low, Taplin, and Scheld speculate that the NPS was a willing ally to those efforts.

> Eager to extend its domain further to the populous East, the NPS advocated establishing national seashores and even urban recreational parks in the 1930s. Only one national seashore, Cape Hatteras, was established before World War II. Cape Cod National Seashore entered the system in 1961, followed by Point Reyes, California, in 1962; Fire Island, New York, in 1964; and Indiana Dunes National Lakeshore, near Chicago, in 1966 (Foresta, 1984).
>
> The proximity of these national seashores to metropolitan areas fit in with [President Johnson's] the Great Society's mission of evening out the unfair distribution of public goods (Foresta, 1984). The procession of national seashores was also a response to the rapid suburban growth of the postwar era.... Plans were advanced in the late 1960s and 1970s for a new form of national park, the "national recreation area." Both presidents Johnson and Nixon strongly favored the idea, as did their secretaries of the interior. National recreation areas [NRAs] were initially proposed for New York and San Francisco. President Nixon saw the two as demonstration projects for state, county, and municipal park programs. He called them Gateway East and Gateway West, hoping to create the impression of a single project. Other states soon demanded national recreation areas, however, and new NRAs followed in the south of Cleveland [Cuyahoga Valley NRA], on the Chattahoochee River in Atlanta, and in the Santa Monica Mountains of Los Angeles (Foresta, 1984)...

These parks bring the resources of the National Park System to urban populations who, it is thought, would not otherwise have national park experiences. Rather than reserving a contiguous space solely as a park, the NRA typically consists of noncontiguous collections of separate properties, including surplus military installations, nature reserves, and sites formerly operated by local park agencies. Gateway also includes residential "inholdings" ... that proved too difficult for the Park Service to acquire.[2]

While some managers within the NPS may have been looking to expand the domain of the agency into "the populous East," that view was not necessarily shared by all. Expressing opposition to "park barrel" initiatives that diverted funds from western "crown jewels" such as Yellowstone, NPS Director Ron Walker (1973-1975) is reported to have declared, "I will tell you one thing. [The Cuyahoga Valley] will be a park over my dead body!"[3]

Regardless of the support that existed within the NPS for creation of the new urban parks, one thing is certain. Most of these proposed areas did not fit the traditional model of a national park. They were a far cry from the magnificent landscapes associated with places like Yellowstone, Yosemite, Grand Canyon, and Grand Teton. But with a large measure of local support and a sense of urgency to save what undeveloped lands still existed in those areas, in the twenty year period from 1952 to 1972, Congress authorized the creation of twenty-eight entirely new recreational park areas, and directed the NPS to purchase private lands needed for the parks. This process marked a real change in how national parks were created, a new and more controversial approach, fraught with a record of political conflicts that endure into the twenty-first century.[4] According to the National Research Council,

> Acquisition of private lands did not become an important concern of NPS park managers until the 1960s. Before then, most new parks were created from the public domain or from national forests, or in a few cases by donations. In 1961, Congress created the Cape Cod National Seashore and authorized federal money for parkland acquisition from private owners....
>
> Parks authorized after 1959 often include considerable inholdings, and the acquisition program is more systematic....
>
> But the biophysical and social contexts of urban park management were new to NPS, and although the urban parks created a new avenue for system expansion, they also created new problems for the agency (Foresta, 1984).[5]

Many of those problems were a direct result of the charge Congress handed to the NPS to acquire – to purchase – private lands and structures in order to fulfill the statutory mandate and create the new park areas. Efforts were frequently strained over time, as private residents and other inholders, many of whom had initially supported and even petitioned their local and Congressional representatives to support park creation, found themselves surprised, overwhelmed, and alienated by the new government regulations and restrictions they encountered. Many were left with a sense of broken promises and expectations not realized. In some of these communities, matters escalated to violence directed against NPS personnel, likely as not field rangers who interacted with the community on a daily basis, rather than the senior managers who called the shots. These conflicts also created opportunities for outside agitators and militants, as well as opportunistic groups of squatters, to insert themselves into the fray, escalating tensions to the boiling point. As just one example, a ranger at Delaware Water Gap National Recreation Area in Pennsylvania was the target of a firebomb that had been placed in his residence, previously a park inholding purchased and converted into government housing.[6] Another was confronted by a shotgun-wielding squatter who butt-stroked the ranger in the head during a heated argument over court-ordered evictions.[7]

Any agency tasked by Congress with the implementation of policies that are locally controversial or unpopular will inevitably incur at least some community resentment. But individual agencies and their employees should not be faulted or vilified for responsibly and impartially implementing the laws that Congress enacts.[8] This important distinction is far too often dismissed or simply ignored by opponents (including politicians) who may express their displeasure through both words and acts of intimidation, threats, and violence directed at agency personnel engaged in the lawful and good-faith discharge of their duties. Law enforcement officers or not, rangers and other government employees are not paid to be personally harassed or to get hurt, and no agency employee should have to endure that type of treatment. The full force of the law should be applied against any individual or group that pursues those types of actions in the expression of their displeasure with government policies.

But while it's one thing to implement locally unpopular policies, it's an altogether different thing for agency managers to unnecessarily aggravate conflict by exceeding or abusing their authority and discretion.

In many instances community relations were strained by NPS managers who displayed an autocratic or indifferent posture. Worse still was the inconsistent manner in which the NPS frequently operated or communicated with different groups within communities, creating distrust through secret deals or by telling different segments of the community different things in an effort to win support and placate criticism.

A 1978 article in *Newsweek* magazine reported:

The NPS has come under fire for clumsy and heavy-handed tactics, such as threatening to condemn land if a property holder tries to add a bathroom or bedroom to his home. Landowners also complain of being offered unrealistically low prices, of annoying phone calls from park officials, of late-night visits from government land-acquisition officers, and even strong arm tactics ... for example ... residents ... complain that park operated plows shoved snow on top of older porches and rooftops, causing them to cave in – and forcing some owners to sell to the government after they were denied rebuilding permits. And ... the park service stalled for a week before clearing town roads blanketed by a 40-inch snowfall that came two days after the residents petitioned to secede [from the park]. NPS director William Whalen [1977-1980] concedes that from time to time his staff may have been a bit overzealous, but only because he felt he had Congressional support for "stronger policies."

Elsewhere in this same article is revealed some of the disconnect that existed in the position held toward inholders by some NPS officials.

The park service defends its constitutional right of eminent domain to buy out private landowners in the public interest of creating more park land. Also, says NPS assistant director Phillip Stewart, the government offers "fantastic benefits" to landowners, including deals whereby property owners can sell to the government and then stay on as renters for 25 years or until they die. In Stewart's view, those who don't sell are "thwarting the aspirations of 225 million Americans." "The parks are set aside for all Americans to enjoy," adds Whalen. "If the average citizen understood there was a privileged class of people allowed to live in parks and expand their homes, they'd be on our side."[9]

This last comment reflects the widely-accepted management principle that national parks (as well as national forests and other public lands) belong to the whole American people, and not just to residents of local communities. As such, agencies like the NPS are rightly obligated to manage these sites without favor or deference to those who might otherwise view these areas as there for their privileged use; private, commercial, or otherwise. Time and again, however, questions have arisen over whether a measure of deference, or at least extra attention to transparency, consistency, and honesty is warranted and might ease tensions and improve support for the NPS mission in circumstances where those very parks have been carved and created *not* out of the pre-existing lands in the public domain, but out of the private property once held by individual families and then transferred to the government, willingly or otherwise, for the creation of new parks.

The spring 1982 edition of the *Harvard Environmental Law Review* contains a paper by John F. Lambert, Jr. titled "Private Landholdings in the National Parks: Examples from Yosemite National Park and Indiana Dunes National Lakeshore."[10]

Lambert's paper contains detailed accounts of the controversy surrounding congressional policies (i.e., laws and regulations) and NPS efforts to address the management of private lands within these parks, acknowledging that controversies related to federal land acquisitions have frequently been aggravated by the official interpretation of policies that some agency managers have drawn. As one example, he cites past policies in favor of condemnation of private lands if owners even "planned additional living accommodations," as well as condemnation of undeveloped tracts "if owners planned even relatively small dwellings." In another instance in 1977, "The Park Service threatened condemnation" when "an inholder attempted to add a storage room and bathroom to his house."

Lambert continues, observing that

> Compounding the tension between inholders and the NPS was the Park Service's use of the properties it acquired. Over the years, the NPS had acquired about half of the 640 private acres in Wawona [in Yosemite National Park], ostensibly with the goal of returning the land to its natural state. By June of 1978, however, none of the acquired dwellings had been removed. Some had been made available to NPS employees, and others had been converted to rental units operated by [the park's concession operator] the Curry Company.

In summation he adds,

> The history of private land holdings [in parks] has not been a happy one. The Park Service has been unable to decide on a consistent policy toward ... inholders; it has shifted from one policy to another, none completely satisfactory.

In 1993, the National Academy of Science's National Research Council published *Setting Priorities for Land Conservation*, prepared by the Committee on Scientific and Technical Criteria for Federal Acquisition of Lands for Conservation.[11] The 262-page report contains an entire chapter titled "Assessing the Social Effects of Federal Land Acquisition," including a segment devoted specifically to inholders. With respect to "Land-Acquisition Opponents," the authors maintain that

> Opponents to land acquisition often are advocates of private property rights and are often landowners concerned about land-use restrictions that might result from land-acquisition and protection strategies.... Other concerns include effects on the local tax base

and loss of jobs and revenue from lands used for timber, mining, and grazing. Some opponents also object to federal land acquisition as a matter of principle and advocate the use of conservation incentives for private-property owners or nonprofit organizations.

One of the top goals of the "wise use movement," a coalition that includes inholders, is opposition to all use of eminent domain to acquire inholdings. Other opponents fear the loss of access to federal lands for production of commodities; deterioration of rural culture; federal inattention to maintenance, improvement, and development of existing public lands before acquiring additional land; regulatory land-use restrictions that might result from nearby public acquisition; and potential benefits to certain interest groups and nonprofit intermediaries. Many opponents find intellectual support in the writings of the new resource economists and political support in groups such as the National Inholders Association ...

Inholder concerns are an important part of American federal land policy. The national media frequently report on property owners angered over diminished property rights in and around federal landholdings, and several accounts present inholder perspectives in detail.... Membership in the National Inholders Association and kindred organizations is on the rise....

Elsewhere, however, the authors clarify, acknowledging that:

Not all inholders oppose federal ownership of land, nor are they necessarily opposed to conservation per se. Inholder concerns and issues, however, can have far-reaching social and political effects that could be addressed if SIA [Social Impact Assessments] routinely accompany federal land acquisition.[12]

Another study, *A Wolf in the Garden: The Land Rights Movement and the New Environmental Debate,* is a 1996 collection of essays written by diverse authors from all sides of the debate; from Wise Use Movement co-founder Ron Arnold and Cato Institute senior fellow Karl Hess, Jr., to the Wilderness Society's Ray Rasker and Jon Roush.[13] In chapter one, the book's co-editors, Philip Brick and R. McGreggor ("Greg") Cawley, acknowledge that:

There is much to be learned from the rise of the land rights groups ... Jon Roush, president of the Wilderness Society, suggests that the recent congressional assault on the environment reflects shortcomings in environmental strategies, including inattention to social and economic problems, especially in rural areas: "If we can't sustain communities around wilderness areas, then we can't have sustainable wilderness areas." ... In most cases, this means ... paying more attention to social-justice issues.[14]

Perhaps nowhere was the schism and conflict between the local residents and the NPS more visible than at Cuyahoga Valley National Recreation Area in Ohio (established 1974), where matters reached such a fevered pitch that the NPS was forced to move and replace the park superintendent who had spearheaded land acquisitions. The events and controversy there drew national attention, as residents who had once supported and even lobbied for the creation of a national recreation area in their home community, found themselves angry and mobilized against NPS efforts to expel them from their own homes and buy up their land to make way for the new park. The Public Broadcasting System (PBS) aired a documentary as part of their *Frontline* program, titled "For the Good of All." The documentary, narrated by reporter Jessica Savitch, was seen across the country, and highlighted the controversy, painting a very disturbing picture of NPS management practices.[15]

More recently, in 2004 and continuing all the way through 2014, similar controversy surfaced at Point Reyes National Seashore in California. What made the situation at Point Reyes noteworthy was the level of discord and attention it drew a full half-century after the national seashore was created in 1962, and the division that developed within the environmental community itself.

Most of the controversy at Point Reyes was associated with "wilderness status" subsequently declared for a portion of the seashore in the Drakes Estero, and the impacts that status should have on, of all things, an historic oyster farm that had been in operation there for more than eighty years.

* * *

Provisions for the designation of legal wilderness are contained within the 1964 Wilderness Act, which creates special protections for designated public lands administered by a wide variety of federal agencies. The purpose of the Wilderness Act is summarized in Section 2 of the Act:

> In order to assure that an increasing population, accompanied by expanding settlement and growing mechanization, does not occupy and modify all areas of the United States and its possessions, leaving no lands designated for preservation and protection in their natural condition, it is hereby declared to be the policy of the Congress to secure for the American people of present and future generations the benefits of an enduring resource of wilderness. For this purpose there is hereby established a National Wilderness Preservation System to be composed of federally owned areas designated by the Congress as "wilderness areas" ... [to be] ... administered for the use and enjoyment of the American people in such manner as will leave them unimpaired for future use as wilderness, and so as to provide for the protection of these areas, the preservation of

47

their wilderness character, and for the gathering and dissemination of information regarding their use and enjoyment as wilderness.[16]

In essence, the Wilderness Acts requires that federal agencies charged with the management of areas designated by Congress as wilderness or potential wilderness, do so with a special sensitivity to the preservation of purely natural conditions, "where the earth and its community of life are untrammeled by man, where man himself is a visitor who does not remain."

As one can easily imagine, definitions and guidelines like these are still subject to interpretation, not only within the environmental community, but between different agencies and even *within* individual agencies. *High Country News* once described the situation in the NPS as "Park Service Wilderness in disarray."[17] Conflicts over how the Wilderness Act should be implemented are frequently encountered between agency purists who may, for example, argue against the presence of any form of technology or man-made artifacts whatsoever, even by agency personnel engaged in official duties. On the other side of the argument, but even within the same divisions, may be resource managers who see a need to apply modern tools and techniques to at least restore already-disturbed habitat to its natural condition, to accommodate historic uses, or to accommodate some visitor and employee needs. For example, within the potential wilderness of Yosemite National Park, there are High Sierra backcountry camping facilities that have been maintained for decades, providing "an opportunity to experience the remote backcountry in relative comfort of tent cabins with wood floors, beds and small woodstoves, fresh home-cooked meals, and hot showers."[18] Photographer Ansel Adams defended the camps, observing "The present High Sierra Camps do not, in my opinion, violate wilderness qualities as they now exist."[19] Removal of these facilities would allow for conversion of the area to full wilderness status, but there are no plans to do so. Some have argued that the presence of such facilities is not (or should not be) permitted without the enactment of special legislation. Nevertheless, there are wilderness and potential wilderness areas within parks where local managers, out of a sense of practicality or political expedience, have at various times made the decision to accommodate or at least tolerate certain non-conforming uses and man-made facilities; a reflection of the inconsistent manner in which different parks are frequently managed.

* * *

In the case at Point Reyes, controversy over the impact wilderness designation should (or should not) have on operations of the oyster farm resulted in a heated and very public 7-year legal battle that *Newsweek.com* (on-line magazine) called "one of the ugliest environmental fights in the country."[20]

Like other urban parks from that period, establishment of Point Reyes National Seashore received broad community support. Key to the creation of the seashore was the support that existed within the local ranching community.[21] By that time, state officials and developers already had plans for a four-lane highway to run through the area, with subdivisions and other developments scattered along the adjacent landscape. But Marin County, where the seashore is situated, is known for its level of affluence and political influence, not to mention environmental advocacy and "green" lifestyles. Point Reyes would not have become a national seashore were it not for a concerted community effort to protect those areas against urban and suburban sprawl. But in the second decade of the 21st century, many residents – inholders – who long ago agreed to sell their farms or ranches to the government in an effort to preserve their rural lifestyles, found themselves battling the same NPS whose efforts they once supported and lobbied for.[22]

The oyster farm was located in a portion of Drakes Estero within the national seashore, operating as one of many inholdings in the area "leased back" from the government as a working farming or ranching enterprise. Among the allegations leveled against the NPS was that senior officials inexplicably reversed the long-standing management position that had permitted and encouraged the continuing operation of the farm since the government purchased the site as part of the national seashore.

In the 1960s, NPS land use surveys and economic feasibility studies conducted as part of the proposal and public relations campaign to create Point Reyes National Seashore had supported continuation of the oyster farm, observing:

> Existing commercial oyster beds and an oyster cannery at Drakes Estero, plus three existing fisheries, should continue under national seashore status because of their public values. The culture of oysters is an interesting and unique industry which presents exceptional educational opportunities for introducing the public, especially students, to the field of marine biology. Continuation of commercial fishing, with expansion of existing facilities to include sea food restaurants and markets and charter boat services for deep sport fishing would be compatible with the seashore concept.[23]

Similar language with respect to cattle ranching appeared in the same NPS proposals, noting that

> Some 20,000 acres of land situated in the central part of the Peninsula would be leased for ranching purposes to preserve the present pastoral scene.[24]

Establishment of Point Reyes National Seashore was authorized in 1962. Supplemental legislation designating a portion of the seashore as wilderness was passed in 1976.

Since establishment of the national seashore in 1962, the historic oyster farm continued operations under a forty-year "reservation of use and occupancy" (RUO) issued in 1972. The initial term of that RUO expired in November of 2012, but that same RUO also contained provisions for the issuance of a supplemental permit under which the oyster farm could legally continue to operate, thereafter.[25]

The farm was located within the pastoral zone, adjacent to, but not within, the designated wilderness area. Its operations, however, relied upon access to an 8,000 acre area of congressionally designated "potential wilderness." In theory, and in most cases, potential wilderness is supposed to convert to full wilderness status at such time that obstacles to conversion can be eliminated. In the case of Drake's Estero, two obstacles to conversion existed. The most conspicuous, and the one that received the most attention, was the oyster farm operation. The other was commercial fishing and mineral rights that the state of California retained in perpetuity (as mandated by state law) when it conveyed some 10,000 acres of tide and submerged lands to the federal government for the seashore.

But provisions of the Wilderness Act and Interior policies also allow for the continuation of some pre-existing non-conforming uses. That point was stressed in an October 6, 1975 letter of support for wilderness designation submitted by no less an entity than the San Francisco Bay Chapter of the Sierra Club, noting that

> One aspect of concern which the State has expressed in considering wilderness for Drake's Estero is the Johnson Oyster Company Operations. Wilderness status does not mean an end to the harvesting of oysters in the Estero, or a prohibition on the use of motorboats by the company in carrying out is operations ... The Wilderness Act permits prior non-conforming commercial uses to continue, and the Secretary of the Interior can authorize the continued use of motorboats in support of the enterprise. Departmental memoranda express this quite clearly and the regional solicitor has interpreted the act to permit specifically this commercial operation."[26]

Later, in hearings considering the bill to designate wilderness at Point Reyes National Seashore (S. 2472), sponsor Senator John Tunney (D-CA) testified that "Established private rights of landowners and leaseholders will continue to be respected and protected. The existing agricultural and aquacultural uses can continue."[27] In those same hearings, Congressman John L. Burton (D-CA), sponsor of the bill on the House side, reiterated that point, stating, "This legislation is intended to preserve the present diverse uses of the Seashore ..." and "There are two areas proposed for wilderness which may be included as wilderness with 'prior, non-conforming use' provisions. One is Drakes Estero where there is a commercial oyster farm..."[28]

That same position was echoed by California 9th District Assemblyman Michael Wornum, who, in a letter of support for the wilderness legislation, stated, "Finally, I believe everyone concerned supports continued operation of oyster farming in Drakes Estero as a non-conforming use."[29] The Marin County Planning Commission affirmed this position, noting in its own letter that "We accordingly hope that the tidal zone will be managed as a wilderness area and we find this approach consistent with the State's reservation of fishing and mineral rights. We wish to note the following points in this regard: A. S. 2472 would allow the continued use and operation of the Johnson's Oyster Company in Drake's Estero ..."[30]

Finally, the members of the Golden Gate National Recreation Area Citizen's Advisory Commission, appointed by the Secretary of the Interior to consider the possible designation of a portion of Point Reyes as a wilderness area, offered the following statement regarding "nonconforming uses":

> Two activities presently carried on within the seashore existed prior to its establishment as a park and have since been considered desirable by both the public and park managers. Because they both entail the use of motorized equipment, specific provisions should be made in wilderness legislation to allow the following uses to continue unrestrained by wilderness designation:
>
> 1. Ranching operations on that portion of the "pastoral zone" that falls within the proposed wilderness....
>
> 2. Operation of Johnson's Oyster Farm including the use of motorboats and the repair and construction of oyster racks and other activities in conformance with the terms of the existing 1,000 acre lease from the State of California....[31]

After enactment of the Point Reyes Wilderness legislation, the park's General Management Plan seemed to also support that position. In letters prepared in 1996, the park superintendent confirmed that

> The Point Reyes National Seashore General Management Plan (1980) clearly states th[at] an oyster farm would continue at the northern end of Drakes Estero.... Therefore, continuation of an oyster operation has been discussed publicly and approved by the National Park Service.[32]

But in May 2007, the NPS released another report, titled "Drakes Estero – A Sheltered Wilderness Estuary." In that document the NPS seemed to reverse its position on the oyster farm, stating that:

> The issuance of a new lease cannot be extended beyond 2012 because of the GMP, NPS Management Policies, and the enacted Wilderness legislation.

Notably, the General Management Plan cited as requiring termination of the lease in 2012 was the very same document previously cited by the park superintendent in his letter affirming the NPS position that "an oyster farm would continue at the northern end of Drakes Estero ..."[33]

That same report, "A Sheltered Wilderness Estuary," noted that:

> The waters of Drakes Estero were designated by Congress as potential wilderness by the 1976 Point Reyes Wilderness Act (Public Law 94-544). It designated 25,370 acres as wilderness, and 8,002 acres as potential wilderness. The legislative history (House Report 94-1680) indicates Congressional intent: "it is the intention that those lands and waters designated as potential wilderness, to the extent possible, with efforts to steadily continue to remove all obstacles to eventual conversion of these lands and waters to wilderness status."[34]

In support of its new position, the NPS cited recent studies it had conducted, concluding that the operation of oyster farm boats disrupted and threatened the activities of harbor seals that frequent the adjacent wilderness area within Drakes Estero. The agency also cited a new 2004 "memorandum of opinion" requested from the DOI Office of the Solicitor supporting the new NPS position that:

> The Park Service is mandated by the Wilderness Act, the Point Reyes Wilderness Act and its Management Policies to convert potential wilderness, i.e., the Johnson Oyster Company tract and the adjoining Estero, to wilderness status as soon as the non-conforming use can be eliminated.[35]

This language, along with language contained in subsequent documents released by the NPS, alarmed not just the owner of the oyster farm, but other ranchers in the area, who viewed this new interpretation as threatening the very institutions, lifestyles, and pastoral landscapes they had sought to preserve in their own support of the establishment of the national seashore. They couldn't understand how the very same 1980

Point Reyes GMP could one day be cited by the superintendent to justify and support the continuation of oyster farming at Drakes Estero, and then just a few years later be cited by the NPS as legal justification for the farm's closure. Equally perplexing was the apparent change in the government's interpretation of the park's wilderness legislation, away from that cited by the Sierra Club in 1975, in their attempts (then) to allay concerns over the impacts that wilderness designation would have on future operations of the oyster farm, to one (now) compelling closure.[36]

Release of those documents sparked a wave of controversy and outrage in the immediate Point Reyes community. The entire matter was complicated when county commissioners asked a member of the National Academy of Sciences to review the studies and reports that had been submitted by NPS officials in support of its decision to shut down the oyster farm. The Academy review was highly critical of the methodology and findings reached by the NPS, raising questions related to the concealment of exculpatory evidence and the manipulation of data. The NPS then paid for a separate review, which concluded that the agency had "selectively presented, over-interpreted, or misrepresented the available scientific information on potential impacts of the oyster mariculture operation." The chairman of the review committee added that "political pressure, funding issues and conflicting mandates, not deliberate misconduct, are concerns." The director of the NPS (and former NPS Pacific West Regional Director) credited the review in 2009, noting that "the research will be valuable to the Park Service to guide scientific studies that will assist it in making future decisions." But the director was apparently unmoved by the underlying findings, reportedly telling reporters "he does not intend to extend the oyster farm's lease in 2012." Distancing himself from the compromised NPS environmental reviews that had been cited to justify the closure, he explained, now, that "The permit of use and occupancy expires in 2012 ... and that really is a policy and law issue, not a science issue."[37]

Adding to the magnitude and the visibility of the controversy was the support local farmers, ranchers and other families secured from a number influential political figures, including Senator Diane Feinstein (D-CA, 1992 to present), as well as former Representative Paul "Pete" McCloskey (R-CA, 1967 to 1983) and other local officials who were instrumental in introducing and passing federal legislation first establishing the seashore. McCloskey is an environmental heavy-weight by any standard, having co-authored the Endangered Species Act and having also supported any number of other significant environmental laws and causes. He co-sponsored the first Earth Day celebration in 1970 that is widely credited as the launch of the modern environmental movement in the United States. McCloskey was also one of the principle co-sponsors of the legislation calling for management of certain areas of the seashore as wilderness (the

Phillip Burton Wilderness) and potential wilderness.[38] Yet he, along with several other key historical political figures (including Phillip Burton's brother John, also a former Congressman) all vocally challenged the Park Service's interpretation of those laws and how Congress intended they should (or should not) restrict pre-existing commercial farming, ranching, and oyster operations within the national seashore.[39]

To resolve the legal dispute over the Park Service's new interpretation of the Wilderness Act and its implications on the oyster farm, that same year (2009), for better or worse, Senator Feinstein sponsored and Congress passed superseding legislation granting the Secretary of the Interior explicit authority to issue a ten-year extension for the oyster farm's operating permit.[40] That move by Feinstein infuriated wilderness advocates, who feared her actions established a dangerous precedent that could "prompt other U.S. senators and Congressional representatives to make similar requests for commercial operations on national parkland in other states." They maintained that "A deal's a deal. Drakes Estero is supposed to become wilderness."[41]

After that, even more environmental reviews, intended to inform the secretary and guide him in his decision, were conducted or contracted by the NPS, claiming environmental damage caused by the oyster farm operation. But those reviews were, in turn, repeatedly challenged, again, by the National Academy of Sciences and other scientists. Even the Interior Department's own attorneys were forced to acknowledge bias and other deficiencies identified in the process used by the NPS.[42] Those findings, in turn, led Senator Feinstein to charge, in 2012, that "The Park Service has falsified and misrepresented data, hidden science and even promoted employees who knew about the falsehoods, all in an effort to advance a predetermined outcome against the oyster farm."[43]

In the end, the Secretary decided against the oyster farm, allowing the RUO to expire without issuing the ten-year extension permit. That, in turn, led to an unsuccessful two-year effort by the farm owners to secure an injunction against the closure, as a precursor to a broader legal challenge to the process and legal interpretations that guided the secretary in his decision.[44] The motion for injunction was denied and then appealed to the 9th Circuit, and subsequently to the U.S. Supreme Court, without success. That was largely because, ironically, the Feinstein law ultimately gave the secretary complete discretion in the matter without regard to the validity of the science or other factors that may have influenced his decision. The oyster farm was forced to cease operations as 2014 came to a close. The entire facility was hurriedly dismantled by the NPS, precluding any benefit for the farm owners that might otherwise have come from additional litigation attempting to address the underlying conflicts in interpretation of the original wilderness legislation, or the allegations of scientific misconduct and abuse of legal processes.

Even more recently, still at Pt. Reyes, tensions have arisen over the impacts an NPS-reintroduced heard of once-rare Tule elk is having on park ranches, as those elk expand their range into historic pastures used for cattle. Families operating within the national seashore's pastoral zone under long-term renewable leases negotiated when they originally sold their ranches, are facing what has been characterized by some observers as a form of NPS "mission creep"; pressure for the agency to now manage the area more as a traditional national park and even wilderness, rather than as part of the originally envisioned "... 20,000 acres of land situated in the central part of the Peninsula ... leased for ranching purposes to preserve the present [1961] pastoral scene."[45]

No matter what position one supports, it is certain that the situation at Pt. Reyes has turned into a genuine public relations disaster for the NPS. That was confirmed as far back as 2008, when officials from the National Parks Conservation Association, advocating for wilderness, acknowledged that "All parties are at fault. It's escalated to a level it should never have reached."[46] The local environmental community has become split. Decent people on both sides of the debate are sharply divided, and not just because of their respective views on operation of the historic oyster farm and area ranches, versus pure wilderness. The different groups appear to have had different experiences and been told different things in their interactions with NPS officials, resulting in different expectations and a genuine erosion of trust in portions of the community for anything the agency now says or does.

Endnotes

1. 16 U.S.C. 460L-4, et seq., Sept. 3, 1964. The fund is also available for use by state and local governments.

2. Setha Low, Dana Taplin, Suzanne Scheld, *Rethinking Urban Parks; public space and cultural diversity*, (Austin, Texas: University of Texas Press, 2005), 30-31.

3. National Park Service, *Cuyahoga Valley: Ohio's National Park*, "Park Idea Meets NPS Resistance," (National Park Service informational brochure).

4. National Park Service, *Shaping the System: Mission 66 and the Environmental Era, 1952 to 1972*, (on-line book, National Park Service).

5. National Research Council, Committee on Scientific and Technical Criteria for Federal Acquisition of Lands for Conservation, *Setting Priorities for Land Conservation*, (Washington, D.C.: National Academy Press, 1993), 59-60. http://books.google.com/books?id=9Kq26MWk7n-sC&pg=PA60&lpg=PA60&dq=urban+parks+NPS+1960s&source=bl&ots=ng-V0m-W7MW&sig=aj3yet3I2Z-qMGzi4AlxLxNOkYc&hl=en&sa=X&ei=PCg4T_z9N6vY-iQLNtvmtCg&sqi=2&ved=0CEUQ6AEwBQ#v=onepage&q=urban%20parks%20NPS%201960s&f=false.

6. USPP Inspector Franklin A. Arthur, National Park Service (Washington Office), "Follow Up Slip," June 3, 1972. *Also*, Congressional Record-U.S. House of Representatives (H 5537), June 13, 1972, p. 19.

7. Warren D. Beach, National Park Service memorandum, June 5, 1972, "Assault on Chief Ranger Hutchison."

8. *See* Administrative Procedure Act, 5 USC, Chapter 5, sections 511-599.

9. Stryker McGuire with Pamela Abramson and Dan Shapiro, *Newsweek* magazine, "National Affairs – Land Grab by the Parks," August 14, 1978, p. 21.

10. John F. Lambert, Jr., *The Harvard Environmental Law Review,* Vol. 6, issue 1 (6 Harv. Envtl. L. Rev. 35, 1982), "Private Landholdings in the National Parks: Examples from Yosemite National Park and Indiana Dunes National Lakeshore."

11. National Research Council, *Setting Priorities for Land Conservation,* (Washington, D.C.: National Academy of Sciences/National Academy Press, 1993).

12. National Research Council, *Setting Priorities for Land Conservation,* (Washington, D.C.: National Academy of Sciences/National Academy Press, 1993), 98-99, 103-106.

13. Phillip D. Brick and R. McGreggor Cawley (editors), *A Wolf in the Garden: The Land Rights Movement and the New Environmental Debate* (Lanham, MD: Rowman and Littlefield, 1996).

14. Phillip D. Brick and R. McGreggor Cawley (editors), *A Wolf in the Garden: The Land Rights Movement and the New Environmental Debate* (Lanham, MD: Rowman and Littlefield, 1996), 9.

15. Valley Film Works, *For the Good of All* (Public Broadcasting System, 1983), for PBS's "Frontline" with Jessica Savitch, Stephanie Tepper, writer/producer; Adapted from the film, *For All People, For All Time.*

16. P.L 88-577 (16 U.S.C. 1131-1136), Sep. 3, 1964.

17. Matt Jenkins, "Park Service Wilderness in disarray," *High Country News,* Feb. 16, 2004.

18. http://www.yosemitefun.com/high_sierra_camps.htm. Also, http://www.yosemitepark.com/high-sierra-camp-lodging.aspx.

19. Ansel Adams to Richard Leonard, June 19, 1971, Carton 163, *Sierra Club Papers*; National Park Service, *Yosemite: The Embattled Wilderness,* https://www.nps.gov/parkhistory/online_books/runte2/chap12.htm; Richard Orsi, Alfred Runte, Marlene Smith-Baranzini, *Yosemite and Sequoia: a century of California national parks,* (Berkeley, CA: University of California Press, 1993), 125.

20. Michael Ames, *Newsweek.com,* "The Oyster Shell Game," Jan. 18, 2015.

21. *Saving Point Reyes National Seashore, 1969-1970: An Oral History of Citizen Action in Conservation,* Interview with "Boyd Stewart – Point Reyes Rancher and Seashore Supporter," An Interview Conducted by Ann Lage in 1990, (Berkeley, CA: The Regents of the University of California, 1993).

22. Ann Lage, *Saving Point Reyes National Seashore, 1969-1970: An Oral History of Citizen Action in Conservation,* [1990] Interview with "Boyd Stewart – Point Reyes Rancher and Seashore Supporter" (Berkeley, CA: The Regents of the University of California, 1993).

23. National Park Service, *Report on the Economic Feasibility of the Proposed Point Reyes National Seashore 1961,* prepared by Region Four Office, Lawrence C. Merriam, Regional Director, February. 1961. p. 2 (incorporating testimony presented by NPS director Conrad L. Wirth, 1961, before the subcommittee considering S. 476, A Bill to Establish the Point Reyes National Seashore).

24. National Park Service, *Report on the Economic Feasibility of the Proposed Point Reyes National Seashore 1961,* prepared by Region Four Office, Lawrence C. Merriam, Regional Director, February. 1961. p. 2.

25. Exhibit C from the 1972 Johnson Oyster Company Reservation of Use and Occupancy, "Upon expiration of the reserved term, a special use permit may be issued for the continued occupancy of the property for the herein described purposes, provided however, that such permit will run concurrently with and will terminate upon the expiration of state water bottom allotments assigned to the Vendor." Those assigned allotments were renewed on June 25, 2004, for a period of twenty-five years (expiring in 2029), with the option, at the discretion of the State of California, for issuance of additional extensions thereafter ("Renewal of Leases, M-438-01 and M-438-02," Dec. 21/25,

2004, between State of California and Johnson Oyster Company; Amendment No. 2 to Indenture of Lease, No. M-438-01, transferring Lease Agreement No. M-438-01 from the Johnson Oyster Company to Drakes Bay Oyster Company).

26. Larry Kolb, Vice Chairman for Wilderness Issues, Sierra Club, San Francisco Bay Chapter, to The Resource Agency of California, Claire Dedrick, Secretary, letter, Oct. 6, 1975. *See also*, Sierra Club, Apr. 1974 Public Comment on Final Environmental Impact Statement for S. 2472, Bill to Designate Wilderness at Point Reyes National Seashore ("... The water can be put under the Wilderness Act even while the oyster culture is continued [as] ... a prior existing, non-conforming use.") p. A-51.

27. John V. Tunney (D–CA), during hearings on S. 1093 and S. 2472 before the Subcommittee on Parks and Recreation of the Committee on Interior and Insular Affairs, 94th Cong. 271, March 2, 1976.

28. John L. Burton (D-CA), during hearings on S. 1093 and S. 2472 before the Subcommittee on Parks and Recreation of the Committee on Interior and Insular Affairs, 94th Cong. 271, March 2, 1976.

29. Michael Wornum, Assemblyman, 9th District of California, to U.S. Senator J. Bennett Johnston, Chairman, Subcommittee on Parks and Recreation, Committee on Interior and Insular Affairs, Nov. 4, 1975.

30. Jerry Friedman, Chairman, Marin County Planning Commission, to Hon. J. Bennett Johnston, Chairman, Parks and Recreation Subcommittee, Nov. 6, 1975.

31. Frank C. Boerges, Chairman, Golden Gate National Recreation Area Citizen's Advisory Commission, prepared statement to Chairman of the Subcommittee,

32. Superintendent Don Neubacher (Point Reyes National Seashore) to Alex Desoto (Specialized Financial Consultants), letter, Jul. 19, 1996 (L1425, 02-106, PORE), and Don Neubacher to Bank of Oakland, letter, Nov. 22, 1996 (L1425, 02-106).

33. Superintendent Don Neubacher (Point Reyes National Seashore) to Alex Desoto (Specialized Financial Consultants), letter, Jul. 19, 1996 (L1425, 02-106, PORE), and Don Neubacher to Bank of Oakland, letter, Nov. 22, 1996 (L1425, 02-106).

34. National Park Service, *Point Reyes National Seashore – Drakes Estero: A Sheltered Wilderness Estuary*, (NPS website, May 22, 2007), 1, 2.

35. Ralph G. Mihan, DOI Field Solicitor, San Francisco Field Office, to NPS Superintendent, Point Reyes National Seashore, letter, Feb. 26, 2004.

36. Larry Kolb, Vice Chairman for Wilderness Issues, Sierra Club, San Francisco Bay Chapter, to The Resource Agency of California, Claire Dedrick, Secretary, letter, Oct. 6, 1975.

37. Peter Fimrite (quoting NPS director Jon Jarvis), "Scientists side with Drakes Bay oyster farm," *San Francisco Chronicle*, May 6, 2009.

38. P.L. 94-544.

39. Pete McCloskey, John Burton, and Billy Bagley to Secretary of the Interior, letter, Aug. 11, 2011; Pete McCloskey (guest columnist), "Neubacher's slashing attack on the oyster farm: Will the bogus science continue?" *Point Reyes Light*, Sep. 22, 2011.

40. H.R. 2996 (111th) : Department of the Interior, Environment, and Related Agencies Appropriations Act, 2010, Section 124 (Point Reyes National Seashore): "Prior to the expiration on November 30, 2012 of the Drake's Bay Oyster Company's Reservation of Use and Occupancy and associated special use permit ('existing authorization') within Drake's Estero at Point Reyes National Seashore, notwithstanding any other provision of law, the Secretary of the Interior is authorized to issue a special use permit with the same terms and conditions as the existing authorization, except as provided herein, for a period of 10 years from November 30, 2012: *Provided*, That such extended authorization is subject to annual payments to the United States based on the fair market value of the use of the Federal property for the duration of such renewal. The Secretary

shall take into consideration recommendations of the National Academy of Sciences Report pertaining to shellfish mariculture in Point Reyes National Seashore before modifying any terms and conditions of the extended authorization. Nothing in this section shall be construed to have any application to any location other than Point Reyes National Seashore; nor shall anything in this section be cited as precedent for management of any potential wilderness outside the Seashore."

41. Robert Gammon, "Dianne Feinstein's War," *East Bay Express* (on-line newspaper), June 13, 2012, quoting Amy Trainer, executive director of The Environmental Action Committee of West Marin.

42. Gavin M. Frost (DOI Office of the Solicitor) to Will Shafroth (DOI, Acting Asst. Sect.), "Public Report on Allegations of Scientific Misconduct at Point Reyes National Seashore," March 22, 2011.

43. Michael Ames, *Newsweek.com,* " The Oyster Shell Game," quoting from a March 2012 letter from Senator Feinstein to Secretary of the Interior Ken Salazar.

44. Alleging violations of NEPA, the Delta Quality Act, the Administrative Procedures Act, and the U.S. Constitution.

45. National Park Service, *Report on the Economic Feasibility of the Proposed Point Reyes National Seashore 1961,* prepared by Region Four Office, Lawrence C. Merriam, Regional Director, February. 1961. p. 2. Laura A. Watt, 2015, "Parks as (Potential) Wilderness," Chapter 4 in *The Paradox of Preservation: Wilderness and Working Landscapes at Point Reyes National Seashore,* unpublished manuscript. *Also,* James Knight, "Wild Meets Mild – Do elk have a place in Pt. Reyes?" the *Bohemian* (Santa Rosa, CA), March 11, 2015; Natasha Geiling, "Cattle Ranching Has 'Hijacked' A Protected Seashore, Environmentalists Say," *Think Progress.org,* Feb. 25, 2016.

46. Bill Meagher, "West Marin's Lunny family struggles to keep Drake's Bay Oysters afloat," *Northbay Biz,* Nov., 2008 Issue (interview with Neil Desai of NPCA).

PART 2

CHAPTER FIVE

A Foot in the Door
(Indiana Dunes)

My own appreciation for public lands developed while growing up on the edges of the expanding suburban sprawl of southern California. I was part of a fortunate generation where a quest for adventure and escape from increasing congestion was fueled by an unprecedented level of mobility. Armed with our driver's licenses and a sense of boundless freedom, my family, friends, and I thought nothing of five-hundred or even thousand-mile trips to the nearby mountains, canyons, and deserts. The national parks, forests, and other open spaces of the West served as our vacation and even weekend playgrounds. Participation in organizations like the Audubon Society, the Sierra Club, and the Student Conservation Association provided me with the opportunity for summer internships working and attending classes in parks like Grand Teton, North Cascades, and the Grand Canyon. By the time I left home for college, I knew those were the kinds of places where I wanted to spend my life and pursue a career.

After nearly eight years working on and off as a seasonal ranger for the NPS, principally at Grand Canyon National Park in northern Arizona, and Lake Mead National Recreation Area outside of Las Vegas, I happily settled on a job as a sheriff's deputy in Boulder, Colorado. In those days, Boulder County was still a relatively undeveloped and beautiful area in its own right. As a highly regarded agency, a position on the sheriff's department was a perfectly acceptable alternative to a hard-to-get permanent job patrolling the national parks.

But before long, an unexpected call came from a former colleague in the NPS. The dense and decaying scene on the south shore of Lake Michigan was certainly not the dream assignment I'd envisioned, but it *would* be another adventure. Even beyond that, I considered myself lucky to finally be offered a permanent job as a criminal investigator at the newly-established Indiana Dunes National Lakeshore (est. 1966). It was, after all, a unique opportunity to pursue a law enforcement career with what had long been my dream agency.

Traveling along the highway approaching East Chicago, Indiana I was struck by the apocalyptic scene passing before me. I still have recollections of the mountain-like silhouette in the dim evening light, created by the endless row of enormous piles of garbage in an open-pit dump extending for what seemed miles. Out of each "peak" extending into the distance were pipes to vent the methane gas. The flames burned throughout the night, giving an eerie orange glow to the evening sky.

The boarded-up, dilapidated buildings lining the streets of Gary, Indiana only reinforced the scene as I made my way through Lake County. Continuing eastward and crossing into Porter County, the view gradually changed to reveal the comparatively lush, green community of Chesterton where park headquarters was located. Over the next several days, settling in, I was shown around the new and developing NPS site.

It's always interesting to look back and reflect on how seemingly unrelated people, places, and events can eventually come together to reveal a hidden connection. With absolutely no hint of its significance at the time, many of the events and unseen characters at Indiana Dunes would figure prominently in a series of what would, for me, be life-changing experiences.

* * *

Indiana Dunes was one of the of new urban parks authorized by Congress in the 1960s and 1970s in an effort to satisfy the political and recreational needs of surrounding metropolitan areas. Like many of these urban national parks, the idea of establishing Indiana Dunes National Lakeshore had been formulated years earlier by forward-thinking citizens of the region. Support for the establishment of a national park along the southern shoreline of Lake Michigan was expressed as far back as 1916. That's the same year the NPS was created as a unifying federal agency to manage the national parks that already existed and those that would later be established. Jens Jensen, a pioneering advocate for the national park, articulated the unique demand for such an area immediately adjacent to Chicago's burgeoning industrial and metropolitan scene, explaining

> The people of the mills, the shops, and the stores are the backbone of the great cities. They are the producers of wealth and the human species; and the opportunity for those people to get the full value of the out of doors is made almost impossible. The great national reservations of the West are beyond their reach and the parks of the cities, valuable as they are, do not possess the wild beauty of the master's hand nor do they inspire the soul in the same degree... The Dunes of Northern Indiana are almost within a stone's throw of perhaps one of the greatest industrial communities in the world. It is the only landscape of its kind within reach of the millions that need its softening influence for the restoration of their souls and the balance of their minds.[1]

No less a figure than Stephen Mather, credited founder of the NPS and that agency's first director, "declared that the Indiana Dunes were unmatched anywhere in the United States, if not the world." Expressing his vision for the park, he noted,

> Here is a stretch of unoccupied beach 25 miles in length, a broad, clean, safe beach, which in the summer months would furnish splendid bathing facilities for thousands of people at the same instant...[2]

NPS Director Stephen Mather (left) surveying Indiana Dunes as a prospective park site. (NPS Photo).

Notwithstanding these types of pronouncements, support for the park was not unanimous. Strong opposition came from segments of the community who preferred the expansion of industry along the valuable Indiana shoreline, and attendant prospects for jobs and economic growth. Many residents, especially those in Porter County, charged that

> It would undermine the tax base of the region and permanently close the lakeshore to industry. Many believed U.S. Steel Corporation was the power behind the park movement because it wished to keep its competitors out.[3]

World War I placed the entire debate on hold. Supporters of a national park, including the group known as the National Dunes Park Association, were forced to change their popular slogan "Save the Dunes," to "First Save the Country, Then Save the Dunes." Still, considerable public support continued throughout the period, as reflected in a 1918 editorial that appeared in a Chicago newspaper:

Unless the State of Indiana or the United States takes the matter in hand, commercial plants will crowd the entire lake frontage. The matter resolves itself into a decision of humanity. Shall the millions of mill workers be condemned to the slavery of labor without recreation in the big plants of the lake shore, or shall they be given the privilege of open-air spaces and pure air in which to renew strength and courage in their brief hours away from the mills?[4]

The prosperity realized in post-war America, accompanied by renewed industrial growth and the attendant influence of powerful business interests, succeeded in further postponing efforts to "save the dunes." Those preservation efforts floundered through the next several decades, up to and all the way through World War II. In the process, much of the twenty-five mile stretch of lakeshore originally envisioned for the park, and once comparatively free of development, became lined with an ever increasing expanse of job-producing heavy industry, including several more steel mills, battery factories, and eventually even plans for development of a nuclear power plant.

Efforts to save what was left of the lakeshore were renewed in 1952, when a group of twenty-one local women led by Bess Sheehan formed the Save the Dunes Council. They faced stiff opposition from powerful economic interests, including:

> a united front of the political and business communities [who] sought to maximize economic development along the limited lakeshore. The idea of setting aside more parkland was an anathema to the economic planners who were working to secure federal funds to construct a gigantic "Port of Indiana" at Burns Harbor (or Ditch). Expanding the existing mills and attracting still other steel companies to the area were other top priorities.[5]

Opposition to the establishment of a park administered by the NPS was fueled by racial tensions as well as fears about access to what had become de facto private beaches for residents of the many affluent suburbs and resort communities that had since sprung up in the area. As one NPS planner observed,

> Rumors are being circulated that the beaches in front of excluded towns within the proposal will be overrun with Chicago negroes. Also, that the National Park Service is planning to fence off the towns from the beach...[6]

Lobbying by the competing interests of preservation versus industry continued all the way through the 1960s. Illinois Senator Paul Douglas (D-IL) and Representative J. Edward Roush (D-IN) supported establishment of a national park. Roush eventually sponsored H.R. 51, arguing that:

> while there may never be a local consensus, Indiana Dunes National Lakeshore was certainly in the national interest.[7]

Response to the proposed legislation was almost immediate:

> Few could have predicted the magnitude of the vehemence unleashed on Senator Douglas. Media, industry, and political organizations combined accusing Douglas with interfering in Indiana's affairs, serving as a Chicago carpetbagger plotting against Indiana's economic development, and working to establish a park to placate the minorities of Chicago. Douglas's opponents derisively referred to him as the "Third Senator from Indiana." Indignant Hoosiers pointed to an underground coalition of Illinois politicians and industrialists who were hiding behind Senator Douglas' "Save the Dunes" movement in order to stop the Port of Indiana. Douglas' nefarious coalition was also believed to be joined by dunes area industry which hoped to keep competitors out.[8]

Leading the opposition was northwest Indiana Congressman Charles A. Halleck, who voiced strong opposition because:

> it would destroy the area's economic potential, thereby depriving his constituents of thousands of jobs.

Ironically, by this time he was also able to cite what he believed was the futility of efforts to preserve the remaining natural landscape:

> As for Park Service plans to establish nature trails near the industrial zones, Halleck scoffed, "I can't conceive of anyone even walking across the street to explore some of those parcels."[9]

Concerns over the already deteriorated landscape resulting from delays in the protection of the lakeshore would continue to plague park efforts for years to come. Over time, those concerns would be cited as justification to restrict expansion of proposed park boundaries. On May 26, 1976, Assistant Secretary of the Interior Nathaniel P. Reed reluctantly echoed this sentiment during hearings of the Committee on Interior and Insular Affairs concerning the acquisition of additional acreage for the Lakeshore.

> We are 50 years, 70 years late. We are in a numbers game with tremendous supporters, dedicated men and women and children,

who have worked to preserve this area and who have seen their chances erode over the years. They are in a numbers game with us. They want us to buy acres, regardless as to the quality of the acres because in some way, it makes up for the lost opportunities.

He added,

I cannot believe that a slag dump is a worthwhile addition to a National Park area.[10]

The Lakeshore faced even more unique challenges, including strained efforts by resource managers to somehow address "...the obnoxious odors emanating from the Continental Can Company plant near Dune Acres and Bethlehem Steel."[11]

But over the course of time, political compromises were reached and a victory was realized by the Save the Dunes Council and their supporters. On October 14, 1966, H.R. 51 was passed in the House of Representatives. The Senate thereafter concurred. Indiana Dunes National Lakeshore came into being on November 15, 1966, with the passage of P.L. 89-761, signed into law by President Lyndon Johnson.

Though plagued with controversy throughout its long conception process, the victory realized in the authorization to establish a national park along the south shore of Lake Michigan was widely celebrated throughout the region. One supporter would later observe,

The Dunes National Park, I think, is going to be one of the finest parks in the System for one very basic reason, and that is that this wasn't a park that a President of the United States decided to start because he had gone camping there when he was a little boy or that somebody started because of pressure from a certain area or political group or ecological group. The Dunes National Park actually was created by citizen pressure, and it has actually been planned by citizen pressure. So while it may not be the biggest park and it may not be the first urban park, as we sometimes refer to them, it is the first citizens' park.[12]

Included within the authorized boundaries of the new park were the lands adjacent to the tracks of the Chicago South Shore and South Bend Railroad, and the open fields near the decaying buildings and apartments of Gary. Beyond that, in Porter County, there were the numerous gated and un-gated communities, including the incorporated towns and communities of Dune Acres/Porter Beach, Ogden Dunes, Pines, Burns Harbor, and Beverly Shores, populated by both long-term residents and wealthy seasonal refugees from the adjacent metropolitan areas. The park's headquarters and administrative offices would eventually move into an abandoned NIKE missile compound. The areas actually intended for public use as part of the national park were the remaining sand dunes and beaches that lined the lakeshore, historic areas in the interior, and at least one biologically unique wildlife preserve known as Cowles' Bog.

* * *

As I toured the area and was shown around and introduced to my new assignment, the overall scene was certainly not what I had envisioned when I left Boulder to accept the job, and it was certainly not my western idea of what constituted a national park. Planners in the NPS apparently agreed with that assessment, acknowledging that:

> Indiana Dunes National Lakeshore simply did not fit into any of the traditional molds for a national park.[13]

Indiana Dunes National Lakeshore. (NPS Photo).

In establishing the Lakeshore, Congress had authorized an aggressive land acquisition program, asserting eminent domain to acquire and then demolish many of the homes and other buildings within the boundaries of the park. That same type of authorization and authority was provided to the other developing lakeshores and recreation areas of the period, including Cuyahoga Valley National Recreation Area (1974) and Sleeping Bear Dunes National Lakeshore (1970).

Predictably, these and other land acquisition programs resulted in considerable tension with home owners, many who opposed establishment of the NPS site in the first place, and whose property was now targeted for incorporation into, and in many instances, acquisition by the newly created national lakeshore. Disputes over restrictions on the use of private property retained as inholdings were common. Equally common were disputes over government purchase prices, as well as contractual details relating to rights retained by the sellers to continue their use and occupancy under "leaseback" agreements.[14] Where agreements could not be reached, the NPS asserted its authority to acquire the properties through condemnation and "declaration of taking" proceedings.[15] Even those sales that occurred "voluntarily" were often tinged by a sense of pressure and coercion, and the inevitability of a legal confrontation with NPS land acquisition officials.

This process was made all the more controversial by the inevitable gaps that emerged between funding available to acquire these homes and other property, and resources needed to later clear the sites and restore the land to its "natural state." Entire subdivisions sequentially acquired through either voluntary sale or condemnation proceedings subsequently sat vacant for years, decaying into dens for everything from feral dogs to drug addicts. Vacated homes were frequently burglarized and pilfered for their remaining parts; from cabinetry, to kitchen and bathroom fixtures, to lumber, to internal copper wiring and pipe. Some homes were torched, either by reckless junkies or angry former owners. Where the original intent may have been to turn these areas back into natural, park-like landscapes, the overall effect for many years was to turn them into newly blighted neighborhoods and slums, confirming for many their worst fears about the effects from establishment of the Lakeshore.

Consequently, while some advocates for establishment of the Lakeshore may have believed Indiana Dunes would be "one of the finest parks in the System," at least a portion of the resident population viewed the matter differently. Some perceived it as a conspiratorial attempt to limit the expansion of industrial-based economic development in the region. Others perceived the NPS as an unwelcome, heavy-handed government agency, dismissive of their property rights and bent on destroying their way of life.

The aggressive land acquisition process at Indiana Dunes and many other developing park areas across the country provided fuel for the establishment of organizations and lobbies representing the interests and advocating for the rights of private inholders. Contentious meetings and even rallies were convened where angry citizens, led by community organizers, vented their rage and opposition to the government's incursion into their backyards. Citing the brazen attitude often reflected in NPS land acquisition practices, leaders of the growing opposition movement were able to generate extensive media interest, resulting in a wave of negative publicity for the NPS. Meanwhile, lawsuits and other efforts initiated by those individuals and advocacy groups were effective in pressuring Congress and the White House to order the investigation and subsequently the revision of many NPS land acquisition regulations and practices, service-wide.[16] The effects of those investigations, pressures, and legal battles continue to be felt throughout the NPS to this day, as many of those same opposition groups have long since matured into extremely efficient and well financed organizations whose sole mission is to oppose government restrictions on the use of public lands and to oppose the expansion of park and wilderness areas.

* * *

Like most other low-level employees, I was oblivious to the maneuvering going on behind the scenes in the establishment and management of the Lakeshore. I was motivated simply by the chance at a permanent law enforcement position with the NPS. I was there and willing to pay my dues and do my time at Indiana Dunes with the hope of an eventual transfer back West to what I viewed as a "real" national park, free of the corrupting influence of urban development. Those were the places I wanted to live and work, superior in my own mind for their vast, rugged, unpopulated landscapes and wild, expansive vistas. In fairness, I may have also viewed those areas in the West as superior because they had received federal protection in time to prevent the widespread encroachment of industrial and residential development.

In the meantime, a major part of my own duties focused on investigating the theft of component property from empty houses slated for salvage contracts, and the investigation of arson and a host of other crimes made opportune by the presence of a vast expanse of vacant houses and adjacent lands acquired by the NPS. Those lands were frequently used for drug dealing and marijuana cultivation, as party sites, or for the disposal of stolen cars, car parts, and the bodies of murder and overdose victims. Those investigations were frequently punctuated with the unpleasant duty of actually serving civil papers on residents whose homes were undergoing condemnation, and responding to threats directed at government officials from disgruntled residents and local opposition groups.

Another unique aspect of this assignment was my firsthand exposure to entrenched regional corruption. I had long heard and read stories about the politics of areas like Chicago, Illinois, and Lake County, Indiana. I had seen movie depictions of both mob and police corruption in the greater Chicago and northern Indiana area that locals refer to as "The Region." Lake County, in particular, was known as a suburban hang-out for mobster Al Capone. Another famous gangster, John Dillinger, spent time in The Region, bringing notoriety to the jail in Crown Point, Indiana, when, according to legend, he made his escape using a fake gun carved out of wood.

But I never really considered that those depictions of regional crime and corruption might be more accurate than not, and that I might actually be in a position to see some of that corruption in my own lifetime and career. It was fascinating to witness the extent to which graft, nepotism, and the patronage system influenced local politics as well as police and other government activities. Many of the local officers with whom I worked thought nothing of taking handouts and payoffs from business owners. Connected residents and community members were virtually immune to arrest and prosecution for offenses ranging from traffic violations to drug dealing. Brutality and racism were an accepted part of the prevailing police culture. Seasoned detectives openly bragged and laughed about tricking, coercing, and even beating confessions out of prisoners and other suspects, while simultaneously rejecting and ridiculing new and more sophisticated interviewing techniques advanced in training sessions sponsored by the Department of Justice.[17] Apprehensions over who could actually be trusted in the local law enforcement community added to the challenge experienced as an outsider already resented for the manner in which property for the Lakeshore had been acquired and for the way the NPS was perceived by a sizeable portion the resident population.

Ironically, the few agencies in the area that did strive to maintain professional standards within their ranks were reluctant to work with the Park Service's own law enforcement personnel. Those local officials had been alienated, early on, as their recommendations for law enforcement staffing levels and infrastructure at the new Lakeshore were summarily ignored by NPS planners and managers. Alienation and isolation were compounded as the better police administrators in the area observed the frequently incompetent manner in which the NPS attempted to staff and manage its own developing law enforcement program.

While frustrated by the manner in which we were frequently received by our local counterparts, most of the transplanted and relatively young law enforcement staff at the Lakeshore were oblivious to the background politics. We just wanted to do our jobs, get some experience, and get a good enough performance evaluation to effectively compete for positions in one of the "real parks" out west.

The entire situation was a 180-degree contrast to what I had seen with the Boulder County Sheriff's Department, where *we* set the standard, and where it appeared to me that even the slightest hint of dishonesty or abuse of authority would result in an immediate investigation, including polygraph examination. There, discipline for violations was swift and severe, often as not resulting in outright dismissal. That posture, and the culture it contributed to, had an undeniable effect on behavior throughout the department. But here in the Region, checks and balances were so out-of-whack or completely absent, and abuses so prevalent that the local office of the FBI, in Hammond, maintained a full-time squad of agents largely dedicated to investigating and prosecuting both mob figures and government officials with ties to organized crime, as well as law enforcement officers engaged in graft and civil rights violations. It was something reminiscent of the old black-and-white mobster movies from the 1940s and 1950s, except what I was seeing was first-hand in the present tense, and for real.

An article by Mark Kiesling summarized the evolution of organized corruption in Northwest Indiana from the 1950s through the 1990s. Writing for *The Times of Northwest Indiana* in 2002, and citing the colorful names of real-life figures that could have come straight out of an old mobster movie, Kiesling observed:

> The organized crime, once pervasive in the south suburbs in Northwest Indiana, has become a shadow of its once-fearsome former self, replaced by other legal and illegal operations.
>
> The last major prosecution of the "Godfather"-style mobsters in Northwest Indiana was the December 1990 indictment of 15 people from Chicago crime boss Dominick "Tootsie" Palermo's crew...

Kiesling discussed other Indiana-based members of the "Chicago Outfit," such as "crime boss" Frankie LaPorte and "kingpin" Gaetano "Tommy" Morgano, who was deported to Italy after a 1963 conviction for gambling. Then he continued,

> From the 1960s through the mid-1980s, it was Frank Nick Zizzo, and when Zizzo died in 1986, his mantle was assumed by Tommy's son, Bernard "Snooky" Morgano, indicted in the Palermo investigation, convicted and released in 1996.
>
> Since Morgano's indictment, federal authorities say, the Chicago Outfit that has controlled Northwest Indiana has stayed so far under their radar as to be invisible...
>
> "We've legalized everything the mob used to do," said Gary Police Deputy Chief Jeffrey Kumorek with a wry laugh. "Either that, or it's gone in a different direction."

The article concluded with one official, a friend of mine, James Mesterharm from the Hammond office of the U.S. Attorney, confirming the influence of the mob on local law enforcement in Northwest Indiana up until the late 1990s:

We're not having that any more, and you don't have any longer, as you once did, the tainted law enforcement who were on mob payrolls. I think the prosecutions have sent a very strong message to law enforcement officers who might have been inclined to go that way. [18]

My own brief exposure to that culture of corruption reinforced my desire to get back west where I believed most things were better and where, it seemed to me, law enforcement was approached as a true profession and practiced to a much higher standard and level of integrity. Surely things would be better there, away from the big cities and their big-city corruption, in the great national parks of the West.

Life at Indiana Dunes was a scenic and cultural shock and an eye opening experience for a western boy. And while I don't necessarily agree with the assessment that it was "one of the finest parks in the System," I can understand the important role that Indiana Dunes National Lakeshore plays for residents of "The Region" and the greater area known as "Chicagoland."[19] Looking back now, I don't regret any of the four years I spent there, seeing first-hand what life was like in the rust belt of America, making many wonderful new friends, and developing my own law enforcement views and skills in that challenging environment. Nevertheless, in February 1982, at the age of 28, I was thrilled when I received a rare competitive promotion and transfer to work as a criminal investigator in Yosemite National Park.

Now *that* was a dream assignment.

Endnotes

1. Ron Cockrell, *A Signature of Time and Eternity: The Administrative History of Indiana Dunes National Lakeshore* (Omaha: Office of Planning and Resource Preservation, Midwest Regional Office, USNPS, 1988), Part 1, Introduction.

2. David Turello, National Park Service, *Indiana Dunes National Lakeshore Administrative History*; Part 1, Chapter 1.

3. National Park Service, *Indiana Dunes National Lakeshore Administrative History*; Part 1, Chapter 1.

4. National Park Service, *Indiana Dunes National Lakeshore Administrative History*; Part 1, Chapter 1.

5. National Park Service, *Indiana Dunes National Lakeshore Administrative History*; Part 1, Chapter 1.

6. National Park Service, *Indiana Dunes National Lakeshore Administrative History*; Part 1, Chapter 4.

7. National Park Service, *Indiana Dunes National Lakeshore Administrative History*; Part 1, Chapter 4.

8. National Park Service, *Indiana Dunes National Lakeshore Administrative History*; Part 1, Chapter 2.

9. National Park Service, *Indiana Dunes National Lakeshore Administrative History*; Part 1, Chapter 3.

10. National Park Service, *Indiana Dunes National Lakeshore Administrative History*; Part 1, Chapter 8.

11. National Park Service, *Indiana Dunes National Lakeshore Administrative History*; Part 1, Chapter 9.

12. Greg Reising of the Miller Citizens' Corporation, speaking before a public meeting on the General Management Plan, Gary, Indiana, Jan. 16, 1980.

13. National Park Service, *Indiana Dunes National Lakeshore Administrative History*; Part II.

14. The term "leaseback" is short for sale-and-leaseback, and refers to a financial transaction where one sells an asset, including property, and leases it back from the purchaser for a long term, during which period he or she is able to use the asset, but no longer owns it.

15. A declaration of taking vests property in the United States immediately upon filing papers in the court and depositing what is considered to be just compensation for that piece of property.

16. E.g., In 1987 President Reagan issued Executive Order 12630, authored by [then] Department of Justice staff attorneys Mark Pollot and Roger Marzulla. Under the caption of "Governmental Actions and Interference With Constitutionally Protected Property Rights," the order requires a "takings impact analyses" of all new government regulations, "to reduce the risk of undue or inadvertent burdens on the public fisc resulting from lawful government actions."

17. *See* CBS News, *60 Minutes*, first aired Dec. 9, 2012, "Chicago is False Confession Capitol," http://www.cbsnews.com/8301-18560_162-57557685/chicago-the-false-confession-capital/. *Also see*, Aamer Madhani, "Chicago To Pay For Police Torture," *USA Today*, Apr. 15, 2015.

18. http://editorialmatters.lee.net/articles/2003/04/21/stories/top_stories/anews052.txt , *The Times of NW Indiana*, Mark Kiesling.

19. As of this writing, legislation has been introduced in Congress by U.S. Rep. Pete Visclosky (D-IN) to re-designate Indiana Dunes National Lakeshore as Indiana Dunes National Park.

CHAPTER SIX

Paradise (Yosemite)

Yosemite is one of the oldest, largest, and most famous national parks in the world. In contrast to sites like Indiana Dunes, Yosemite benefited from the success of early preservation efforts dating as far back as 1855. But those early efforts were not without their own controversy and competition from early settlers, including park inholders.

Native Americans knew and inhabited Yosemite before that, and records suggest the first white men to enter Yosemite Valley were members of the Mariposa Battalion, in 1851, pursuing hostile Indians as part of the Mariposa Indian War.[1] Just a few years later, in 1855, the first tourists reportedly came to Yosemite on horseback and by stagecoach. That same year businessman and publisher J.M. Hutchings wrote an article appearing in the *Mariposa Gazette* and the San Francisco *California Chronicle,* describing Yosemite Valley. That article, accompanied by a picture by noted artist Thomas Ayres, drew national attention to the spectacular scenery of Yosemite. Thereafter, a number of cabins and even crude hotels were erected in Yosemite Valley and the surrounding area by surveyors, loggers, and settlers staking their claim; J.M. Hutchings among them.

One of those early homesteaders was Galen Clark, who had settled in the southern portion of Yosemite. When he came upon what is now known as the Mariposa Grove of Giant Sequoias, he launched his own crusade to preserve the trees from logging. In concert with photographer Carleton Watkins and U.S. Senator John Conness, Clark was instrumental in rallying support for the introduction of legislation to protect both the Mariposa Grove and Yosemite Valley through creation of the Yosemite Grant. The act was signed into law by President Abraham Lincoln in 1864, deeding those areas to the State of California as a park to be held in trust for the American people, with the stipulation "that said State shall accept this grant upon the express conditions that the premises shall be held for public use, resort, and recreation ... inalienable for all time."[2] Galen Clark was appointed Guardian of the park by the new park commissioners. He served in that capacity for fourteen years.

It was under the management of the State of California that Yosemite first experienced resentment and resistance to government land acquisition practices, though under circumstances somewhat different experienced more than 100 years later at urban parks like Cuyahoga Valley, Sleeping Bear Dunes, and Indiana Dunes National Lakeshore. Ironically, the most forceful resistance came from the same J.M Hutchings who had come to Yosemite with his family after purchasing a claim, who had publicly extolled the spectacular scenery of Yosemite, and for whom noted naturalist and conservationist John Muir thereafter operated a sawmill for nearly two years. But Hutchings had purchased his claim from another speculator who had, himself, made claim before Yosemite had ever been surveyed, and therefore before legal title had been (or could be) acquired. Upon enactment of the federal grant creating the park, Hutchings refused to surrender his inholding. Naming California governor Frederick F. Low, Hutchings filed a lawsuit in state court, resisting efforts to force a surrender of "his" land. Hutchings prevailed before the California Supreme Court, but his victory was short-lived. The state appealed the decision to the U.S. Supreme Court, winning in their effort to incorporate Hutchings land into the park when the state court decision was reversed.[3] That case, *Hutchings v. Low*, is noteworthy not only for its denial of Hutching's untitled claim, but also for the manner in which the court affirmed the constitutionality (under the Property Clause) of Congressional action to retain and set aside public lands as parks "for public use, resort, and recreation ... inalienable for all time."[4] Meanwhile, in an alternative strategy, Hutchings, a powerful political force, petitioned the state legislature to pass a separate bill granting him a 160-acre tract within Yosemite Valley. The legislature passed that bill, but that grant to Hutchings was, once again, subject to the approval of Congress, which in authorizing the original Yosemite Grant had clearly stipulated the "public use" conditions under which the State of California was required to abide. That Congressional approval would never come. In 1875, Hutchings' claim was incorporated into the Yosemite state park. Hutchings received $40,000 from the State of California as compensation for his land. But in yet another irony, Hutchings and his political allies succeeded in ousting the entire body of state park commissioners. Hutchings was named by the new board of park commissioners to replace Galen Clark as Guardian of Yosemite, from 1880 to 1882-1883.[5]

John Muir's name will forever be associated with Yosemite and the Sierra Nevada, or "Range of Light." But in the mid-1860s, Muir supported his geologic studies working as a both a sawyer and a guide. He was employed by J.M. Hutchings for nearly two years, operating the sawmill Hutchings owned near Yosemite Falls. It was there, in 1870, that Joseph Le Conte, a practicing surgeon as well as professor of natural history, chemistry, and geology, sought out Muir while exploring the Yosemite region. Years later, in 1892, Le Conte, Muir, and others would direct their shared passion for the protection and preservation of the Sierra Nevada and Yosemite to establishment of the Sierra Club, one of the first and arguably the most influential conservation organization in America. Le Conte described his first meeting with Muir in his 1870 journal:

> To-day to Yosemite Falls.... Stopped a moment at the foot of the falls, at a sawmill, to make inquiries. Here found a man in rough miller's garb, whose intelligent face and earnest, clear blue eye, excited my interest. After some conversation discovered that it was Mr. Muir, a gentleman of whom I had heard much from Mrs. Prof. Carr and others. He had also received a letter from Mrs. Carr, concerning our party, and was looking for us.... Mr. Muir is a gentleman of rare intelligence ... He has lived several years in the Valley, and is thoroughly acquainted with the mountains of the vicinity. A man of so much intelligence tending to a sawmill! ... not for himself, but for Mr. Hutchings. This is California![6]

John Muir emerged as a driving force behind the creation of a Yosemite *National* Park and also, eventually, the return of Yosemite Valley and the Mariposa Grove to federal administration. But those efforts were significantly aided by officials from the Southern Pacific Railroad. In his *Sunset Limited: The Southern Pacific Railroad and the Development of the American West 1850-1930,* California State University Professor (emeritus) Richard Orsi discusses that unique and little-known alliance, as well as some of the challenges Muir and others faced in their efforts to protect the greater Yosemite region:

> Americans were accustomed to exploiting resources as rapidly as possible. To most people, preserving wilderness was a new, strange, even unpatriotic idea. Moreover, powerful local interests strenuously opposed protecting Yosemite. Instead, they wanted free rein to log the forests or graze their livestock in the lush summer meadows. A host of park concessionaires also fought to retain their lucrative monopolies over lodging and transportation, while other developers proposed converting the valley itself into a gaudy tourist carnival along the lines of Niagara Falls. All of these groups preferred dealing with a lax, easily manipulated state commission rather than unpredictable federal authorities. With much influence in the state legislature, the governor's office, and Congress, the enemies of Yosemite preservation repeatedly blocked programs to increase protection of the region, to transfer it to federal jurisdiction, or to vote sufficient funds to enforce existing regulations. Like many other natural landmarks, Yosemite appeared doomed.
> The Southern Pacific's leaders had long appreciated the company's stake in preserving Yosemite. ... as a tourist attraction ... In the 1870s, the company's people began to assist John Muir in his

conservation work, particularly in the protection of Yosemite ...
One was William H. Mills, longtime railroad land agent and editor
and the railroad's partner in the *Sacramento Record-Union*. ... Mills
opened up the columns of the *Record-Union* to the great naturalist's
first major public appeal for wilderness preservation ...[7]

The Yosemite Grant had charged the State of California with responsibility for administration of Yosemite Valley and the Mariposa Grove.
But the state struggled in that role, succumbing to pressures for development and exhibiting many deficiencies in protecting those areas. Mills
secured a position on the Yosemite Valley Commission (1880-1888), and
in that role opposed development and commercial exploitation, while advocating for increased enforcement of regulations and the implementation of scientific management policies.[8] But he eventually resigned from
the commission in protest over policies he believed conflicted with the
state's obligation to protect the area, accusing the state of "ignorance, stu-
pidity, and vandalism" and violating a "trust on behalf of the lovers of nature throughout the world."

Meanwhile, Muir and his ally, Robert Underwood Johnson, conservation editor of *Century Magazine*, focused efforts on preserving the
still-federally owned high country that surrounded Yosemite Valley. They
"turned for help to Southern-Pacific leaders.... The railroad provided the
political muscle to extend federal protection over the larger Yosemite region." Southern Pacific land agent Daniel K. Zumwalt played a key role
in lobbying for legislation to create a *national* park even larger than that
proposed by Muir, "marching from office to office in the capitol pushing
for the passage of the amended Yosemite Sequoia Bill before congress ad-
journed."[9]

The Yosemite Act, signed into law on October 1, 1890, extended protection to approximately 1,500 square miles of federal lands, including
"all timber, mineral deposits, natural curiosities and wonders," from "settlement, occupancy, or sale" by the establishment of Yosemite National
Park.[10] But, as Orsi also explains,

[by] the 1890s, environmental depredations continued unabated
in the valley, and the state commission proved incapable of dealing with the problems. Meanwhile, Muir and his cohorts were im-
pressed by the U.S. Army's success in driving poachers from the
surrounding national park. When a sympathetic governor, George
C. Pardee, took office in 1904, Muir resumed the assault on state
control of the valley. By this time, to build public interest in wilderness and to organize conservation battles, Muir had in 1892 founded the Sierra Club, with substantial support from business leaders.
Southern Pacific executives were especially prominent among the

Sierra club's charter members ... Led by Muir as president and William Colby as secretary, the club decided to press the California legislature to return the valley to the federal government for inclusion in the national park....

The California State Board of Trade had for nearly a year been at work in Sacramento and around the state on behalf of Yosemite Valley retrocession. Ancestor to the present-day California State Chamber of Commerce, the Board of Trade had been founded in 1887 largely through the efforts of Southern Pacific land agent William H. Mills ... Now a committee of the board led by Mills ... was preparing a bill to protect Yosemite Valley by returning it to federal jurisdiction....

Thus, the Board of Trade and the Sierra Club joined forces. Mills and Colby co-authored a retrocession bill ... The retrocession bill passed the Assembly easily on February 2 [1905].[11]

A greater challenge was faced in the state senate, where newspaper mogul and Southern Pacific archenemy William Randolph Hearst applied pressure to stop the bill. Fierce opposition was also brought by state senator John Curtin, who had already battled federal authorities in his attempts to graze his own cattle in Yosemite National Park, and who had also been retained by valley concessionaires to protect their business interests.

State opposition was eventually overcome when, on February 23, 1906, the bill for retrocession passed the California senate by a single vote. Thereafter, following approval in both houses of Congress to accept California's grant, on June 11, 1906, President Roosevelt signed the legislation accepting Yosemite Valley and the Mariposa Grove – lands previously included in the Yosemite Grant – for inclusion into an expanded Yosemite National Park.[12]

Yosemite National Park now spans nearly 1,200 square miles, of which approximately 95% is designated wilderness. The total acreage comprising the park, today, reflects a reduction from the original size. That occurred in accommodation to other influential interests tied to mineral lands and timber within the initially established boundaries and, incidentally, in an attempt to redefine park boundaries along natural features and landmarks, rather than the arbitrary straight lines that had first been drawn.[13]

The park, today, receives between 3-4 million visitors every year. The majority of those visitors come to stay in the seven square mile area known as Yosemite Valley. That relatively small portion of the park is the center of activity and development; a full-blown tourist town in its own right (John Muir's efforts notwithstanding), with a supermarket, restaurants, bars, hundreds of campsites, and nearly a thousand hotel, motel, and other rooms available as lodging for the thousands upon thousands of tourists who spend the night during peak seasons. Also within the Valley is the park's

Law Enforcement Office (LEO), a full-time staffed jail, and full-time federal courtroom with dedicated United States Magistrate Judge.

Yosemite is considered one of the icons and "crown jewels" of the National Park System, not only for its size, history, and spectacular scenery, but also for its prominence and high-profile reputation both within and outside of the agency. If you are interested in law enforcement, it is one of a handful of parks in the country where an employee wants an assignment. It long had a reputation for being on the cutting edge of not only law enforcement, but also search and rescue and emergency medical operations, and was where other parks across the country turned for advice on how things should really be done. That was particularly the case during the 1970s and 1980s, when nearly any incident that occurred there, and particularly crime and crime fighting activities, received instantaneous national publicity and media coverage.

Adding to the reputation of Yosemite National Park and its rangers was the short-lived television series, *Sierra,* patterned after a line of other highly romanticized police dramas of the time, such as *Adam-12, Emergency,* and *CHiPS. Sierra* took place in the fictional Sierra National Park, but was actually filmed in Yosemite, where park management all too willingly bent over backwards in support of the Music Corporation of America (MCA) production and their fantasized depiction of the NPS and its rangers. MCA held the lucrative concessions contract for Yosemite, and exercised considerable influence over park activities and operations. In the course of filming, MCA actually utilized the services of the park's chief ranger as a technical assistant, and even employed NPS rangers as extras on the set.[14]

Filming a scene for the 1973-74 TV show, *Sierra*. (NPS Photo)

79

Author Tim Palmer described MCA's influence over the NPS and the production of *Sierra* in his book, *The Sierra Nevada; A Mountain Journey:*

> In 1973, the Music Corporation of America (MCA) bought the Yosemite Park and Curry Company, a commercial monopoly operating the lodges, restaurants, gas stations, bars, horse stables, and gift shops. At the same time, professional management of the park slipped to an abysmal low because of directives from the top. Richard Nixon appointed Ron Walker, his advance man who had arranged for public appearances during the 1972 campaign, as head of the Park Service. At a time of unprecedented stress, the agency that had remained distinguished even in times of gross government mismanagement was led by one of the few nonprofessional directors in its history.
>
> The Yosemite superintendent was instructed to cooperate with MCA. Its largest subsidiary, Universal Studios, filmed a television series called 'Sierra,' and while the park faced an entirely new era in matters of visitation, crime, environmental awareness, back-country use, and almost everything, a TV show that producers later aborted stole priority. Universal Studios closed roads, paid rangers to act, and took over entire campgrounds.
>
> When the cliffs were the wrong color for the TV show, Universal painted them darker, and that was the limit. Photographs of the 'painted rocks' were broadcast nationwide. The paint was soluble in water and would wear away, but the principle was the thing. Environmental groups were outraged, an entire park plan was eventually halted because it catered to MCA, and Congress launched an investigation into concessionaires. In 1976, the report was issued; "National Park Service Policies Discourage Competition, Give Concessionaires Too Great A Voice in Concession Management." Today, this experience is behind MCA and the Park Service. Each presumably learned important lessons.[15]

Time would prove Palmer's assessment of the isolated and partisan nature of that situation to be naïve, and the expectation of lessons learned during that period to be optimistic, at best. That sad truth was confirmed at Glen Canyon National Recreation Area in 1990, when the Arizona Attorney General's office conducted its own felony investigation into a long list of environmental crimes committed by the park's concession operator, Del Webb, and then ARA Services, who later purchased the concession contract. Special agents found that the park's own concession chief had for years orchestrated efforts to conceal the violations, lied, and even instructed subordinates to lie to state investigators. When confronted, the concession chief acknowledged it was "standard practice" to allow the powerful concession operator to review and edit their own annual evaluations, but justified his actions by claiming "it would be political suicide" to document concession violations in written reports, because "all the concessions have strong political friends in government."[16] The influence maintained by corporate concessionaires and their "political friends" may explain how and why the NPS subsequently promoted the disgraced concession chief to the regional office, first as regional chief of concessions, and ultimately deputy regional director.

In the years since the filming of *Sierra* in Yosemite National Park in the 1970s, and then the scandal at Glen Canyon NRA in 1990, the NPS has become even more susceptible – or receptive – to influence by powerful financial interests, especially as Congress has failed to properly fund the agency. That, in turn, has led many park managers to actively solicit donations from an ever-growing list of wealthy commercial and non-profit "partners" in exchange for special consideration; in some instances allowing those entities to dictate park policies and practices, and to even influence criminal and internal investigations.[17] To that extent, *Sierra* and the influence of MCA over the NPS in Yosemite was not so much an anomaly or a learning moment, as it was precedent-setting. At the same time, *Sierra* signaled a turning point for the NPS, demonstrating the agency's willingness to at least participate in efforts to craft its own public image. And as part of that image, according to actor James G. Richardson (who starred as ranger Tim Cassidy), "the series would downplay the role of park rangers in policing national parks, because 'the Park Service is very sensitive about its law enforcement job.'"[18] Those imaging efforts, along with a series of other events that we will discuss next, helped to propel Yosemite, the NPS, and its rangers to the forefront of the American psyche.

Endnotes

1. Controversy exists over this date, with an entry in the diary of gold-seeker William Penn Abrams indicating that he and a friend first gazed upon Yosemite Valley in 1849 from a spot near Inspiration Point. *See* Shirley Sargent, *Wawona's Yesterdays (1961): A Short History of Yosemite National Park.*

2. U.S. Statutes at Large, Volume 13, Ch. 184, P. 325, "An Act Authorizing a Grant to the State of California of the Yo-Semite Valley and of the Land Embracing the Mariposa Big Tree Grove" [S. 203, Public Act No. 159]. (1864).

3. 82 U.S. 77, "The Yosemite Valley Case Hutchings v. Low (1872). " *Also*, James M. Hutchings, *In the Heart of the Sierras*, Chap. XII, "Congressional and State Enactments Concerning Yo Semite," http://www.yosemite.ca.us/library/in_the_heart_of_the_sierras/12.html

4. *Hutchings v. Low*, 82 U.S. 77 (1872).

5. Ansel F. Hall (w/ Ralph S. Kuykendall), *Handbook of Yosemite National Park* (New York, NY: G.P. Putnam's Sons, 1921) 20-23. *Also*, Alfred Runte, *Yosemite The Embattled Wilderness* (Omaha, NE: University of Nebraska Press, 1990), Ch. 3; Tom Bopp, *The Yosemite Commissioners 1864-1906*, 2012.

6. Ralph Kuykendall (N.S.G.W. Fellow in Pacific Coast History, University of California), *History of the Yosemite Region; Handbook of Yosemite National Park (1921).*

7. Richard J. Orsi, *Sunset Limited: The Southern Pacific Railroad and the Development of the American West 1850-1930* (Berkeley, CA: University of California Press, 2005) 359-360.

8. Tom Bopp, *The Yosemite Commissioners, 1864-1906,* 2012.

9. Richard J. Orsi, *Sunset Limited: The Southern Pacific Railroad and the Development of the American West 1850-1930* (Berkeley, CA: University of California Press, 2005) 361-364.

10. U.S. Statutes at Large, Vol. 26, Chap. 1263, pp 650-652, "An act to set aside certain tracts of land in the state of California as forest reservations," (H.R. 12187).

11. Richard J. Orsi, *Sunset Limited: The Southern Pacific Railroad and the Development of the American West 1850-1930* (Berkeley, CA: University of California Press, 2005) 364-365.

12. It should be noted that elsewhere in the country, railroad executives played an active role in opposition to protection of parks. *See* testimony of Lewis Payson, addressing the House Committee considering HR 5880, "granting a right of way through Yellowstone National Park to the Cinnabar and Clark's Fork Railroad Company." *Congressional Record (House of Representatives),* Dec. 14, 1886, p. 149-153 ("I can not understand the sentiment which favors the retention of few buffaloes to the development of mining interests amounting to millions of dollars"). Also, Roderick Nash, *Wilderness and the American Mind* (New Haven, CN: Yale University Press, 1967), 114-115.

13. Ansel F. Hall (w/ Ralph S Kuykendall), *Handbook of Yosemite National Park* (New York, NY: G.P. Putnum's Sons, 1921) 32-33.

14. Jack Morehead was brought in as Yosemite's chief park ranger after the Yosemite Riot, and served as a technical consultant to the TV series, *Sierra.* Not coincidentally, the show's chief ranger character was named Jack Moore.

15. Tim Palmer, *The Sierra Nevada; A Mountain Journey* (Washington, D.C.: Island Press, 1988), 95-96.

16. Ron Everhart (as Glen Canyon NRA concessions chief, subsequently promoted to Intermountain Region chief of concessions, and then deputy regional director), multiple interviews conducted in 1990 by special agents from the State of Arizona Office the Arizona State Attorney General, Special Investigations Section, AGI case no. 90-0250.

17. E.g., *see* Paul Berkowitz, *The Case of the Indian Trader: Billy Malone and the National Park Service Investigation at Hubbell Trading Post* (Albuquerque, NM: University of New Mexico Press, 2011) 72-74, 83-85, 122, 128-130, 138-139, 236-239, 264, 289-291, 293, 296, 303; Kurt Repanshek, "Are National Parks an Appropriate Backdrop for Sport's Illustrated's Swimsuit Issue," *National Parks Traveler,* Aug. 7, 2016; Kurt Repanshek, "Subaru Given Access to Film Commercials in Shenandoah National Park During Peak Foliage Season," *National Parks Traveler,* June 28, 2016; Kurt Repanshek, "Park Advocates Concerned by NPS Plans to Revise Fund-Raising Guidelines," *National Parks Traveler,* May 17, 2016.

18. *Television Obscurities,* "Sierra," http://www.tvobscurities.com/spotlight/sierra/, citing Richard Shull, "There's a New Webb show," *Lakeland Ledger* (Lakeland, FL), TV insert, Aug. 25, 1974.

CHAPTER SEVEN

Seeds of a Legacy (The Ranger Image)

Yosemite first achieved notoriety for its law enforcement activities in the summer of 1970, when hundreds of counter-culturally inclined youths illegally congregated to party in Yosemite Valley's fortuitously named Stoneman Meadow. Yosemite's proximity to San Francisco as well as Southern California has long made it an attractive site for an odd assortment of visitors, including refugees from the "establishment" as well as individuals pursuing a chemically enhanced back-to-nature experience. That 4th of July, things got out of hand as rangers tried to restore order and close the meadow. Those efforts led to fighting, and fighting led to what is now known as the "Yosemite Riot," as park rangers and other employees on horseback wearing construction hard-hats, using baseball bats, axe handles, and even lassos, made a strained attempt to confront and disperse the rowdy crowd of nearly 500. With the assistance of nearby state and county law enforcement personnel (and contemplation of calling in troops from the National Guard), more than 150 individuals were ultimately arrested and transported from the scene. Several law enforcement officers were injured during the altercations. Still more civilians were injured, predictably resulting in well-publicized claims of police brutality.

AND MARIPOSA MINER

RNIA   THURSDAY, JULY 9, 1970   -   NO. FIFTEEN

Yosemite Valley Is Scene Of 4th Of July Hippie Rioting

Calm has returned to Yosemite Valley after a wild weekend of hippie rioting, injuries, arrests and evacuation of tourists from camping areas around Stoneman Meadow the gathering point of an estimated 500 persons.

U. S. Border Patrolmen with U. S. Marshals are working with Park Rangers

Rock, Wawona, Crane Flat and Tioga Pass.

Rumors of anticipated trouble had spread earlier in the week, but the first definite sign of trouble came at 8:00 p.m. Friday night when Mariposa Sheriff Norman Garrett received a report from Yosemite that the Rangers were beginning to have trouble with a gathering in one

but at that time no help was needed. A teletype was sent out, alerting Fresno, Merced and Madera counties Sheriffs Depts.

At 7:35 that same evening, a radio dispatcher sent out a call that the Rangers were being attacked and surrounded and they needed all the help they could get. It was later learned that Rangers and park em-

(Mariposa Gazette and Miner, July 9, 1970).

Three years later, on August 5, 1973, 200 miles west of Yosemite, the mystique of the NPS and the ranger image was again shattered at Point Reyes National Seashore. There, ranger Ken Patrick was brutally gunned

2 Independent-Journal,   Monday, August 6, 1973

Seashore Ranger Slain
On Fog-Shrouded Road

FBI Called In; Killer Possibly A Poacher

A ranger at Point Reyes National Seashore was shot and killed Sunday as he searched for deer poachers in the fog-shrouded park.

The Federal Bureau of Investigation was called in and clamped an immediate lid on information.

Investigators for the Marin Coroner's Office said it appeared Ranger Kenneth Carmel Patrick, 40, a father of three, was finished off at close range after having been shot once in the left hand near his jeep on Mount Vision Overlook Road.

Patrick, a 10-year veteran of the National Park Service and

a former highway patrolman, ran about 180 feet into thick underbrush and fell, whereupon the killer finished him off with shots to the left and right chest, the coroner's office said.

A trail of blood led from the road to the body. One empty cartridge was found near Pat-

rick's jeep, and two others close to where his body was discovered.

An FBI spokesman in San Francisco today declined to elaborate on the investigation. "Anything I could say would be speculation, and we don't like to speculate," he said.

Patrick left his house at the Estero housing area near Point Reyes Lighthouse at 5 a.m. Sunday to look for game poachers, the park service said.

When he did not return at 6:30 a.m. for breakfast, his wife, Tommie, tried unsuccessfully to call him by radio, then called ranger Daniel Whittaker who went to look for him.

Whittaker found Patrick's patrol jeep, its red police lights on and engine running, on the

Mount Vision road. A trail of blood led through the thick fog to Patrick's body, lying against a large bush.

Patrick's flashlight was found in a shallow ditch near the jeep. The National Park Service said Patrick worked for a year as an officer of the Arizona State Highway Patrol in the 1960s and so "was experienced in law enforcement."

Nevertheless, the ranger's service revolver still was strapped in his holster when Patrick was found. "He never had a chance," one investigator said.

Officers of the FBI, the Marin Sheriff's Office and the park service still were on the scene of the slaying today, looking for clues.

"We don't know if it was a poacher (who killed Patrick). We're not ruling anything out," an FBI agent said.

Patrick, who had worked for one year at Point Reyes, also had served at Organ Pipe National Monument and Grand Canyon National Park, both in Arizona.

He is survived by his wife, and three sons, Kenneth Jr., 13, Jamie, 4, and Clay, 18 months. Funeral arrangements were pending today at Keaton's Chapel of Marin, Novato.

A park service spokesman said there have been about a half-dozen incidents of poaching in the seashore in the past 12 months but there have been no arrests that he knew of.

San Francisco Chronicle ★★   Mon., Aug. 6, 1973

RANGER SLAIN

From Page 1

radio several times, then finally called Ranger Daniel Whittaker, who went to find his colleague.

When Whittaker drove up Mount Vision Overlook road, he spotted Patrick's car in the thick mist. The red police lights were on, and the engine was still running.

Whittaker then scoured the area, and 150 feet away he found Patrick's body in the wet brush next to the windy road.

Authorities theorized that one of the two shots in his chest knocked the ranger down and the final two shots were fired as he lay dying.

His service revolver was still strapped in its holster, indicating, as one investigator said, "He never had a chance."

Patrick, a veteran park ranger, had served with the National Park Service for ten years. Before duty at Point Reyes Seashore —

which he began about a year ago — he had worked at Organ Pipe National Monument in Arizona and at Grand Canyon National Park.

Orville E. Rogers, a Ranger supervisor in the Bear Valley area, described Patrick as "a very competent, very mild-mannered individual."

Teams of Marin sheriff's officers and FBI investigators spent all day combing the wind-blown hillocks for clues.

The death scene, remote and chilly, is about a mile east of Sir Francis Drake boulevard. The overlook road, winding through grasslands that are bristled with occasional clusters of low, weatherbent cypress trees, leads to a Federal Aviation Administration facility atop Mount Vision.

Patrick is survived by his wife Tommie and sons Cray, 18 months old, Jamie, 4, and Kenneth Jr. 13. Funeral services are pending.

RANGER KENNETH C. PATRICK
Slain during 5 a.m. investigation at Pt. Reyes

Upper: *Independent Journal.* Lower: *San Francisco Chronicle* (August 6, 1973).

down by a member of the notorious Black Panther movement.[1] Patrick had been conducting a typical early morning poacher patrol; alone, with no back-up and no dispatcher yet on-duty, and only his small revolver for protection, concealed under his zipped uniform jacket. His bullet-riddled body was discovered several hours later, after he'd failed to return home to pick up a new ranger scheduled for an orientation patrol. Just hours earlier, the evening before, lamenting the sorry state of the NPS law enforcement program and lack of adequate training, ranger Patrick had commented that the agency was "due" to have one of its rangers murdered. And prior to that, acknowledging his own inadequacies and outdated training, Patrick had submitted repeated requests – all rejected – to attend a contemporary law enforcement academy, to update his knowledge and skills.[2] Thereafter, compounding the tragedy, either as a face-saving move or out of blind ignorance of its own history, the NPS falsely claimed that Ken Patrick was the first ranger ever to be murdered in the line of duty.[3]

In the wake of Ranger Patrick's murder, a "board of review" was convened to evaluate the incident and submit a report identifying factors, both local and national, that may have contributed to the tragedy.

The overall report, which is only five pages long, "represents a consensus opinion of all members of the Board," and seems to focus almost entirely on deficiencies of individual park employees. But, "Additional comments of individual Board members are attached."

Significantly, one (and only one) member of the board was a senior law enforcement official from another agency, and not part of the NPS organization; supervisory criminal investigator William G. Wilson of the Bureau of Indian Affairs (BIA). Wilson's comments, alone, contained harsh criticisms of the Park Service's approach to law enforcement, along with remarkable insights into the magnitude and over-arching nature of the problem, citing an agency bias that, if acknowledged and properly addressed, could have paved the way for real improvement.

Wilson's eight-page memorandum, submitted to Western Regional Director Howard H. Chapman on November 19, 1973, addressed a wide-range of deficiencies in the NPS law enforcement program, including the absence of any requirement for chief park rangers to possess "substantial law enforcement background," along with the accepted practice of vesting employees with "law enforcement responsibilities for which [they] are not well trained or, in some instances, not physically or mentally suited…" Wilson also took exception to what appeared to be the agency's abandonment of basic public safety responsibilities, taking the concept of "selective law enforcement" to extremes:

> Statistical reports at Point Reyes a couple of years ago indicated that about 70 narcotics violations were reported to the Rangers

[yet] last year's report reflects no narcotics violations reports. As an explanation for this situation, we were informed the enforcement program elected to ignore such violations. To leave discretionary authority with the enforcement program itself on what criminal statutes it will enforce is a grave mistake ... [that] violates the trust and confidence placed in the Park Service on the part of the general public.

From there, Wilson took on the broader issue of an agency culture that is fundamentally dismissive of its overall law enforcement responsibilities, and the consequences of such an approach to resource protection and both public and employee safety:

There appears to be a general reluctance in the Park Service to readily accept and visibly support the fact that effective law enforcement services are vital to the successful operation of the Parks and their enjoyment by the many visitors.

With the hundreds of thousands of people visiting the Parks, serious problems arise concerning criminal activity involving assaults, larcenies, narcotics, intoxicants, firearms, traffic, and other related acts of misconduct. If the general public is to enjoy the Parks, then a high priority must be given by the Service to protect them while they are there from criminal activity, harassment and molestation. An efficient and effective enforcement program can and will, through both preventative and enforcement measures, provide the climate and stability in the Parks that will permit the public to enjoy their benefits in a peaceful manner.

The level, and caliber of law enforcement services in the various Parks rests largely with the discretion of individual Park Superintendents. In all probability, such services will range from good to poor. There needs to be a descriptive national law enforcement policy dealing with the protection of life and property of Park visitors and the operation of effective Park enforcement programs to carry out this objective....

Terms like 'soft-image' and 'low profile' ... have been adopted because some officials feel that a uniformed enforcement officer carrying a sidearm is offensive to the public. This is an erroneous premise.... The most serious problem with such general descriptive terms are they leave many unanswered questions as to actual operating procedures. Thus, officers on borderline cases will try to maintain a 'low profile' and get themselves involved in incidents which can escalate into dangerous situations for themselves and/ or others they are trying to protect. ...

The question concerning the responsibility for Mr. Patrick's death needs to be answered. The major share of responsibility must rest with the Service ... who by omission, neglect, or inattention, operates an inadequate or substandard enforcement program.... It is the Service, whose laxity in its ... enforcement program, allowed Mr. Patrick to place himself in the position and circumstances that resulted in his death. It is incumbent, therefore, upon the Service to take prompt affirmative action to correct and strengthen its enforcement program.[4]

As well-informed and well-reasoned as all of these observations and recommendations were, time would reveal (as we shall see) that almost all of them were summarily ignored; dismissed because, as NPS management saw it, Wilson was "coming from out in left field"; an "outsider" from another agency, who didn't understand the NPS.[5] That same rationale would be repeatedly invoked by the NPS over decades to follow in response to similar findings made by other entities – from the National Academy of Public Administration, to the International Association of Chiefs of Police, to the DOI Office of the Inspector General – each independently tasked with reviewing the NPS law enforcement program.[6]

Still, in the early 1970s, both the Yosemite Riot and the murder of Ranger Patrick made national news. The NPS suffered a severe blow to its benign image, reinforced by the public perception that when it came to law enforcement, the agency had failed to keep up with the times, and that its rangers were neither trained nor equipped to deal with serious law enforcement problems.

But, ironically, that was not entirely the case.

* * *

Inconsistency was then and to this day remains a hallmark of how the NPS manages park operations. It's almost impossible to characterize various programs in the NPS, including but not limited to its law enforcement program, as either good or bad because, beyond wearing the same basic uniforms, there is so little similarity in how these programs are managed from one site to another.

As Wilson had so accurately observed in his comments about the murder of ranger Patrick, that characteristic is a direct outcome of the deliberately decentralized manner in which parks are managed under the supervision of a local park manager – a superintendent – who functions with near-complete autonomy and little if any real accountability. In a very real sense, most parks and other NPS operations are more personality driven than they are program driven. Superintendents with big egos and the right connections are empowered to ignore or circumvent policies, and juggle and manipulate funds and programs in virtually any manner that they see fit. As a consequence, some parks in the system actually did then – and some do today – have extremely capable law enforcement programs, with well-trained and equipped rangers who are allowed and even encouraged to perform their law enforcement duties professionally, unmolested by unqualified supervisors and managers clinging to the ranger image. At the same time, other parks and park law enforcement programs can and frequently do bear absolutely no resemblance to those at other sites, compromised by local policies and attitudes imposed by a superintendent with a different set of values and priorities.

So, while in 1970, Yosemite's rangers may have been untrained, poorly equipped, and unprepared to deal with something as serious as "hippie" riots or other disruptions, a handful of other parks actually did have their act together.

Rangers at Lake Mead National Recreation Area in Nevada had long gone about their business with a serious attitude and access to defensive equipment, under what was then the local management philosophy that "lawlessness will not be tolerated." By the 1960s, rangers at Lake Mead were being sent through the Clark County Police and Sheriff's Academy, which evolved into the Las Vegas Metropolitan Police Academy in 1973.[7] Some of Lake Mead's own rangers were used as instructors at that same academy, teaching both NPS rangers and Las Vegas police officers, side-by-side.[8] By 1973, some of Yosemite's rangers were also being sent there for training.

Even before then, in the early 1960s – years before the Yosemite Riot – some parks in the West were sending their rangers through the San Diego Police Academy. Around that same period, the chief ranger at the Natchez Trace Parkway in Mississippi, Gil Calhoun, was sending his rangers through the state highway patrol academy and even the state criminal investigator school, and required them to participate in tactical training that included full riot gear and tear gas. Those same rangers were authorized to carry shotguns, tear gas, and other riot gear in their patrol cars, and openly carried their own side-arms, including .357 revolvers and 9mm semi-automatic pistols, with which they qualified at least twice a year.[9] None of that compromised their ability to project a positive, friendly image as members of a resource and people-serving agency. Other parks across the country, at various times and under the right circumstances (i.e., a supportive superintendent and/or chief ranger) might have had equally well developed law enforcement programs, often matching or exceeding the capabilities of counterparts in local sheriffs' and police departments. But again, that was entirely dependent on the interest and support of local management. Whether a national park like Yosemite, a national monument like Death Valley or Joshua Tree (both of which were later designated national parks), or a recreation area like Lake Mead or Point Reyes National Seashore, a change in any key administrative position could result in a reversal, leading to an almost instantaneous roll-back of those programs, stripped of funding, personnel, and other support necessary to maintain an effective, professional law enforcement presence.

Rangers at Natchez Trace Parkway participating riot training, 1967. (Author's Collection, courtesy of Wes Kreis).

NPS rangers graduating from the San Diego Reserve Academy, 1969. (NPS photo).

Rangers at Lake Mead National Recreation Area. (Author's photo).

NPS Rangers at Grand Canyon N.P., Sep. 4, 1971. (NPS Photo).

Rangers at Lake Mead National Recreation Area, early 1970s. (NPS photo).

Still, with the bad press and outside pressure coming out of the Yosemite Riot and the subsequent murder of ranger Patrick at Point Reyes, the NPS was forced to respond by beefing up its law enforcement training and resources, nationwide. Yosemite was a focal point for much of that emphasis, receiving a huge infusion of money, personnel, and other resources to address the problem, all the while struggling to maintain a benign image for its rangers as something other than real "cops" or full-time, professional law enforcement officers. In the process, with that as its model, the NPS made up its own rules about how to manage a law enforcement program. Out of that effort came what is commonly referred to as the "Yosemite Mafia," to this day depicted in NPS mythology as "...an elite corps of rangers hand-picked to 'clean up' after the 1970 Yosemite Riot"; hand-picked and indoctrinated to fit into the mold of the ranger image.[10]

That name – the "Yosemite Mafia" – was probably used first by an official in the Alaska regional office as a disparaging reference to rangers from Yosemite National Park. Those rangers, and rangers from other areas, were being detailed to Alaska in the 1970s to help establish an NPS presence in the state's several new national park sites.[11] The manager was unimpressed with the attitude and approach he saw in the young recruits from Yosemite, reportedly declaring that he didn't want any more of those "Yosemite Mafia" rangers assigned to his area. Today, that account is discounted by some members of the Yosemite Mafia for the negative characterization it conveys. Still, there is general agreement that the name was coined by an "outsider," but was soon embraced by original members of the group as a badge of honor; not unlike a clique, club, fraternity, or (in a more nefarious sense) a gang seeking an identity and recognition laced with a humorous and fanciful air of rakish intrigue or mystery. There is nothing official about the group, but membership in the Yosemite Mafia is generally self-acknowledged with a measure of pride, denoting the unique friendship, stature, and consequent recognition they and their descendants enjoy within the NPS. What is certain is the role that its various members, as products of the turbulent 1960s, the counter-culture era, and the environmental movement (a sort of NPS Mod-Squad) played from the 1970s and thereafter in influencing and perpetuating the ranger image both within and outside of the NPS. That generational distinction and the attitudes reflected by those who were recruited to lead and be a part of that "elite corps of rangers" may explain a great deal about the aversion and negative views so many NPS managers still seem to have of law enforcement, and the genuine offense so many contemporary and recently retired NPS officials (as compared to their predecessors like Woodring and Townsley, a half-century before) seem to take at being labeled or compared to "police" or "cops."[12]

* * *

Prior to 1976, literally all employees of the NPS were vested with arrest authority. That antiquated condition resulted from the 1905 enactment of legislation proclaiming

> All persons employed in the forest reserve and national park ser-
> vice of the United States shall have authority to make arrests for
> violations of the laws and regulations relating to the forest reserves
> and national parks, and any person so arrested shall be taken before
> the nearest Unites States commissioner. ..."[13]

That authority had been preceded by similar legislation enacted as far
back as 1897.

But on the heels of the Yosemite Riot and then the murder of Ken
Patrick, in 1976, overcoming intense resistance from within the management of the NPS, new legislation was enacted that rescinded that authority. That move signaled a strong congressional rejection of the NPS "generalist" concept, where a ranger was considered to be a jack-of-all-trades.
Instead, the new legislation limited the delegation of re-defined and far
more specific law enforcement authorities to only certain specially designated employees who were required to meet new training and other standards imposed on the NPS by the Department of the Interior.[14] That shift,
however, led to resentment among many park managers who thought
they already knew all they needed to know about law enforcement. And
stripped of their own authority, those managers (including many chief
park rangers) felt threatened by the prospect of a cadre of rangers among
their ranks who would be vested with authorities they no longer had.

Within the House committee report (part of the Congressional Record) accompanying the legislation, Congress recognized that "Effective
law enforcement in the Park System has been severely hampered by the
remoteness of many areas" and that "isolation of these areas from conven-
tional federal, state, and local law enforcement has made law enforcement
dependent primarily on employees of the National Park Service." And so,
Congress charged these personnel with a duty to "maintain law and order
[and] protect persons and property," under "a single clear mandate authorizing designated employees performing law enforcement functions
within the National Park System to bear firearms; enforce all Federal laws
including serious criminal violations as well as misdemeanors applying
specifically to parks; execute process; and investigate offenses ... consistent with the authority exercised by other Federal personnel having law
enforcement responsibilities, such as the Federal Bureau of Investigation
and United States Marshals." "The authority to enforce all Federal laws
would under appropriate circumstances, include authority to enforce the
laws of States in areas of the National Park System under the exclusive or
concurrent legislative jurisdiction of the United States through assimilation of those laws into Federal law (18 U.S.C. 7(3), 13)."[15]

But the NPS strenuously resisted implementation. Such requirements
and restrictions might mean that rangers delegated with the new law en-

forcement authorities were somehow special, and if there's one thing the NPS eschews, it's specialization in its corps of rangers, especially where that specialization runs contrary to the traditional ranger image. To support that view, the NPS omitted from its own records and internal documents all references to those Congressional directives (above) relating to "a single clear mandate ... to bear firearms; enforce all Federal laws," etc. Equally critical language identifying personnel to whom the new authorities did *not* apply, was also ignored.[16] The NPS, instead, selectively invoked and over-interpreted only those parts of the Congressional record that urged the NPS to assure it continued to be perceived as a resource and people serving agency.[17] NPS management also attempted to syphon off a full $1 million that had subsequently been authorized by Congress to support the new authorities with law enforcement training. The director's office had diverted the funds to projects totally unrelated to law enforcement, expending more than half before being forced by Congressional inquiries to restore the balance to the NPS law enforcement training program.[18]

The effects of this approach were amplified through establishment of a formal "Ranger Image Task Force," chaired by Western Regional Director Howard Chapman; the same official who had received the reports documenting conditions and practices that had contributed to the murder of ranger Patrick. In practical terms – in reality – the mission of the task force was to propose new policies and procedures to dilute and diffuse the effects of the new legislation, and limit damage to the ranger image that might otherwise result from enactment of new law enforcement authorities and specialized training requirements.[19] That effort was widely applauded by superintendents and other managers who voiced strenuous opposition to what they saw as "police-type rangers" they feared were being produced through participation in the formalized law enforcement training mandated by the Department of the Interior. Writing to task force chairman Chapman, the superintendent of Mount Rainier National Park argued that "The 400 hour police training should be dropped ... Rangers should have a *less* extensive basic training which includes lots of emphasis on how *not* to write a ticket.... Perhaps 80 hours of training and no weapons would be OK."[20] [emphasis added]. The general manager for the Bay Area National Parks (and future NPS director) weighed in on the subject, arguing that "We cannot continue sending 'our rangers' to 'their school' [i.e., the consolidated federal law enforcement academy] and expect them to return with the proper attitude. I would suggest that we immediately look for a way to train 'in house.'"[21] Attitudes and efforts like these would signal the beginning of an unfortunate legacy of resistance to real professionalization, the effects of which are felt in the NPS to this day.

But others questioned the emphasis the task force recommendations seemed to place on the ranger image over real-world conditions and the growing demands of professional law enforcement, including the protection of people.[22] One veteran ranger, Carl Christensen, who was assigned to the Washington office at the time, observed:

> It can be debated whether, up until now, the "single most important aspect of the ranger image is resource preservation." It may be that we would like to think this is the case, but it cannot be demonstrated to be true without rather extensive surveys of what park visitors expect of rangers, surveys which I do not believe exist. Be that as it may, I think it is important to bring into the open the thinking which motivates this discussion of the "image." I see this as an effort to separate the public conception of the National Park Service from our actual function. It has long been said, and I think has been universally accepted, that protection of *people* is the function which takes precedence over all others. If we do, in fact, accept this ordering of priorities, are we being honest in attempting to either perpetuate or create a public image which differs from this? I think we do a disservice to ourselves and to the public if we attempt to disguise or downplay the fact that rangers are protectors of people, as well as resources, since this tends to create a situation where a visitor is surprised when a ranger must deal with him in the context of a law enforcement situation. In 60 years of managing the parks, the ranger's role has changed; why should we attempt to conceal this fact from the public through manipulation of our "image"?[23]

Two other veteran rangers assigned to the Washington Office, Andy Hutchison and Wes Kreis, were more blunt in their criticism of the task force report. Both men were graduates of the FBI National Academy, and both had put their careers on the line by working quietly behind the scenes to push through the new legislation and then attempting to develop national law enforcement policies – subsequently reduced to mere "guidelines" – known as "NPS-9."

Hutchison challenged the authors of the task force report, asking, "With all this concern about Ranger image, why doesn't somebody ask the Ranger how he perceives himself? Let's deal with real Rangers, not imaginary ones." Hutchison also raised a series of important questions related to the impacts the task force recommendations might have on proper position classification for rangers, their prospects for twenty-year law enforcement pay and retirement benefits and, ultimately, employee morale and workforce retention.[24]

Expanding on these comments, Kreis summed up his own thoughts and concerns:

> Prevailing attitudes convey the impression that law enforcement is something we should not be involved in, a function that will only

sully the Ranger image. This type of monastic and ill-conceived thinking has served to create a credibility gap of serious proportions between management and the protection ranger ... we find ourselves living in the past, yet attempting to cope with modern problems. Management has failed to recognize that the public does not have a hang-up with the Ranger image. Only management is afflicted with this misguided notion....

Instead of recognizing that the protection ranger is faced with potential hazard to his personal, as well as the public safety, the report only widens the previously mentioned credibility gap. The task force needlessly tortured itself with operational considerations when it should have recognized that this was outside of their policy making purview. This report has only served to notify our field personnel that management has little understanding nor sympathy for the problems besetting the protection ranger....

We carp endlessly about concern for a "low profile" so as not to "offend" the visitor with a law enforcement image. In our misguided notions with what the visitor might think, we have neglected our basic safety responsibility to the employee who is faced with a potential hazard each time he attempts a law enforcement response.[25]

In hindsight, these comments from Christensen, Hutchison, Kreis, and others seem almost prophetic, illuminating the extent to which NPS managers were too self-absorbed to understand what the evolving field of professional law enforcement was all about, and foretelling any number of serious problems for the NPS, including a disproportionately high number of assaults that rangers across the country would suffer in the years that followed.[26]

Nevertheless, the task force recommendations were adopted. The result was a tide of new national policies, guidelines, and procedures reinforcing the NPS position that *none* of its rangers were to be viewed internally or by the public as law enforcement officers. Access to legitimate law enforcement and other defensive equipment was even further limited – an ironic turn, given that one of the factors identified as contributing to Ranger Patrick's murder was his own limited access to his sidearm.[27] At the same time, law enforcement training curriculum was even further diluted, a process that came to be known and endorsed by training managers (including what the NPS considered its own "law enforcement specialists") as "defanging."

Adding insult to injury, some park managers seemed to go out of their way to confirm the validity of Kreis's observation that the task force report "has only served to notify our field personnel that management has little understanding nor sympathy for the problems besetting the protection ranger."

VOL. XXXIV, NO. 43   Tuesday, July 10, 1979

Burgeoning Issue

Ban On Ranger Sidearms Provokes Debate Within National Seashore

By JOHN R. LEANING

Law enforcement rangers in the Cape Cod National Seashore are not happy with a policy now being enforced that bars rangers on routine daytime patrol from wearing weapons.

The policy, announced last week by park superintendent Herbert Olsen, says that unless confronted by "emergent" situations, patrol rangers during the daytime should not wear their sidearms.

Concerned that the policy will remove patrol rangers the final decision on whether a potential situation warrants wearing a sidearm, several top rangers in the park have requested an official clarification of the no-arms policy from National Park Service regional headquarters in Boston.

Superintendent Olsen emphasized the policy was not new; he said he was simply implementing pre-existing policy set down by the regional office, and enforced by his predecessor, former park superintendent Lawrence Hadley.

"The primary purpose of National Park Service rangers is not law enforcement," Mr Olsen explained. He said the principal function of rangers was protection of U.S. government land for the enjoyment of visitors.

The regional headquarters in Boston backed up Mr Olsen's no-arms emphasis.

"Rangers are not to wear firearms unless in circumstances involving potential danger," explained Leonard Frank, chief of resource management and visitor protection for the region. He added it was "up to supervisors to determine conditions" under which a ranger may be armed.

Mr Olsen indicated some concern over making the no-arms policy more of an issue than it actually is, but

A National Park Service ranger shows how the .38 caliber service revolver is carried unobtrusively, discernible from the side, out of sight from the front. Carrying sidearms during daylight hours has become an issue in the Cape Cod National Seashore following orders from Superintendent Olsen banning sidearms from daytime patrols. This ranger agreed to wear the weapon for picture purposes only; it was removed after photo was taken.   TCC—Leaning

there are rangers too happy with

PE

"I would pr firearms left enforcement

Another ran be used, said th NPS Nine — ultimate decis daytime patrols see the situation

"We're not to be cops," people we enc up, it's proba

"It's that with that can going to happe

By coincide rangers in the recreational ve area just after man removing in a sheath.

Upon confi learned the " insisted the car. During onlookers gath

While incide firearms are involved alleg another a dista loaded shotgun Beach.

The no-arms circumstances not to wear patrolling the weapons.

Mr Olsen, policy has ca when dealing

Cape Cod National Seashore, MA. (*The Cape Codder*, July 10, 1979).

    In the summer of 1979, a group of rangers from the Madison Sub-District of Yellowstone National Park were summoned to park headquarters to answer for openly violating the superintendent's policy against wearing side-arms and other defensive equipment while on their patrols.[28] Instead, according to the superintendent and new NPS polices, service revolvers were to be stored in the glove-box of their patrol cars or in a briefcase, where they could be retrieved if a ranger found himself subjected to gun-fire during a car-stop or other "visitor contact."

    Bracing for the meeting, the rangers brought along copies of Department of the Interior policies.[29] As the meeting began, the superintendent reiterated his position that the rangers were not permitted to wear their side-arms. One of the rangers responded, telling the superintendent "You don't have the luxury to be able to order us not to wear our handguns," reminding him that "Departmental policy supersedes you. We're duty bound to follow our departmental manual." Those superseding policies actually mandated the wearing of side-arms and other defensive equipment by personnel engaged in law enforcement duties, directly conflicting with the superintendent's own interpretation of the new NPS policies. When confronted with that discrepancy, the superintendent dismissed the argument, telling the rangers, "If you think you're going to be shot, call the sheriff or the highway patrol; that's what they're there for."

The rangers were stunned by the response. They tried to reason with the superintendent, pointing out the preposterous nature of his suggestion and the obvious safety implications of such an untimely response if help ever did arrive, at all. But beyond that, the rangers tried to explain that as an area of exclusive federal jurisdiction, neither the sheriff's office nor the highway patrol had jurisdiction in Yellowstone National Park. In the absence of a cooperative agreement (which did not exist at the time), those state officers lacked authority to take any action, whatsoever, within park boundaries. Unable to challenge that reality, the superintendent then bluntly summed up his position, telling the rangers, "Well, then, if you're shot and killed, you'll go out in a blaze of glory like a man, *without* a gun."

The disagreement ended in a stalemate. The rangers remained defiant. Erring on the side of safety over their own career prospects, they continued to wear their side-arms on their patrols, earning a reputation in the park (and beyond) as members of what came to be known as the "Blaze of Glory Society," or "BOGS." For years thereafter, in celebration of the stance taken by the rangers, whenever the superintendent was heard talking on the park radio, other personnel would tauntingly chime in with their own anonymous transmissions, one after another echoing the name, "Bogs, bogs, ..." etc.[30] Meanwhile, the superintendent remained equally outspoken in his opposition to arming rangers. Justifying his position during what was supposed to have been one of the first training sessions to familiarize NPS managers with the legal and ethical complexities of law enforcement, the superintendent defiantly stood up and declared to his colleagues and classmates, "It's easier to explain a ranger being killed than it is to explain a ranger shooting a visitor."[31]

Callous indifference aside, this management approach to law enforcement could be further justified by the extent to which the real history of crime and crime fighting in parks had been obscured and even manipulated, along with any record of assaults and even murders suffered by NPS rangers. At that time, according to the NPS, only one ranger (Ken Patrick) had ever been killed in the history of the agency (a fiction stubbornly perpetuated by the agency all the way into the early 21st century), and none of its rangers had ever needed to defend himself with deadly force.[32] Parks were safe places where serious crime almost never occurred, and where bad people magically became good. What rare crime did occur was only the result of misguided souls in need of a polite educational warning from a friendly ranger wearing a Smokey Bear hat. It was the GIGO principle in action; "garbage in – garbage out." Only in this case, instead of data generated by a computer, the outcome was the development and acceptance of some genuinely bad policies that were both unrealistic and dangerous, and not just for employees, but for the public as well.

In a very real and lasting sense, the agency succeeded in obstructing efforts to reform and professionalize its law enforcement program. Many old-timers were merely grandfathered in and issued a law enforcement commission based upon minimal training and experience they were able to piece together to meet the required number of credit hours. Meanwhile, although it might run contrary to reason, absolutely nothing in the new legislation specifically called for law enforcement programs and rangers to be supervised by counterpart law enforcement personnel. Academy-trained rangers could be and frequently were (and still are) directly supervised by non-law enforcement counterparts who might have little or no training, experience, understanding, or even sympathies for law enforcement activities. This left new law enforcement rangers and programs subject to all manner of manipulation, enabling local managers to obstruct investigations and other law enforcement activities where they saw fit, or alternatively to abuse law enforcement personnel and other resources for purely political purposes.

There was yet another "advantage" to this approach, as viewed by agency managers. As a part of the effort to maintain the ranger image, the NPS steadfastly resisted any form of position specialization or program management that would properly have included the application of government background, hiring, and classification standards for law enforcement personnel.[33] That had the simultaneous benefit of circumventing requirements to afford employees enhanced law enforcement pay and retirement benefits otherwise prescribed by federal regulations. Instead, for decades, standards applied to rangers for recruitment, pay, and retirement were artificially suppressed as part of official agency policy.

Both of those deficiencies had been poignantly noted back in 1973 by the same senior law enforcement official from outside of the NPS organization (BIA special agent Wilson) who had offered the other damning comments about the Park Service's own role in the murder of Ken Patrick:

> Administrative actions should be initiated to control time worked by Rangers in excess of their regular tour of duty. Serious consequences can result where employees decide on their own to go on patrol or perform other job-related actions when such actions have not been authorized or directed by supervisory personnel. In the event an employee under these circumstances becomes injured, damages property or becomes involved in an automobile accident with a government vehicle, it is extremely doubtful that it can be said or supported that he was properly on duty in any authorized pay status, or performing responsibilities within his official scope

of duties. The consequences will not only effect the Park Service, but also benefits to the employee and/or his family in the case of injury or death…. It is recommended … the Regional Director review the provisions of Title 5, United States Code, Section 5545(c)(2) and the Federal Personnel Manual Section 25.261 which provide for payment of premium compensation for investigative and police personnel whose time cannot be controlled administratively and who must at times exercise independent judgment in responding to requests for enforcement activities….

Law enforcement is a hazardous profession. For this reason Federal law enforcement personnel are entitled to more liberal retirement benefits than other Federal employees. It is my understanding that Rangers are not classified in an enforcement series and therefore are not now eligible for these benefits. If Rangers are expected to be enforcement officers, and as such meet the demands of the profession and operate in accordance with contemporary enforcement standards and practices, then certainly they are entitled to the benefits offered by the Federal Government to Federal law enforcement officers."[34]

But none of these comments were given serious consideration. As Ranger Image Task Force Chairman – and recipient of the above letter – Howard Chapman was forced to acknowledge, years later, when questioned under oath during legal proceedings supported by the U.S. Park Ranger Lodge of the Fraternal Order of Police, the NPS was

squarely opposed to recognizing and/or implementing the provisions of 5 USC 8336 [defining the provisions of law enforcement retirement] for any of its employees … regardless of duties actually performed in the field by its employees. … Field offices such as the Western Regional Office were not to prepare, classify, or submit for determination positions which might qualify for … Law Enforcement Officers enhanced retirement credit.[35]

As another interesting strategy to avoid specialization, many rangers with only minimal responsibilities for law enforcement were sent to the new law enforcement academy. Law enforcement commissions were handed out like candy. Nobody was special or specialized if everybody had a law enforcement commission. And since law enforcement was not a real profession in the NPS, anybody, regardless of their aptitude or interests, could be trained and assigned to do it. And since no one was special or had special skills or duties to face special hazards, no one needed to be awarded special pay or retirement benefits for doing so. Rangers with absolutely no interest and no desire to work in law enforcement were either grandfathered or sent through the academy where, upon graduation, they were issued an NPS law enforcement commission; a ticket to be punched in the compilation of the ranger's resume. Not surprisingly, many of those who subscribed to this approach have been among the most successful in the agency, rapidly rising through the ranks to senior positions where they, in turn, are positioned to perpetuate that management model.

In most agencies, candidates are rigorously screened and tested – academically, physically, and psychologically – long before they are hired and sent through the academy. Upon graduation, they are viewed as raw recruits and trainees, on probation for at least a year as they are closely monitored and supervised. Thereafter, it generally takes years of experience, proven performance, and still more rigorous testing in the form of both oral and written exams, before an officer is even considered for promotion. This was true in progressive agencies as early as the 1970s. By the 1980s, it was standard practice in major law enforcement agencies across the country. But in the NPS, graduation from a basic academy – *any* academy – placed a ranger at the top of the heap where, with nothing more than a graduation certificate and a flimsy law enforcement commission card for credentials, they were internally viewed as a trained professional, a "law enforcement (or protection) specialist," and frequently even a law enforcement supervisor to be let loose on the park and the public, stumbling, fumbling, and far too often making up their own rules, all the way.

The result was only a handful of maverick employees in the agency with any real interest in law enforcement, and even fewer with any credible experience or expertise. Left, instead, was a large workforce with mixed and often dubious backgrounds, lifestyles, and personal agendas, that received law enforcement training and delegation of law enforcement authorities, but very little credible oversight, experience, or genuine expertise as measured by contemporary standards. Many bad habits and bad practices, along with some truly bizarre attitudes about law enforcement – both passive and aggressive – were subsequently passed on from one generation of rangers to the next, becoming institutionalized into training and even written policies. The entire approach was a formula for self-fulling prophecy, as the many bad examples that inevitably came to light – usually in the form of overreaction to minor incidents, or abuse of authority – served only to reinforce the existing agency bias against law enforcement, generally, rather than the actual need for more stringent hiring and promotion practices, and increased training.

All of this simultaneously served to further limit development of expertise in law enforcement through any form of position specialization. The ranger image would rule. Any personnel left over whose duties and careers did, in fact, tenuously focus on law enforcement – positions where the opportunity to develop expertise actually existed – were relegated to the non-professional "park technician" job series. Classification standards for park technicians placed employees several grades beneath their "professional" non-specialized park ranger counterparts, or counterparts in other agencies; an artificial, inverted system of second-class rangers that for years held back many highly educated and skilled employees from advancement.[36] Utilization of other available job series that might otherwise have accurately described those duties and acknowledged proper grade-levels for law enforcement professionals – job series utilized by most other federal agencies – were outright prohibited by NPS policy.[37]

Not surprisingly, this led to disturbingly high rates of employee turnover. In one region alone over a three year period, twenty-two of the twenty-six total authorized commissioned positions were vacated through transfers or resignations. Ten of those twenty-two employees transferred to law enforcement positions in other agencies. As one of those employees explained, "Why should I keep applying for jobs within the Service, when I know that even if I'm lucky it will be at least 10 to 15 years before I could even begin to think of getting to the GS-12 level, when I can go to another agency, and be a GS-12 in four or five years?"[38] Equally disturbing but no more surprising were the disparaging comments openly voiced by supervisors and others who viewed those types of "defections" as nothing more than good riddance of employees with bad attitudes that the agency was better off without, since they obviously weren't sufficiently loyal to the NPS in the first place and who, after all, really only wanted to be "cops" and not "real rangers." Sadly, this condition still exists today, resulting in the continuing loss for the agency of many enormously talented employees who were initially drawn to the NPS by their own idealism and a desire to make a real contribution, but have subsequently been compelled to seek out positions elsewhere, where their interests and their talents might be more appreciated. As one such "defector" explained, "I didn't quit the NPS, the NPS quit me."[39]

Meanwhile, the NPS continued to cling to terms and concepts such as "low profile" and "soft image" law enforcement that had been cited as significant contributing factors in the 1973 murder of Ken Patrick. Reflecting a continuing aversion to anything "cop" or police-related, trained and commissioned rangers would not be viewed as law enforcement officers, but "resource protectors," "resource educators," and "generalists" (aka, "multi-specialists"), tasked, wherever possible, with a variety of other "traditional" ranger duties, including fire-fighting, resource management, and "interpretation," all of which duties officially precluded wearing defensive equipment (e.g., firearms, handcuffs, etc.) or otherwise presenting the appearance of a law enforcement official.

Of course, these terms and attitudes toward law enforcement create very complex but real disincentives for rangers to document crime that does occur in parks, particularly those incidents that require an armed response or the use of force. As just one example, the same official who, in 1989, had told reporters "it's surprising rangers haven't used deadly force before [the three ranger-involved shootings that year]," years later acknowledged and described the account of a ranger he knew on the Natchez Trace Parkway, in Tennessee, who in the early 1960s had emptied the unauthorized revolver he carried, firing at suspects in a fleeing vehicle after they attempted to run him down. The suspects got away and he didn't know if he had hit anyone, but the ranger had certainly never filed an official report on the incident.[40] And though he failed to mention it, that same official speaking with the press in 1989, had been the law enforcement specialist at Lake Mead National Recreation Area in 1970, when a seasonal ranger shot and killed a disorderly young man who was partying in a campground.[41] Omissions like these from just one revered NPS official raise a host of questions about the accuracy of statistics and other representations made by the agency in support of the ranger image. That troubling pattern was acknowledged by a senior law enforcement official in the Department of the Interior who years later observed that many of the statistics and programmatic reports generated by the NPS were "'not worth the paper they were sent in on,' ... under-reporting crime information to protect their image..."[42]

This entire approach to law enforcement has left its own unfortunate legacy, characterized by genuine confusion both within and outside of the NPS over the role and function of rangers.

An example of internal confusion over the ranger image can be found hidden in the records from an April 9, 1986 shooting incident at Cape Hatteras National Seashore. There, a ranger found himself subjected to gunfire from a suspect who had stolen an airplane in Rocky Mount, NC, and flown it to a landing strip at Mitchell Field, within the national seashore. When confronted, the suspect opened fire, emptying his .25 ACP pistol at the ranger. The ranger, who was fortunately armed at the time, returned fire, emptying his own .38 caliber revolver, reloading, and firing six more rounds at the fleeing suspect; all without effect. In the board of review that followed, the ranger acknowledged his own surprise and lack of mental preparedness for the shooting, honestly but naively declaring,

> This thing just doesn't happen very often to park rangers. We're not conditioned to expect someone to, without provocation, just open up and start shooting at you. And so, naturally, you're going to question your role as a protection personnel that works for an agency where our primary duty and obligation is to protect resources and be of service to visitors.[43]

At the very same time, externally, rangers are widely seen as something less than legitimate police officials possessing real law enforcement authority That confusion is exacerbated by NPS policies requiring all employees to wear almost exactly the same uniform, even though that practice conflicts with Interior policies requiring that "uniformed law enforcement personnel are easily recognized as law enforcement officers by the general public" and that "uniforms of non-law enforcement personnel shall be plainly distinguishable from the uniforms of law enforcement officers."[44] Those Interior policies notwithstanding, the ranger image and NPS management demands that all agency employees – from clerical personnel to entrance-station attendants to scientists and even maintenance workers – are viewed by the public as rangers, virtually indistinguishable from one another in their duties and authorities. That intransigent position is even acknowledged within policies related to other NPS programs such as fee collection, where employees are cautioned, "To the public, there is little obvious difference between commissioned law enforcement rangers and other park employees. All NPS uniforms are similar, and the only difference on the LE ranger's uniform is the defensive equipment and badge."[45] As a consequence, a sizeable portion of the American public, and particularly the criminal or merely intoxicated population, see park rangers as something closer to overgrown boy scouts; cartoonish figures in funny uniforms, lacking real authority to enforce laws; whose requests, instructions, and even orders can be ignored and challenged. That aspect of the ranger image was noted in 1963, by Rocky Mountain National Park ranger Jack Moomaw. Writing in the introduction to his *Recollections of a Rocky Mountain Ranger,* Moomaw lamented, "It has always been something of a puzzle to me why all of the books that I have read about rangers have been slanted toward teenagers, and rangers presented as being overgrown boy scouts, or as Simon-pures."[46]

Evidence of this perception can be found daily in parks across the country, where some of the most common phrases heard in confrontations and other interactions between rangers and the violating public are "you're not a real cop," "you can't arrest me," or "you can't tell me what to do." Challenges like that, in combination with remote working environments, a lack of back-up, and an accumulation of agency-imposed psychological baggage over their own identity, helps explain the extraordinarily high levels of resistance and accompanying assaults perpetrated against NPS rangers, nation-wide; a rate of assaults that is frequently higher than that suffered by any other category of officials in federal government.[47] That rate of assaults is just one of the unintended consequences of NPS success in crafting and manipulating the ranger image. But there are still more consequences to this management approach, where professionalism takes a back seat to concerns over image.

Over the decades, the NPS obsession with the ranger image has resulted in dangerously disparate levels of performance agency-wide. It is true that many rangers have risen to the challenge, demonstrating real competence, especially those whose interests and aptitude for law enforcement were complimented by time spent in assignments at recreation areas or other active sites with well-developed law enforcement programs. Some of the smartest, most professional, and most experienced law enforcement officers in the country can be found among the ranks of the Park Service's rangers. That said, even today there is little if anything in the way the NPS manages its law enforcement program to assure real proficiency. By avoiding those types of assignments (because, among other reasons, they really didn't want to be law enforcement officers, in the first place), many commissioned rangers are able to go through their entire careers merely dabbling in law enforcement, deprived of the opportunity to develop the kind of judgment and skills that can only be acquired through extensive experience under competent and critical supervision in a taxing environment. Some have never even made an arrest, much less a felony arrest, not to mention testified under rigorous cross-examination during a suppression hearing or trial in U.S. District Court.

Consequently, contrary to popular perception, the mere fact that a ranger (up to and including many chief park rangers and superintendents) has received academy training or has been delegated with law enforcement authority, does not necessarily mean that he or she has a professional level of knowledge, experience, or ability in law enforcement. The result is that most dangerous of conditions where a lot of supervisors and managers with a little knowledge and even less experience are empowered to make critical decisions relating to law enforcement operations and programs. That deficiency has been perpetuated over the years through the cultivation of a provincial agency mindset that is passionately resistant to the acceptance of models and standards advocated by "outsiders" (i.e., professional law enforcement organizations) for how to run a law enforcement program. Internally, the Service brands this as "NPS law enforcement" or "visitor and resource protection"; its own special, proprietary approach that de-emphasizes law enforcement as a distinct profession and instead approaches it as something closer to a "collateral duty." As such, inexperience and poor performance in law enforcement doesn't necessarily matter all that much and can be readily tolerated because it is, after all, only one of many other duties such as search and rescue, EMS, firefighting, and interpretation, all of which are more valued because they are perceived as more traditional and in keeping with the ranger image.

The result of this model and approach to law enforcement can be found in the sometimes baffling mix of over-reaction, under-reaction, and even no reaction (reminiscent of the selective enforcement practices previously noted by BIA investigator William Wilson) by some reluctantly commissioned rangers to a wide range of incidents that occur in parks.

The following true account of an incident from the early-1980s is just one example out of many that can be cited to help illustrate this problem.

A family – mother, daughter, and step-father – were staying in one of the campgrounds in the Tuolumne Meadows area of Yosemite's high country. Nearby, but outside of the designated campground, one of Yosemite's many young "climbing bums" was set up in his own illegal campsite. The daughter, an attractive girl of legal age, had developed a quick friendship with the climber, wandering off one afternoon to spend time with her new male acquaintance. Later that evening (but a little later than expected), the girl returned to her parent's campsite, accompanied by her new, scraggily-looking friend.

The girl's stepfather took immediate umbrage, concluding that the young man had taken inappropriate advantage of his ward. Though both the girl and her friend denied that anything untoward had occurred, the stepfather took hold of a convenient cooking knife and grabbed the young man by his hair, pulling him back as he pressed the knife across the climber's throat. The stepfather told his wife to summon the rangers, as he detained the young man at knifepoint until law enforcement officials arrived to sort things out.

A commissioned backcountry ranger, highly regarded for his own climbing and rescue skills, was dispatched to the scene. When he arrived, the matter was quickly investigated and resolved with an arrest. The prisoner was transported down to the jail in Yosemite Valley, where he sat overnight.

The next morning, the prisoner was brought in to a holding cell for an interview where, as was normal procedure, he was questioned by NPS investigators about the incident and his pending charges.

The investigators were as baffled as the prisoner, not understanding why he was there and, quite reasonably, believing that *he* was the *victim* of an aggravated assault and unlawful detention. The young climber had been arrested the night before and charged by the backcountry ranger with illegal camping! Meanwhile, the stepfather who had illegally held the young man at knifepoint, had been issued ticket for assault with a deadly weapon, and was released at the scene. The ranger's report documenting the entire incident had passed through and been co-signed by all of his supervisors without question or comment, signifying their concurrence that reasonable and appropriate action had been taken.

Endnotes

1. FBI Case #SF89-141, Marin County (CA) Coroner Case #73292.

2. Tomie (Patrick) Lee to the author, email, Jan. 17, 2014; Tomie Lee to the author, email, Jan. 23, 2016.

3. Tom Wilson (NPS Public Information Officer, Washington Office), "NPS Pays Respects To Ken Patrick," *NPS Newsletter*, Vol. 8, No. 17, Sep. 3, 1973. At least two other NPS rangers had died from felonious gunfire prior to the 1970 killing of Ranger Ken Patrick: Ranger James Carey at Hot Springs, AK in 1927, and Ranger Karl Jacobsen at Acadia N.P. in 1938.

4. William G. Wilson, Supervisory Criminal Investigator, Bureau of Indian Affairs, Phoenix, Arizona (Board of Review member) to NPS Regional Director [Howard Chapman], National Park Service, Western Region, Attention: John M. Moorehead, Acting Assistant Regional Director, memorandum, regarding "Kenneth C. Patrick," Nov. 19, 1973. This memorandum supplements and is made part of the full board's December 14, 1973 report from the NPS Board of Review examining the Aug. 5, 1973 murder of NPS ranger Ken Patrick at Point Reyes National Seashore.

5. Tomie (Patrick) Lee, interview with the author, May 2, 2014.

6. *See* DOI Office of the Inspector General, *A Disquieting State of Disorder; An Assessment of the Department of the Interior Law Enforcement*, Jan. 2002.

7. Records maintained by the LVMPD Training Division document NPS rangers attending the academy by at least 1968. The Las Vegas Police Department and the Clark County Sheriff's Department were merged, July 1973, into the Las Vegas Metropolitan Police Department.

8. E.g., Dave Montalbano and John Townsend, interviews with the author, July 27, 2013. Peter Allen taught report writing, Bill Larson provided firearms instruction, and John Townsend taught defensive tactics.

9. Weston Kreis, interview with the author, July 27, 2013. Kreis carried his personal S&W .357, and Glen Voss carried his own 9mm pistol. Kreis was also sent to criminal investigator school at the Mississippi Highway Patrol academy in 1967.

10. Melody Webb, *A Woman in the Great Outdoors: Adventures in the National Park Service* (Albuquerque, NM: University of New Mexico Press, 2003) 86.

11. *See* Alaska Claims Settlement Act (1971) *and* Alaska National Interest Lands Conservation Act (1980).

12. J.T. Reynolds, interview and email exchange with the author, Mar. 15-16, 2014.

13. 16 USC 10, 10A (Act of Mar. 3, 1905). These sections were repealed in 1976 through enactment of P.L. 94-458. *See, also,* 16 USC 9a (repealed), government of parks, etc. under Secretary of the Army.

14. Weston Kreis, interview with the author, Aug. 16, 2013. *Also,* Andy Hutchison, interview with the author, Apr. 14, 2015. The NPS had attempted to limit the curriculum and number of hours of required training. That effort was countered by DOI Chief of Law Enforcement, Security, Col. Robert Smoak, who was able to get language inserted into the legislation requiring the NPS to comply with training standards established by the DOI.

15. P.L. 94-458 (codified at 16 USC 1a-6). West's *U.S. Code, Congressional and Administrative News*, 94th Congress, Second Session, 1976, Jan. 19 – Oct. 2, Vol. 4l Legislative History. See, also, 94th Congress, Second session, Committee Report to accompany H.R. 11887, p. 17-18. State traffic, boating, fishing, and hunting laws are also enforced by NPS rangers throughout the National Park System, through adoption into NPS regulations (36 CFR).

16. The committee report contained the explicit admonition that " *"This bill would not affect the functions or authorities of the United States Park Police, whose law enforcement mission has been defined by the Act of March 17, 1948, as amended (62 Stat.81). Presently the Park Police are authorized to arrest for Federal offenses committed in the District of Columbia and on Federal reservations in its metropolitan area. This special authority of the Park Police is adequate for them to perform their responsibilities, and we do not believe there is a need to alter that authority in this bill."* [Emphasis added] (West's *U.S. Code, Congressional and Administrative News* for the 94th Congress, Second Session, 1976, Jan. 19 - Oct. 2, Volume 4: Legislative History).

17. "The Committee intends that the clear and specific enforcement authority contained in this subsection, while necessary for the protection of the Federal employees so involved, will be im-

plemented by the Secretary to ensure that law enforcement activities in our National Park System will continue to be viewed as one function of a broad program of visitor and resource protection. Law enforcement duties should be a function of the National Park Ranger, along with a diversity of other protection concerns. It is not intended here that law enforcement responsibilities should fall on a small number of individuals as their exclusive duty. In like manner, the carrying of firearms and other defensive equipment should be done with a view toward maintaining the appearance of all designated employees as representatives of a resource and people-serving agency, and not as members of an organization whose only function is law enforcement."

Cleveland "Cleve" Pinnix, interview with the author, Oct. 3, 2011, and related email exchanges (Sep. 9 – Dec. 12, 2011). Pinnix was the principle author of the committee report accompanying P.L. 94-458. Pinnix was a NPS ranger, who left the NPS to work for Rep. Roy A. Taylor, sponsor of the House legislation (H.R. 11887).

A detailed analysis of this and related portions of the committee report, subsequently reviewed and confirmed by Pinnix, is contained in my self-published 2000 essay, "A Ranger's Field Guide to Myths and Misinformation (debunking 10 common misperceptions about U.S. Park Rangers)."

18. Andy Hutchison, interview with the author, June 22, 2015.

19. The "Task Force on the Ranger Image" chaired by Western Regional Director Howard Chapman, was established by NPS Director Gary Everhardt in August of 1976, and issued its report the following year. See memorandum from the Director (Gary Everhardt) to all employees, "Law Enforcement in the National Park Service, Aug. 13, 1976. Also, see memorandum from the Director (Gary Everhardt) to all employees, "Law Enforcement (Ranger Image) Task Force Report," Apr. 18, 1977; memorandum from Weston P. Kreis, Staff Park Ranger to Assistant Director, Park Operations, "Report – Ranger Image Task Force," (FNP: WPKreis;ck:4/11/77), with attachments by Andy Hutchison (FNP:AEHuchison[sic]:ck:2/2/77 and 4/4/77), and Inspector Jack M Sands (USPP) (4/1/77), and Carl Christensen (FNP:CChristensen:ck:3/31/77). Also, misc. interviews by the author, 2011-2013, with Weston Kreis and Andy Hutchison.

20. Daniel J. Tobin, Jr. (Superintendent, Mount Rainier National Park) to Howard M. Chapman, Chairman, Law Enforcement Task Force, "Law Enforcement in the National Park Service," Sep. 3, 1976.

21. William J. Whalen, General Manager, Bay Area National Parks, to Howard Chapman, Regional Director, Western Region, "Ranger Image," Sep. 3, 1976. Whalen was appointed Director of the NPS in July of 1977, and served in that capacity through 1983.

22. Paul D. Berkowitz, "letter to the editor," *Courier: The National Park Service Newsletter,* Jan. 1978, p. 11.

23. Carl Christensen (Park Ranger) to Chief, Division of Ranger Activities and Protection, "Report of Law Enforcement Task Force," memorandum, Mar. 31, 1977.

24. Andy Hutchison (staff Park Ranger) to Acting Assistant Director for Park Operations, memorandum, Feb. 24, 1977, "Ranger Image," (FNP:AEHutchison:ck:2/24/77). *See also,* Robert J. Byrne (Chief Ranger, Independence National Historic Park) to Chief, Resource Management & Visitor Protection, Mid-Atlantic Region, memorandum, Mar. 23, 1984, subject "Employee Turnover."

25. Weston P. Kreis to Assistant NPS Director, memorandum, Apr. 11, 1977, "Report – Ranger Image Task Force" (FNP-WPKreiss:ck:4/11/77).

26. *See* Michael V. Finley (Law Enforcement Specialist, Grand Teton N.P.) to Western Regional Director [Howard Chapman], memorandum, Oct. 7, 1976, subject "Law Enforcement in the National Parks."

27. Andy Hutchison, *The Ken Patrick Murder (A Case Study),* Applied Criminology, FBI National Academy, 103rd Session, Nov. 11, 1975.

28. Rangers Chuck Pesta, Ken Hay, and Al Viara. Superintendent John Townsley.

29. Departmental Manual 446.

30. Chuck Pesta and Ken Hay, misc. interviews with the author, early 1990s. Chuck Pesta and Ken Hay, re-interviewed by the author, Feb. 24-25, 2014. Chuck Pesta, follow-up email to the author, May 1, 2015. Chuck Pesta eventually left the NPS to pursue a career with the U.S. Marshals Service.

31. Andy Hutchison, interview with the author, Apr. 14, 2015, Rapidan, VA. The statement was made during one of the first "Law Enforcement for Managers" classes held at the Federal Law Enforcement Training Center (FLETC). Hutchison was the NPS FLETC representative (1977-1987) and class coordinator, present when superintendent John A. Townsley made this statement. Also attending this session was regional director Howard Chapman.

32. NPS news release, "Man Convicted of Killing Ranger to be Paroled," May 27, 2005.

33. It is noteworthy that official aversion to the application of proper position classification for NPS law enforcement personnel persisted long after the adoption of proper position classification for counterpart fire-fighting personnel.

34. William G. Wilson (Supervisory Criminal Investigator, Bureau of Indian Affairs, Phoenix, Arizona) to Regional Director [Howard Chapman], National Park Service, Western Region, memorandum, Nov. 19, 1973, subject, "Kenneth C. Patrick" [supplement to findings of the Board of Review of the Ken Patrick murder].

35. Howard H. Chapman (NPS Western Regional Director), sworn testimony, hearing before the Merit Systems Protection Board in the matter of Lady D. McClaren (widow of deceased NPS ranger Richard McClaren) v. Office of Personnel Management, *The Protection Ranger* (newsletter of the U.S. Park Ranger Lodge of the Fraternal Order of Police), Jan./Feb. 1992.

36. The "park technician" series progressed at single-grade intervals from already-low entry grades (e.g., GS-3,4,5,6,7, 8), as opposed to the "park ranger" series that progressed from higher entry levels, at two-grade intervals through the GS-11 level, and single-grade levels thereafter (e.g., GS-7, 9, 11, 12, 13, etc.).

37. Most federal agencies place their law enforcement personnel in the "1800" series; e.g., 1811 for criminal investigators, etc. Use of those job series was prohibited by internal NPS policies.

38. [Robert J. Byrne] Chief Ranger, Independence National Historic Park, to Chief, Resource Management & Visitor Protection, Mid-Atlantic Region, memorandum, Mar. 23, 1984, subject "Employee Turnover." *Also*, Andrew E. Hutchison, USDI/NPS Representative, FLETC, to Chief, Division of Training, "FLETC Graduate Survey," Feb. 22, 1985, documenting the high rate of transfers to other agencies of NPS graduates of both basic and advanced curriculum at the Federal Law Enforcement Training Center.

39. David Montalbano, undated conversation with the author,

40. Rick Gale, undated interview with the author (est. 1993), about Natchez Trace Parkway sub-district ranger Jake Hamilton. Gale served as president of the Association of National Park Rangers from 1988-1994. He was also the first ranger to receive the park service's prestigious "Harry Yount Lifetime Achievement Award," in 1994, in recognition of being "on the cutting edge of innovation in almost every major ranger program area for the last two decades, a period when ranger work became truly professionalized in the NPS."

41. May 30, 1970, Lake Mead NRA seasonal ranger Leland Lamoreaux shot 18 year old Theodore Goodwin in the back, as he was walking away from the ranger. Lamoreaux had drawn and cocked his service revolver, pointing it at Goodwin, and (according to witness accounts) warning that he would shoot if the he didn't stop, as ordered. The gun discharged, striking Goodwin in the spine. Goodwin died from his gunshot wound a few days later. Lamoreaux was charged by county officials with an open count of murder, but was acquitted at trial.

42. DOI-OIG "A Disquieting State of Disorder: An Assessment of DOI Law Enforcement," Jan. 2002 (interview with Irving Tubbs).

43. Ranger Mike Anderson, during the recorded Board of Review for his April 9, 1986 shooting incident (versus suspect Gary Peterson) at Mitchell Field, Cape Hatteras National Seashore, NC.

44. Department of the Interior, Departmental Manual (DM) 446, Chap. 12, 12.4A, Law Enforcement Equipment, Uniforms. National Park Service, Law Enforcement Policies, Reference Manual (RM) 9, Chap. 29, Uniform and Appearance Standards.

45. National Park Service, Reference Manual 22A, Recreation Fee Collection, Appendix D, Introduction.

46. Jack C. Moomaw, *Recollections of a Rocky Mountain Ranger* (Longmont, CO: Times Call Publishing Co., 1963) and (Estes Park, CO: YMCA of the Rockies, 1994) 18.

47. F.B.I. Uniform Crime Report, "Law Enforcement Officers Killed and Assaulted, 2010" etc. *See, also,* Paul Berkowitz, "The Middle of Nowhere Syndrome," (*The Protection Ranger,* publication of the NPS Ranger's Lodge of the Fraternal Order of Police, 1993).

CHAPTER EIGHT

Trouble in Paradise

The 1970s and 1980s were a period of dramatic changes and reforms in law enforcement throughout the United States. Those
changes and reforms were in large measure the result of a series
of historic rulings such as *Mapp, Brady, Gideon, Escobedo, Miranda,* and
Terry, handed down by the U.S. Supreme Court during the 1960s, affecting police procedure and rights of the accused.[1] Criminal procedure became "constitutionalized," as police officers across the country, in every
jurisdiction, were expected to study, understand, and perform within the
ever-evolving constraints of both criminal and constitutional law.[2]

The demand for change was compounded by public dissatisfaction
generated by law enforcement response to the civil rights movement, the
Viet Nam War protests, the so-called "hippie" movement, and related un-
rest throughout the turbulent 1960s and 1970s. Incidents like the1965
Watts Riots in Los Angeles, the 1968 Democratic National Convention
in Chicago, and disclosures about widespread corruption in agencies like
the New York Police Department (NYPD) as disclosed by Officer Frank
Serpico, all had a widespread impact on American law enforcement.

Serpico was the first officer in the history of the NYPD to step forward and report "widespread, systemic corruption." His heroic efforts
made him the target of all manner of reprisal and outright retaliation, up
to and including being abandoned and left to die by fellow officers after he
was shot in the face during a drug raid. The shooter was never identified,
and questions remain about whether Serpico was set up and then shot
by fellow officers. Serpico later testified before the Knapp Commission, a
five-member panel convened by New York Mayor John Lindsay to investigate allegations of corruption within the NYPD.[3] Included in Serpico's
opening statements to the Commission were the following comments:

> Through my appearance here today ... I hope that police officers
> in the future will not experience the same frustration and anxiety
> that I was subjected to for the past five years at the hands of my
> superiors because of my attempt to report corruption ... We cre-
> ate an atmosphere in which the honest officer fears the dishonest
> officer, and not the other way around.... The problem is that the
> atmosphere does not yet exist in which honest police officers can
> act without fear of ridicule or reprisal from fellow officers.[4]

Those events, along with the entire Watergate Scandal of the Nixon administration, added fuel for the push to reform not only law enforcement, but government, generally. For all its turbulence, it was simultaneously a promising time, accompanied by a series of efforts in law enforcement agencies across the country to professionalize, modernize, and practice law enforcement at an elevated set of standards.

While the acceptance and implementation of reforms certainly was not – and clearly is still not – uniform across the country, the Boulder County Sheriff's Department from which I had come was one of the progressive agencies where that approach seemed to be embraced. A number of other agencies throughout the West, and particularly in California, acquired a similar reputation (deservedly or not) for being on the cutting edge of these types of changes, adopting elevated standards for education, training, and conduct, and a renewed respect and sensitivity for civil rights and legal standards prescribed by the courts. Accompanying those changes came the incremental establishment across the country of state commissions on Peace Officer Standards and Training, or POST.[5] In addition to the physical challenges faced in law enforcement, this approach emphasized a real intellectual component in the list of demands placed on law enforcement professionals. Brains, creativity, communications skills, and an even temperament became every bit as important as size and strength. That was the kind of law enforcement I wanted to be involved in, and was one of the reasons I had been excited to leave Indiana Dunes and "the Region," and return west.

* * *

With all these references to "professionalism" and the law enforcement "profession," it's probably worth taking a moment to clarify what these terms mean. Recalling my own university classes in criminal justice and public administration, the definition goes far beyond endeavors that are merely done for money as a career.

A true professional – no matter what the field – possesses experience and expertise in that field, stays knowledgeable, proficient, up-to-date and skilled in state-of-the-art standards and practices related to that field, and is held to account by a body (e.g., an agency) or an empowered group of peers for his or her performance and conduct. These last components are critical to professionalism. Generally speaking, real professionalism is not seen where professionalism is not demanded. How rigorous the standards are, the level of scrutiny maintained to detect variations from standards, how consistently those standards are applied, and the level of accountability that is maintained can either make or break a profession. Where law enforcement officers are concerned, it is certain that they must first know the law and the court's interpretation of those laws, and then abide by those laws and interpretations, themselves, in both the performance of their duties and in their own lives.[6]

But there are still more qualifications imposed on true professionals, relating to the ability to maintain composure and objectivity in the performance of one's duties. Ideally, the professional is able to divorce him or herself from whatever biases or prejudices may exist toward a "client" or about a particular subject, undertaking the task at hand with the same high standards without regard to personal feelings. In the medical profession, we expect doctors and nurses to render the best care possible to all patients, regardless of their social standing, whether, for example, they are innocent and sympathetic victims of violent crimes, or despicable suspects accused of the most heinous crimes. As a real-life example in law enforcement, I know one NPS ranger who, after shooting a suspect who was trying to kill him, rebounded from the trauma of his own significant injuries to render aid to the dying suspect by performing CPR until other units arrived to take over. It may be the scientist who meticulously documents and then publishes his methodology and his findings, even when those findings do not support his thesis. It's the police officer or investigator with a comprehensive knowledge of the criminal laws and the case law that applies, who operates within those bounds and includes every statement and every known detail about other evidence in her report and her testimony, even when that includes mistakes made by the police and other facts that might favor a suspect. In other settings involving strained interactions between government officials and citizens, professionalism manifests in the form of treating all constituents honestly, fairly, and with impartiality, no matter what the nature of the conflict and without regard to personalities, emotions, personal agendas, political persuasion, or other distractions.

It's any and all of these types of people taking a stand and resisting the efforts of others who would try to influence them to compromise their standards by undertaking their assignment with anything less than best practices. Nobody is perfect and certainly everyone will fail at some point in time, but all of these are essential elements and the goals of any individual or group that wants to be recognized as "professionals" and of any endeavor or occupation that seeks to be recognized as "a profession."

* * *

At the time of my 1982 transfer, Yosemite's "Law Enforcement Office" (LEO) was managed by Chief Law Enforcement Officer Leland "Lee" Shackelton. Shackelton had been appointed to that position back in 1971, as one of the original members of the "elite corps of rangers" that would come to be known as the Yosemite Mafia. He had two other supervisors working directly under him. The first was Norm Hinson, who had served as the park's chief (i.e., supervisory) criminal investigator since 1976. He was the one who had selected and hired me for my position, and was technically my direct supervisor. The other was "court officer" M. (Marshal) Scott Connelly. He, too, was an original member of the Yosemite Mafia, having been a ranger there since the days of the 1970 riot. He was promoted to his position in the LEO in 1974. Along with supervising and participating in some investigations, Connelly oversaw the supervisor and staff that ran the jail (capacity of 22 prisoners) and evidence storage facilities. More importantly, Connelly was the park's local prosecutor who presented cases in the federal court located in Yosemite Valley. He was authorized by the United States Attorney to make preliminary case presentations and handle misdemeanor trials and plea agreements before Yosemite's resident judge, the United States Magistrate. He also served as the primary agency liaison with actual federal prosecutors (Assistant United States Attorneys, or AUSAs) at the federal courthouse in Fresno. And because most of Yosemite is an area of "exclusive federal jurisdiction," where all crimes ranging from littering to murder are exclusively federal (as opposed to state) offenses, both Connelly and Shackelton wielded enormous power and influence over local law enforcement activities.

Within the first year of my arrival in Yosemite, I was assigned to work nearly full time on what was commonly referred to as the "special drug investigation" or "Curry Case" (for Yosemite Park and Curry Company, or YPCC, the park's primary concessionaire). This was a specially funded, long-term, far-ranging investigation and undercover operation targeting illegal drug trafficking within the park. Among the allegations precipitating the investigation was that "YPCC management was providing a 'protective umbrella' for YPCC employees who were engaging in drug trafficking, prostitution, and embezzlement..."[7] The special investigation was managed and supervised by both Shackelton and Connelly, and I reported directly to these two officials (rather than Hinson) when engaged in activities related to that case.

I'd already been through – and graduated with honors from – two full-blown law enforcement academies. The first was the Colorado POST certified Boulder County Sheriff's Department Academy. Then, upon beginning my assignment at Indiana Dunes, I was sent to the Federal Law Enforcement Training Center (FLETC) for several months to attend Criminal Investigator School, the same basic training program to which most of the government's other new federal agents sent by agencies like the Drug Enforcement Administration, Secret Service, Bureau of Alcohol, Tobacco, and Firearms, U.S. Marshals Service, and the various offices of the Inspector General.[8] Now, with my new assignment in Yosemite, I was sent to yet another specialized course in Managing Informants and Undercover Operations, sponsored by the California Department of Justice. That curriculum focused on federal and state legal standards and procedures required in the effective use of both undercover officers and informants as part of criminal investigations.

As I became more familiar with how the Law Enforcement Office in Yosemite was run, and as I became more involved in the Curry Case, I became increasingly concerned about what I was seeing. On a daily basis I was observing what I believed were improper and probably illegal practices and techniques employed by both Shackelton and Connelly in the routine management of the special investigation. There were any number of other highly questionable practices unrelated to the investigation that seemed to be accepted as routine. These ranged from the use of "buy money" for unauthorized personal expenditures, to unlawful manipulation of evidence and reports, to the use of their positions for personal gain and gratification and the targeting of personal and political enemies for investigation.[9]

Thousands of dollars were being used to cover routine household expenses for salaried undercover agents and informants who were already being paid and employed full-time to infiltrate the drug community and make drug purchases. These same funds were being applied toward registration fees, tuition, and travel expenses to send at least one paid informant with a criminal background, and not yet a federal employee, to a seasonal NPS law enforcement academy, so he could subsequently be placed on government payroll and represent himself in court as a commissioned law enforcement officer. At that time and for many years to follow, the NPS did not require or conduct background investigations on its law enforcement personnel, arguing that the standard investigations used by other federal agencies were too expensive and, furthermore, were not warranted for NPS personnel. Those standards and procedures that did exist for the delegation of law enforcement authority were not being followed. This same operative, along with several others, had been recruited from a network of informants who circulated across the region, from agency to agency, working in exchange for either cash or, at least initially, prosecutorial leniency. The NPS-certified academy attended at government expense *prior* to being placed on government payroll, was managed by a retired NPS Ranger.

It appeared that imprest funds were also being used, and overtime pay requests were being fabricated, to pay off one former informant who had hired an attorney to initiate a lawsuit against Shackelton for alleged breach of contract. The informant claimed that Shackelton had promised more money than he was actually paid when he came to work in Yosemite. In apparent retaliation, Shackelton once boasted that he had initiated inquiries about tax withholdings on cash payments made by other agencies that had employed the informant. Shackelton threatened that he would have the Internal Revenue Service initiate a tax audit on the informant if he didn't drop the lawsuit.

Even more troubling was the routine practice of ordering staff (myself included) to violate established procedures by signing blank imprest vouchers and requests for "buy" funds, which Shackelton and Connelly would subsequently fill in and then "authorize," themselves, for dispersal. This was intended to bypass the required checks, balances, and oversight process established to ensure drug enforcement funds were properly expended.

I also learned that exculpatory evidence was being deliberately destroyed, including urine samples taken from informants and "agents" for testing, to guard against and detect their own prospective (illegal) use of controlled substances. Connelly acknowledged that he sometimes simply poured those samples down the drain instead of submitting them for testing. Shackelton once admitted that letters and reports containing exculpatory information sometimes just "fell" into the shredder. Independent reports from other law enforcement personnel documenting allegations that our own informants and undercover agents were using as well as selling drugs, were not investigated. I believed those written reports were among the documents being destroyed.

Meanwhile, it was common knowledge and apparently accepted that Shackelton periodically drove a government vehicle to Santa Rosa Junior College on regular paid government time to teach at the NPS-certified seasonal law enforcement academy, where he was simultaneously paid for his services by the State of California. Equally common was the falsification of work schedules and overtime pay requests. And in a manner frighteningly reminiscent of what I'd seen in northern Indiana, the practice of "badging" waiters in the local restaurants to have meals "comped" was reportedly also occurring.[10]

Another sensitive but well-known subject was Connelly's predilection for underage boys and young men. Connelly already had a reputation for a lifestyle and social life on the fringes of society. One of the first things I was told about when I first arrived was an incident involving one of Connelly's friends who had stolen a car in Fresno and driven it up to the park, where he was caught and arrested by rangers. I was told about another incident where Connelly was allegedly beaten up under suspicious circumstances while cruising or partying in Fresno. The living room of Connelly's small Yosemite house resembled the lounge of a B-movie brothel, with velvet curtains, glow lamps, and a dominating wet-bar. It was widely suspected, but apparently accepted, that Connelly took advantage of his position by recruiting young men in the Yosemite community as paid informants to satisfy his personal sexual desires. These were among the informants who were constantly being caught in possession of personal drugs and even arrested by rangers, but never prosecuted. But once again, with no requirement for background investigations and no apparent concerns over character, the matter of how these issues might impact upon investigations and prosecutions was never pursued.

One particularly significant event unrelated to the Curry Case occurred after I had been in Yosemite just over a year. It would signal for me a serious escalation of ethical and legal breaches within the Law Enforcement Office and even higher in the park organization, raising my own concerns over my personal safety and who I could trust, and the absence of any credible channels through which I could direct my concerns.

The first week of March 1983 was hectic, with virtually everyone in the park tied up in preparations for a high profile visit by Queen Elizabeth II of England. I was assigned to be part of the dignitary protection team working with the Secret Service. Complicating operations was the tragic death of three of those Secret Service agents on March 5; the day of the Queen's arrival. The agents had been conducting a security sweep, driving the entrance route on a specially closed section of highway approaching the park. But for reasons that were never fully explained, a sergeant from the Mariposa County Sheriff's Department took it upon himself to drive that same route at high speeds while crossing into the oncoming lane. When he rounded a blind curve, his cruiser hit the vehicle driven by the Secret Service agents. The three agents were killed, instantly. The sheriff's sergeant survived his injuries, but his involvement would eventually tie into an entirely separate controversy involving on-the-job drug use, drug distribution, and cover-up in his own department. Still, that single episode that day put a dark cloud over the Queen's visit – and the entire park.[11]

Nevertheless, shortly after the Queen's departure, Connelly directed me to gather up our new body-wire kit (containing electronic surveillance equipment), and meet him at the van we used to conduct surveillance and monitor drug buys.

Endnotes

1. *Mapp v. Ohio*, 367 U.S. 643 (1961), affirming rights under the 4th Amendment to be secure from warrantless search and seizure, and imposing an "exclusionary rule" to evidence in criminal cases that is obtained in violation of the 4th and other amendments (also see *Weeks v. U.S.*, 1917). *Gideon v. Wainwright*, 372 U.S. 335 (1963), affirming rights under the 14th and 6th Amendments for indigent state criminal defendants to be represented by court appointed counsel in all felony and capital cases. *Brady v. Maryland*, 373 U.S. 83 (1963), imposing on prosecutors an obligation to learn about exculpatory evidence from police and to make timely disclosure of it to the defense. *Escobedo v. Illinois*, 378 U.S. 478 (1964), affirming a state criminal defendants' right under the 14th, 5th, and 6th Amendments to remain silent and be represented by counsel, and that incriminating statements made by defendants are inadmissible as evidence unless the accused is

informed of his rights before making statements. *Miranda v. Arizona*, 384 U.S. 436 (1966), affirming police duty to advise a criminal suspect held in custody of his 5th Amendment right to remain silent and 6th Amendment right to counsel, before questioning. *Terry v. Ohio*, 392 U.S. 1 (1968), identifying "reasonable suspicion" as a legitimate basis to temporarily detain and frisk a suspect where an officer "observes unusual conduct leading to the reasonable conclusion that criminal activity may be afoot and that the suspect may be armed and presently dangerous."

2. Akhil Reed Amar, *The Constitution and Criminal Procedure – First Principles* (New Haven and London; Yale University Press, 1997) p. ix.

3. The Knapp Commission, named for its chairman, Whitman Knapp, was officially known as "The Commission to Investigate Alleged Police Corruption."

4. Frank Serpico, testimony before the Knapp Commission, Oct. 1971.

5. The first POST commission was actually established in July of 1959, in California, "as a special fund agency to develop and administer selection and training standards for the betterment of Californian law enforcement. ... Since then, all states have created similar organizations to improve and professionalize their law enforcement agencies." ("POST Celebrates 50th Anniversary," www.post.ca.gov/post-50th-anniversary.aspx).

6. *See* Article III, Section I, U.S. Constitution, " ... The judicial power of the United States, shall be vested in one Supreme Court, and in such inferior courts as the Congress may from time to time ordain and establish," *and* Section II, "The judicial power shall extend to all cases, in law and equity, arising under this Constitution, the laws of the United States, and treaties made, or which shall be made, under their authority;--to all cases affecting ambassadors, other public ministers and consuls;--to all cases of admiralty and maritime jurisdiction;--to controversies to which the United States shall be a party;--to controversies between two or more states; between a state citizens of another state; between citizens of the same state claiming lands under grants of different states, and between a state, or the citizens thereof, and foreign states, citizens or subjects. In all cases affecting ambassadors, other public ministers and consuls, and those in which a state shall be party, the Supreme Court shall have original jurisdiction. In all the other cases before mentioned, the Supreme Court shall have appellate jurisdiction, both as to law and fact, with such exceptions, and under such regulations as the Congress shall make. *Also*, Article VI, U.S. Constitution, " ... This Constitution, and the laws of the United States which shall be made in pursuance thereof; and all treaties made, or which shall be made, under the authority of the United States, shall be the supreme law of the land; and the judges in every state shall be bound thereby, anything in the Constitution or laws of any State to the contrary notwithstanding. The Senators and Representatives before mentioned, and the members of the several state legislatures, and all executive and judicial officers, both of the United States and of the several states, shall be bound by oath or affirmation, to support this Constitution; but no religious test shall ever be required as a qualification to any office or public trust under the United States." *Also*, Alexander Hamilton, *The Federalist Papers*, No. 78, "... the interpretation of the laws is the proper and peculiar province of the courts. A constitution is, in fact, and must be, regarded by the judges as the fundamental law. It therefore belongs to them to ascertain its meaning as well as the meaning of any law proceeding from the legislative body." See *Heien v. North Carolina*. In that case the court held that a police officer who stops a car based on a reasonable though mistaken understanding of the law does not violate the Fourth Amendment to the United States Constitution.

7. DOI-OIG Case #4VI-090, "Background." Also, 08/27/81 *New York Times* (UPI), "Yosemite Staff Accused of Embezzling For Drugs."

8. As part of the Department of Justice, in 1985 the Drug Enforcement Administration's basic training program was co-located with the FBI's training facilities at Quantico, VA. A separate DEA training facility was opened in 1999.

9. Special imprest funds appropriated to the park from the Regional Office for the controlled purchase of drugs and other evidence, including "information."

10. Displaying one's badge and law enforcement credentials to obtain complimentary (free) meals or services. Telephone interview with Andy Hutchison, Feb. 19, 2008.

11. U.S. Secret Service Agents George P. LaBarge (41), Donald Robinson (38), and Donald A. Bejcek (29) were killed. Mariposa County Sheriff's sergeant Rod Sinclair (43) sustained broken ribs and a fractured knee. See, Cheri Seymour, *The Last Circle* (Walterville, OR: TrineDay LLC, 2010) 17-27; A.P., "Investigator in Crash Tells of Tranquilizers," *New York Times,* Apr. 16, 1984.

CHAPTER NINE

Technicalities[1]

Abody-wire or "wire" is commonly used in undercover operations, including "controlled" drug buys made by law enforcement personnel from suspected drug dealers. Recent technological advances allow mobile "smart" phones to perform many of the functions that decades ago required a dedicated body wire kit. But those systems still exist, and are usually made up of three distinct components.

The first is the miniature radio transmitter with attached microphone and antennae (AKA the "bug"), designed to be concealed on the body; either taped to the skin or secreted in clothing. Current technology allows both the microphone and radio transmitter to be extremely small, even the size of a pen, button, or cuff-link. But in the 1980s, the smaller units were closer in size to a pager or a pack of gum. Factors of size and concealment are always made in exchange for power and range. But because of the overriding need for it to be concealed, the "bug" is the smallest component of the entire kit, distinct from the other components in both its size and appearance.

Next is the receiver. Where concealment is not an issue, such as where back-up or monitoring personnel are in a nearby car or van, a basic police radio, programmed to the right frequency could serve. Otherwise, the receiver must be miniaturized so that it, too, can be concealed (usually on the person) and monitored through a small earpiece. However, in most instances, and often because of cost, the dedicated receiver is just small enough to be mounted inside a fitted briefcase.

The last component of a standard body-wire kit is an attached recording device, mounted beside and wired into the radio receiver to record the signal. Digital recorders are used today; but in the 1980s, they were almost all cassette tape recorders.

There are a number of different companies that manufacture and sell body-wire kits to law enforcement agencies across the country. Our body-wire was a newer version recently purchased from Audio Intelligence Devices, Inc., or "A.I.D." (both of these terms will appear later in this story).

---

1. This chapter contains a discussion about federal and related state laws regulating surreptitious electronic monitoring, or "eavesdropping," on private conversations. Some of this information is technical in nature, including citation of criminal statutes and related court opinions. This legal discussion is intended to aid in understanding the scope and seriousness of events described in this book, including attempts at cover-up. Some readers may elect to initially gloss over this chapter, referring back to it later for clarification as related issues are encountered in the unfolding story.

Funding for the A.I.D. kit had been approved for the special investigation, and constituted a welcome addition to our cache of electronic surveillance equipment. When the kit finally arrived, Shackelton was so proud of the new state-of-the-art acquisition that he reportedly showed if off for a select group of officials, including the park superintendent.[1] That display and demonstration would have made clear the difference between a basic portable tape recorder and a sophisticated body-wire kit of which the tape recorder is only one component, physically distinct and separate from the actual "wire" or "bug" that captures and transmits the original signal.

A.I.D. Body Wire Kit. "Bug" in lower left slot

Regardless of its cost, size, or technology, the entire body-wire kit serves at least two critical functions. First, and arguably most important, it allows back-up officers to remotely monitor the activities of an undercover operative. If a problem occurs and the safety of the undercover officer is threatened, the back-up team is positioned to know about it and immediately respond.

The second function of a body wire is to remotely and secretly record conversations occurring between the undercover officer and the suspect(s). Those recordings, if lawfully obtained, can then be used as evidence in the criminal investigation and subsequent prosecution.

No matter what the technology used to either monitor or record the conversation, certain legal requirements must be met. Each state has its own laws restricting the surreptitious monitoring or recording of private conversations and communications.

Some states such as California and Washington are so-called "all party" states. In those jurisdictions, unless court-authorized, *all parties* to a private conversation (as opposed to public meetings and other gatherings open to the public) must first consent to be monitored or recorded. It is otherwise illegal. One may *not* legally record a conversation to which he or she is a party unless *all* of the other participants to the conversation also consent. Violation of this requirement typically carries felony penalties.

Other states such as Arizona are "one party states" and require that only *one party* to a private conversation have knowledge, and consent to be monitored or recorded. In those one-party states, under most circumstances one may legally record a conversation to which he or she is a party without notifying the other participant(s) to the communication.

121

Most states, and also the federal government, authorize law enforcement personnel acting legally within the scope of their employment to secretly record and monitor conversations as part of approved criminal investigations, so long as at least one government agent is a party to the conversation. Strict procedures generally apply to these applications, almost always carrying requirements for documentation of case-by-case request and approval through senior supervisors, prosecutors, or the courts.

The secret monitoring and recording of conversations where *none* of the participants has knowledge almost always requires court authorization. The surreptitious monitoring or recording by government officials of conversations outside of established procedures and not as part of an authorized criminal investigation is generally considered a serious violation, carrying severe administrative, civil, and criminal penalties often exceeding those prescribed by state or federal laws for private citizens.[2]

Federal law addressing "eavesdropping" comes out of Title III of the Omnibus Crime Control and Safe Streets Act of 1968, codified within Title 18 of the United States Code, or USC (the federal criminal code), sections 2510 and 2511. The Congressional Record clarifies that

> [The Act] ... sets forth a comprehensive legislative scheme regulating the interception of oral and wire communications. This legislation attempts to strike a delicate balance between the need to protect persons from unwarranted electronic surveillance and the preservation of law enforcement tools needed to fight organized crime.[3]

The various provisions of the federal law span several pages. The first section, 18 USC 2510, contains applicable definitions. The subsequent section, 18 USC 2511(1), parts (a) through (e) sets out the prohibitions (and penalties) against the secret monitoring or recording of private conversations. Section 2511(2) parts (a) through (i) contains certain limited exceptions.

Section 2511 begins,

> (1) Except as otherwise specifically provided in this chapter any person who –
> (a) intentionally intercepts, endeavors to intercept, or procures any other person to intercept or endeavor to intercept, any wire, oral, or electronic communication...
> ...shall be punished as provided in subsection (4) or shall be subject to suit as provided in subsection (5)...

The 8th Circuit Court of Appeals summarized the major provisions of the Act in the case of *United States v. William Fred Phillips*:[4]

[Title 18 USC] Section 2511(1)(a) generally prohibits the willful interception of any wire or oral communication.

Section 2511(2)(d) provides an exception and subexception to the general rule. That section reads as follows:

"It shall not be unlawful under this chapter for a person not acting under color of law to intercept a wire or oral communication where such person is a party to the communication or where one of the parties to the communication has given prior consent to such interception *unless such communication is intercepted for the purpose of committing any criminal or tortious act in violation of the Constitution or laws of the United States or of any State or for the purpose of committing any other injurious act.*" [Emphasis added].

The court explained the limitation on permitted "one-party" consent interception (the "subexception"), noting that,

> Whenever a private person acts in such situations with an unlawful motive, he will violate the criminal provisions of title III and will also be subject to a civil suit. *Such one-party consent is also prohibited when the party acts in any way with an intent to injure the other party to the conversation in any other way.* For example, the secret consensual recording may be made for the purpose of blackmailing the other party, threatening him, or publicly embarrassing him. The provision would not, however, prohibit such activity when the party records information of criminal activity by the other party with the purpose of taking such information to the police as evidence. [Emphasis added].

Citing yet another case, the 8th Circuit Court summarized this same provision:

> The effect of [18 USC] 2511(2)(d), then, is to prohibit any interception, use or disclosure of oral or wire communications by a person not acting under color of law where the purpose is to commit any criminal, tortious or injurious act. Meredith v. Gavin, supra, 446 F.2d at 798. This determination must be made on a case-by-case basis. Id. at 799.

The federal law applies throughout the country and is not limited in application to federal reservations or enclaves. However, as acknowledged and referenced in 2511(2)(d), state laws can and often do augment the federal law, creating additional requirements and further restricting the surreptitious monitoring or recording of private conversations. In the case of California, section 632 of the Penal Code articulates those additional restrictions with the following:

> Every person who, intentionally and *without the consent of all parties to a confidential communication,* by means of any electronic amplifying or recording device, eavesdrops upon or records the confidential communication, whether the communication is carried on among the parties in the presence of one another or by means of a telegraph, telephone, or other device, except a radio, shall be punished by a fine not exceeding two thousand five hundred dollars, or imprisonment in the county jail not exceeding one year; or in the state prison, or by both that fine and imprisonment. [Emphasis added].

Even though Yosemite is an area of "exclusive federal jurisdiction" located entirely within the boundaries of the State of California, state criminal law is *assimilated* into federal law under a unique provision known as The Assimilative Crimes Act, or "ACA" (18 USC 13).

The Assimilative Crimes Act states:

> Whoever within or upon any of the places now existing or hereafter reserved or acquired as provided in section 7 of this title...is guilty of any act or omission which although not made punishable by any enactment of Congress, would be punishable if committed or omitted within the jurisdiction of the State...in which such place is situated by the laws thereof in force at the time of such act or omission, shall be guilty of a like offense and subject to a like punishment...[5]

Where the Assimilative Crimes Act cites "section 7 of this title," it refers to 18 USC 7, which defines the areas of "Special maritime and territorial jurisdiction of the United States." Included among those areas are "any lands reserved or acquired for the United States, and under the exclusive or concurrent jurisdiction thereof..." Virtually all of Yosemite National Park is such an area of exclusive federal jurisdiction, where the provisions of the Assimilative Crimes Act apply.[6]

"The Act provides for the assimilation of state law to federal enclaves when no 'enactment of Congress' criminalizes an act proscribed by the law of the state in which the enclave is located."[7] Stated more simply, though a person may not be charged by the State of California for a violation of state law occurring within Yosemite National Park, that same person *can* be arrested by federal officials and prosecuted through the federal courts for the same "state" offense. They risk the same penalties prescribed by the State of California, so long as a federal criminal statute does not already prohibit the same "precise" conduct, and the relevant federal statute does not contain language specifically preventing application of assimilated state law to address the broader illegal conduct.

Lawyers and the courts have argued at length over when the Assimilative Crimes Act applies. But throughout the period of events we are discussing, there was no argument within the offices of the U.S. Attorney for the Eastern District of California, which includes Yosemite. Prosecutors there were aggressive in their application of the ACA, in many instances straining legal limits by applying the Act for the sole purpose of securing more severe penalties than could be obtained through the application of federal statues not reliant on the assimilation of state law.[8]

The 3rd Circuit Court of Appeals provided a succinct explanation of the reasoning behind the Assimilative Crimes Act in *U.S. v. Hall* (979 F.2d 320, No. 92-7265), noting that

> Under the ACA [Assimilative Crimes Act], if conduct prohibited by state law occurs on federal land, the state criminal law is assimilated into federal law so long as that conduct is not already made punishable by any enactment of Congress.... In other words, the ACA fills gaps in the law applicable within the federal enclave and within the surrounding state, and provides residents of federal enclaves with the same protection as those outside its boundaries.

Endnotes

1. Leland "Lee" Shackelton, written statement, Feb. 4, 1986, DOI-OIG Case #6VI 055 (Amended).

2. Among the limited exceptions are situations where individuals have no reasonable expectation of privacy, such as in police custody in the back of a patrol car or in prison settings.

3. 1968 U.S.C.C.A.N. 2112. (S.Rep.90-1097, U.S. Code Cong. & Admin. News, 1968).

4. *U.S. v. Phillips* (8th Cir. 1976) 540 F.2d 319.

5. 18 USC 13.

6. A small portion of Yosemite National Park, known as El Portal, lies outside the area of exclusive federal jurisdiction. El Portal is an area of proprietary federal jurisdiction. Also, in large measure as a result of Cushman's efforts, a portion of the park's Wawona District was converted from exclusive federal jurisdiction to concurrent jurisdiction (shared with the State of California). None of the activities described in this account occurred in El Portal or Wawona.

7. *U.S. v. Braxton Harold Yates, III*, 11th Circuit Court of Appeals, No 06-12550, Dec. 22, 2006.

8. *U.S. v. Palmer*, 9th Circuit Court of Appeals, 956 F.2d 189, No. 90-10630. Also, *U.S. v. Johnson Jr.*, 967 F.2d 1431. *U.S. v. Lewis*, 523 U.S. 155, 118 S. Ct. 1135 (1998); defendant was initially tried and convicted in federal court for the first degree murder of a child, as the result of a beating, occurring on a military base. Federal prosecution and conviction was under the special child-victim provisions of Louisiana's first degree murder statute, pursuant to the Assimilative Crimes Act (ACA). The court found that the defendant should *not* have been charged under the assimilated state law because existing provisions of the federal murder statute (18 USC 1111) already made the defendant's actions punishable. The federal murder statute, applicable within areas of special maritime and territorial jurisdiction of the U.S. (e.g., the military base) specifically addresses <u>all</u> forms of murder, including murder in the first degree (e.g., "the unlawful killing of a human being with malice aforethought ... [as well as] ... any other kind of willful, deliberate, malicious, and premeditated killing") and murder in the second degree ("any other murder ..."). There was no

"gap" to be filled by the ACA because the language of the federal statute expressly encompassed all forms of murder, including "the unlawful killing of a human being ... committed in the perpetration of ... child abuse ... or assault or torture against a child." Assimilation of the special child-victim provisions of the state law was inappropriate because the conduct of the defendant was already punishable under federal law.

CHAPTER TEN

Eavesdropping

When Connelly directed me to gather up the body-wire and meet him, I assumed I would simply be assisting in yet another completely legal and approved undercover purchase of drugs, using one of his own informants.

Connelly took a seat in the van and told me to drive to Yosemite Valley headquarters. Arriving just a few minutes later, I pulled into a parking space just west of the building. There, we checked out our electrical equipment to make sure that it was functioning properly. Connelly took the transmitter for the body-wire (the bug), exited the van, and told me to remain inside to await a transmission verifying that the bug was in place and functioning. When I asked what was going on, Connelly said only that the superintendent wanted to use the body wire. He then reiterated his instructions for me to wait in the van while he went inside the building.

Yosemite headquarters and superintendent's office. (Courtesy of Carol Moses).

A few minutes later I heard the transmitter for the body-wire switch "on," and could clearly hear Connelly speaking with another individual whose voice I immediately recognized as the park superintendent, Robert "Bob" Binnewies.[1] In their conversation I could "hear" Connelly showing the transmitter (the bug) to Binnewies, and explaining to the superintendent how it worked. I specifically recall Binnewies expressing surprise at how small the device was. Connelly and Binnewies continued to discuss a suitable place to locate the transmitter and microphone, and apparently decided on a location underneath a desk or table within the superintendent's office.

At one point Connelly contacted me on the regular park radio to verify that I was receiving a clear signal from the bug. I then heard Connelly conclude his conversation with Binnewies. He exited the building a short time later and returned to accompany me in the van. Connelly again directed me to simply monitor the receiver and recorder and make sure that they were functioning properly and capturing the conversation.

A minute or two later we heard Binnewies greet one or two other men and welcome them into his office. Over the next several minutes to an hour or more, it became apparent that the conversation we were monitoring had nothing to do with illegal drugs, prostitution, or any other criminal activity, but was instead a political conversation about the Wawona District of the park and the interests of people who owned private tracts of land and cabins – inholdings – within Yosemite's boundaries. When I again asked Connelly what was going on, he said that Binnewies was meeting with the head of an organization called the National Inholders Association to discuss issues related to private residences in the Wawona District, and wanted to have the meeting recorded.

I couldn't tell how many people were actually in the meeting. At the time, I did not clearly hear or understand the name of the party (or parties) with whom Binnewies was meeting and whose conversation was now, apparently, being illegally monitored and recorded in violation of national policies, executive orders, and both federal and state criminal statutes.[2]

At the conclusion of their conversation I heard Binnewies and the others exchange closing comments and then heard at least one person depart. The tape recorder was stopped. Connelly took the tapes on which the conversation had been recorded and exited, again directing me to wait in the van. A minute or two later I heard Connelly, over the body wire, enter the superintendent's office, greet him, and hand the tapes to Binnewies. If the tapes had ever been intended as evidence, they were no longer. There was no formal transfer, and they were no longer in law enforcement custody. Binnewies thanked Connelly and asked if the recording had worked. Connelly confirmed that it had, and then dismantled the transmitter and turned it off.

A short time later Connelly exited the building and again returned to the van. As he entered the van I protested what had just occurred. That's when Connelly responded very clearly and concisely, ordering "This never happened. Don't *ever* tell *anybody* about this."

Endnotes

1. "Binnewies came to Yosemite in 1979, 'by pure luck,' when Bill Whalen, President Carter's director of the Park Service, made an 'impulsive offer.' Binnewies had started working in the parks in 1961, and when Whalen appointed him, he was a vice president

for the National Audubon Society." Tim Palmer, *The Sierra Nevada: A Mountain Journey,* (Island Press, 1988) "Yosemite," Page 98.

2. U.S. Attorney General to Heads and Inspectors General of Executive Departments and Agencies concerning "Procedures for Lawful, Warrantless Interceptions of Verbal Communications," memorandum, Nov. 7, 1983; U.S. Department of Interior "Departmental Manual" (DM) 446, Chapter 3; Title 18 USC 2511(1)(a), Title 18 United States Code, Section 13, assimilating California Penal Code Section 632.

CHAPTER ELEVEN

System Failure

T here is always the possibility that things are not what they appear to be. But I knew what I was seeing and hearing, and those things caused me enough concern that I felt a responsibility to report them; but to whom? Also, if things really were as bad as they seemed and the situation ever blew up into a public scandal, I wanted to be sure no one could accuse me of being complicit or being derelict in my duty to report serious misconduct. Over this first year or two, I attempted to report and discuss many of my observations and concerns with a variety of officials, ranging from personnel in the NPS Western Regional Office, all the way up to the D.C. offices of the Department of the Interior (DOI), which theoretically oversees the NPS. However, because of my own apprehensions about who I could really trust and who else might have been a party to the already high-level conspiracy, I didn't mention the bugging incident to any of the NPS or DOI officials with whom I spoke. I first wanted to see what kind of reaction and support I'd get in response to my other concerns, before trusting anyone with that information.

In June or July of 1983, and again on August 11 of 1983, I made a series of telephone calls to U.S. Park Police (USPP) Captain Dave Lennox, attempting to report my observations and seek his assistance.

The U.S. Park Police is a sort of urban or metropolitan law enforcement arm of the NPS, based principally in Washington, D.C. with expansion over the years into areas beyond their statutorily defined home turf of the District of Columbia and "its environs."[1] The USPP was absorbed into the Park Service in 1933, when the national capital parks and monuments in and around the District were also transferred to the NPS. Through skillful lobbying and creative interpretations and even abuse of legal authorities, in the 1970s the organization was able to expand its scope of operations into New York City as well as San Francisco.[2] That organizational expansion was accompanied by expanded influence over the broader NPS law enforcement and "protection" program. Capitalizing on the Park Service's already ambivalent attitude toward law enforcement and its insistence on maintaining the ranger image for its own uniformed "protection" personnel, the USPP succeeded in siphoning funds to establish half-a dozen or so entirely new Captain positions assigned to the various NPS regional offices across the country as "regional law enforcement specialists."

Captain Lennox was the Western Region's law enforcement specialist in San Francisco, responsible for managing and conducting audits of
the funds used to support Yosemite's special investigation. In a practical
sense, with respect to this investigation, he superseded the role of Yosemite's chief park ranger as well as the park superintendent. Neither of those
individuals was privy to the details of the Curry Case.

I cautiously shared information with Lennox about my concerns and
what I was observing, emphasizing irregularities related to management
of the imprest fund for which he was responsible. I expressed additional
concerns about how to remove myself from any form of culpability for
illegal practices I was seeing, in which I was being pressured to participate. By this time, my own relationship with Shackelton and Connelly
was becoming strained, as I repeatedly challenged or refused orders to
participate in what I believed were illegal activities and practices; including signing off on blank imprest fund requests, and falsifying reports or
deleting exculpatory information.

On September 1, 1983, I met in person with Lennox while he was in
Yosemite for a routine audit. I reiterated my concerns and presented him
with copies of signed vouchers and other documents supporting many of
my allegations. In spite of the seriousness of the reports I was making and
their recurring nature (especially the misuse of funds and falsification of
vouchers), the only advice Lennox ever offered was "make sure you don't
do anything illegal." This type of feeble advice was usually accompanied
with an apology that "there isn't anything I can do to help you." In fact, my
efforts to report these incidents and practices to Lennox only made things
worse. What few follow-up inquiries Lennox did make in the course of his
audits only backfired, resulting in reprisal and even more difficulties in my
relationships with Shackelton and Connelly, as they, in turn, questioned
my loyalty and the source of Lennox's information.

Lennox would eventually acknowledge his own inaction nearly a year
later, explaining that "he did not take any action against Shackelton …
because he did not feel he should have to baby-sit Shackelton." He also
claimed that "he advised [me] to explain the situation to the Yosemite
Chief Ranger or someone above the Chief Ranger. Lennox declined to
get involved initially until [I] had followed the proper chain of command
and contacted the appropriate people in the Yosemite Park."[3]

It was well known, however, that the park's chief ranger, William "Bill"
Wendt, had issues of his own, and exercised little if any real supervisory
control over Shackelton. This point was confirmed in a confidential report
prepared by Lennox's predecessor, U.S. Park Police Captain John Crockett:

> There is some basis to this statement that Lee Shackelton has been
> operating separate from the Chief Ranger. Shackelton's special

investigation has been ongoing with the Assistant U.S. Attorney White, utilizing the Federal Grand Jury (in Fresno) under the indictment process. It is recognized that Shackelton has privied [sic] the Superintendent on matters prior to the Chief Ranger being told, if at all…

The Chief Ranger (Bill Wendt) is kept at a distance in the investigation, not being privileged to all the particulars. He does have a law enforcement commission but has never been through the full basic training program for law enforcement (being grandfathered into the system), and is obviously overshadowed by Shackelton. To determine the definition of strong law enforcement background, he would be weak in the eyes of a police officer or criminal investigator. Personality conflicts are a matter of fact in Yosemite.[4]

Wendt, himself, acknowledged that "no one told [him] to conduct internal controls or administrative reviews of the Imprest Fund," and "[He] did not get any support from the Superintendent's office."[5] The chief ranger was a non-player in the situation. Instead, as Lennox, himself, correctly observed,

Shackelton functioned autonomously at Yosemite and did not answer to anyone.[6]

In light of what I had already witnessed involving everybody else in my chain of command all the way up to the superintendent, it's difficult to imagine who the "appropriate people" were that Lennox thought I should first have contacted.

Suspicious of the level of support I might receive from anybody else in the regional office, I made a number of other inquiries with trusted colleagues elsewhere in the NPS and in other agencies. It was suggested I contact Harry DeLashmutt, Chief of Law Enforcement in the DOI's Division of Enforcement and Security Management.

DeLashmutt was, himself, a former NPS employee. He and I already had a passing acquaintance, having spoken previously about an effort Chief Investigator Norm Hinson was spearheading for himself and the two other full-time investigators who worked for him (myself included) to have our positions audited by the Office of Personnel Management (OPM). We were seeking a reclassification of our positions into the government's "criminal investigator," rather than "ranger" job series. Each of our position descriptions, or PDs, were actually criminal investigator PDs, but the proper classification of "criminal investigator" had literally been crossed out and replaced with "park ranger," handwritten in its place.[7] The assigned pay-grade simultaneously reflected the lower park ranger pay-scale that deemphasized law enforcement as a professional endeavor. The NPS was the only agency in the DOI that did not utilize the proper job series for its specialized criminal investigators. Our classification appeal was meant to challenge that practice. That effort ran directly against the tide and the will of NPS management, otherwise bent on perpetuation of the ranger image. But if we succeeded in the classification appeal, all three of us would realize an immediate increase in both pay and retirement benefits. DeLashmutt was quietly using his own position in the DOI to support our efforts.[8]

I made preliminary contact with DeLashmutt on March 7, 1984. In that first of several conversations I cautiously shared many of the same concerns previously reported to the Regional Law Enforcement Specialist. By mutual agreement, both DeLashmutt and I separately tape recorded our conversation as a way to document my allegations.

I described my observations related to the misuse of the imprest fund and falsification of imprest fund vouchers, failure to investigate reports of drug use and distribution by our own undercover agents and informants, and destruction of exculpatory reports and other evidence. But I simultaneously tried to impress upon DeLashmutt that I was in no way questioning the need for drug enforcement activities in the park. Rather, I was simply questioning and raising concerns about the manner in which those drug enforcement activities were being conducted, and potential ramifications for the NPS law enforcement program. I told him

> I want to make sure, again, that it doesn't fall back on any of us who are subordinates to Shackelton and Connelly, and [are] being asked to compromise our ethics. And also, again, if this thing blows up, I don't want it to fall back on the Park Service's face and give anybody the opportunity to say, well the rangers, obviously, are incapable of professional law enforcement conduct and, therefore, ya know, take away responsibilities from the good people, as well…
>
> There's no question but that there's a drug problem here, there's a need for this type of investigation. And that I'm sure 99 if not a 100% of the people that we've arrested, indicted, and have subsequently pled guilty did what we claim they did. But I think that we could have attained the same thing through much more professional conduct on our own part. I don't believe that it's necessary to use anybody and to allow just anybody and anything to justify the ultimate result. And that's basically my impression of what the managerial philosophy has been here. If you question it, you're verbally reprimanded for taking the initiative to question it, and that's a pretty strong compromise they're asking a lot of people to do…

I added

> It's a little bit ironic that the initial allegations were of obstruction of justice by Curry Company, and yet I think a reasonable case could made for obstruction of justice on the part of the managers of this operation.

At the end of our conversation I asked DeLashmutt to assist me in contacting the DOI-Office of the Inspector General (OIG). That organization functions independently from the rest of the Interior Department, and has statutory authority to investigate violations occurring *within* Interior agencies (including the NPS). DeLashmutt acknowledged the seriousness of my allegations, stated that he understood my concerns, and assured me that he would relay my report to the OIG and arrange for them to contact me to initiate an investigation. I thanked DeLashmutt for his assistance, and promised him that "I'll cooperate fully in pursuing this matter."[9]

At the time of this conversation with DeLashmutt, I had never before contacted or communicated with the OIG. I didn't really know what authority or jurisdiction they had over activities in the NPS. By no means did the NPS go out of its way to educate employees about the oversight role of the OIG, or employee responsibility to report suspected acts of fraud, waste, abuse, misconduct, and corruption occurring in the workplace. That same situation still exists, and even today the NPS discourages employees, through both subtle and overt ways, from going to the OIG or anyone else outside the NPS organization with complaints or reports of misconduct.

But I was quickly learning that the NPS lacked the capacity and the desire to regulate itself or address issues of serious management misconduct. That compelled me to undertake my own research and learn at least a little about the OIG as a prospective outlet for my concerns. Still, I was not yet entirely comfortable striking out on my own by going outside the chain-of-command of the Interior Department. Also, given what I was learning about how the NPS operated, I wasn't all that confident about how much better any of the other Interior agencies might be, including their OIG. That accounted for my hope that DeLashmutt would assist me in making contact with someone he might already know in the Inspector General's office who was honest and competent, and who might actually be willing and able to undertake an investigation.

Months had elapsed since my first communications with DeLashmutt. I continued to be frustrated by my observations of the same types of practices within the Law Enforcement Office. But I received no word, no relief, and no assistance from anybody within the NPS, the DOI, or the OIG.

Having heard nothing at all from the OIG since my first calls to the DOI Office of Enforcement and Security, in early May of 1984, I re-contacted DeLashmutt to inquire about the status of my request. I was dismayed to learn that my request for involvement of the OIG had been reconsidered. Instead, the Department wanted to keep the matter in-house and handle the complaint internally. My report and complaint had been referred directly back to the NPS! I objected, citing the previous lack of response or support from the Regional Office. But DeLashmutt convinced me to go along with this course of action so that I would be perceived as cooperating in allowing the DOI and the NPS to handle the matter at the lowest possible level.

A week or so later, on the afternoon of May 16, 1984, I was summoned into the office of Yosemite's personnel officer, Mary Sargent.[10] Ms. Sargent said she was aware I had been in contact with officials in the DOI. Contrary to what DeLashmutt had last told me, Sargent said that the OIG was, in fact, starting an investigation in response to my complaint, relayed through DeLashmutt's office. Sargent said that she had been requested to assist the OIG by soliciting details of my complaint, which she would in turn document and hand over to OIG investigators. Sargent also assured me that OIG agents would be arriving in the park to meet with me by or before June 4, 1984, to begin their investigation. Already apprehensive, I had Sargent confirm for me that the OIG was actually launching an investigation, and that she had specifically been asked to assist them by soliciting information from me and then preparing briefing materials for their exclusive use. With her assurance that this was, indeed, the case, I gave her a general accounting of my categorical concerns and allegations, but I did not share or discuss any supporting details.

When the week of June 4, 1984 arrived, it became apparent that Sargent's promised visit by agents from the OIG was not going to happen. No one had contacted me to arrange or schedule such a meeting, and no one had notified me of any change in plans. A colleague with contacts in the regional office was able to confirm that the OIG was, now, not coming. A call to Mary Sargent re-confirmed that news.

On June 5, 1984, going through the OIG hotline, I made my first contact with Steve Lunsford, Senior Resident Agent in the Sacramento office of the OIG. Acknowledging that I was recording my call, I introduced myself, explained my concerns and allegations, and asked why agents from his office had failed to contact me or show up in Yosemite, as I had been promised. Agent Lunsford said he didn't know what I was talking about. He had no knowledge of any investigation that had been initiated by the OIG in or regarding Yosemite National Park.

In speaking with Agent Lunsford, I tried to convey the extent of my frustration experienced in my previous attempts to address the situation through NPS and DOI channels. I told Lunsford that from this point on, I hoped I'd be able to deal only with the OIG, explaining

> This thing has been so mishandled by everybody in the Park Service to this date, that I have absolutely no confidence in them.
>
> I'm extremely frustrated with the situation because, like I said, I've tried to be, as much as I know how, to be an ethical employee and do the things that they always tell you are right to do. If you see an illegal, or possibly illegal activity, to report it. I've made every

effort to go through channels on this thing, to date, and in doing so have suffered nothing but grief for it. They [those reports] haven't been hair raising, they haven't been wild rantings or anything like that; but civil, rational reports to the people that I thought were responsible. And to this date, not a damn thing has been done. And there have been career repercussions for having done [reported] it. There's been absolutely nobody who's taken any initiative to remedy any of this ... [11]

Over the next day or two, Agent Lunsford made extensive inquiries within his organization and confirmed that the OIG had never been contacted by anybody in the NPS or the Department of the Interior about my allegations or concerns. I also learned that the OIG didn't know who Mary Sargent was, and had never authorized Sargent to represent their office in the solicitation of information from me.

Mary Sargent's misrepresentation – the claim that she was acting on behalf of the OIG – seemed to really capture Lunsford's attention. He confirmed that this was an area on which he intended to focus as part of his investigation. Lunsford said,

Well one person that I'm going to want to talk to is the young lady [Sargent] that works over at the personnel office. I want to know why she told you that we were coming when, in fact, there was no intention of anyone ever coming in. I'm more than curious as to why.

I responded by speculating that the idea may have originated at a much higher level.

Understand that park management has a pretty big stake in this thing not really getting out. At its furthest extreme, if a case is made on this, it's conceivable that there could be enough information to support an indictment for obstruction of justice. And additionally, were that the case, it could conceivably give cause to reverse about fifty convictions for drug dealing based upon a special investigation that the region has authorized, so they would look like complete idiots. I think there may be some motive there for them not to want it to be fully investigated. [12]

I finally met with agents from the OIG on June 15 & 16, 1984. This was a full year after my first inquiries to officials in the Western Regional Office, more than three months after my first attempts to report the situation to officials in the Interior Department, and precisely one month after being lied to by Yosemite's personnel officer. The meeting with officials from the OIG took place in secret at my home in the government housing compound in Yosemite Valley. There, I provided Agent Lunsford and his supervisor, Dave Smith, with details and documents to support my charges. I also provided a list of suggested witnesses who could corroborate my claims and concerns. And now, for the first time, I specifically provided the agents with a detailed account of the bugging incident in the superintendent's office, targeting the head of the National Inholders Association.

Over the next six months I engaged in no less than twenty-two separate, secret meetings and phone conversations with OIG agents to provide them with information and documents to assist in their investigation. Agent Lunsford confirmed that I should not mention or discuss the OIG investigation with any of my supervisors or other NPS managers. For the time being, the OIG investigation was to remain a secret. An agent from the U.S. Secret Service, Ralph Curtis, also participated in the investigation to address abuses of government imprest funds and falsification of time, attendance, and payroll records. He was present on one of several occasions when I discussed the bugging incident. Hearing that account, he seemed surprised and exclaimed, "That's a fucking felony!" Meanwhile, acknowledging the extraordinary sensitivity of that incident, Agent Lunsford cautioned me, "Don't discuss this with *anybody*."[13]

The fact that the OIG had *actually* opened an investigation was revealed on June 23, 1984. U.S. Park Police Captain John Crockett had been dispatched from Washington, D.C. to Yosemite to interview me and finally begin an investigation for the NPS. Seeking advice about how to proceed, I alerted OIG Agent Lunsford about the forthcoming meeting and interview. Lunsford told me not to volunteer any information about his case. But if specifically asked, I could acknowledge that I had spoken to the OIG and they had opened a case file and initiated an investigation.

As far as I was concerned, Crockett blundered in his investigation the moment he arrived in the park. His assignment was to follow up on a memorandum that Harry DeLashmutt had written to the NPS, summarizing some of the information I had shared in our recorded telephone conversation. One of the first things Crockett did when he arrived at the park, even before contacting me, was to contact Shackelton and let him see the memo. That immediately made the situation horrible for me and my family. But there was nothing I could do about it.

Sitting with me at my kitchen table, with his as well as my own tape recorder running, Crockett asked me a series of basic questions about my background and my report. At the beginning of the interview, Crocket acknowledged that we were both recording our conversation, declaring,

We are taping this conversation.

Curiously, he added,

There is no monitor transmitting our conversation out of this house, is there?

I answered,

Not that I know of.

Crockett produced a copy of the memorandum that Harry DeLashmutt had prepared, summarizing our conversation of March 7, 1984. Crockett asked me to review the memorandum. I pointed out a few errors and inaccuracies, making notations where those existed. I also noted to myself that DeLashmutt's notes were incomplete and did not contain all of the allegations and other information I had provided.

Then, Crockett asked why I contacted Harry DeLashmutt in the DOI, in the first place, to make my report. I answered,

Because I went to Lennox and didn't get any response.

Crockett seemed genuinely surprised. Our conversation continued:

(NOTE: *The following transcription is intermittently supplemented with brief explanations of what was occurring in the room, as well as my own thoughts and comments about what was being said. Those observations and comments appear in distinct text*).

CROCKETT: You *did* go to Lennox?

BERKOWITZ: Yeah.

CROCKETT: When did you go to Lennox?

BERKOWITZ: About ten months to a year ago.

CROCKETT: What did you do with Dave Lennox? Was this telephonic, in person, or what?

BERKOWITZ: I tracked him down. As I recall he was not in San Francisco, but someplace else, and asked him to call me here at home. That's because I was concerned about confidentiality talking in the office. He called me here at home. And then I made arrangements to have a subsequent meeting with him, which we did for about an hour and a half here in the park, and pretty much in secrecy.

CROCKETT: And what was discussed there, generally?

BERKOWITZ: Generally, the same things that are reflected in that [DeLashmutt's] memo.

CROCKETT: Do you know when that was?

BERKOWITZ: Again, I'd say it was approaching a year ago.

CROCKETT: And you discussed your concerns?

BERKOWITZ: That's correct.

CROCKETT: Anything in particular?

BERKOWITZ: Nothing in particular. But again, all the general issues I addressed in that memo from Harry [DeLashmutt].

CROCKETT: And when was this now?

BERKOWITZ: I'm guessing that it was anywhere between eight months and a year ago, that I had the meeting with him.

CROCKETT: So June of '83?

BERKOWITZ: Since June of '83, I would say. In essence, what I was trying to do was go through the chain-of-command, as much as possible, without compromising things here.

CROCKETT: Then when you left Lennox you weren't satisfied? And you went to DeLashmutt?

BERKOWITZ: That's correct.

CROCKETT: Why?

BERKOWITZ: Because nothing had been done here.

CROCKETT: No, I understand that. But why DeLashmutt?

BERKOWITZ: Well, I had contact with DeLashmutt previously through friends, on other matters. I knew he was with Interior. People who were mutual friends of DeLashmutt's and mine said he was an OK guy, and that he was somebody who wasn't in awe of the National Park Service, and wouldn't necessarily do anything to protect the Park Service when it didn't warrant it.

CROCKETT: Other friends advised you?

BERKOWITZ: Well, they didn't advise me to go to him. It's just that he had a good reputation. And as somebody in Interior I thought, perhaps, I could approach him, ask him for guidance on finding somebody in the I.G.'s Office who was credible and would do a good job here, if they were to look in to it.

CROCKETT: That was my next question. Why didn't you go to the Inspector General?

BERKOWITZ: I have.

CROCKETT: You have?

BERKOWITZ: That's correct.

CROCKETT: OK. When was that?

BERKOWITZ: Right after I found out that the I.G. wasn't coming here.

Notably, Crockett did not question this response in any way, or ask me to clarify what I meant. Our conversation continued without interruption.

CROCKETT: Do you have any idea when?

BERKOWITZ: A couple, three weeks ago.

CROCKETT: OK. Who'd you talk to?

BERKOWITZ: I talked to Steve Lunsford and Dave Smith.

CROCKETT: OK. What did they tell you? That they'd look into it?

BERKOWITZ: Yes.

CROCKETT: Good enough.

Crockett's voice raised in pitch as though ending our conversation. But I continued.

BERKOWITZ: They also wanted to make sure that nothing was done here that would compromise the investigation that they're going to conduct.

CROCKETT: OK.

Crockett paused, and then continued.

CROCKETT: You got anything else to tell me?

BERKOWITZ: Well, I have several questions I'd like to ask you.

CROCKETT: Well, before we get into that in a minute. What I'm trying to get into the record is do you have anything further than this as far as, that is criminal?

BERKOWITZ: I have nothing further, there. I've related quite a bit of information to the IG. And until such time as I get some further clarification on matters, I would prefer to leave it with them.

Crockett's voice became raised, suggesting his own level of frustration, and he said,

No problem.

Crockett ended our interview with one final question:

Would you be willing to support anything you say with a polygraph?

My answer was short and simple. I replied

Sure.

After a few more purely administrative questions, Captain Crockett reached over to turn off his tape recorder. I turned off mine. Crocket exclaimed,

This fucking park.

Crockett's interview and the Service's own internal investigation ended then and there.

Endnotes

1. P.L. 80-447 (1948): "Be it enacted ... that on and within roads, parks, parkways, and other Federal reservations in the environs of the District of Columbia over which the United States has, or shall hereafter acquire, exclusive or concurrent jurisdiction, the several members of the United States Park Police force shall have the power and authority to make arrests.... Such police officers shall also have the power upon such roads and within such parks, parkways, and other reservations to execute any warrant or other process.... For the purposes of this Act, the environs of the District of Columbia are hereby defined as embracing Arlington and Fairfax Counties and the city of Alexandria, Virginia, and Prince Georges, Anne Arundel, and Montgomery Counties in Maryland."

2. P.L. 94-458 (1976), codified at 16 USC 1a-6 affirmed statutory law enforcement authorities for "certain officer or employees ... [designated by the Secretary of the Interior] ... who shall maintain law and order and protect persons and property within areas of the National Park System. In the performance of such duties, the officers or employees may: 1) carry firearms and make arrests without warrant for any offense against the United States committed in his presence, or for any felony cognizable under the laws of the United States if he has reasonable grounds to believe that the person to be arrested has committed or is committing such felony, provided such arrests occur within that system or the person to be arrested is fleeing there-from to avoid arrest; 2) execute any warrant or other process issued a court or officer or competent jurisdiction for the enforcement of provisions of any Federal law or regulation issued pursuant to law arising out of an offense committed in that system, or where the person subject to the warrant or process is in that system, in connection with any Federal offense; and 3) conduct investigations of offenses against the United States committed in that system." However, in passing this legislation Congress expressly excluded application of these law enforcement authorities to members of the USPP, declaring "This bill would not affect the functions or authorities of the United States Park Police, whose law enforcement mission has been defined by the Act of March 17, 1948, as amended (62 Stat.81). Presently the Park Police are authorized to arrest for Federal offenses committed in the District of Columbia and on Federal reservations in its metropolitan area. This special authority of the Park Police is adequate for them to perform their responsibilities, and we do not believe there is a need to alter that authority in this bill." [Emphasis added] (West's U.S. Code, Congressional and Administrative News for the 94th Congress, Second Session, 1976, Jan. 19 - Oct. 2, Volume 4: Legislative History). Nevertheless, the director of the National Park Service disregarded this admonition when he formally designated the officers or employees who are authorized to maintain law and order and protect persons and property within units of the National Park Service. The officers and employees so designated were: "(1) *all officers of the United States Park Police* and (2) all other employees of the National Park Service who possess law enforcement certification as specified by Department of Interior and National Park Service regulations and guidelines. Each designee is authorized, when acting according to orders, instructions or policy, to exercise the authorities set forth in section 1(b) of the Act." [Emphasis added]. *41 Federal Register 44876* (October 13, 1976).

3. Dave Lennox, OIG interview, Jul. 12, 1984, DOI-OIG Case #4VI-090.

4. [Signed by] USPP Captain John S. Crockett, Jr., undated statement captioned "Complaint B", items #4 & #6, DOI-OIG Case #4VI-090.

5. Charles W. "Bill" Wendt, OIG interview, Aug. 22, 1984, DOI-OIG Case #4VI-090.

6. Dave Lennox, OIG interview, Jul. 12, 1984, DOI-OIG Case #4VI-090.

7. My position description at Indiana Dunes had also been prepared in the "1811" criminal investigator series, but artificially assigned and downgraded into the NPS "026" park technician series at the GS-7 level.

8. Telephone conversation between Paul Berkowitz and Harry DeLashmutt, Feb. 10, 1984.

9. Consensually recorded telephone conversation between Paul Berkowitz and Harry DeLashmutt, Mar. 7, 1984.

10. Mary Sargent later changed her name to Mary Martin, following her marriage to a prominent NPS Ranger and Superintendent.

11. Consensually recorded telephone conversations between Paul Berkowitz and Steve Lunsford, June 5 and 6, 1984.

12. Consensually recorded telephone conversations between Paul Berkowitz and Steve Lunsford, June 5 and 6, 1984.

13. Paul Berkowitz to Congressman Tony Coelho, complaint letter, Jan. 15, 1986.

CHAPTER TWELVE

Fallout

It didn't take long for word of the OIG investigation to leak out to the community. I was labeled a traitor; disloyal to the NPS and to the management of Yosemite National Park.

A series of other disturbing incidents occurred after that. On specific instructions from Agent Lunsford, I made copies of imprest records and ledgers, to be turned over to the OIG. Lunsford had arranged for me to convey the documents to him, sealed as evidence, through the park's administrative officer, Arthur "Butch" Abell. We were told to follow an explicit process that included the use of receipts to document the exchange. But when the actual meeting with Abell took place, he completely deviated from pre-arranged procedures, and refused to follow the instructions that he and I had both been given. When I protested his actions, he became hostile and violent. He demanded that I give him all of the records I possessed (beyond what had been arranged), exclaiming that the OIG had no business investigating NPS affairs. He told me that I was not even authorized to talk to the OIG without the superintendent's approval. Then he threatened me, saying that if I didn't surrender everything I had to him, he would "order a dozen rangers to hold [me] down and break into [my] house to get the documents." Remarkably, while making his threats, Abell argued that it was my responsibility to obey all orders given to me by my superiors, even if those orders were illegal.

Even with the OIG's investigation now exposed, it didn't appear that anything had really changed in the Law Enforcement Office. There were certainly no improvements. But making matters worse, the OPM position audits initiated long ago by Chief Investigator Hinson were finally resolved with the determination that all three of our criminal investigator positions needed to be reclassified back into the official criminal investigator job series, instead of the park ranger series.[1] NPS management and the Western Regional Director, in particular, were not pleased. Relying on its benign image and the cultivation of powerful political allies, the NPS has long taken comfort in its ability to function autonomously and free of meaningful outside oversight. In being overruled by another government agency (OPM), our classification victory was not only a blow to that autonomy, but an embarrassment, especially since that ruling highlighted the Park Service's abuse of federal position classification standards and simultaneously threatened the fictitious ranger image the agency worked so hard to perpetuate.

That ruling only exacerbated resentment at my having already gone outside of the agency to report misconduct in Yosemite's Law Enforcement Office. Management had had enough of uppity troublemaking investigators. Their response was swift and severe. The three of us, the only full-time investigators in Yosemite, had our positions summarily eliminated. Hinson was left dangling with no position description and no meaningful duties, at all.[2] The other investigator, Kim Tucker, was sent to work in the concessions management office. Neither Shackelton nor Connelly was affected by the classification ruling and the resulting organizational restructuring. They remained in their positions within the Law Enforcement Office, and continued to manage the Curry Case utilizing newly recruited seasonal investigators who were willing to do almost anything to earn Shackelton's favor and, hopefully, a permanent job. I was reassigned to a position as a uniformed patrol ranger in Yosemite Valley where, I was told, I would learn to improve myself and my career opportunities by becoming a professional "generalist" ranger.[3]

Just months later, a young Danish woman was murdered – stabbed to death – adjacent to a paved footpath leading to Mirror Lake, on the east end of the Valley. With the complete disbandment of the park's only dedicated team of full-time investigators, the NPS response was chaotic, at best; a case study in the ugly politics of homicide investigation in an organization where image takes precedence over substance. That case remains unsolved, to this day.[4]

* * *

James "Jim" Loach was the new Valley District Ranger, a comparatively prestigious position due to the high visibility and intensity of operations there. Prior to that, Loach had supervised the Wawona District, known for the Badger Pass ski area as well as the large number of private homes and inholdings located in that portion of the park. Having secured the coveted transfer, Loach became my new second-line supervisor. Loach's best friend, Bill Blake, was assigned as my direct supervisor. Both were delighted with the shake-up in the law enforcement office, and the opportunity that restructuring afforded them to expand their own control.

With no alternative and no recourse, I assumed my new patrol duties, initially receiving glowing performance appraisals along with several special assignments, such as dedicated firearms officer and range master for the park, and eventually rotational assignments as District investigations coordinator. I also retained my credentials as one of the park's deputy coroners. Those collateral duties made the reassignment somewhat more palatable. And ranger image or not, the initial transition to Valley District patrol was made easier still by the striking similarity I found between my basic duties there and those I'd had as a deputy in the sheriff's department. Only it seemed to me that the sheriff's department was a more professional operation; equally committed to a positive image and good community relations, but far more consistent in its approach to policing, with seasoned pros (including full-time detectives) throughout the organization to both supervise and mentor new recruits. By contrast, in Yosemite Valley and even more so throughout the rest of the park, it seemed like the various rangers and even supervisors were freelancing; doing their own thing to the best of their ability (or not), based upon their own personal agenda or beliefs about their proper role as "rangers vs. cops"; almost a free-for-all approach to law enforcement. Not surprisingly, as a consequence, it also seemed to me that back in Boulder we were generally received and treated by the public with more respect.

These and other observations about the similarities as well as the differences between my new patrol ranger position and my earlier position as a sheriff's deputy contributed to my developing suspicions about the myth of the NPS ranger image. Those suspicions, in turn, led to my interest in researching the actual history of law enforcement in the NPS. That, at least, was one positive outcome from my personal Yosemite "ranger experience."

Still, the patrol job was not one I had applied for or come to Yosemite to pursue. The manner in which I had been reassigned and not even consulted smacked of reprisal and left a very sour taste in my mouth.

More than two years had passed since my first efforts to report my observations and concerns through a variety of official channels within the NPS, the DOI, and the OIG. After seeing absolutely no corrective or disciplinary action taken at Yosemite National Park, no change in the practices that had originally motivated me to report my concerns, and no change or relief in the reprisal I was experiencing, I seized upon an opportunity to elevate my complaint.

Endnotes

1. "GS-1811" is the official government job series identified for federal criminal investigators. "GS-025" is the job series broadly applied to "rangers" who perform a wide variety of duties, from providing nature walks and visitor center contacts, to law enforcement, to fire fighting and resource management. Hinson's position description differed from my own and that of the other full-time investigator only in that his contained additional supervisory duties (over the two of us), and ours did not; therefore, our positions would also be reclassified into the 1811 series as non-supervisory criminal investigators.

2. Tragically, Hinson would never benefit from his classification victory. Even years later, after the NPS had finally relented on the matter of position classification and law enforcement retirement benefits, when Hinson finally retired he was not awarded those benefits.

3. Gene Rose, "Yosemite rangers say park service took job reprisals (Investigators get hearing in Fresno)," *Fresno Bee*, May 9, 1985.

4. The Helle Olsbro murder, March 16, 1985.

CHAPTER THIRTEEN

Troublemaker

A subcommittee of the House Committee on Interior and Insular Affairs was scheduled to hold public hearings in Yosemite on October 15, 1985, to listen to community opinions and concerns about issues facing the NPS and Yosemite National Park. It had been nearly a year and a half since the OIG launched their investigation. But as far as I could tell, nothing had really changed, at least not for the better.

In the hope that some action might still be forthcoming, five days before the hearing, on October 10, I re-contacted OIG Agent Lunsford to inquire about the status of his investigation and his report. I told him I was considering presenting voluntary testimony before the Subcommittee on National Parks, Forests, and Public Lands that was scheduled to hold hearings in Yosemite the following week. But I also told Lunsford that I didn't want to do anything that might in any way compromise his case or the possibility for improvements, administrative actions, or even criminal prosecutions. Still, I expressed concerns about how much longer I could endure the reprisal that I was already experiencing for filing a report with his office and cooperating in his investigation. I questioned him about how long it had been since the OIG began its investigation, and the absence of any apparent corrective action. I also reminded him of the level of obstruction I had encountered from NPS officials even before I made contact with his office, expressing my hope that the full extent of the Service's efforts to prevent an outside investigation was documented in his report, along with details of the other issues I'd reported.

I indicated, however, that if there was no real hope for his investigation to affect a change in the practices at Yosemite or in the NPS, then I intended to voice my concerns in testimony presented to the Subcommittee. Lunsford was cautious in his answer, but admitted he couldn't offer any reason not to proceed. He acknowledged that both his investigation and his report were finished, and that no further investigation was being considered. What he did not tell me till much later, was that a complete copy of his report had already been provided to the NPS nearly two months earlier, on August 28th. Among the recipients of the report were Western Regional Director Howard H. Chapman and newly appointed NPS Director William Mott. That information would have made it even more clear that there truly was no reason to hope for a change.

I had told only a few of my closest friends about the testimony I was planning. But on one of my days off while I was typing (on a typewriter!) the printed transcript to be submitted at the time of my presentation, I was contacted by Valley District Ranger Jim Loach. He asked what I was doing. I told him. Loach asked me to come with him to "take a walk." He put his hand on my shoulder and escorted me to an isolated location in the maintenance compound. Loach told me he'd heard rumors that I intended to present testimony during the upcoming Congressional hearings and that my testimony would include references to an illegal bugging that had occurred in the superintendent's office. I acknowledged that what he had heard was true. It was then that Loach told me about his own involvement in the bugging, and inadvertently identified for me the name of the man whose conversation had been secretly recorded.

That man, I would learn, was Charles "Chuck" Cushman.

Loach explained that back when he was the Wawona District Ranger, he'd had a variety of interactions with Cushman, who was president of the National Inholders Association. Loach characterized Cushman as unscrupulous and dangerous; an enemy of the park and, even more so, an enemy of the NPS. He failed to mention that Cushman was also one of President Ronald Reagan's appointees to the National Park System Advisory Board.[1]

Loach told me that a couple years earlier, a meeting had been arranged between Cushman and Yosemite Superintendent Binnewies to discuss issues relating to private inholdings in the Wawona District of the park, where Cushman owned his own cabin. Loach continued, explaining to me that as a part of his responsibilities as then-Wawona District Ranger, he had counseled the superintendent to be extremely cautious in his dealings with Cushman, and suggested that Binnewies secretly record the meeting. That suggestion had led to the 1983 bugging incident in which I had become an unwitting participant. Loach, it turns out, had been the third person present at the meeting between Cushman and the park superintendent.

Even with Chuck Cushman identified as the man targeted in the bugging, I didn't really know who he was or just how controversial a figure he was. At that point I didn't even make the connection between Cushman's National Inholders Association, and my own experiences interacting with inholders back at Indiana Dunes.

In fact, Chuck Cushman had a long history of contentious relations with the NPS, and an even longer history before that in Yosemite National Park.

* * *

Cushman grew up in Southern California where his father, Dwight, was a teacher in the Los Angeles city school system. But Cushman also spent most of his summers in the historic Wawona District of Yosemite

National Park, where his father worked as a seasonal ranger-naturalist. There, Cushman's family owned and lived in a historic cabin as a private inholding they had purchased in the 1950s. The entire Cushman family was devoted to the NPS and its environmental mission. While his father worked for the Park Service, a young Chuck Cushman assisted. He was actually among the first group of students to participate as a volunteer in the newly established Student Conservation Corps, which would later evolve into the Student Conservation Association. But in 1962, the park used its leverage over Ranger Cushman, as one of its employees, to pressure him into selling the cabin to the NPS as part of the agency's land acquisition program. Ranger Cushman's supervisors told him that if he refused to sell, he would not be hired back.

Ranger Cushman was resigned to his situation and the power the NPS exercised over him. The park acquired the cabin, for years used it as a seasonal residence, and eventually burned it to the ground as part of a fire training exercise. Meanwhile, the elder Cushman resigned from his ranger position. Using money from the sale of his summer home, he purchased another cabin – another inholding – located in the Klamath National Forest in northern California.

Left: Ranger Dwight Cushman leading a Yosemite N.P. nature walk in the 1950s. Right: Yosemite campfire program in the 1950s. (Photos courtesy of the Cushman family).

Years later as an adult in 1970, Ranger Cushman's son, Chuck, along with a business partner, purchased another cabin in Wawona. It, too, was an inholding within the park. Chuck Cushman and his family stayed in the cabin on vacations. It was (and is) also available as a rental property the rest of the year, as part of a cluster of cabins managed under the business name "Redwoods in Yosemite."

During one of his vacations staying in Wawona, Cushman saw that several other cabins in the area had recently been burned to the ground.

Chuck Cushman in Yosemite National Park (early 1970s). (Photo courtesy of the Cushman family).

The NPS, he learned, had purchased those cabins as part of its ongoing land acquisition program, and burned them down. Cushman later read in a local newspaper that the NPS had announced plans to buy out the remaining inholdings in Wawona and clear the area of all those cabins over the next five years. Cushman acquired a copy of the Master Plan for Mariposa County, which includes Wawona. The plan contained absolutely no mention of private homes and residences held as inholdings within the park, suggesting that county and park planners had already decided the fate of the historic community that actually pre-dated the park. Outraged, and mindful of how his father had been treated years before, Cushman organized a group of Wawona residents to attend the next meeting of the Mariposa County planning commission, where they vocally protested what was happening in their community. The planning commission relented and agreed to expand their Master Plan to once again include Wawona.

In what has to stand as one of the more ironic moves in private land-rights advocacy, Cushman also organized the Citizens to Save Wawona.

They hired a successful Southern California property lawyer to sue the NPS for its failure to comply with the National Environmental Policy Act, or NEPA.[2] They alleged that the NPS had not conducted the required environmental impact analysis when it acquired and then burned down the historic cabins. That, claimed the Citizens to Save Wawona, was a violation of NEPA.

The Citizens to Save Wawona eventually lost their case when it was presented in federal District Court.[3] The presiding judge ruled against Cushman and his group, finding that a change in title, alone, did not require an environmental review. That meant that no NEPA violation occurred when the NPS merely purchased private homes in Wawona, or even when they were acquired through condemnation and "taking," under the principle of eminent domain. However, in his ruling, the judge did warn the NPS that they *might* need to satisfy NEPA and conduct an environmental review if they intended to burn down or otherwise remove any more historic cabins in the District. For the time being, that clause satisfied the interests of the inholders, and they did not appeal the ruling. In Cushman's mind, they had succeeded, sending a clear signal to the NPS that they intended to fight to protect their cabins and their property interests within the park.

Then, in September of 1977, NPS Director Bill Whalen sent letters to inholders across the country, cautioning homeowners against making any significant improvements to their property. Implied in Whalen's letter was the threat of the NPS seizing homes through condemnation. That letter, along with memories of his father's experience years before, prompted Cushman to make a career change.

Up until that point, Cushman worked as a successful insurance agent in Southern California. Now, he changed his focus to fighting NPS land acquisition practices. Out of that initiative was born the National Park Inholders Association, later changed to simply the National Inholders Association. Years later, Cushman's organization evolved into the American Land Rights Association (ALRA). That organization has the expanded mission of broadly opposing virtually all forms of government land acquisitions throughout the country, and opposing application of federal wilderness designation to restrict the use and development of adjacent areas and private lands maintained as inholdings.

Starting in 1978, Cushman began traveling across the country to represent the interests of other inholders and to participate in public planning meetings held by the NPS. At each meeting, Cushman would hand out materials and encourage community members to write their Congressional representatives to protest land acquisition "abuses" perpetrated by the NPS. Congress was flooded with protest letters. In response, Representative Sid Yates (D-IL) temporarily stripped the NPS of its authority to seize property through condemnation, until hearings could be held and an investigation could be conducted by the Interior Department's Office of the Inspector General, to assess the conduct of the NPS.

Cushman attended all of these meetings. After each hearing, he filed a Freedom of Information Act (FOIA) request, seeking NPS transcripts of the hearings along with a list of hearing attendees. In the spring of 1978, he also filed a FOIA request with every park superintendent across the country, attempting to secure from the NPS the names and mailing addresses of every single inholder within every park, with the goal of including those names on his mailing list.

The NPS attempted to consolidate all of Cushman's FOIA requests into a collective response from the Washington, D.C. office. That consolidation resulted in significant delays, and also constituted a violation of FOIA laws and regulations. Cushman then threatened to file suit against each individual superintendent, one a week, until they individually responded and provided the information he wanted. Cushman's strategy worked. The NPS eventually provided Cushman with a list of 34,000 names. Since that time, according to Cushman, the National Inholders Association (now the American Land Rights Association) list of supporters has grown to more than 2 million. In the meantime, Cushman has become an active and conspicuous political force opposing the NPS throughout the country, coordinating opposition to the manner in which lands for the parks are acquired. He had actually visited and organized meetings with inholders of the Lakeshore during the time I was at Indiana Dunes. His efforts there earned him prominent (if unflattering) mention in the prologue to Kay Franklin's and Norma Schaeffer's definitive history of Indiana Dunes National Lakeshore, *Duel for the Dunes: Land Use Conflict on the Shores of Lake Michigan:*

> The second antigovernment movement emerged from within the national parks. There, inholders – owners of property inside of the parks – took issue with proposed new legislation that recommended accelerated purchase by the NPS of private property in the older parks and that intended the gradual elimination of all inholdings. A self-styled activist named Chuck Cushman founded the National Inholders Association, a group initially dedicated to "protect[ing] the environment of our national parks and property rights from blind bureaucracy." Inevitably, Cushman and the Sagebrush Rebels found each other, and with Sagebrush support, Cushman expanded his operation still further.
>
> Moreover, [Secretary of the Interior] Watt and Cushman sang in perfect harmony. The National Inholders Association provided a ready-made lobbying constituency for Watt's policies. In gratitude Watt appointed Cushman to the prestigious and influential Nation-

al Parks Advisory Board, thus legitimizing the man, his methods, and his mission. Cushman's tactics emasculated new preservation legislation and persuaded Watt to crusade against the NPS and any additions to the national park system.[4]

As part of his effort, Cushman has used what opponents characterize as guerilla tactics, subjecting NPS managers to public scorn and ridicule and, according to some sources, threats and intimidation generated from the crowds incited by Cushman's rhetoric.

Even Cushman's staunchest opponents, however, acknowledge his success in forcing changes in the way the NPS has pursued land acquisitions. Describing the inception of Cushman's Inholders Association in *The War Against the Greens,* Sierra Club author David Helvarg observes,

> On September 14, 1977, [Cushman] received a letter from the National Park Service saying cabin owners in Yosemite were prohibited from modifying their homes or building on their property and that new laws and regulations were under consideration to limit development inside national parks. In Chuck's mind this was a repeat of the abuse his father had suffered, although he claims not to have been immediately aroused to action. "I didn't pay much attention to it until January of seventy-eight," he recalls, "when a group of six or eight of us met in a room at the Holiday Inn in Sacramento and decided to form the Inholders Association. I had the time to work on it. Using Freedom of Information requests and threatening to sue one regional [sic] park superintendent a week until I got the names, I got lists of other inholders from the Park Service."
>
> With those names, Chuck began a campaign of lawsuits and protests targeting the Park Service. The Inholders Association grew rapidly, forcing the Park Service bureaucracy to reform some of its more arbitrary activities; to open up hearings on land acquisitions and limit the use of condemnations against unwilling sellers. But Chuck also developed a reputation for shooting from the hip and the lip and for creating conflicts where none had previously existed.[5]

By the early 1980s, the National Inholders Association had grown into a serious political force with close ties and relations with elected as well as business officials across the country. Cushman, himself, developed a reputation as a fierce and outspoken opponent of government land management and acquisitions practices, with powerful conservative political allies across the country. He used his reputation and his resources to support candidates who, in turn, supported his own cause. Among those candidates was conservative California governor and presidential candidate

Ronald Reagan, who declared himself to be "a Sagebrush Rebel." That term was reportedly coined by *Washington Post* reporter Lou Cannon to identify individuals and groups supporting the widespread transfer of federal lands in the West to state as well as corporate control.[6]

John McClaughery was a conservative political activist with ties to the film industry. He worked as a full-time special assistant in the 1981 White House of President Ronald Reagan. Shortly after receiving his appointment to Reagan's staff, McClaughery called Cushman to see if the new administration could do anything to support his cause. Cushman asked for an appointment to the (then) twelve-member National Park System Advisory Board. That body has no direct authority over the NPS, but is able to influence policy and operations through recommendations provided to the White House and the Secretary of the Interior. And while Cushman found his appointment to be less useful than he had hoped, the very fact that he had secured a position on the Board infuriated many officials in the NPS.

In the very success of his efforts, along with the aggressive, often in-your-face tactics he used, Cushman made a great many enemies, especially among the ranks of NPS managers and allied Congressional representatives. Representative Bruce Vento (D) of Minnesota, chairman of the House Natural Resources Subcommittee on National Parks, Forests, and Public Lands, was conspicuous among the group of individuals identified as Cushman's enemies, and vice-versa.

Over the years, Cushman has been a significant enough force in his interactions – or battles – with the NPS, to have earned prominent mention in the published administrative histories of Indiana Dunes NL, Sleeping Bear Dunes NL, Cuyahoga Valley NRA., and a host of other old and new NPS areas.

The Administrative History for Cuyahoga Valley NRA contains its own interpretation of the circumstances surrounding establishment of the National Inholders Association:

> During the tenure of NPS Director George B. Hartzog (1964-1972), NPS produced a study comparing the cost of fee acquisition versus permitting the development of private inholdings into townsites. The analysis determined that long-term costs were considerably higher to "allow these environmental cancers to remain than it would be to eliminate them." In the late 1970s, Interior Secretary Cecil D. Andrus, backed by a group of congressmen led by Phillip Burton (D-CA), instructed the NPS to acquire in fee the inholdings in western parks. The aggressive policy resulted in grassroots organizing of affected landowners and the formation of what became known as the National Inholders Association (NIA). The NIA nurtured this discontent to such a fevered pitch that the

protest movement, which became known as the "Sagebrush Rebellion," effectively scuttled this policy...

The Sagebrush Rebellion came in reaction to two decades of unprecedented expansion of the National Park System. It soon became apparent that the tremendous growth of the System had outstripped NPS's ability to protect and maintain it. Carving parks out of privately owned lands only encouraged the cries against big government interfering in the interests of individuals and private enterprise. [7]

On a larger scale, Cushman, along with his friend and author Ron Arnold, is also known as one of the two co-founders of the so-called Wise Use Movement. In that and related capacities, Cushman is variously known as both a hero to his supporters, and arch-enemy number one to environmental interests. Among the titles bestowed on him by conservation groups and advocates for public lands and wildlife preservation is "right-wing extremist" and "Mr. Rent-a-Riot." *California Magazine* labeled him "The man environmentalists fear most" and "The Most Dangerous Man in America."[8] Among the management of the NPS, he is also, arguably, the single most hated man in America.

But I didn't know any of this at the time of my conversation with Jim Loach.

American Land Rights Association
(Formerly National Inholders)
P.O. Box 400
Battle Ground, WA 98604
Phone 206-687-3087 Fax 206-687-2973

A6—THE DAILY NEWS
Port Angeles, Wash., Thursday, July 23, 1981

'Park buster' Chuck Cushman is a

By TONY WISHIK
Peninsula staff writer

A Sierra Club official, denying a recent charge by West End residents that his group is an "outside agitator organization," countered that Chuck Cushman "could aptly be described that way."

Chuck Cushman agrees.

An aide to Rep. Don Bonker, D-3rd Dist., recently commented that "Cushman's interest is controversy. If there's no controversy there's no reason to have him around."

Chuck Cushman agrees.

The president of the Wild Rivers Conservancy Federation, which hired Cushman to help fight a bill to study seven Peninsula rivers for possible Wild and Scenic designation, admits that "we've had questions arise within the group about Cushman."

Good, Chuck Cushman says.

Whatever Chuck Cushman is, he's not what you'd expect.

He is a 37-year-old Californian who started his own insurance business at 22. He is a bearded outdoorsman who owns property within Yosemite National Park. He is executive director of the National Inholders Association, which he founded, a group of people with property surrounded by or proposed for federal ownership.

He is, in the words of some environmentalists and legislators, a "park buster." In 1980, Cushman spearheaded battles against federal parks in Big Sur,

CHUCK CUSHMAN
Professional 'outside agitator'

Columbia River Gorge. And the rivers of the Olympic Peninsula.

"If ever there were a place inappropriate for federal land acquisition, the Olympic Peninsula is it," says Cush-

His dad spent summers as a ranger at Yosemite, and owned a cabin there.

As a teen-ager, Cushman joined the Youth Conservation Corps, building shelters, trails and outhouses in Olympic National Park. Later, he purchased land in Yosemite.

In 1977, he got a letter from the federal government, stating park inholders could not modify their property or build on vacant lots.

Cushman and several others gathered to draft a course of action. The National Park Inholders Association — the "park" later was dropped to include inholders on other federal land — was born.

"It was supposed to be two hours a day in my attic," says Cushman.

Instead, he toils from dawn to dusk, for expenses but no salary. He supports himself from leftover insurance profits and the sale of property, and figures he can "last another year or two" without a new source of income.

The inholders have an office next to Cushman's Sonoma, Calif., home and another in Washington, D.C. The group employs one full-time lobbyist and 15 to 20 part-timers.

Cushman previously aided Friends of Lake Crescent, a group of Olympic National Park inholders. In March, a member telephoned about the riverbank landowners.

"He said, 'These people are in trouble, can you come,' " relates Cushman. "I said yes."

Cushman helped the federation

and $1,000 a m
bill.

"For that Representation where we lobby Congress is doir behind them, so in Forks fighti representation, help; and my ab Cushman su affable and a he's the consum

But some legislators say I past land acc would not be potential re character assas Without refer

(Port Angeles (WA) *Daily News*, Thursday, July 23, 1981).

BEST OF CALIFORNIA
MUSIC / EVENTS / ART / THEATER
OUTDOORS / RESTAURANTS / DANCE
CALIFORNIA MAGAZINE

RECHARGING IN DESERT HOT SPRINGS
WILL CALIFORNIA LABOR SAVE JAPAN?
THE MAN ENVIRONMENTALISTS FEAR MOST

CALIFORNIA

NOVEMBER 1990 $2.00

IN THE WINTER OF 1984, AS temperatures were dropping below zero in New York's Upper Delaware River Valley, the population of several villages packed into a small school auditorium. From the stage came the thundering voice of a burly Californian named Charles Cushman: "They're going to come in and strangle you! You're going to lose your valley!"

The locals were already upset. Congress had just decided to zone the river valley "wild and scenic," and the National Park Service was moving in to manage the area. Understanding how his audience felt about this change in their lives, Cushman gripped the podium and kept up his attack. New rules would restrict hunting and fishing, he warned. Farms and stores would be closed, and ancestral lands would be seized. "The Park Service wants to get rid of you!" he shouted.

For three hours, Cushman played to the crowd's fear of change and distrust of big government. At center stage, conspicuous in his buckskin vest, he led the crowd in call-and-response chants. He showed them a film of what had happened to people facing similar circumstances in other parts of the country. And throughout, he raged against environmentalists and the government bureaucrats who, he claimed, cared more about the land than about the

To many rural Californians, Charles Cushman is the man in the white hat, but to environmentalists, he may be the most dangerous man in America....

BY JILL HAMBURG

people who lived off it. When he finished, the agitated crowd filed out of the auditorium, scooping up all of the fliers and bumper stickers he had brought along with him and leaving behind donations to the organization he headed back in California.

Not long afterward, the violence began. Over the next weeks, local residents slashed tires and painted swastikas on Park Service vehicles, and defaced the buildings in which support- ers of the government plan lived and worked. When *The River Reporter*, the local newspaper, exposed inaccuracies

in Cushman's presentation, residents organized a boycott of the paper and threatened to burn down its office.

Soon, a new group, supported by the local canoe liveries and realtors who had sponsored Cushman's visit, formed in the area to oppose the Park Service action. Next, several radical subgroups emerged and continued the harassment of those who did not agree with them. The newspaper's editor, Glenn Pontier, was a particular target, and he continued to receive threats for a period of months and even years. Finally, in 1986, at a time when the fire-alarm system in Pontier's neigh- borhood was disabled, a mysterious fire burned his house to the ground. Arson was suspected in the case but never proved.

Cushman, meanwhile, was long gone from the area. As the violence raged in New York, he was back at his house in Sonoma, preparing for simi- lar battles closer to home.

CHUCK CUSHMAN WEL- comes me through the kitchen door of his home with an enor- mous handshake and a warm smile. After hearing the Delaware River story, and others like it from outraged envi- ronmentalists around the country, I had been expecting to feel intimidated by this man. But instead, I am sur-

(*California Magazine*, November 1990).

THE KATAHDIN TIMES, TUESDAY, APRIL 13, 1999

'Greens' beware,
Cushman is here

By R.J. MacLean

KATAHDIN REGION - Mixing witticism with aversion, the head of the American Land Rights Asso- ...ronmental trust funds and activist groups to convert the Northern Forest of Maine into a series of new national parks, national forests, wildlife refuges and other ...has been fighting political battles against conservation laws and expansion of public parks since 1978. He says he's fighting for the

(*The Katahdin Times*, Tuesday, April 13, 1999).

With his disclosure about his own role in the bugging, Loach appealed to me to consider my sense of loyalty to the NPS. He tried to impress upon me how damaging it would be to the image and reputation of the NPS if the press or the public ever found out about the incident. Loach

155

added that including that subject in my Congressional testimony would probably result in Binnewies getting fired and then replaced by the park's assistant superintendent, Jim Laney. That prospect concerned Loach greatly, because while he had a "direct line" to Binnewies, he did not get along well with Laney. Loach speculated that if Laney became superintendent, he (Loach) would have to leave Yosemite. It was clear that Loach wanted me to omit any reference to the bugging incident in my testimony, suggesting that such testimony would only hurt the NPS, my own career, and, quite significantly, Loach's career aspirations. Reinforcing that latter point, Loach acknowledged that he was asking for my cooperation not only as a loyal NPS employee, but as a personal favor to him.[9]

This was another extremely awkward situation for me. I had already seen what happened when I refused orders from other supervisors and tried to report their misconduct. Now another senior line-supervisor was using his own enormous power in an attempt to influence me and keep me from reporting activities in which he, too, had been a direct participant. I was very much aware of the uncomfortable and dangerous situation I might face if I challenged him and refused his request.

Attempting to mitigate this incredible situation, I flatly told Loach that I would not lie for him and that I had already reported the entire matter to officials from the OIG. Nevertheless, (and regrettably), I acquiesced and agreed to omit from my testimony any specific reference to the bugging incident. Inexplicably, this seemed to satisfy Loach for the moment, as he showed little if any surprise or concern about my report to the OIG. Unfortunately, I did not pick up on the real significance of that lack of reaction. Loach gave me a slap on the back, telling me that he knew he could rely on me to do "the right thing" and not do anything to embarrass the NPS.

On October 15, 1985, I presented thirteen pages of testimony to the House Subcommittee on National Parks, Forests, and Public Lands.[10] Those hearings were held in the Yosemite Valley main auditorium, under the gavel of subcommittee chairman Representative Bruce Vento (D-MN). Also sitting on the panel was Congressman Tony Coelho (D-CA), representative for my home district, and neighboring Congressman Richard Lehman (D-CA). Sitting in the audience was Coelho's and Lehman's close friend, Yosemite Park and Curry Company (YPCC) president, Ed Hardy. All of the players in the bugging incident (Shackelton, Connelly, and Loach) were also in the audience, along with Superintendent Binnewies and NPS Western Regional Director Howard Chapman.

In anticipation of potential problems, friends of mine seated themselves directly behind Shackelton and the others. I took the added precaution of wearing body armor underneath the dress shirt and coat I was wearing.

As the hearings began and the Congressmen made their opening introductions and statements, I was struck by the casual banter put forth by the representatives, directed at prominent members of the audience. Singled out for praise and gratitude was YPCC President Ed Hardy, who had apparently sponsored and paid for a lavish backcountry pack trip on which they had all gone and enjoyed themselves thoroughly. I was new to this type of hearing, but the casual comments and verbal backslapping in which the representatives engaged struck me as inappropriate, sending the wrong signal about what were intended to be "oversight" hearings. Had I been more worldly and wiser to the ways of politics, I would not have been so surprised. That behavior was apparently typical of the group of politicians who openly fraternized with the wealthy business interests of the park. A June 1993 article in the on-line journal, *Washington Monthly* discussed this relationship:

> Concessionaires have, over the years, not only funneled thousands of dollars in campaign contributions to law makers on all the right committees…but, for the more personal touch, have regularly treated leading members of Congress to free excursions at some of America's most beautiful parks. Yosemite Park and Curry Company, for example, hosted Rep. Richard Lehman, who represents Yosemite's district, California Rep. George Miller, and three members of the House Appropriations Committee on excursions, all gratis, of course. "It's a real good way to get people into the park," Lehman said after one of his trips a few years back. "Just familiarizing people with the park is very helpful."[11]

Several other people made their presentations before me, discussing issues as varied as housing, schools and medical care, to over-flights, conservation of resources and the effect of the park on local business communities. When it was my turn to speak, I approached the table, sat down, introduced myself and began with these opening remarks:

> My testimony is presented as that of a citizen and a concerned member of Yosemite's law enforcement community.
> I feel considerable anxiety about testifying here today, as I am certain I will be subjected to reprisal, just as I have already been subjected to reprisal and harassment for having previously attempted to address these same issues to National Park Service management. I also harbor fears for my career as well as personal and family safety. A number of people very highly placed in the Park Service as well as the local federal criminal justice system will be implicated by this testimony. However I view this opportunity to speak to you as a last resort directed at drawing attention to what I believe is

grossly unethical, unprofessional, and perhaps criminal conduct on the part of some members of NPS upper management as well as senior law enforcement officials within Yosemite National Park.

From that point on, things became chaotic. I attempted to proceed with the balance of my presentation, making it through only the first several pages. But my testimony effectively shut down the hearings, and before I could finish, Congressman Vento attempted to silence me. At the same time, members of the media raced to the front of the auditorium to grab printed copies of the full testimony I had prepared. The result was a flurry of press, nation-wide.[12] It also resulted in any number of threats directed my way, including statements made by YPCC President Hardy, who, referring to me, reportedly told several of members of his staff that, "He should be shot." The publicity generated by my testimony and further attention to the ongoing investigation of drug use and sales by YPCC employees was, apparently, bad for business. Given the power and influence of YPCC and its parent company, MCA (the Music Corporation

(*San Francisco Chronicle,* October 16, 1985).

(*Merced Sun-Star,* October 16, 1985, front page).

of America), threats like those were not to be taken lightly.[13] Still, inexplicably, Valley District Ranger Loach directed the officer who filed the criminal incident report documenting Hardy's statements, to refrain from conducting any follow-up interviews or other investigation into those "Threats Against a Federal Officer."[14]

Endnotes

1. The National Park System Advisory Board is comprised of members designated by the Secretary of the Interior. Members come from a variety of professional, civic, and academic backgrounds, and advise the Secretary on matters related to NPS programs and policy and, particularly, the designation of national historic landmarks and national natural landmarks.

2. Jerrold Fadem, attorney at law.

3. Myron D. Crocker, presiding judge, U.S. District Court.

4. Kay Franklin and Norma Schaeffer, *Duel for the Dunes: Land Use Conflict on the Shores of Lake Michigan* (Chicago: University of Illinois Press, 1983), xvii. (Prologue).

5. David Helvarg, *The War Against The Greens* (San Francisco, CA: Sierra Club Books, 1994), 148 (Chapter 5, "Grassroots for Sale").

6. David Helvarg, *The War Against The Greens* (San Francisco, CA: Sierra Club Books, 1994), 65 (Chapter 3, "Rebels and Reaganites").

7. National Park Service, *The Administrative History of Cuyahoga Valley National Recreation Area*, Chapter 11.

8. Jill Hamburg, "The Lone Ranger (The Most Dangerous Man in America)," *California Magazine*, Nov. 1990. That label for Cushman was reportedly first coined by Robin Winks when he served as chairman of the National Park System Advisory Board, during Cushman's own tenure on the body.

9. Paul Berkowitz, written statement to OIG citing statements made by Jim Loach on Oct. 10 or 11. 1985, DOI-OIG Case #6VI 055 (Amended), Feb. 3, 1986.

10. The full text of that testimony appears in the appendix to this book.

11. Michael Doyle, "Yosemite Scam – concessionaires reap profits at national parks," *Washington Monthly*, June 1993.

12. Dale Champion, "Yosemite Ranger Accuses Park Officials," *San Francisco Chronicle*, Oct. 16, 1985; Janis McRae, "Yosemite drug cover-up alleged – Park ranger questions use of funds," *Merced Sun Star*, Oct. 16, 1985; "Berkowitz testifies to justice obstruction", *Fresno Bee*, Oct. 16, 1985; Russell Clemings, "Yosemite Park officials named in Interior drug probe"; *Fresno Bee*, Oct. 16, 1985; etc.

13. See, William Knoedelseder, *Stiffed: A True Story of MCA, the Music Business, and the Mafia* (New York, NY: Harper Collins, 1993), and Dan E. Moldea, *Dark Victory: Ronald Reagan, MCA, and the Mob*, (New York, NY: Viking Penguin, Nov. 1997).

14. Yosemite National Park, 10/15/85 Incident Record #85-21125, "Threats Against A Federal Officer."

CHAPTER FOURTEEN

The G.A.O.
("Objective, Fair, and Balanced")

Congressman Vento responded by directing the General Accounting Office (GAO) to undertake its own investigation into the allegations cited in my testimony.

The GAO (renamed the Government Accountability Office in 2004)
is "the investigative arm of Congress," and "the Congressional watchdog."
The GAO is responsible for supporting the Congress in meeting its Constitutional responsibilities and helping improve the performance and accountability of the federal government. In their own words, they fulfill this
mission by "providing [members of Congress with] information that is
objective, fact-based, non-partisan, non-ideological, fair, and balanced."[1]

A team of three auditors from that office were dispatched to the park
during the first half of November.[2] I met with them for several hours on
November 6 and again on November 11, 1985. They asked me to meet
with them in the superintendent's office. I refused, suggesting instead that
we meet at my house. With the consent of all parties, I openly placed a
cassette recorder between us to document our conversations, with only
slight breaks to change tapes when they ran out.[3]

Those conversations provide an intimate glimpse into the real dynamics
of the exchange, almost sparring in my repeated attempts to address critical
issues like the bugging incident, and their efforts at damage control by trying to avoid that and other sensitive topics. Selected transcriptions of those
unedited exchanges, using their words and my own, reveal what was really
going on in a far more graphic and compelling way than I could ever accomplish by attempting to retell this part of the story with a narrative summary.

For the sake of brevity, discussions about routine and less-sensitive
matters have been left out. Brief summaries of those discussions are provided to fill those gaps. Relevant background material, as well as some of
my own thoughts about what was being said, is also included. As before,
those explanations and comments appear in distinct text.

* * *

The Binnewies-Cushman bugging was one of the first things I brought
up during the opening segments of our very first meeting, on November
6, inquiring if the OIG report contained information about that incident.

The lead auditor from the GAO began the conversation.

GAO: We've tried to break up what you put in your testimony into sort of neat allegations, so we can deal with each one. One of the things that we have to understand as well as we possibly can is what examples of what evidence you think exists and where we might find that kind of evidence with regard to each one. Probably the first five of the allegations we've put into the area of obstruction of justice, falsifying records, the exculpatory evidence not being gathered; that sort of thing. And those are probably some of the more difficult things for us to deal with unless there are some records around that you can suggest that would tend to show that.

Before even responding to that initial inquiry, I interrupted.

BERKOWITZ: Let me ask you this. Have you guys read the I.G. Report?

GAO: Yes.

BERKOWITZ: OK.

GAO: Now, have you read it?

BERKOWITZ: No, I have not.

GAO: OK. See that's another one of the problems that we have, is that that hasn't been released. It's got another 30 days, at least another 30 days to go on an exemption seven of the Freedom of Information Act. So we can't release it.[4]

BERKOWITZ: Sure.

GAO: Um, we can talk about it in generalities, though, for sure.

BERKOWITZ: The reason I brought it up is that I'm hoping that the bulk of what I made reference to is covered in that. I have reason to believe that certain aspects of it were not. Among which, is the reason I didn't want to talk over there [in the superintendent's office].

GAO: OK.

BERKOWITZ: Which is the bugging incident.

GAO: OK.

BERKOWITZ: And I am curious to know if that was addressed.

GAO: Well, let me put it in general terms. The allegations with regard to evidentiary and operational kinds of things that were exclusive of the imprest fund are not dealt with to any great extent, in that report.

That was the most he would say for the moment, but it was clear enough that he knew about the bugging. By his response, I suspected the topic was *not* addressed in the OIG Report. The lead auditor continued, discussing Lunsford's report.

GAO: OK. Now he does have interviews with a large number of people. And some of the interviews do touch on certain issues. But in terms of his making a conclusion, he's limited by what evidence he was able to gather. Those areas are not really covered fairly well. So, if you don't mind why don't we go through this [list] first, and then if there's something you want to add to it, in terms of, let's go down the list, and then you can put in the examples. I think the bugging situation might be a really good example of one of the allegations you've got.

That discussion would have to wait until later. But I was not going to let the afternoon pass without getting back to the topic. I went along for the moment.

Their first questions were about incidents related to obstruction of justice and the destruction of evidence or reports. I provided details about occasions where damaging letters and reports had been shredded so that they couldn't be used to discredit informants. I provided the names of legitimate officers and other witnesses who had actually written their own reports – since destroyed – documenting incidents where some of our own informants and undercover officers had been observed using and selling drugs on their own. I speculated that the U.S. Attorney's Office knew about this and other serious problems, noting that Lunsford had even told me about a comment made by one of the federal prosecutors, acknowledging that "Shackelton bends the rules, but he bends them well."

Once again, I found myself forced to explain the same point that I had made to DeLashmutt years before. I was not questioning the need for our drug enforcement operations, but rather the way those operations were conducted and the lack of regard for established procedures and legal standards. I tried to explain the resistance offered by Shackelton and Connelly to the most basic of operational standards, including the requirement to search informants for drugs and other contraband before and after drug operations. That conversation, in turn, led to discussion about Connelly's relationships with some of those same informants.

BERKOWITZ: We had a meeting with [a local high school student] who was an informant. He'd been twisted. We had him, originally, we had him on drug distribution and seven counts of forging checks or something like that. He was twisted, making buys for us. One instance I can recall, at the old Superintendent's house, quarters #1 [used for special events, rather than as a residence], I patted him down, searched him for drugs, found a lid of dope on him, pot. OK. I booked it into evidence; wrote a report on it. It'd be interesting to see if that's around.

GAO: OK, but you did write a report on it, and that should be in [the informant's] file, then?

BERKOWITZ: It should be. And after I did it, Connelly reprimanded me for it.

GAO: OK. Did he do that on paper, or was it all verbal?

The GAO's follow-up question was laughable, revealing the extent to which they really did not understand the situation. Our conversation on this topic continued for several more minutes, as I provided them with several more specific examples.

BERKOWITZ: Yeah. There was an instance where [the very same informant] was busted for possession of hashish by a guy named Tom. Tom was a ranger up here. He now works at Channel Islands National Seashore. And at the time Tom popped him and found him in possession of hashish, [The informant] acknowledged that it was hashish, which would even without a lab test tend to confirm that it was hash. And then somehow or other, in the course events, that evidence was not hashish after Connelly did a presumptive test on it. And I would recommend talking to both Randy [the Evidence Custodian] and Tom about that. Randy was there when Connelly did the presumptive. But Tom was interviewed by Lunsford, and he just couldn't believe that it wasn't hash. When you bust somebody and they admit that it's hashish, it's usually hashish.

The younger auditor picked up on a key point made previously about Connelly's peculiar use of young informants.

2nd GAO: [Name of informant]. I mean, I'm trying to figure a reason they would be doing that. [The informant's] role, again, was what? I mean, you lost me.

BERKOWITZ: Well, originally he was busted for selling drugs, himself, and I had a case on him of I think it was seven counts of forgery. He stole some checks and forged them.

GAO: Well, he was buying for LEO as part of the process?

BERKOWITZ: It's also complicated by the fact that he was homosexual, and so was Connelly.

GAO: Well, I've heard some things about that already.

They most certainly had, as had OIG Agent Lunsford; although the concern was not with Connelly's sexual orientation, per se. Though not openly discussed in the workplace, Connelly's homosexuality was widely known and, for that time in history (the early 1980s), was remarkably well accepted by most of his co-workers. The concern I was attempting to raise had to do with Connelly's reputation for an attraction to underage boys, supported by his pattern of recruiting young gay men in the community to work directly for him as informants, paying them with "buy money" and shielding them from prosecution. The conflict and suspected impropriety was obvious. That topic was discussed in detail, on-and-off-tape, by me and others. But for my purposes it was good to at least finally obtain some confirmation, on tape, that the GAO was familiar with the issue.

As the interview progressed, the fact that the officials from the GAO truly were auditors, and not investigators, became painfully apparent. They were lost in their own little world of paper trails and random samplings. This was reinforced time and again, as the lead auditor either challenged what I was telling him, becoming confused and confrontational, or expressed incredulity at the very notion that Yosemite National Park and the NPS did not fit into his neat little world of accepted policies, procedures, and paper trails. He couldn't grasp the concept of conducting an investigation by pursuing any kind of lead other than a signed receipt or voucher. This point was made, still again, with the following exchange about breaches to the chain-of-custody and prospective destruction of evidence.

GAO: The toughest part is trying to find specifics and then trying to find some documentation that shows them. And of course, one area that's always tough is, was there some sort of criminal intent, in terms of where's the behavior you can document? What was the full intent of their behavior, OK? Now, as far as the actual physical tampering, which we've also got evidence.

BERKOWITZ: That's one in particular that you've got to talk to Randy [evidence custodian] about. OK, Randy's being in charge of evidence, there were a number of situations where evidence was, out of the blue, not there.

GAO: Obviously, any evidence is kept under pretty tight control. How could this happen?

BERKOWITZ: Well, Connelly being [Randy's] supervisor, had access to everything [Randy] had.

GAO: But he'd still have to sign in and out for it.

BERKOWITZ: Well, that's the point.

GAO: But, uh ---

BERKOWITZ: That's the point. Things were not signed in and out by Connelly. There was one instance that Randy related where he went into Connelly's desk, saw a piece of evidence sitting on his desk, and there was no record of it having ever been logged out.

GAO: Are you telling me also that Randy did not have the only key to the evidence room?

BERKOWITZ: Yes, that's what I'm telling you.

The auditor was incredulous, saying he couldn't believe that anyone other than the property officer – not even the property officer's supervisor, Connelly – would have direct access to evidence.

Then the topic turned to reports. As the auditor cited the new category appearing on his list, he appeared already prepared to dismiss one of the categories he had identified.

GAO: Falsifying and embellishing criminal reports. I mean, embellishing I can't do anything with that.

I was starting to show my frustration, and interrupted.

BERKOWITZ: Well, yes you can. OK. Here's the point. [Undercover informant] Bill, and [undercover officer] Craig, particularly [Craig]. He's functionally illiterate. The guy has a third grade education, by his own admission. He could not read or write at a functional level.

GAO: OK. Are you saying neither were functionally, uh, uh ---

BERKOWITZ: [Bill, the full-time, salaried informant], a little more so, but not to any great degree.

GAO: [speaking out loud as he writes]: Neither could use written ---

BERKOWITZ: [Bill] was better than [Craig]. [Craig] was just abominable. You'd look at his stuff and tell this guy had not had an education. Both those guys would turn in this hand scrawled gibberish, and those were their reports.

GAO: OK. So what did you do? You were their supervisor. Did you have to walk them through it and write it for them?

BERKOWITZ: Sometimes we'd be ordered to walk them through it, sometimes Lee [Shackelton] would order myself or other people to out-and-out re-write the whole damn things based upon an interview. And then rather than reflecting them as an interview, they would be reflected as the words of either of those individuals. It's as if you have your five year old daughter - [have] - her scrawl out something, and then that obviously not being adequate for court purposes, you interview her and interpret it onto paper, yourself, and have your daughter sign it as though it were her own product.

GAO: OK. Well now that, um ---

BERKOWITZ: Rather than reflecting it as, in fact, your interview of that subject.

GAO: Now, tell me, from your experience, at least, I'm a little troubled with one aspect of that. That is, it seems to me that if you have someone up on the witness stand, I'm thinking about the impact of this on the people that have to read the report and the people that have to listen to the evidence when you get to a jury trial, if you in fact get there, um, if it's written up as an interview, and you're basically, you're confident that the guy was able to communicate to you what happened and you've accurately written it down, and they signed it. What is the impact, other than the fact that you're not getting credit for having written it down, beyond that, what's the impact upon the validity of the testimony?

I was struggling to make him comprehend what was occurring. Certifiable criminals were being used in drug enforcement operations, but not as mere informants. Individuals with criminal backgrounds, whose records had been destroyed or sealed, were being represented as bona-fide law enforcement officers and government officials. In the process, Shackelton was deviating from established recruitment, screening, training, and certification procedures, and exceeding his own authority on a grand scale by using government funds to pay for their training before they were even hired, and then asserting that he (Shackelton) had independent authority to "commission" these same people as law enforcement officers. In the case of "Craig," he had actually pulled it off, sending him through the NPS seasonal academy run by the retired ranger, and where Shackelton, himself, was double-dipping as a paid instructor. In the other case with "Bill," he was unable to complete the process, but not for lack of trying. "Bill," an acknowledged "former" heroin addict, was simply too much of a physical wreck and too strung out to complete even the most basic of training, which I was ordered to provide in an effort to piece-meal together the necessary number of hours. I was certain that he was still using heroin and other drugs throughout the period that he worked for us. Meanwhile, his real wife, who had also been recruited as a part of his cover, was a former prostitute (in the same way that Bill was a former heroin addict). On one occasion I was even directed to make a run with "Bill", to pick up his wife's sister, also a prostitute, who was coming in from Las Vegas to hide and recover from a beating by her pimp.

Naturally, the fact that Shackelton hired these people as paid NPS employees did not alter their lifestyles or keep them from getting into trouble. I was getting called out at all hours of the day and night to extricate them from their own confrontations with legitimate rangers and other law enforcement personnel both within and outside of the park, after being caught with drugs or getting involved in fights.

There's nothing all that unusual about encountering these kinds of problems when working with informants. That's just a part of the business, and something openly addressed in court if the informant needs to testify. But these were the kinds of people Shackelton was hiring as salaried government employees, and representing as government officials and gun-toting, badge carrying law enforcement officers. I told all of these things to the auditors, and then attempted to explain the significance of the situation.

BERKOWITZ: OK. Here's the impact. If I'm a defense attorney and I see a report that indicates it's written by an officer, it's signed off on the bottom of a criminal incident report, which suggests just by virtue of the format that it's written by an official of the Park Service. OK. And I read this thing, the image I form in my mind is that this is a police officer who wrote this thing. This is a first-hand account ---

GAO: And that it looks like, what you're saying is, it gives him the misimpression that the guy is a lot more capable than, in fact, he is.

BERKOWITZ: That's correct. If I see that, I'm less likely to want to go to trial. Because I see that, well, "this person is very articulate," they really know what they're talking about. I better not challenge it. It's here on paper. As opposed to seeing the idiot that, in fact, provided that information who, like I said, virtually has to scrawl out his own name. Now, if on the other hand, I realize the truth about that person, hell, yeah, I'm going to go to trial, because I realize this person is a blithering idiot. You can make him look like a fool on the stand, and of course that's an accepted tactic of defense.

GAO: OK. OK. I'm just thinking about that, you know, how I react. I'm not, I can understand it, alright. The problem I'm having with that is, um, I think that, I think it's misleading. Falsifying, to me, means something different.

BERKOWITZ: That's a description of embellishment. OK. In addition to that, Dennis, the same guy I told you about [a legitimate seasonal investigator] has related to me that he has seen Shackelton shred the original hand-written reports. Which, of course, would remove the possibility of, normally, hand-written and original copies are available on discovery. That's why we keep all of our notes. OK. If they're destroyed, there's no basis upon which to make a comparison between the end product and the original product to ascertain if the person, hey, maybe the person, maybe this isn't quite right.

GAO: OK. OK. (sighs) OK. I can follow that.

BERKOWITZ: Now, in terms of falsification ---

The auditor broke in, continuing.

GAO: The embellishing, I think, from my standpoint, is a very difficult one to deal with. I think we're almost talking about something beyond embellishment. You're talking about, to an extent, misrepresentation of this as being the report of someone that, in fact, did not prepare it. But that I can deal with a little more easily.

BERKOWITZ: Well, if you want to call it misrepresentation, that's fine with me.

The conversation progressed from embellishment into outright falsification of reports, with detailed discussion of numerous examples, both that I had witnessed and had been witnessed by others. I provided the names of those other officers who could corroborate those second-hand accounts. I suggested they ask to look at the handwritten notes of undercover officers whose reports I believed had been falsified.

The entire recorded interview with the GAO continued this way for nearly three hours. We covered every single topic I had previously reported to everybody from every agency. The tone of the conversations was the same throughout; civil, but with frustrating, almost argumentative exchanges, misunderstanding of basic legal concepts, and resistance to verifiable, factual accounts.

There was at least one more topic I was determined to discuss again before the interview concluded. To their apparent annoyance, I again brought up the bugging. I was sure they already knew all about it. But I wanted to continue this discussion so I could document on tape that I had fully shared the account with them.

GAO: Well, that's the basic list. Is there anything else that you'd like to add that you think that we haven't at least touched on, thus far?

BERKOWITZ: Yeah. One of the biggies is the matter of bugging the superintendent's office.

GAO: Well, was that in your, I didn't see that. Was that in your transcript?

That was a most curious response, since I'd already raised the topic at least twice before in this very conversation.

BERKOWITZ: No, it wasn't.

GAO: OK. Well, why don't we talk about it?

BERKOWITZ: OK. I'm curious to know, was that, well you said tangentially, in the I.G.'s report?

GAO: No. no, no, no. The bugging business, no that wasn't touched on. Although Lunsford. Well, why don't you tell me about it, since I'm not clear? Lunsford talked to me about having some tapes and so forth, and I don't know what they are of [stumbles and fumbles, unintelligibly], I, yet described as saying he had some. ...

Now *that* was an interesting slip. The auditor finally confirmed that the bugging incident was not covered in Lunsford's report. But the GAO did know about the bugging, and they knew that Lunsford, for some reason, apparently already had some tapes related to that incident. Had he somehow obtained the tapes made back in March of 1983, capturing the conversation between Binnewies and Cushman? If that was the case, Binnewies, at the very least, had already been contacted. If that was the case, a concerted effort was being made to cover up the incident without ever having conducted a legitimate investigation.

I didn't expect the auditor to tell me anything more, so I went through the full scenario about the bugging incident, one more time, "for the record." They heard me tell it all, including how pissed off I was for having unwittingly been dragged into the illegal affair.

Throughout the entire account, for what must have been the fourth or fifth time I had by then provided the long version of the story, the auditors sat there, virtually silent. Finally, the lead auditor tried to dismiss the account as beyond the scope of his inquiry. He said,

GAO: Well, I can appreciate your feeling in that regard, no doubt. This one doesn't really have a very good tie-in to the rest of ---

BERKOWITZ: Yeah. But I never claimed that it did.

GAO: Well, that's fine. I understand that. I certainly don't mind receiving the complaint.

That would be, quite literally, the very least he could do. The auditor tried to excuse himself from doing anything more, in the process shedding light on what was going on behind the scenes.

GAO: Miles [my supervisor] wouldn't let me investigate that. What we're doing right now is something specifically for a Committee, they're asking us ---

BERKOWITZ: Well, I did allude to it, still, in my comments, where I said that specific accounts of what I believe would be a violation of criminal law.

GAO: Yeah. OK. I understand that. What I'm just saying to you right now is that I don't know. Do you? [talking to colleague]. This one's gonna be very difficult to deal with. That's all. I'm just telling you I don't know how to deal with this.

That was an understated but prophetic statement. But I persisted in my attempt to impress upon them the significance of that incident, even beyond mere criminality.

BERKOWITZ: But let me draw on that further. The reason I think it's significant is because I believe, firmly, number one, I've heard from people that, if you want, I'll tell you who they are, that Shackelton has used that as a point of potential blackmail against the superintendent. OK.

GAO: Uh-huh.

BERKOWITZ: And I believe that that's a pattern of behavior on Shackelton's part. I think that Shackelton has a lot of stuff similar to that on a lot of people. And that's why he's been allowed to carry on the way he has for so long. And I know that a lot of people in this park share that view.

GAO: [Continued silence]

BERKOWITZ: Obviously, when that incident occurred, that removed the superintendent or anybody in this park from my ability to go to them to report any misconduct on Shackelton's part.

GAO: OK. Is this place bugged other than your tape recorder?

The conversation was becoming almost comical, as the auditor's own paranoia and discomfort over the entire topic started to show.

BERKOWITZ: This is sure as hell why I didn't want to talk in the superintendent's office.

GAO: Well, OK, that's fine. I'm just asking the question.

BERKOWITZ: I hope it's not. But who knows.

GAO: I'm just wondering. You have experience. Did you check the place?

BERKOWITZ: Well, how do you check it? I don't have the equipment.

GAO: OK. Well, I just asked. That's all. I don't know how to check it, either.

BERKOWITZ: But I am concerned, because I reported that to Lunsford. And when I reported it to him, the other guy's name is Ralph Curtis Jr., Lunsford told me not to talk about it with anybody. OK. I understand that. But when I hear that, that impresses in my mind the fact that they may prosecute. That's why I didn't bring it out in the hearing.

GAO: Two things. Something like that, he would probably put a separate report out on. We wouldn't even have seen that. We saw something that was specifically related to the LEO here in the park. And the operation of the imprest fund here in the park. And things that were specifically tied to that.

BERKOWITZ: Point is, I called up Lunsford a few days prior to testifying before Congress, to make crystal clear that anything I would say wouldn't compromise anything that was in the works. Because if they were in fact pursuing an investigation of any kind I didn't want to get up there and ruin it.

GAO: Sure.

BERKOWITZ: And he told me that it was a hundred percent finished, that there was absolutely nothing in the works. And if that's the case, then I'm curious to know why it's not addressed in that report.

GAO: Well, I certainly don't recall seeing anything on that subject in that report. Uh, I wouldn't want to say that it's not covered in an interview or something like that, because he's got interviews with you written up in there and I can't recall them word for word. So I may have missed something. And I've read a pile of documents last week that's about like yay-big.

The auditor was stumbling now, and trying to back-peddle his way out of the entire subject.

BERKOWITZ: But do you understand that aside from it being a problem in and of itself, I think that it branches out further, because, like I said, I have heard that Shackelton said, I think like the week before this hearing, that he could "have Binnewies' job," because of this incident, if he wanted it. OK. And he told that, I believe, to Andy Hutchison and Dave Montalbano, who are two instructors from FLETC [the Federal Law Enforcement Training Center].

Andy Hutchison was the NPS agency representative, a superintendent, assigned to the Federal Law Enforcement Training Center in Brunswick (FLETC), Georgia. That made him a key figure in the Service's law enforcement training program and direct supervisor over the NPS recruits while they attended the academy at FLETC. Hutchison had been visiting Yosemite on business the first part of October 1985, and had at least one discussion over lunch or dinner with Shackelton. It was during that conversation, according to Hutchison, that Shackelton alluded to the bugging incident and boasted that he could "have Binnewies' job," if he wanted. Hutchison later shared details of that conversation with me, adding that instead of paying for their meal, Shackelton "badged" the waiter and handed him back the bill, saying the manager would know that the meal was free.

GAO: [sighs ...]

I was getting tired of the silence and the sighing.

BERKOWITZ: You don't want to hear this, do you?

The auditor sighed some more. He made a few more comments to signal that it was time to end the interview. I persisted, bringing up one final point I was intent on discussing, getting off my chest, and getting it on the record, on tape.

BERKOWITZ: Now the other point which I think that you guys have missed, and the press certainly missed in a lot of the things that I've been reading, when I articulated some of these very general allegations which were made, OK, my purpose in alluding to that before Congress was not to make the allegations in a public forum. But rather, to set a context upon which to complain about the obstacles that were thrown in my way to try to report these matters. And I even say that, that the thing that concerns me, primarily, is what a pain in the ass, what a ripping pain in the ass and all the hassles that I went through to try to report this to anybody.

GAO: OK. Well, I understand your concern there. I don't think we missed that concern. It's just that, uh, that is sort of an overview kind of situation where what you're doing is you're saying are the mechanisms in the broader sense, working? I think you make in your statement, there, you allude that you thought that part of the reason the I.G. in Interior has changed is, at least at the headquarters level, is because of the lack of handling.

The auditor was referring to the recent removal of the actual DOI Inspector General – the top man – who had quietly been removed from his position after the White House learned about the OIG's own mishandling of the investigation.[5]

GAO: Now, without going too far, because I'd have to double check the figures, but, uh, I don't know right now, without double checking, whether the I.G., for example, was even informed when you thought they were going to be informed when you contacted the various people within NPS who said they would deal with it.

BERKOWITZ: Well, here's the point. Somebody's lying, because the I.G.'s office told me that they had not been. And, OK, if they're lying, then that's a problem. If the Park Service was the one who was lying when they said they had reported to them, then they're lying, and that's a problem. Somebody's lying.

GAO: I agree with that, uh, we already touched on that one. You've got also the idea of it, was it Mary Sargent, the personnel officer, who ---

BERKOWITZ: Let me clarify something there, as regards Mary. I don't think in my own mind, I don't have anything to base it on except for what I know about Mary. I don't think that Mary concocted that. I think she was told that and may have accepted it as fact. And Steve Lunsford did, in fact, tell me that Lowell White [the Associate Regional Director] was the one who instigated that story. Now I think that's a real problem, if you've got the Office of the Inspector General, who is supposed to be the one that you can go to, to "blow the whistle," and the hot-line, and all that kind of stuff. If the Park Service is misrepresenting the Office of the Inspector General, then that sounds to me like a real serious problem, because then nobody's going to feel safe going to the OIG. If the OIG is, on the other hand, telling me affirmatively, not simply saying we can't comment, but telling me affirmatively that, "no, we have not been contacted by the Park Service," and in fact they have, then that's a problem, too, because there's no credibility with the OIG, itself.

GAO: OK. I understand your commentary. Mine is directed toward the basis of who was contacted, when, and where. As near as I can tell, until you personally contacted the OIG, yourself, I see no evidence in the reports that I have read, thus far, that indicates the Park Service contacted them at all.

BERKOWITZ: That's my understanding.

GAO: But I'd have to double check to be sure that's so. But that's the way I've seen things, thus far. And ---

2nd GAO: [Chimes in] --- You also called the Office of Enforcement and Safety?

BERKOWITZ: Yeah, Enforcement and Security, I think that's it. Harry DeLashmutt was the guy I called.

2nd GAO: Yeah, that's not part of NPS at all, either. So I mean it's not just NPS ---

BERKOWITZ: No, it's part of Interior.

2nd GAO: ---or the OIG, other elements, as well.

BERKOWITZ: That's true. I alluded, in fact, I went through it. I made three separate contacts with Dave Lennox, who is the person who I understood was supposed to be responsible for supervising this fund and this operation at the regional level. It's a weird situation, because, given the secrecy, which may have been blown up more than necessary, the superintendent and the chief ranger didn't even really know that much about the case and how it was being handled. They didn't supervise a thing, in a hands-on way, at all, or in a knowledgeable way. That meant that Dave Lennox was the nearest supervisor in a position of knowledge. When I went to Dave Lennox, I resent the hell out the fact that all three instances when I went to him reporting this stuff, his response was damn-near verbatim, "Sorry. Nothing I can do for you. Can't help you. Don't do anything illegal. Bye." That seems to me like an entirely inappropriate response to someone trying to report possible misconduct, whether it's founded or not. Just to be responded to in that way I think is wrong.

GAO: OK.

BERKOWITZ: And it put me, like I said, it put me in a real precarious situation of, do I quit and not do anything illegal? Do I simply monitor the activities? Or do I just go along with it and become accomplice to anything that may be wrong? OK. Hearing nothing from him, I call Harry DeLashmutt. I called DeLashmutt just because I'd had some dealings with him before. Don't know the guy personally. He's in a high-ranking office. My feeling was, why should I trust anybody in the I.G.? Maybe they're just as fucked-up as the Park Service is. So I wanted to go to a third party who might know somebody who was responsible in the Office of the I.G. I went to DeLashmutt, specifically saying "please put me in touch with a responsible investigator from the Office of the I.G." He said he would. Then I gave him a very, very long and relatively detailed account over the phone of what the problems here were. He tape recorded it. I tape recorded it. We both have copies of that conversation. Then, in turn, whether on his own prerogative or not, took that information, wrote a memorandum and sent it right back to the Park Service, [Chief Ranger's] office. OK. [The chief ranger], his office or maybe it was the Director's office, appoints John Crockett to investigate the thing for the Park Service. Comes out here. What's he do, first thing, with the memorandum? Shows it to Lee Shackelton! OK.

GAO: OK. Keep on going.

BERKOWITZ: OK. An idiotic move to show, ya know, to divulge what is supposed to be in confidence, a secret investigation. I don't know of anybody else in the Park Service that's been given that privilege to see all the allegations like that for an internal matter.

GAO: Oh Yeah. I understand. The I.G.'s report is very closely controlled.

BERKOWITZ: OK. Why the hell did they show him? And that created all kinds of internal problems here. And, ya know, my wife [who also worked at the LEO] had to go find another job, like "then" [snap my fingers]; no place to go.

2nd GAO: By the time Crockett was out here, though, had you already talked to the I.G.?

BERKOWITZ: Yeah.

2nd GAO: OK.

BERKOWITZ: But it was in secret. Park Service didn't know about it at that point. OK. Did that. Then he comes in here, I think the next day I had an interview with Crockett. We sat down. I called the I.G. saying, "Well, what the hell do you want me to do? Do you want me to tell him that I've been talking to you guys?" And he said, well, don't lie to them if they ask you, but don't volunteer anything. And it came down to that. And he said, "Well, why haven't you called the I.G.?" And I said "Well, I have." And John Crockett closed his books up and said let's turn these tapes off and really talk about what's happening. And we did. And he showed me a memorandum written by [Regional Director] Howard Chapman saying that, "Crockett, look at this thing. I want you to consider whether or not we should call the I.G." OK. The point is, that by that time, of course, way back, I'd already been told by the Park Service that the I.G. was entering into the case ---

GAO: We, we, we've ---

BERKOWITZ: --- to elicit information.

GAO: We got that call. Apparently Crockett did turn over whatever he had to the I.G. and also to the Secret Service.

BERKOWITZ: Well, no doubt. But my point, ya know, that was the main point I was trying to address to these guys in Congress. What the hell kind of system do they have when people who are trying to report misconduct, whether it's legitimate or not, have to go through this kind of a hassle, and this kind of personal aggravation to do what's right?

The auditor fumbled and stumbled for several more minutes, pointing out that it was probably a mistake for me to have first tried to report my concerns through channels, before contacting the OIG directly. I replied:

BERKOWITZ: That's well and good. But, ya know, the other response that you're going to get is why didn't you try to resolve the matter at the lowest level? That's what I ---

GAO: You said you did.

BERKOWITZ: I know that I did. But I think, had I not gone that route, that would have been the attack that was turned upon me. What the hell did you go out and make a big fucking deal out of it? Why didn't you just go through the chain?

Once again, it was the second, younger auditor who jumped into the conversation, offering a more reasoned observation.

2nd GAO: It is kind of a no-win situation. You go the I.G. first off, or you seek to resolve it at a low level. And if you go to a low level ---

GAO: You already tried the basic thing you're supposed to do. You brought it up to your supervisor. You had an argument or two with the guy, at the very least, saying here's what's going on and I don't think that's right. I don't want any part of it. You've done that a couple times.

BERKOWITZ: Yeah.

GAO: Uh, I don't know how much more you have to do. It's uh, that's uh, anybody could, and anybody will ---

BERKOWITZ: Yeah, but it's more than a passive problem. From what I read in the situation with Butch Abell, where the guy tells me it's my obligation to obey illegal orders, the I.G. has no fucking business in the park, ya know, investigating things. That he's going to have a dozen rangers kick down my door and hold me down. That sounds to me like it goes, ya know, way the hell to the other extreme in terms of trying to encourage any kind of a professional operation.

Exchanges like these made the entire three hour interview painfully frustrating. It was also apparent that the investigation being conducted by the GAO auditors was a waste of time. They were either incompetent or under orders from Congressman Vento to make it a white-wash, or both.

That point was further reinforced during my second meeting with these same officials the following week, on November 11. On that occasion, I handed over, and we discussed, copies of many of the same documents I had previously given to Steve Lunsford. Toward the end of that taped conversation, I once again raised the issue of the bugging.

BERKOWITZ: I'm still concerned about the matter of the bugging of the office. I'd like to know where that's going, and why nothing has been done so far. It seems to me that's a pretty serious matter.

The lead auditor replied,

GAO: I'll tell you what is going to happen on that right now. We're going to go back and tell the guy that requested us to do the work [Vento], he said "you look at these particular things." And we're going to tell him which ones we've been able to look at and how much, and, how much we've been able to come up with thus far on those things, and ask him if he wants us to do more, or he does not want us to do more. We will mention to him [Vento] that initial one. That goes beyond the scope of what he asked us to do originally. We're having a hard time getting done what we'd like to get done on all the things you've given us, thus far. Quite frankly, the biggest problem with doing what we're trying to do now is that are *so* many things that are being looked into that it's hard to cover all of them.

That last honest comment was revealing. The GAO was under a severe time-line to finish their inquiry. The lead auditor was acknowledging that his investigation would, at best, be limited to a cursory review and only a limited number of interviews; something not acknowledged when their report was released. I responded.

BERKOWITZ: My question is, what the hell do you need to do to get a violation of criminal law looked at when Lee Shackelton and Scott Connelly do it?

The auditor gave another big sigh and answered,

GAO: Ya know, I wish I --- When you get into criminal law, generally speaking you're getting beyond us, 'cause as soon as we get a hold of a criminal violation, usually, what we do is simply hand it over the FBI and say "it's yours."

BERKOWITZ: Well, is that going to happen?

The auditor stumbled some more and said,

GAO: Oh, as far is it goes I don't think that there's any problem saying that Lunsford, Lunsford's report, uh, it's gone two directions. It's not just gone to the Park Service. And that's about as much as I can say right now because we aren't authorized to talk about it, even.

That answer was a dodge. The auditor had already told me that Lunsford's report didn't mention the bugging. So even if his report did go to the U.S. Attorney, there would be no consideration of a prosecution for the bugging. That decision had evidently been made before the auditors were ever dispatched to the park.

I made my final point in the form of a question.

BERKOWITZ: Yeah. I just want to know, have I wasted my time in trying to address that issue, the bugging?

GAO: What, the bugging? Uh, with us right now, it's beyond what we can do this week. If the guy [Vento] sends us back, that's another story. If he wants us to do some of that, that's another story.

I wasn't satisfied, and continued,

BERKOWITZ: What about Steve [Lunsford] though? I mean, that was related to him.

GAO: OK. I don't know. I haven't had but a couple of, one conversation with Steve I think, a great talk, was trying to talk to him again.

I tried to impress upon him one more time what my own position was on the subject.

BERKOWITZ: I'd be real interested in getting feedback. Because, I'll be honest with you, because of the implications of that particular act, I'm not going to feel comfortable until somebody documents the thing and really looks at it.

2nd GAO: You did discuss that with Steve?

BERKOWITZ: Absolutely, from the very beginning.

GAO: In terms of us, it's just a case of how much can we accomplish. And what this guy wants to know is "what's the story as of right now?" And then he's going to make a decision. I'm not going to make a decision as to what if any additional work he wants to do.

The GAO auditors were contradicting themselves, first acknowledging that they (and, therefore, Vento) knew about the bugging (and even the location of the tapes) and that I had reported the incident to the OIG, and then coyly asking if I had discussed the incident with Lunsford.

It was clear, now, that Vento was pulling the strings. If he wanted to know "what's the story as of right now," that probably included finding out who else I had already told about the bugging. Vento undoubtedly knew about it. But he considered Chuck Cushman an enemy, so at the very least was sympathetic to the officials who had orchestrated and pulled it off. And if he knew about it, so did the top management of the NPS. As Chairman of the House Subcommittee on National Parks, Forests, and Public lands, if Vento wanted to squash an investigation and protect people like Connelly, Shackelton, Loach, and Binnewies, then absolutely nothing was going to happen as long as he could keep it a secret. But just a minute before, I'd made my position clear when I told them *"I'm not going to feel comfortable until somebody documents the thing and really looks at it."* I continued.

BERKOWITZ: The message I get as a grunt at the field level is that, hey, this is too hot to handle. "We don't want to do anything to this guy anyway. Drop it."

GAO: Well, I can't, uh, you know. Your feelings are as legitimate as anybody else's feelings about how your organization operates. In dealing with Congressional types, what I have to do is, *"what they want is what I do."*

Now *that* was a quote worth remembering.

Endnotes

1. GAO website, GAO "mission statement."

2. Al Voris, Richard Griffone, and Greg Kosarin.

3. One side of this taped interview did not properly record.

4. Exemption 7 of the Freedom of Information Act provides for the withholding of "records compiled for law enforcement purposes." Time is allowed for redaction of information from reports before release to the public.

5. *See* Appendix One: "Testimony of Paul Berkowitz, presented before the House Subcommittee on Parks, Forests, and Public Lands, Oct. 15, 1986, Yosemite, California."

CHAPTER FIFTEEN

A Certifiable Cover-up

By the time the auditors left the park, it was apparent that the entire GAO investigation was a cover-up and sham. Almost none of the other officers or members of the community whose names I provided were contacted for corroborating interviews. The GAO report came out just a short time later, confirming that they had not pursued even the most basic of leads they were provided.

Consequently, a widely circulated press release issued on January 15, 1986 by Congressman Vento, accompanying the nine page GAO report, left the false impression that no serious improprieties had occurred at Yosemite and that my allegations were unfounded.[1]

Vento publicly declared,

> The GAO found no evidence of criminal conduct and, more importantly, found no basis to support such allegations.[2]

The resulting headlines read,

2 Yosemite officers cleared in drug probe.[3]

(*Fresno Bee*, January 16, 1986).

Predictably, the GAO report contained absolutely no mention of the illegal bugging, or of the many other violations that were actually confirmed within the unreleased OIG report. In fact, the GAO made no reference, at all, to the earlier year-long investigation conducted by the OIG into the same issues, or to the existence of the related OIG report that contradicted just about everything claimed by the GAO and Congressman Vento.

But with only the GAO report released and distributed to the public and the news media, I experienced still further isolation in Yosemite, and was subjected to open ridicule by members of the NPS fraternity. At one point, I was called in for a counseling session by my new supervisor, Bill Blake. Citing Vento's press release and the GAO report, he admonished me that I would have to "swallow the pill," acknowledge that I had been wrong in my allegations, and move on to a trusting working relationship with my former supervisors, Leland Shackelton and Scott Connelly.

The only fortunate aspect of the entire process for me, however, was my earlier decision to openly record and document not only my telephone calls and other contacts with OIG agents, but also the hours of interviews in which I had participated with Captain Crockett, as well as the GAO auditors. Not all of the tapes had properly recorded. But those that did, along with my own copies of the records I had turned over to the OIG and to the GAO, contained virtually all of the details about my allegations. At the very least, I could prove that the OIG and the GAO had been told about everything, including the Binnewies-Cushman bugging incident. Those tapes and related documents would eventually provide the ammunition I needed to prove the NPS, OIG, GAO, and Congressional cover-up. And even more than I realized at the time, in conjunction with the OIG report (that I had not seen, but Vento and the GAO had), they could prove the GAO report was a lie, and that Representative Bruce Vento, Chairman of the House Subcommittee on National Parks, Forests, and Public Lands, was a liar.

Endnotes

1. "Fact Sheet for the Chairman, Subcommittee on National Parks and Recreation, Committee on Interior and Insular Affairs, House of Representatives: NATIONAL PARKS, Allegations Concerning Yosemite National Park Drug Investigation," Dec. 1985.

2. Press release, "New For Release", Committee on Interior and Insular Affairs, House of Representatives, "Vento Announces GAO Findings in Yosemite Probe," Jan. 15, 1986.

3. Gene Rose, "2 Yosemite officers cleared in drug probe," *Fresno Bee*, Jan. 16, 1986.

CHAPTER SIXTEEN

Outrage and Defiance

D oes a citizen have the right to know that he is the victim of a crime, or that his rights have been violated? Stated another way, does the government have an obligation to tell a citizen when it knows that person's rights have been violated by an illegal act? From a moral and ethical standpoint, the answer seems simple, yet I've never received a clear *legal* answer from any of the dozens of government and private attorneys I've asked over the years. But these are questions with which I struggled as I contemplated my next move.

In response to the widespread release of the GAO report by Congressman Vento's office, and in an effort to clear my own name and reputation, I sent two separate, detailed letters to Representative Coelho, reminding him that I still had proof of my many allegations, including the consensually made recordings of my interviews with the GAO. This time, however, I copied the letter to a number of other congressional representatives.

By now, I'd come to realize that Representatives Vento, Coelho, and Lehman were all unduly allied with the interests of the NPS as well as officials at MCA, and were, to say the least, disinclined to openly address the issues I was reporting. In frustration, I made a key decision. I tracked down the phone number for Chuck Cushman, and gave him a call.

When Cushman picked up the phone, I sheepishly introduced myself by name, explaining that I was an NPS employee who possessed information that might interest him – information *about* him – but which I could not immediately share. I asked if he could recommend the name of someone in Congress he trusted, and with whom I could communicate to pass along what I knew. Cushman provided me with the name and address for Congressman Chip Pashayan who, prior to redistricting, had represented residents in the Wawona District of the park. I then called Representative Pashayan's office to brief him on the situation, advising that I would be including him on the list of recipients of correspondence I was sending to Congressman Coelho.

In the first of those letters, heatedly written January 15, 1986, the same day as Vento's press release and my subsequent call to Chuck Cushman, I stated,

> I have read Congressman Vento's press release of 01/15/86 and I am disappointed to see that he appears to have missed many of the

primary points of my testimony. I would ask that the subcommittee take the time to re-read its content. I stand by that testimony and reaffirm its accuracy and my commitment to its content. I further remain convinced that my presentation before the sub-committee was an entirely appropriate forum in light of the exhaustive efforts I and others have made to have these issues addressed at lower and less public levels. Please don't lose sight of the fact that my stated primary intention in addressing your sub-committee was to apprise you of obstacles and resistance with which initial and even subsequent attempts to report these matters were met.

As for Mr. Vento's statement that "the GAO spent considerable time looking into Mr. Berkowitz's charges…" I take exception to that conclusion. I note that by their own admission the GAO was under severe time constraints to conduct their inquiry and did not even have time to speak to the primary persons to whom they were directed to corroborate incidents I related. I note that my interviews with the auditors for the GAO were consensually and openly tape recorded and remain available for your review to confirm these deficiencies.

As you should by now be aware, not all allegations were brought forth to you in the public forum of October 15, 1985. *Significant deletions were made in my testimony in the interests of saving the National Park Service from substantial political and lasting operational damage. Nevertheless, ALL such allegations were related at length to both the Office of the Inspector General and the G.A.O…* [Emphasis in original].

I direct your attention to the incident I reported wherein Supt. Binnewies requested that the Law Enforcement Office staff assist him by placing a miniature radio transmitting device in his office for the purpose of having a *political* private inholder's negotiation meeting surreptitiously monitored and tape recorded…

The letter continued for another full page, concluding,

Mr. Coelho, I request that you apprise me of what specific progress has been made into all of the relevant matters. I would also ask that you provide me with what guidance you can, so that I might equitably balance my desire to defend my reputation and credibility, along with my desire to save the Park Service and affected individuals from further embarrassment by my being compelled to make additional public disclosures of the details of this matter, in order to refute incomplete and misleading pronouncements made by Mr. Vento and others, about my testimony.[1]

That first letter was copied to Representatives Robert Kastenmeier (D-WI), Charles Pashayan (R-CA), Pete Visclosky (D-IN), and Sid Yates (D-IL). Those officials were included in the mailing in an effort to prevent a further cover-up by Congressmen Vento, Coelho, Lehman, and any others pre-disposed to protect the interests of NPS and YPCC officials. A copy of the entire letter was also sent to recently appointed NPS Director William Mott.

Within a matter of days, Superintendent Bob Binnewies was "reassigned" to the Western Regional Office in San Francisco. The January 25 & 29 headlines accompanying that action read, *Yosemite Park Chief Replaced*,[2] and *Yosemite Chief's Firing Tied to Ranger Morale, Crime*[3]

(*San Francisco Chronicle*, January 25, 1986).

(*Los Angeles Times*, January 29, 1986).

Then, in an effort at damage control, Congressional and NPS officials fabricated a series of press releases claiming that my first report of the Binnewies-Cushman bugging incident was made only *after* the GAO investigation and report had exonerated the NPS on my other allegations. The resulting headlines on January 30, 1986 read, *Berkowitz Makes Further Allegations*,[4] and *Park Chief Allegedly Made Secret Taping*.[5]

Berkowitz makes further allegations

In a letter dated January 15th to William P. Mott, and five congressman including Charles Pashayan, R-Fresno and Tony Coelho, D-Merced, Paul D. Berkowitz, park ranger, alleged that he was ordered by Scott Connelly, a Yosemite National Park law enforcement personnel, to secretly tape a meeting conducted in park superintendent's office shortly after Queen Elizabeth's visit a few years back.

Robert O. Binnewies, park superintendent, met with Charles Cushman, a Wawona and private land-holder within park boundaries to discuss the problems occuring between park officials and private inholders.

The allegations come on the heels of a prior investigation made by the U.S. Inspector General's office, also as the result of Berkowitz's allegations.

Last summer, Berkowitz wrote a letter outlining what he believed to be injustices, unethical, unprofessional and perhaps criminal conduct on the part of some of NPS' upper management as well as senior law enforcement officials within Yosemite National Park.

A congressional hearing was later scheduled to be heard in the park about issues affecting Yosemite National Park. Berkowitz asked to testify at that hearing and was given the ok. Meanwhile, based on Berkowitz' original letter last summer, and investigation was begun.

In that hearing at the Park, Berkowitz testified that he felt "considerable anxiety" as well as "fear for his career and the safety of himself and his family," as a result of giving testimony before the congressional committee. Berkowitz's original communication was in June of 1982 to the U.S. Park Service Captain in San Francisco. Berkowitz alleged misuse of special funds which had been established to buy drugs and information. He claimed the funds had been used to supplement the income of officers and informants.

Although the Inspector General's report of the investigation has not been made public, the General Accounting Office has given Yosemite a clean bill of health of some of these matters.

It is believed that Berkowitz, upon hearing of these findings, wrote the January 15th letter alleging the possible misconduct of Robert O. Binnewies in the "secret taping of a political conversation." However, the key factor is that the impression of NPS spokespeople of Berkowitz's letter is not that Binnewies told him to secretly tape the meetings, but that Scott Connelly, senior law enforcement officer, told Berkowitz that Binnewies said to tape the meeting.

Duncan Morrow of the NPS Washington DC office clearly states that Binnewies is not being transfered because of some alleged misconduct. Binnewies, himself, chose the move and was not asked to move. "At this point, while an investigation is pending, there is not and cannot be the inference that the transfer is in any way punitive," Morrow said.

After Berkowitz's allegations had been made, NPS director William Mott, demanded a full investigation. According to Morrow, "if the investigation bears out grounds for disciplinary action, it will be dealt with at that time.

(*Mariposa Gazette*, January 30, 1986).

.. or bee

Bee

25¢

VALLEY EDITION

Copyright 1986 The Fresno Bee ★ ★

Park chief allegedly made secret taping

By GENE ROSE
Bee staff writer

Yosemite Superintendent Robert O. Binnewies was relieved of duties last week for allegedly ordering park rangers to secretly record a March 1983 meeting with Charles Cushman, a longtime critic of the park service's handling of private land within parks boundaries.

National Park Service Director William Penn Mott removed Binnewies pending an investigation by the Department of Interior, the parent agency for the park service.

The allegations were made by Paul D. Berkowitz, a park ranger who claims he was ordered to participate in recording the conversations. Berkowitz made the charges in a Jan. 15 letter to Mott and five congressmen, including Charles Pashayan, R-Fresno, and Tony Coelho, D-Merced.

Berkowitz wrote that he and Scott

Connelly of the park's law enforcement had been ordered to record a conversation between Binnewies and Cushman held in the superintendent's office.

The subject was one the two men had disagreed about for seven years — the treatment of people who own private land in Yosemite. Cushman believes the park service uses a heavy hand with those property owners. He organized National Inholders Association in the late 1970s to address his concerns.

The meeting was held to discuss Wawona, an area of private ownership within Yosemite. Cushman owns property in Wawona.

According to Berkowitz's letter, "Superintendent Binnewies requested that the law enforcement staff assist him by placing a miniature radio transmitting device in his office for the purpose of having a political private inholders negotiations meeting surreptitiously monitored and tape recorded."

"Law enforcement office personnel installed the transmitter and were then situated outside the building in a van where they monitored and recorded the radio broadcast conversation utilizing electronic surveillance equipment normally reserved for use in undercover drug operations" in Yosemite.

Berkowitz said he participated in the operation because he was ordered to by Connelly.

"At the conclusion of this incident, Mr. Connelly turned the recording directly over to Mr. Binnewies. Upon returning to the van, Mr. Connelly addressed me by command, 'This never happened!' and 'Don't ever tell anybody about this".

Duncan Morrow, a parks service spokesman in Washington, D.C., said Mott learned of the allegations Thursday morning and ordered a full investi-

See Yosemite, back page

(*Fresno Bee*, January 30, 1986).

Those headlines and stories reflected a complete distortion of the actual chronology of events, concealing the fact that I had first reported the bugging incident to the OIG more than one-and-a-half years earlier. I was unable to publicly challenge any of these lies, having been placed under an official gag order by Regional Director Chapman, and instructed by my supervisors to not speak with members of the press.

Further frustrating my own and any other efforts to get the true story out to the media were the captivating accounts of the January 28th space shuttle *Challenger* disaster that understandably dominated the news headlines for weeks. That tragic event pushed any and all accounts about the scandal in Yosemite to the back pages of even state and local newspapers.

Nevertheless, as part of their spin and distortion of the facts, the Washington office of the NPS also made the preposterous assertion that Binnewies' hasty "reassignment" to San Francisco was unrelated to the bugging. They tried to make it appear that they had not previously known about the incident. In its January 30 story, the *Fresno Bee* related

> Duncan Morrow, a parks service spokesman in Washington, D.C., said [Director] Mott learned of the allegations Thursday morning and ordered a full investigation. Binnewies was then offered and accepted a transfer to a management position in the parks service western regional office.
>
> "At this point, while an investigation is pending, there is not, and cannot be the inference that this transfer is in any way punitive," Morrow said. "If the investigation bears out grounds for disciplinary action, it will be dealt with at that time."
>
> One park official, who spoke only on the condition that he not be identified, said Mott wanted to fire Binnewies on the spot, but was advised not to because it would be a violation of civil service guidelines.

William Mott had assumed the position of NPS Director only seven months earlier, in May of 1985. He succeeded Russell E. Dickenson, a Carter appointee who was the only Interior Department bureau chief to be retained by the Reagan administration in 1981. Dickenson was director of the NPS when I transferred to Yosemite, and he served in that position throughout most of the period that I was attempting to file reports of misconduct with both NPS and Interior Department officials. Dickenson almost surely knew about the bugging incident, but it's possible that Mott did not.

The OIG had known about the bugging since at least June of 1984, when I first met with Agent Lunsford. The GAO knew about it since at least November of 1985. I even had them on tape saying they would tell Vento about the incident.

The OIG is supposed to report its findings to both Congress and to the Secretary of the Interior, who directly oversees the Director of the NPS. The first OIG report – the one prepared by Lunsford – had been provided to the NPS and Director Mott (as well as Regional Director Chapman) on August 28, 1985. But that report made no mention of the bugging.

The GAO has a statutory responsibility to report its findings to Congress; in this case, Congressman Bruce Vento, who had ordered the GAO investigation. Given the relationship between the Director of the NPS and both the Secretary of the Interior as well as Representative Vento, it is inconceivable that Director Dickenson did not know about the bugging. But Mott might not have *fully* known about what was going on in Yosemite if the GAO and Representative Vento, along with the other senior NPS officials in the D.C. and Western Regional offices, had kept it a secret from the new Republican director.

On a broader agency scale, if Mott and the rest of the NPS directorate were truly furious and "wanted to fire Binnewies on the spot," it was probably not so much because the bugging had actually occurred, but because the incident could no longer be contained and had finally been made public. The real focus of Mott's displeasure was clarified in a January 27, 1986 memorandum regarding "the Yosemite situation" that he sent to Western Regional Director Howard Chapman. Within days of receiving a copy of my letter to Congressman Coelho, Mott euphemistically concurred with the decision that had previously been made to permanently eliminate my own and the other two Yosemite investigator positions (mine, Hinson's, and one other) because, as Mott phrased it, "it is my feeling that they cause conflicts."[6] But Mott expressed no concerns over "conflicts" created by Lee Shackelton or Scott Connelly, much less Jim Loach. Their conduct in orchestrating, carrying out, and concealing the bugging was, apparently, of no concern and was not perceived as any form of conflict, whatsoever. None of their positions were adversely affected.

Further outraged, on February 3, 1986, I hastily sent a second heated letter to Congressman Coelho, copying the same mixed group of Congressmen. This letter began,

> Having received no written reply from your office, I perceive the recent "press-leak" of my January 15, 1986 letter as a form of response on your part. It is unfortunate that these leaks and releases have been less than complete and have, therefore, resulted in misleading press coverage which conveys the misimpression that the Superintendent's Office bugging is an incident that I only recently reported…prompted by supposed vindictiveness and vengeance. Such accounts are, in my opinion, both unfair and destructive. These press spurred misconceptions have been the source of considerable anxiety for – and hostility directed toward – my wife… and me. As you well know, the incident related in my January 15 letter was first reported long ago – 1-1/2 to 2 years ago – to the Of-

fice of the Inspector General, and was subsequently again reported to your G.A.O. auditors when I spoke with them November 6 and 12 [11], 1995. Attempt was made to report this and other matters even earlier... but sadly, no one at any level of the National Park Service or Department of the Interior seemed willing to listen or investigate my claims.

The letter continued for another two pages, and included selected quotations from my October 15, 1985 testimony, reinforcing my concerns over the lack of accountability in the NPS and the absence of any credible avenues through which to report misconduct.

In many respects, my impassioned, if awkwardly worded letters to Representatives Coelho and Vento were a waste of time and energy. It was clear by now that they were a part of the problem and more than likely orchestrating the cover-up. But by copying those letters to any number of non-allied members of Congress, both Republican and Democrat, I apparently forced their hand. Also, the suggestion that I was prepared to make the full content of my taped GAO interviews available to the press, was more than Coelho and Vento could deal with. They were forced to finally acknowledge my report about the bugging, and at least create the appearance of an investigation.

Endnotes

1. Paul Berkowitz to Congressman Tony Coelho, complaint letter, Jan. 15, 1986.

2. Dale Champion, "Yosemite Park Chief Replaced," *San Francisco Chronicle,* Jan. 25, 1986.

3. Ronald B. Taylor, "Yosemite Chief's Firing Tied to Ranger Morale, Crime," *Los Angeles Times,* Jan. 29, 1986.

4. "Berkowitz makes further allegations," *Mariposa Gazette,* Jan. 30, 1986.

5. Gene Rose, "Park chief allegedly made secret taping," *Fresno Bee,* Jan. 30, 1986. Also, "Binnewies transfer followed accusations of bugging," *Merced* (CA) *Sun-Star* (McClatchy News Service), Jan. 28, 1986.

6. "Bill" Mott (NPS Director), "Note to Howard Chapman, Western Region," Jan. 27, 1986.

CHAPTER SEVENTEEN

Double Cover
(The O.I.G. Covers Its Tracks)

T he very same day that my second letter went out to Congressman Coelho marked the beginning of the OIG's long-overdue investigation into the bugging. By that time both Superintendent Binnewies and Chief Park Ranger Wendt had been replaced; Binnewies for his involvement in the bugging, and Wendt for other unrelated issues.[1] But all the other players in the scandal remained, unaffected.

On February 3, 1986, OIG Agent Richard Berta arrived in Yosemite to begin his investigation. We met that afternoon. The consensually taped interview begins with Agent Berta declaring:

> My visit here is prompted by a letter that you wrote on January 15, 1986 regarding allegations of bugging of this particular office, Mr. Binnewies' office, by law enforcement personnel from Yosemite Park, the Ranger Service. Can you shed some light on that incident other than what is already given in your correspondence?

My first words were to remind him,

> First of all, it should be pointed out that that letter indicates that it was reported to [OIG Special Agent] Steve Lunsford about a year and half to two years ago. So that is not a new revelation; it should not be for the I.G., nor for the Park Service, for that matter, assuming that they communicate with you guys.

From there, I described in detail the entire sequence of events, beginning with Connelly instructing me to gather up the surveillance equipment and drive with him to the parking area in front of the superintendent's office. As the story unfolded, Agent Berta probed one aspect that I had not previously addressed.

BERKOWITZ: Connelly told me to wait in the van. He was going to go in and he told me he was going to be setting up a bug in this office, that the superintendent had requested that that occur.

BERTA: The superintendent requested that a bug be planted in his office. Who did he make that request to?

BERKOWITZ: I don't know specifically. I know that Connelly related to me that this was being done at the request of Superintendent Binnewies. I can speculate if you want to hear it. But I'll leave that for later if you want to ask it.

BERTA: Go ahead and speculate.

BERKOWITZ: I would speculate that Lee Shackelton, being the Chief Law Enforcement Officer, would be the person that he would go to, to request assistance or guidance in how to pursue something like that. Besides which, just with the structure of the Law Enforcement Office being the way it was, nothing happened up there that Shackelton didn't know about and sanction. He made perfectly sure that he knew, or tried to know, about what everybody was doing.

BERTA: So Shackelton would have had to have known about this and sanctioned it?

BERKOWITZ: Logically, yeah. And I did subsequently learn that even if he did not know about it prior to its occurrence, he did know about it subsequent to its occurrence...

As it turned out, my assessment of the power structure and office dynamics, and my speculation about who had actually helped arrange the bugging, was dead-on.

The interview continued, as I once again related the details of how Binnewies assisted Connelly in selecting a location to plant the bug, how we monitored and recorded the entire meeting, how Connelly took the recorded tapes and turned them over to Binnewies, and then ordered me, "This never happened. Don't ever tell anybody about this." I continued, still attempting to emphasize my frustration over the larger "system failure" and obstruction I experienced nearly every step of the way in my efforts to report what had occurred.

BERKOWITZ: OK. A long, long time passed. I knew that this had happened. I knew that it was shady. I knew that, at that point, I knew that basically you couldn't go to Binnewies to report any kind of misconduct by Shackelton or Connelly or any of those guys. In my mind that just compromised things completely. And I didn't do much about it except try to find somebody to report it to, as was detailed in the testimony of October 15th, 'cause there was nobody to tell it to. However in very open senses, I talked about that I knew there were lousy things going on here, and that the superintendent was compromised, and that there was a bugging incident involved here, and spoke about it relatively freely, especially in the group of people that I worked with and felt, more or less, trust in. And so, we're talking now, a couple years passing. I, well, whenever I first called up Steve [Lunsford] and he came here, and I *did* tell him about it. I told him the first time he was here with [his supervisor] Dave Smith. And then I think about a week later he was here with a Secret Service agent from Fresno, Ralph Curtis.

BERTA: The issue here, of course, is, was there a bugging contrary to Departmental policy.

I should have, but did not at the time pick up on Berta's curious omission of a reference to any inquiry into a potential criminal violation.

BERKOWITZ: OK. When I told it to Lunsford when Curtis was here, Curtis's reaction was something like, "Jesus, that's a serious felony." OK. Lunsford, essentially, echoed that sentiment and very explicitly told me not to talk about that to anybody. OK. That's all that happened. Then all this other stuff, you know, went down, and I never did get interviewed about that incident, even though Steve [Lunsford] knew about it, Ralph Curtis knew about it, Dave Smith knew about it. So in my mind, when they started coming out with this stuff that there was no evidence of any wrong doing and stuff like that, the only conclusion I could reach was that they hadn't even addressed this thing. I knew they hadn't investigated it, because they didn't ask me enough questions to pursue it. OK. I wasn't going to, at that point then approaching October, I had the opportunity to testify before Congress. On my day off, I think probably five days before the hearing, which would have been a Thursday or Friday night or afternoon, I was up at my desk on my off time, working on my testimony for Congress. And Jim Loach, who is the, was the Wawona District Ranger prior to ---

BERTA: [Interrupting] That's something I want to ask you. You mentioned his name. You talked about Mr. Binnewies being in here, and Mr. Cushman being in here. But I talked to Steve about it, and he said he went back and he had some notes and Jim Loach was on there.

BERKOWITZ: I didn't give Steve [Lunsford] Cushman's name 'cause I didn't remember it.

BERTA: You didn't know it, I know. But there was Jim Loach, was in his notes. Was Jim Loach in here with ---

Though I didn't realize it at the time, Agent Berta (like the GAO auditors before him) was now inadvertently confirming that the OIG had, indeed, quietly looked into the bugging incident, long ago, but took no action and kept their inquiry a secret. I had never mentioned Jim Loach in any of my conversations or interviews with Agent Lunsford, because I had not really known Loach, at the time, or that Loach was a party to the bugging. That meant that Lunsford must have learned about Loach's involvement through inquiries he made back in 1984, after I first told him and his boss about the bugging incident. So Lunsford had known about Loach (and, therefore, Chuck Cushman) even before I did, which was not until Loach, himself, made the admission to me just prior to my testimony. That would explain why Loach was not alarmed when I told him that I'd already reported the bugging incident to the OIG. He was not alarmed because he *knew* the OIG already knew, and that they weren't going to do anything more about it – *hadn't* done anything about it for the past two years. That would also explain the GAO comment about Lunsford having somehow secured the tapes. But no official acknowledgement or action of any kind had been (or would be) taken about any of it until I pressed the matter in my letters to Congress, challenging the GAO report and Bruce Vento's press release. It was only then that the charade of an "official" investigation and disciplinary action was initiated, leading to Agent Berta's arrival in the park.

I jumped in before Berta could finish his sentence.

BERKOWITZ: Here's how Jim Loach gets tied in. And I didn't know about it until before the testimony. I was getting ready to testify. Jim was up there in the office, too. He said, "What are you doing?" I said I'm preparing my testimony for next week. He said "Let's take a walk." OK. So we took a walk. He was obviously agitated. Not agitated in a hostile sense, but very nervous. And through the grapevine, he acknowledged, in fact, through Bill Blake [who] is probably his best friend here, and I had told Bill Blake that I knew about a bugging incident involving the superintendent. Jim acknowledged, in essence, that that's how he had heard about it. And, he expressed his very deep concern that if I testified about that, that he would be compromised. And at that point he told me that he had been the one who had initially recommended to the superintendent that he have the conversation recorded. OK. So when Jim was still the Wawona District Ranger, dealing with Cushman and dealing with private lands up there, anticipating this meeting that Cushman was going to have with Binnewies, Loach told me that he had recommended to Binnewies that he tape record the conversation, because he said that you couldn't trust Cushman. He also, because of that, because he felt that he might be implicated in this thing, expressed concerns for his career. Further, [he] expressed concerns because he realized if that got out, that Binnewies would be dumped in a second and that once Binnewies was out, that would make [assistant superintendent] Laney, I guess Jim Laney, the [now] Acting Superintendent, quite possibly a permanent superintendent, and that he didn't think he'd be able to work and have the direct line to Laney that he did with Binnewies, if there were political considerations. And he expressed them in terms of being able to benefit the District, since he had a direct pipeline to Binnewies, he could get directly to him and get the things he wanted. But he felt that he wouldn't have that with Laney and that he would, in essence, if Laney became superintendent, have to leave the park. OK. My response to him was, as a quote, "Jim, I'm not going to lie for you," and that I've already reported this, and whatever happens is going to happen, assuming anybody investigates it.

BERTA: What is Loach's position?

BERKOWITZ: He is now the Valley District Ranger. He is my second-removed supervisor, and was at the time.

BERTA: He works for [the new Chief Park Ranger]?

BERKOWITZ: Yeah. He would be one of the three district rangers under [the Chief Ranger]. Right. [Loach is] basically the ranger in charge of Yosemite Valley, which is probably the biggest district ranger job in the country.

BERTA: So he's responsible for law enforcement and ---?

BERKOWITZ: Law enforcement, search and rescue, fire presently is an independent function that he doesn't have. But, yeah, campgrounds, law enforcement, search and rescue, virtually anything. And for that matter, he even has some measure of input to maintenance on matters that affect the Valley. So he asked me, he didn't come right out and ask it. He was definitely two-stepping it. He was saying, "I don't want to tell you what to do. I don't want to ask you what to do. But here's what's going to happen if you talk about this before Congress." And that he would certainly appreciate whatever consideration I could give him for his career. And I told him, again, "I'm not going to lie for you. It's already been reported," and all that. "But for the sake of not embarrassing the Park Service any further, I will not bring it up, specifically, before Congress, because presumably they already know about it, by my having related it to Steve [Lunsford]." And, therefore, I did not. However, in the testimony, I did allude to it, because I said and I believe, in specific statutory violations. Well, I may be wrong about that, but it's certainly one that I believe, and it was reinforced by [Secret Service agent] Curtis and Steve [Lunsford] when they heard about. That's basically it, except for this...

I finished up the interview with yet another overview of what Andy Hutchison from FLETC had told me about Shackelton saying he could "have Binnewies' job" if he wanted it, pointing out to Berta, "That's why I know that Shackelton was privy to the incident." Berta replied, "Well, I'm going to be talking to Mr. Shackelton."

The entire meeting and interview with Berta lasted about an hour as, once again, I related every detail of the entire incident, from start to finish.[2] Subsequently, Agent Berta also finally interviewed Binnewies, Loach, Connelly, and Shackelton. But there was at least one other critical witness that Berta did *not* interview; a *victim* interview he did *not* conduct that would ultimately confirm the predetermined course of his investigation.

* * *

Agent Berta's 27-page report, identified under file #6VI 055 (amended), is dated May 9, 1986; more than three years after the bugging occurred, two years after I first reported the incident to the OIG, a year after Agent Lunsford's (first) OIG report was completed (but not released); seven months after my Congressional testimony, six months after my recorded meetings with the GAO, and five months after release of the GAO report. It is this latter OIG report, alone, that contained documentation of allegations and any investigation and findings related to the Binnewies-Cushman bugging incident.

However, even *that* document – the second OIG report, prepared by Agent Berta – made absolutely no reference to the initial detailed report I personally related to Agent Lunsford and his colleagues two years earlier, in June of 1984, or to the subsequent recorded report I made to GAO investigators in November of 1985. Instead, for its genesis, that second report relies solely upon (and cites only) the January 15, 1986 letter I directed to Representative Coelho, poignantly challenging the credibility of the GAO "Investigative Report" and their failure to pursue the majority of my allegations, including the bugging incident. That letter is cited (but not included in the report) as the sole source of the complaint leading to Agent Berta's investigation into the bugging incident. The dates reflected in file #6VI 055 confirm that the OIG failed to document my complaint and did not pursue an *official* investigation of the bugging incident for nearly two years, until that story was about to break in the press. To at least that extent, the second OIG report – the one finally documenting the bugging incident – was also a cover-up.

The initial (unreleased) version of Agent Berta's report #6VI 055, was hastily finished and dated February 19, 1986. That report documented the exact same events and written statements as a later, amended version, and included the notation that,

> Superintendent Binnewies...did not obtain approval from the U.S. Department of Justice Attorney. Therefore, the interception conducted at his request failed to comply with the Attorney General's memorandum to Heads and Inspectors General of Executive Departments and Agencies...

But the first version of the report contained no reference to NPS or Interior policies that were simultaneously violated. That omission was corrected in the report, modified and re-issued on May 9, 1986, as "6VI 055 (amended)," citing violation of Interior Department Manual 446, Chapter 3 (09/29/86). At the very least, then, the findings contained within the OIG report *did* confirm that the bugging violated both executive order and Departmental policy. That point was reinforced when Binnewies, at least, lost *his* job over the incident.

But even that amended May 9, 1986 report contained absolutely no clear reference or accurate citation of *criminal statutes* that might have been violated. Instead, the report actually misstated the law by reciting only selectively edited portions of 18 USC 2511(2)(d), incorrectly dismissing a violation because, according to Agent Berta's narrative, that section "clearly exempts the interception of oral communications where one of the parties to the communication has given prior consent, even though he is not acting under color of law." In fact, however, the only way Agent Berta's summation would have been true was if the statute did not also include the critical "subexception" that continues in the very same sentence,

> unless such communication is intercepted for the purpose of committing any criminal or tortious act in violation of the Constitution or laws of the United States or of any State or for the purpose of committing any other injurious act.

The summation and analysis contained in Agent Berta's narrative report inexplicably omitted that entire, critical, second half of that very same subsection. The investigation apparently did not probe – and the report offers absolutely no commentary on whether that critical qualifying component of the statute might have been violated.

The report, and apparently the investigation, gave absolutely no consideration to the exploration of an "unlawful motive" or state violation that might have triggered the curiously omitted "subexception," and the accompanying violation of criminal and civil provisions. In fact, the manner in which the law is misstated (by omission) in the narrative report suggests an attempt to conceal, or at least ignore, the fact that those additional elements are even contained in the statute! The only place where an accurate reflection of the statute appeared was as an attachment buried at the very back of the report.

As I had tried to impress upon Agent Berta, 18 USC 2511 did *not* excuse the interception and recording under the dubious circumstances of the Binnewies-Cushman incident. Furthermore, the statute did not preclude consideration of other additional laws, federal as well as state, regulating eavesdropping activities. But Agent Berta's investigation never even examined or looked into what federal or assimilated state criminal laws might actually have been violated, including violation of 18 USC 241, Conspiracy Against Rights, or 18 USC 242, Deprivation of Rights Under Color of Law.[3]

In fact, there was nothing in the report indicating that the investigation was ever brought to the attention of federal prosecutors or that they were ever consulted on the case; at least not in writing. The OIG's failure to consult with anyone in the Department of Justice was subsequently confirmed in a June 24, 1986 letter signed by Danny P. Danigan, Assistant Inspector General for Administration.

Acting on my behalf, Sonora (CA) attorney John Paul Hollinrake had previously submitted a Freedom of Information Act request, seeking, among other documents,

> Any communications, i.e. letters, memorandum, etc. between the Office of the Inspector General and the Department of Justice concerning the filing of criminal charges against any individuals who were the subject of the investigation [6VI 055], and specifically any communications concerning violation of 18 USC 13; Calif. Penal Code section 632.

Responding to that request, Danigan acknowledged that,

> The files of the Office of the Inspector General do not contain any of the requested documents.[4]

A criminal investigation was never conducted. Agent Berta's investigation was purely an administrative inquiry, and an incomplete one, at that.

That the OIG did not want to investigate the bugging, at all, is highlighted by their failure to do so until forced by public disclosures made nearly two years after the matter was first brought to their attention. Then, when finally left with no choice, they attempted to conceal their own early inaction, and pursued their investigation only half-heartedly, giving no consideration whatsoever to potential criminal or civil violations. All of these factors add strength to the theory that the OIG, itself, actively participated in the cover-up of the bugging incident even *after* the purported shake-up and reform of their own office arising from their early mishandling of the case.[5] That approach has proven to be a long-standing problem for the OIG. As recently as 2012, a survey of the OIG's own workforce found a disturbingly high number of employees (including their own special agents) who, themselves, questioned whether the OIG conducts its work in a manner that is free from improper influence from the Department of the Interior and its subordinate agencies.[6] Findings like that led at least one independent watchdog organization to conclude that "Under the current system, IG's revel in petty scandals and flee profound corruption."[7] That summation aligns very closely with my own experiences and observations made independently, and not just "under the current system," but over the last several decades.

And so the simple explanation of what was going on is probably the closest to the truth, and has nothing to do with legal issues. Given the players and the politics behind the scenes, no matter what the law might have prohibited or allowed, it's far more likely that no one in power really wanted to touch the case or pursue a prosecution; not the U.S. Attorney, not the NPS or the Department of the Interior, and certainly not Bruce Vento or anyone else on his Subcommittee. Not one of these individuals or organizations, including the supposedly independent Office of the Inspector General, could stand the thought of officially labeling Chuck Cushman the victim of a federal criminal conspiracy.

Still, this second OIG report did finally confirm that the bugging incident had occurred, and that Loach, Binnewies, Shackelton, and Connelly had all knowingly planned and/or participated in the incident. When finally interviewed by the OIG and asked for written statements, all four of these individuals admitted some level of knowledge and participation in the incident, but accusingly pointed fingers at one another in their various attempts to place blame for the inception and implementation of the plan.

The handwritten statement signed by Binnewies, presented here in its entirety, is dated February 4, 1986.

> In March 1983 I scheduled a meeting with Mr. Charles Cushman,
> who claimed to be representing the Board of Directors of the

Wawona Property Management, Inc. Prior to that meeting, District Ranger James Loach warned me to be guarded in my conversation with Cushman, and he recommended that I tape record the meeting. I agreed to his recommendation and contacted the Law Enforcement Office to request a tape recorder. I don't recall who I talked to, but Scott Connelly arrived at my office a short time later and placed a device out of sight in a roll top desk in my office. I assumed he placed a tape recorder in the desk. I didn't realize that he placed a transmitter in my office and that the transmission was being recorded in a van. Jim Loach and I knew the conversation was being taped. I did not inform Cushman that it was being taped (Loach indicated no surprise because he had recommended the taping). At the conclusion of the meeting, Scott Connelly appeared in my office and handed me two tapes, and removed the listening device. It was at this point that I realized the conversation had been transmitted outside the office. I would like to add that this is the only time in my professional career that I have ever recorded a conversation without the knowledge of all participants. The prompt reaction to the Berkowitz letter, resulting in my removal and the attendant widespread media coverage has caused me public disgrace and acute personal embarrassment. This action on my part was a lapse in judgement [sic], but my intentions have always been to further the interests of the N.P.S. [8]

Loach, in his written statement, contradicted not only the superintendent, but what he had also told me; first emphatically denying, and then claiming he merely did not "believe" he had suggested that Binnewies tape the meeting. He acknowledged that he knew the meeting was being secretly recorded, but only because Binnewies had told him before the meeting began:

At no time prior to the meeting between Binnewies and Cushman did I recommend that Binnewies record the meeting. I cautioned Binnewies to be guarded in his conversation with Cushman, but it would have been presumtious [sic] of me to recommend tape recording the meeting. I don't recall specifics of the discussion between Binnewies and I; however, I don't believe that I ever suggested recording the meeting.

When I walked in the door to attend the meeting Binnewies informed me that he was going to record the meeting. I was not disturbed, but I know it was news to me that a recording was being made. I never saw the device planted in the office and I left prior to anyone bringing tapes into the room.

On at least two occasions Berkowitz and I discussed the covert recording of the Binnewies-Cushman meeting. In those discussions we talked about the implications for the N.P.S. and the magnitude of the potential problems for future dealings with the National Inholders Association. I never discussed Jim Laney, nor the possibility that Binnewies could be fired. I certainly didn't tell him that I recommended that the meeting be taped.[9]

Connelly, in his statement, claimed he was only acting under instructions from his own supervisor, Lee Shackelton. Connelly denied, however, that he had ever told me "this never happened" and "don't ever tell anybody about this."

In approximately March 1983 I was assigned to the special drug investigation team. The team had various types of surveillance equipment available including covert transmitters and receiver/recorders. During this time my supervisor Lee Shackelton informed me that he had a request from the superintendent to use an Audio Intelligence Device to record a meeting that the superintendent was having with a Mr. Cushman. Shackelton said Cushman represented the Wawona Property Owners and there was a fear that Cushman might employ coercive or underhanded tactics. At Shackelton's direction, I and fellow employee Paul Berkowitz left the office to deploy the listening device (Berkowitz, like myself, was supervised by Shackelton). Binnewies and I discussed the placement of the microphone, and I eventually taped it to the bottom of a coffee table. The table was located in front of a sofa which Binnewies stated would be occupied by Jim Loach and Cushman. Binnewies intended to sit on the opposite side of the table. I returned to the van where Berkowitz was monitoring the receiver and insured [sic] that everything was working. I then returned to the office leaving Mr. Berkowitz to monitor and record the meeting. Towards the conclusion of the meeting I once again returned to the van. When the meeting had ended I removed the tape(s) from the recorder and carried them to Binnewies' office. When I arrived at his office I asked Binnewies what he wanted me to do with the tapes. He told me that he would take custody of it (or them). I gave him the tape or tapes, removed the bug and returned to my normal duties. I never told Mr. Berkowitz "This never happened" and "Don't ever tell anybody about this."[10]

Finally, in his statement, Shackelton claimed that he was able to recall only that Binnewies had called to request use of the A.I.D. body wire to record a meeting. Shackelton denied that he had done anything more than respond to the superintendent's request for assistance and the use of law enforcement personnel and (specifically) electronic surveillance equipment ("the Audio Intelligence Device"). Instead, according to Shackelton, he "put Connelly and Binnewies in contact [with each other] to work out the details" of the bugging:

I don't recall the date, but I do remember Bob Binnewies telephoned me at my office to request the loan of recording equipment. In late 1982, and prior to this telephone call, I received an Audio Intelligence Device through a government purchase order. I showed the equipment to most of my supervisors, and I believe Binnewies was included. I recall that Binnewies said he wanted to use the equipment to tape record a meeting, but I don't remember any other details of the conversation. Because Connelly was technically more proficient in the use of the equipment, I informed Binnewies that Connelly would handle it. I don't recall the circumstances, but I put Connelly and Binnewies in contact to work out the details. I never suggested or recommended that Binnewies use this equipment.[11]

Elements of truth and a measure of lies (or at least selective memory) are present in the accounts provided by all four of these individuals (Binnewies, Loach, Connelly, and Shackelton). Notably, however, while all four individuals indisputably knew that the bugging had taken place, apparently none of them took steps to report the incident; a violation in and of itself.[12] To the contrary, most if not all went to great pains to keep the incident secret and prevent its disclosure to officials having jurisdiction over the violation(s).

I was never re-interviewed or requested to assist the OIG in making sense of the discrepancies. Agent Berta, in his investigation, apparently never attempted to reconcile those conflicting statements, at least some of which had to have been lies amounting to "false statements" made during an investigation; a separate federal offense punishable under felony provisions.[13] Andy Hutchison was never interviewed about the boast attributed to Shackelton. The prospect that the bugging incident might at some point have been used to manipulate or even blackmail Binnewies was never explored.

But even more significant as proof of the government's reluctance to pursue a legitimate investigation of any kind is that the target/victim of the bugging, Chuck Cushman, as an "aggrieved person" was never interviewed or even officially notified about this incident, at all.[14] He was never queried about the circumstances leading up to the meeting, or why or how the meeting was arranged. He was never asked about follow-up conversations or negotiations with Binnewies, Loach, or other NPS officials after the meeting, or if he had ever been pressured or threatened. In fact, he did not learn that his conversation had been secretly recorded until after I had contacted him, and the story was about to break in the newspapers, more than three years after the fact! But even then, he was never interviewed or even contacted by the OIG or by investigators from any other agency.

Cushman has speculated that Binnewies, Loach, and the NPS were looking for a way to embarrass or blackmail him; hoping that something would be caught on tape that could be used to force Cushman off the National Park System Advisory Board, or to diminish his capacity to run the National Inholders Association or represent the Wawona inholders.[15] If so, that could have triggered both the criminal and civil provisions of 18 USC 2511. But again, none of these potentially "tortious" or "injurious" motives was ever explored. It's almost certain that Cushman *never* would have known that he was the victim of an illegal government bugging and that his rights had been violated by government officials, if the NPS, the OIG, the GAO, and Representative Vento had been more successful in their efforts to control the scandal and maintain their cover-up. *They*, apparently, believed they had no obligation tell Chuck Cushman, and believed that Cushman had no right to know about any of it.

The controversy that resulted from the new OIG report and these purportedly new revelations resulted in another flurry of media attention to conditions at Yosemite National Park. For the first time, details of the bugging were receiving national press coverage, and the names of NPS officials implicated in that and other previously "un-reported" incidents and activities were appearing on the front pages of newspapers throughout the West.[16] Among the names now receiving attention was Jim Loach, who had first suggested to Superintendent Binnewies that he record their meeting with Cushman. Also implicated in the bugging, for the first time, was chief law enforcement officer Leland Shackelton and park prosecutor Scott Connelly, both of whom were identified as having assisted Binnewies in the bugging.

(*Fresno Bee*, Friday, May 9, 1986).

In truth, Binnewies was probably the most innocent player of the group, to the extent that he was most certainly naïve about what was really going on. In my own limited interactions with him, I had always found him to be a soft-spoken and decent man who seemed to truly care about national parks, far more than he did about power and prestige. My guess is that in spite of his many years with the NPS (25 years, in all), he did not fully understand the Yosemite Mafia and how some of the real pow-er-players in the agency operated. More than anything, he was guilty of heeding very bad advice from some very bad and manipulative people who worked for him.

Prior to his appointment as Yosemite's superintendent, Binnewi-es was vice president of the National Audubon Society. Like most NPS managers, he did not have any real background in law enforcement, and he was not vested with law enforcement authority (although he could and did supervise law enforcement personnel). In fact, in an interview for a television documentary, he openly voiced the popular view about NPS law enforcement held by virtually every other superintendent and senior manager in the agency. Attempting to justify why law enforcement should not (and would not) be managed or practiced as a profession within the NPS, Binnewies claimed that "The park ranger career is definitely a pro-fession [but] it is not a police profession. It is not a criminal investigator profession. It's not purely a law enforcement profession." As much as Bin-newies' comments reflected a passionately-held attachment to the my-thology of the ranger image, they were, even more, a revealing expression of what amounted to the realization of a self-fulfilling prophecy, if ever there was one.

I was interviewed for that same documentary. More than hinting at widespread deficiencies in the NPS law enforcement program, I offered a somewhat more controversial – and heretical – dissenting view.

> They call it "ranger law enforcement" or "Park Service law enforce-ment," as opposed to any other kind of law enforcement, which is a fallacy. Basically, if you want to classify it, it ought to be classified as "professional law enforcement" and "unprofessional law enforce-ment." To say that there is a special "Park Service" type of law en-forcement is to create something out of the sky that doesn't exist. You're either a professional or you're not. [17]

So although Binnewies was not really trained or experienced in law enforcement activities, someone needed to take the fall and pay the price for what was internally viewed as an unfortunate public disclosure about NPS law enforcement; and that would be him. Ironically, Binnewies was also the only one to express regret for what had occurred and to offer an apology to Chuck Cushman (albeit three years after the fact). [18] None of the other three officials, all senior commissioned law enforcement offi-cers involved in suggesting, planning, and carrying out the bugging, was disciplined or suffered negative repercussions. In the meanwhile, almost immediately, I was subjected to a significant escalation in reprisal and vil-ification, labeled "responsible" for the superintendent being fired and for embarrassing the NPS.

Particularly memorable for me is a conversation I had with my [new] immediate supervisor, Bill Blake, the day that Loach's name appeared in the national newspapers. Blake approached me at work, at the foot of the stairs that led up to the District Ranger and Shift Supervisor's offices, with a somber and disgusted look. He advised me that he had seen the newspaper accounts about the bugging and mention of his friend, Jim Loach. He stated to me that "This is a sad day for the National Park Service." I paused for a moment, and then defiantly responded that I thought it had been a sad day when the bugging incident occurred.

From that point on, with Loach's role exposed, my life in Yosemite became impossible. My shifts and work assignments were manipulated to affect maximum disruption to my life. Previously approved leave for a long-scheduled vacation was canceled without explanation. All of the collateral duties I previously enjoyed (investigations coordinator, park firearms officer and range master, acting shift supervisor, etc.) were revoked. Those changes, I was told, could result in the downgrading of my position. Both Blake and Loach subjected me to frequent counseling sessions, reminding me that my loyalties must lie first with the NPS family and the "team" that was led by these two supervisors. Adding to their attempts at intimidation were their constant reminders that all of my actions were being closely scrutinized at the highest levels, because I was "in the focus," a phrase I heard time and again. My car was vandalized and our garden was torn up. I received anonymous phone calls at all hours conveying death threats along with disparaging comments and slurs. My then-wife and I became increasingly isolated in the community, as many of our friends were afraid to be seen with us, for fear that they, too, would be subjected to reprisal and swept up in my own acts of "career suicide."[19] It was clear that the NPS wanted me to quit my job and go away. But I was becoming increasingly incensed and stubborn. If I resigned, they won. Besides, under the conditions that had been created for me, I really had nowhere else to go and certainly no references with which to get a job in another agency. Though NPS officials formally denied that such a thing even existed, I was firmly positioned at the top of the NPS "blacklist."

I initiated a series of requests for a directed re-assignment out of Yosemite. These efforts were met with orchestrated resistance at virtually every level, with politicos (and even a future lobbyist) from one of the non-profit NPS partners reportedly weighing in, in an attempt to drive me out of the agency. One friend, a superintendent, confided that the Rocky Mountain Regional Director had issued orders prohibiting any parks in her region from accepting me through a reassignment. Another superintendent in Hawaii acknowledged that he received similar instructions from his own regional director.

* * *

Situations like these make for strange alliances.

Prior to these events, I didn't even know who Chuck Cushman was, and I had never heard of the National Inholders Association. To this day, I don't agree with most of Cushman's views. But whatever his views and however much they may conflict with my own (or those of the NPS), I still believe that he and his supporters deserve to be treated honestly, fairly, and legally in their interactions with government officials, including NPS managers and law enforcement personnel.

Knowing who Chuck Cushman was would not have made a difference in anything I did or said. It would, however, have explained a great deal for me about the political significance of what was occurring and why there had been such enormous resistance to my efforts to have the incident exposed. But for me there was never anything all that complicated or political about it. I wasn't taking sides in the conflict between Cushman and the NPS, or even in the debate over NPS land management policies and park inholders. The actions I took were a simple reflection of my own sense of integrity and my duty as a law enforcement officer. Unfortunately, what I saw as an attempt to honor and fulfill my constitutional oath of office, the management of the NPS saw a demonstration of betrayal and disloyalty to the agency. It was a unique situation highlighting the conflict between two competing sets of values and priorities (about what is "America's best idea"?) where I was fundamentally out of step with the values and priorities espoused and practiced by my employer, the National Park Service.

In the fall of 1986, with the assistance of Congressman Pashayan and pressure from Chuck Cushman, the NPS relented in providing me with a directed re-assignment to Whiskeytown National Recreation Area, located near Redding, California. The superintendent there, Ray Foust, had offered to take me, boldly stating he had nothing to hide and wasn't afraid to have a whistleblower and an honest law enforcement officer working for him. His willingness to assist created a unique opportunity for me to escape a horrible situation while still working for the NPS. In spite of the best efforts of many other officials in the agency, and though I have continued to be a "troublemaker," I somehow managed to advance over the years as a Special Agent, and eventually a Supervisory Special Agent for the last twenty years of my career.

Endnotes

1. Chris Cameron, recorded interview with the author, Nov. 14, 1984, discussing pending removal of Yosemite chief ranger Bill Wendt. Binnewies was replaced by Jack Morehead, the same person who had been brought in as chief park ranger (1971 to 1974) after the 1970 Yosemite Riot.

2. Recorded interview with Paul Berkowitz conducted by OIG Agent Richard Berta, Feb. 3, 1986.

3. 18 USC 241 states, "If two or more persons conspire to injure, oppress, threaten, or intimidate

any person in any State, Territory, Commonwealth, Possession, or District in the free exercise or enjoyment or any right or privilege secured to him by the Constitution or the Laws of the United States, or because of him having so exercised the same ... they shall be fined under this title or imprisoned not more than ten years, or both." 18 USC 242 states, "Whoever under color of any law, statute, ordinance, regulation, or custom, willfully subjects any person in any State, Territory, Commonwealth, Possession, or District to the deprivation of any rights, privileges, or immunities secured or protected by the Constitution or the laws of the United States ... shall be fined under this title or imprisoned not more than one year, or both."

4. Danny P. Danigan (DOI Office of the Inspector General, Assistant Inspector General for Administration) to John Paul Hollinrake (Attorney-at-Law), letter, June 30, 1986.

5. In the four year period that I was in Yosemite, the OIG went through a succession of five (5) different appointments to the position of Inspector General, starting with Robert W. Beuley (appointed "acting" 5/1/81), Arthur J. Dellinger Sr. (appointed "acting" 5/20/84), Robert W. Beuley (appointed "acting' 5/2/85), Thomas T. Sheehan (appointed "acting" 9/8/85), and James R. Richards (appointed I.G. 1/6/86).

6. DOI Office of the Inspector General, *2012 OIG Annual Survey Results*. Optional comments included, "I think there is a widespread distrust and low morale in the organization right now. There are at least perceptions the acting IG and COS [Chief of Staff] did not do the right thing, i.e., improperly quashed investigations and have not been forthright with Congress." Also, "Be careful with how much reports get softened to avoid 'slamming' the Department [of the Interior] in the interest of maintaining a good relationship."

7. Jeff Ruch, Executive Director, Public Employees for Environmental Responsibility, *Rising Doubts on Independence of Interior Inspector General*, Oct. 9, 2012.

8. Robert O. Binnewies, handwritten statement to OIG (complete and unedited), Feb. 4, 1986, DOI-OIG Case #6VI 055 (Amended).

9. James A Loach, handwritten statement to OIG (complete and unedited), Feb. 3, 1986, DOI-OIG Case #6VI 055 (Amended).

10. M. (Marshal) Scott Connelly, handwritten statement to OIG (complete and unedited), undated, DOI-OIG Case #6VI 055 (Amended).

11. Leland ("Lee") Shackelton, handwritten statement to OIG (complete and unedited), Feb. 4, 1986, DOI-OIG Case #6VI 055 (Amended).

12. 18 U.S.C. 4, Misprision of Felony.

13. 18 USC 1001.

14. 18 USC 2510(11); "aggrieved person" means a person who was a party to any intercepted wire, oral, or electronic communication or a person against whom the interception was directed.

15. Gene Rose, "Park chief allegedly made secret taping," *Fresno Bee*, Jan. 28, 1986.

16. Gene Rose, "Park chief allegedly made secret taping," *Fresno Bee*, Jan. 28, 1986; "Binnewies Admits Ordering Recording," *Fresno Bee*, May 9, 1986.

17. *Law of Nature: Park Rangers in Yosemite Valley*, 1986, John Philbin – "Philbin Philms," interviews with Superintendent Robert Binnewies and "law enforcement ranger" Paul Berkowitz.

18. Bob Binnewies to Chuck Cushman, letter of apology, May 6, 1986.

19. Albert D. Lauro, written statement documenting conversations with other NPS employees, Mar. 9, 1986.

PART 3

CHAPTER EIGHTEEN

Noble Cause Corruption

O ver the course of time, almost all of the allegations I first presented to the NPS, the DOI, the OIG, and the GAO, were proven to be true. Part of that proof would materialize only through the recurrence of the same conduct I first reported. But the bulk of the evidence supporting my claims had already been documented by the OIG in their initial (secret) investigative report, along with internal NPS memorandums. Unfortunately, by the time the press finally got ahold of that first report, the story was old and most of the players had moved on. I first saw the actual reports late in 1986, only after I'd left Yosemite, and newspaper reporter Gene Rose had written his last article on the affair. He subsequently reached out to me and gave me his own un-redacted copies, somehow obtained by the *Fresno Bee*. The NPS and the DOI succeeded in burying the story until the smoke had cleared, assuring that no one would ever learn about what had really happened. The damning findings contained in that report were never fully covered in the state or national news.

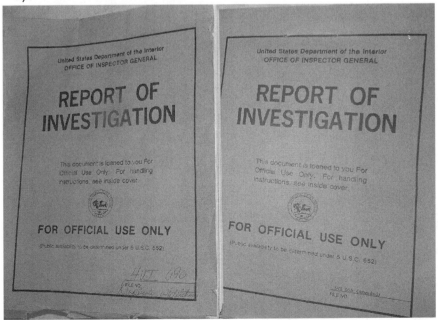

The two OIG reports. The first, Agent Lunsford's report #4VI 090, dated July 9, 1985, and the second, Agent Berta's report #6VI 055 (amended), dated May 9, 1986.

That first (unreleased) OIG Report, prepared by Agent Lunsford and identified under file #4VI 090, was finalized July 9, 1985, predating my Congressional testimony by several months. The report is several hundred pages long, and substantiated virtually every allegation I had made, going back as far back as 1983 (misappropriation of funds, falsification of reports and vouchers, expenditure of federal funds to send informants through the law enforcement academy, etc.). But the report contained absolutely no reference to the Binnewies-Cushman bugging incident, and made no mention of any inquiry into the concealment of exculpatory information or to the destruction of exculpatory evidence. Also absent from the report is any mention of the Park Service's efforts to obstruct the OIG investigation.

For some reason, that first OIG report focused almost exclusively on Lee Shackelton, and offered little if any reflection on the misconduct of others. Among the official conclusions presented in the report summary were the following points:

> Shackelton borrowed $1,000 ... from the Yosemite Natural History Association (YNHA), purportedly for the purpose of purchasing evidence. ... Shackelton used those monies to create a slush fund and pay travel expenses for a Confidential Informant. Procurement of those funds were [sic] in violation of NPS guidelines, NPS-32, dated June, 1981. ...
>
> Shackelton also used those funds to pay for 200 hours of seasonal law enforcement training and living expenses at Santa Rosa Junior College for an undercover operative, who was not a Government employee at the time. The training was to qualify the individual for a law enforcement commission. Shackelton used those funds to provide training without NPS authorization and in violation of Federal Personnel procedures. ... [1]
>
> Shackelton and other involved NPS personnel did not adhere to the established guidelines for the operation of the SIF [Special Imprest Fund], nor did they establish or maintain the appropriate accounting records for the fund....
>
> Shackelton was deliberately excluded from those who had authority to request or approve the obtaining of funds from the SIF, however, he performed those functions on a number of occasions that resulted in the improper expenditure of funds from the SIF....
>
> Shackelton authorized, approved, or spent, at least $3,829.99 from the SIF in non-compliance with existing NPS regulations and special procedures. Other NPS personnel failed to conduct required evaluations of the operation of the SIF that would have disclosed the misuse of the moneys by Shackelton....
>
> Investigation also revealed that Shackelton taught law enforcement related classes at Santa Rosa Junior College and received payment from the State of California while his time and attendance

records show full-time work status with the NPS. Between April 1978 and September 1984, Shackelton taught on 22 occasions totaling 176 hours without claiming annual leave. This does not include 11 occasions, 44 hours, when Shackelton took four hours annual leave instead of eight....

Damning as they may be, these and other summary statements prepared by the OIG are comparatively mild and incomplete when viewed next to witness statements and NPS memorandums contained in the body of the report:

> The reason Crockett read the guidelines to Shackelton was because of a history of poorly run (sloppy) operations by Shackelton....
>
> Lee Shackelton's philosophy was "it is easier to take punishment than to ask permission." ...
>
> Hinson told him that Shackelton was using informants that Hinson considered, from his experience, "not to be any good."
>
> Undercover narcotics purchases had to be performed by commissioned Law Enforcement Officers ... Shackelton used people to perform undercover narcotics purchases who did not have commissions. Shackelton used the noncommissioned operatives until he was told to stop....
>
> Shackelton ..."milked the account" by purchasing things that were not necessary for the investigation as well as overtime not on the investigation....
>
> Shackelton did not have authority to finance training for anyone, especially someone who was not a Government employee. Further, Shackelton did not have authority to use the Special Imprest fund to advance travel funds or pay personal expenses for anyone.[2]

Another witness reiterated that,

> Shackelton had a long history of poorly run operations and of not following instructions....
>
> Shackelton had extended law enforcement credentials to someone ... without going through the Regional Office.[3]
>
> Shackelton was under some pressure by ['Bill'] with the threat of a suit over money promised in the assignment as 'Willie' ["Bill's undercover name] vs. money earned. Under the circumstances, the timekeeper's actions were justified in questioning the overtime. ...[4]

Yet another witness, the retired ranger who ran the seasonal NPS law enforcement academy at Santa Rosa, acknowledged that,

> He considered it unusual and questionable that Shackelton would send a person to school before they were hired. [He] stated that he

asked Shackelton why he wanted to make [the undercover informant] a Ranger. Shackelton told [him] that he had gotten it from a good source that being a Park Ranger lended credibility to testimony in court.[5]

As to the success of the overall operation, another official acknowledged,

the main objective of the drug investigation, to penetrate the protective umbrella of YPCC management, was never achieved.[6]

Finally, the position taken by the U.S. Attorney's Office regarding these and other violations was confirmed with the following observation:

Assistant United States Attorney James White, Fresno, California, declined prosecution [of Shackelton, et al.] based upon his appraisal that the LEO [Law Enforcement Office] narcotics investigation was successful since it resulted in numerous guilty pleas or convictions and the OIG investigation did not show any personal profit or gain by NPS employees in the improper use of the SIF.[7]

That last comment is noteworthy for at least a couple of reasons.

* * *

Rationalizations like that offered by AUSA White are a reflection of what is today referred to as "Noble Cause Corruption."

Noble Cause Corruption has been described as "a mindset or sub-culture which fosters a belief that the ends justify the means ... adopt[ing] a philosophy that supports the notion that ... it is morally right to do whatever it takes to imprison those who prey on society, [a philosophy] sometimes embodied in the battle cry, "never let the truth stand in the way of justice." That synopsis was offered by retired Miami-Dade Police Department chief of criminal investigations Steve Rothlein, who is also an in-demand consultant and instructor on matters related to internal investigations and police corruption.[8] Another authority on police corruption, Wayne State University Professor Thomas J. Martinelli, has added that "each action [of Noble Cause Corruption] violates the U.S. Constitution, the officer's oath of office, and the public's trust in the policing profession."[9]

Though it did not yet have a name, this type of government conduct was identified and challenged as far back as 1928, by Justice Louis D. Brandeis, in *Olmstead v. United States.* That case involved a bootlegger whose lower court conviction in the Western District of Washington relied upon the admissibility of evidence obtained illegally by federal agents through a warrantless wiretap. On appeal, the majority ruled in favor of the government, allowing the conviction to stand. But writing for the minority, Brandeis offered what has since been recognized as one of the most important and subsequently validated dissents in Supreme Court history.

> By the laws of Washington, wire-tapping is a crime ... To prove its case, the Government was obliged to lay bare the crimes committed by its officers on its behalf. A federal court should not permit such a prosecution to continue ...
>
> Decency, security and liberty alike demand that government officials shall be subjected to the same rules of conduct that are commands to the citizen. In a government of laws, existence of the government will be imperilled [sic] if it fails to observe the law scrupulously. Our Government is the potent, the omnipresent teacher. For good or for ill, it teaches the whole people by its example. Crime is contagious. If the Government becomes a lawbreaker, it breeds contempt for law; it invites every man to become a law unto himself; it invites anarchy. To declare that in the administration of the criminal law the end justifies the means—to declare that the Government may commit crimes in order to secure the conviction of a private criminal—would bring terrible retribution. Against that pernicious doctrine this Court should resolutely set its face.[10]

The term Noble Cause Corruption was not coined until years later, in recognition of a pervasive approach to law enforcement that tolerates and even promotes a disregard for established legal process and procedures – including the rights of citizens to due process and other constitutional safeguards – in favor of arresting "bad guys" and assuring a conviction by whatever means necessary, up to and including law enforcement officials, themselves, breaking the law. The concept was exemplified not only in the conduct of Shackelton and his Yosemite associates, but also in AUSA White's rationale for declining a prosecution of Shackelton and others for that very conduct. Of course, none of this even comes close to addressing the motives behind acts such as falsifying time and attendance reports, accepting payment from both the NPS and the state of California for the same time spent instructing at the seasonal law enforcement academy, not to mention the use of government funds to pay off an extortion attempt. Noble Cause Corruption can and often does open the door to other forms of abuse and corruption, whether out of a sense of entitlement, a quest for power and prestige, or just raw greed.

But the concept of Noble Cause Corruption has application beyond just the law enforcement circles of government. The term can equally well be applied to superintendent Binnewies' justification for his own role in the bugging incident, reluctantly explaining to the OIG that "This action on my part was a lapse in judgment, but my intentions have always been to further the interests of the NPS." That, too, exemplifies Noble Cause Corruption; breaking or bending the rules of government for the good of the agency. The same can be said about actions supporting closure of the oyster farm at Point Reyes National Seashore (discussed in chapter four), where an independent review determined that agency personnel had "selectively presented, over-interpreted, or misrepresented the available scientific information on potential impacts of the oyster mariculture operation," but where "political pressure, funding issues and conflicting mandates, not deliberate misconduct, are concerns."[11]

This is a concept encountered far too frequently in a close examination of the hidden record of misconduct in the NPS. Other common examples include park superintendents ignoring NEPA and other environmental laws and policies in order to fast-track a pet construction project; the manipulation of agency reports to reflect a desired finding or to conceal issues of liability; and even the concealment of facts about incidents or agency decisions that might prove embarrassing or damaging to the image of the NPS (the ranger image). All of these examples are borne of a culture that frequently places greater emphasis on a desired outcome rather than on the process ("due process") that is prescribed by law and policy to reach that outcome, and the mistaken belief that the short-term benefits of such an approach somehow outweigh any long-term harm created through the erosion of public trust and the alienation of impacted groups and individuals. But as Professor Martinelli has observed, Noble Cause Corruption does, indeed, have consequences, however unforeseen; and not just for law enforcement organizations that "violate the public's trust in the policing profession." Noble Cause Corruption has negative consequences even for a beloved agency like the National Park Service and its genuinely noble resource protection mission. *Every* noble cause is diminished when pursued through less than honorable means.

* * *

Assistant United States Attorney James White, Fresno, California, declined prosecution based upon his appraisal that the LEO [Law Enforcement Office] narcotics investigation was successful since it resulted in numerous guilty pleas or convictions and the OIG investigation did not show any personal profit or gain by NPS employees in the improper use of the SIF. [12]

AUSA White's comment deserves close examination for yet another reason, particularly against Congressman Vento's claim that "The GAO found no evidence of criminal conduct and, more importantly, found no basis to support such allegations."[13] A contradiction exists between the two statements, and while Vento's GAO may conveniently have "found no evidence of criminal conduct," the OIG most certainly did. The statement attributed to the federal prosecutor seems to confirm that the U.S. Attorney's Office believed criminal laws *had* probably been violated by the people running the investigation. In other words, they *could* have been charged but were not, simply because the other "narcotics investigation was successful...and the OIG investigation did not show any personal profit or gain by NPS employees..."

The conflict in findings between the GAO and the OIG reports was actually noted, but not resolved, in an article published April 27, 1986, in the *Fresno Bee*. After finally obtaining a copy of the first OIG report, staff reporter Gene Rose wrote a piece titled "Report Indicates Yosemite Drug Funds Misused." The article begins,

> An inspector general's report on the undercover drug investigation in Yosemite National Park supports many of the charges made by park ranger Paul Berkowitz – even though an earlier government investigation had found no basis for those charges.

Notable, of course, is the manner in which even the *Fresno Bee* was confused about the actual chronology of the investigations and reports; the "earlier government investigation" by the GAO having actually been conducted nearly two years *after* the OIG investigation was initiated. After outlining some of the findings contained in the OIG report, Rose continued, noting in frustration that,

> Efforts by the *Fresno Bee* to determine the reasons for the discrepancies between the inspector general's and the GAO report on the same investigation have been unsuccessful.

The same *Fresno Bee* article was the first to also address the repercussions from my whistle-blowing efforts.

> One of [Berkowitz's] co-workers, who asked not to be identified, said the fallout from his efforts to bring the situation to light has ruined his park service career. The co-worker added that Berkowitz has been the subject of contempt and scorn from some Yosemite residents who consider him responsible for Binnewies' fall from power.[14]

Another article captioned "Ranger's Yosemite Drug Report Supported" appeared the next day, April 28, in the *Merced Sun-Star* (McClatchy News Service), picking up where the Fresno Bee story had left off:

Berkowitz had accused park officials of misusing a special fund used for obtaining information and of bugging telephone conversations with a longtime critic of National Park Service policies in the park.

The Inspector General's report, which was obtained by the Fresno Bee, says that Lee Shackelton, Yosemite's chief law Enforcement officer, made illegal disbursements from the fund, and did not use accepted accounting methods in handling the fund. But the report adds that he did not profit personally from the disbursements....

The Department of the Interior is investigating allegations that Binnewies ordered park drug investigators – including Berkowitz – to bug a phone conversation with Chuck Cushman – a longtime critic of park policies.

The Inspector General's report also stated that:

The National Park Service hired former drug users – some with criminal backgrounds – and used $31,872 from a special Yosemite imprest fund and other park service funds from Washington, D.C., to buy narcotics and information between October 1982 and June 1984.

Urine tests required of the informants were not handled in a professional manner. Samples were allowed to evaporate or were handled unprofessionally.

The U.S. Attorney's Office in Fresno declined to prosecute Shackelton because the overall investigation was successful ...

Berkowitz, an eleven-year veteran of the park service, was assigned to Yosemite in 1982 to join the drug investigation.

He had testified at public hearings that his supervisors obstructed justice, suppressed or tampered with evidence, gave perjured or misleading testimony to a federal grand jury and falsified or embellished crime reports.

Efforts to determine the reason for the discrepancies between the inspector general's and GAO report on the same investigation have been unsuccessful....

At congressional oversight hearings at Yosemite in October, Berkowitz testified that he had been subject to "repeated incidents of harassment" in his efforts to correct what he thought was unprofessional conduct on the part of his superiors.

Berkowitz said he tried for two years to bring the situation to light through regular park channels – but his reports ended up in the hands of those he was reporting about.

He said if he had remained silent as to what he considered the illegal recordings of Cushman conversations, he could have been held culpable.[15]

Allowing for a few inaccuracies that were subsequently corrected (e.g., "bug a *phone* conversation"), the articles appearing in the *Fresno Bee* and *Merced Sun-Star* were the only two to take note of what had really occurred: a full-blown cover-up of a wide variety of crimes.[16]

20 Merced, Ca. Sun-Star Mon., April 28, 1986

Ranger's Yosemite drug report supported

By McClatchy News Service

FRESNO — An inspector general's report on an undercover drug investigation in Yosemite National Park supports many of the charges made by park ranger Paul Berkowitz — even though an earlier government investigation had found no basis for those charges.

Berkowitz had accused park officials of misusing a special fund used for obtaining information and of bugging telephone conversations with a longtime critic of National Park Service policies in the park.

The inspector general's report, which was obtained by The Fresno Bee, says that Lee Shackelton, Yosemite's chief law enforcement officer, made illegal disbursements from the fund and did not use accepted accounting methods in handling the fund. But the report adds that he did not profit personally from the

disbursements.

The report also states that General Accounting Office investigators who compiled the initial report failed to act on allegations that former park Superintendent Robert O. Binnewies bugged telephone conversations with park critics.

The Department of the Interior is investigating allegations that Binnewies ordered park drug investigators — including Berkowitz — to bug a phone conversation with Charles Cushman, a longtime critic of park policies.

The inspector general's report also stated that:

The National Park Service hired former drug users — some with criminal backgrounds — and used $2,369 from a special Yosemite interest fund and other park service funds in Washington, D.C. to buy narcotics and information be-

tween October 1979 and June 1981.

Urine tests required of the informers were not handled in a professional manner. Samples were allowed to evaporate or were handled unprofessionally.

The U.S. Attorney Office's in Fresno declined to prosecute Shackelton because the overall investigation was unsuccessful.

The original inspector general's investigation was launched to determine if the management of the park drug investigations engaged in either illegal drug activity or prostitution at Yosemite. Such allegations were never proven during the investigation, the inspector general's report indicates.

Though the GAO did not support Berkowitz's charges, it did recommend indirectly that any future criminal investigations in the park should be led by investigators from the FBI or the U.S.

Drug Enforcement Agency.

Berkowitz, an 11-year veteran of the park service, was assigned to Yosemite in 1982 to join in the drug investigation.

He had testified at public hearings that his superiors obstructed justice, suppressed or tampered with evidence, gave perjured or misleading testimony to a federal grand jury and falsified or embellished crime reports.

Efforts by to determine the reasons for the discrepancies between the inspector general's and GAO reports on the same investigation have been unsuccessful.

Berkowitz refuses to discuss the issue.

One of his co-workers, who asked not to be identified, said the fallout from his efforts to bring the situation to light has ruined his park service career.

The co-worker added that Berkowitz

has been the subject of contempt and scorn from some Yosemite residents who consider him responsible for Binnewies' fall from power. Binnewies was relieved of his duties in January, pending completion of Interior's investigation.

At congressional oversight hearings at Yosemite in October, Berkowitz testified that he had been subject to "repeated incidents of harassment" in his efforts to correct what he thought was unprofessional conduct on the part of his superiors.

Berkowitz said he tried for two years to bring the situation to light through regular park channels — but his reports ended up in the hands of those he was reporting about.

He said that if he had remained silent as to what he considered the illegal recordings of Cushman conversation, he could have been held culpable.

(*Merced Sun-Star*, April 28, 1986).

But the inconsistency between the OIG and GAO reports, and the actual existence of prospective criminal violations was subsequently confirmed, though downplayed, in a May 11, 1986 article in the *New York Times*. The article also addressed deficiencies in the Park Service's overall approach to law enforcement (and its "ranger image"), where "rangers who lead nature walks and campfire songfests double as law enforcement officers ..." Citing an interview with the newly appointed DOI Inspector General, reporter Robert Lindsey wrote that

> James R. Richards, the Interior Department's Inspector General, said in an interview that two recent investigations by his agency at Yosemite National Park, 185 miles east of San Francisco, had convinced him that using park rangers as police investigators was inadequate to deal with the most serious crimes now occurring increasingly in public parklands.

Addressing the findings of those investigations, Lindsey quoted Richards, who observed,

> This drug operation, while it resulted in some arrests, was a pretty sloppily run type of operation.... I think it's obvious they were in over their heads.

Focusing more specifically on the conduct of the NPS officials who were the focus of those OIG investigations, Lindsey wrote,

> Although the Inspector General concluded that Mr. Berkowitz's supervisors had technically violated regulations, it noted that the Justice Department had considered the violations too minor to prosecute.[17]

A number of criminal statutes (and not just regulations) apply to the misuse of federal funds and making false statements, including the falsification of vouchers, time and payroll sheets, and other government records and reports. Most of these statutes do not require proof of personal profit or gain. Were these among the charges the federal prosecutor declined to file against law enforcement officials, because their violations were committed while successfully targeting others for prosecution? And was this same rationale perhaps also applied but not documented in deciding what to do about the bugging incident, itself? And what about the documented profit or income realized from the State of California while simultaneously being paid by the federal government? Finally, to what extent did the standing relationship and mutual interests between the Assistant United States Attorney and the prospective defendants influence the decision to decline prosecution?

The conflict of interest that existed in allowing AUSA White to evaluate and make a decision regarding prospective prosecution of the people running the Special Investigation is inescapable. AUSA White openly socialized with those same people. He was the same prosecutor who had worked for years with Shackelton and Connelly in not only their Grand Jury "Curry Company" investigation, but any number of other routine prosecutions generated out of Yosemite National Park. As much as anyone, White had a vested interest in the outcome of those prosecutions, and assuring that nothing compromised those cases, especially the documentation of ethics, credibility, and prospective criminal issues with any of the officers or informants involved in the investigations.

Beyond that, it was White's own office that would have been responsible for *defending* Shackelton, Loach, Connelly, and Binnewies for involvement in the bugging, had Cushman pursued a civil suit against those government employees for a violation of section (2)(d) of 18 U.S.C. 2511 (the "subexception"). Certainly the U.S. Attorney's office did not want to contribute to that prospect by openly confirming, or even suggesting that "such communication [had been] intercepted for the purpose of committing any criminal or tortious act in violation of the Constitution or laws of the United States or of any State or for the purpose of committing any other injurious act."

Reviewing the first OIG report in its entirety, including the hundreds of pages of incorporated supporting documents and attachments, it becomes clear that while NPS and DOI officials were fully aware of the magnitude of the problems in Yosemite, little if any consideration was given to correcting the situation until it was too late and the cat was out of the bag. Numerous internal memoranda suggest that all of the parties to whom I had confidentially spoken in search of support were sharing information with one another in an effort to contain the situation and handle the matter internally. By the time the NPS realized the problem was bigger than they could handle or conceal, I had already gone to the OIG and filed my own complaint. But the acknowledged strength and seriousness of my allegations was confirmed in a confidential internal NPS memorandum prepared by Captain Crockett:

> in investigating this complaint [from Paul Berkowitz], we have found major discrepancies in procedures and methodology that deem further examination by both the Inspector General's Office (of Interior) and the United States Secret Service.[18]

But even Captain Crockett was surprised when, during his June 23, 1984 interview with me, he learned that I had *already* abandoned hope for an NPS response and intervention, and had contacted the OIG, directly.

The Service's and Interior Department's desires to quietly handle the entire affair internally were dashed when, out of sheer frustration and perhaps an excess of idealism, I presented my testimony before the House Subcommittee on National Parks, Forests, and Public Lands. No longer able to keep the problem secret, NPS, DOI, and even Congressional officials launched a new campaign to at least spin the story in an effort to minimize the damage and the embarrassment. They partially succeeded in those efforts, concealing evidence and delaying an official investigation into the Binnewies-Cushman bugging incident for another year, and then creating the appearance that they had only recently learned about that incident.

Predictably, after learning that he was the focus on an internal investigation, Shackelton attempted a face-saving counter-attack. When interviewed by the OIG in 1985, he claimed that I had developed an "irrational vendetta" against him after my investigator position was eliminated and I was reassigned to patrol duties. At nearly the same time, he claimed, I must have somehow found out about, or inexplicably anticipated that he was getting ready to launch his own internal investigation against me for my "poor level of performance and attitude with co-workers," my own "mismanagement of funds," and "...the theft of Government files and records from the Law Enforcement Office."[19] Shackelton told the OIG that the complaints I had filed with them must have been a smoke screen, intended to distract from the investigation I somehow knew he was about to initiate against me!

Of course, at the time Shackelton fabricated this account, early in 1985, he did not know that I had initiated reports as far back as June of 1983, well before the OIG initiated their investigation and well before my investigator position was eliminated. Shackelton was also, apparently, oblivious to my documented above-average performance ratings from my actual supervisor of record (Hinson), and the fact that I was not a supervisor or even remotely in a position to manage or supervise the expenditure of funds of any kind. But he certainly did know that the "Government files and records" to which he referred and claimed had been "stolen," had been legally accessed and secured at the specific request of the OIG. Shackelton's hastily fabricated claims never got off the ground. They did, however, reinforce the extremely ugly nature of internal NPS politics, and the peril faced by those who go up against powerful NPS officials. It also sheds a very scary light on how the authority to conduct its own internal investigations can be abused in an agency like the NPS.

Whether with or without the assistance of the U.S. Attorney's Office, the NPS did apparently succeed in preventing investigation – or at least the release of findings – into two other troubling issues that I had raised with both the OIG and the GAO. Lunsford had eventually told me, privately, that the regional office was behind personnel officer Mary Sargent's false claim that the OIG had asked her to solicit information from me. But in all of the records that eventually were released or secured though legal action, there is no report documenting an interview with Sargent or anyone else on that topic, even though Lunsford had told me, on tape,

> Well one person that I'm going to want to talk to is the young lady that works over at the personnel office. I want to know why she told you that we were coming when, in fact, there was no intention of anyone ever coming in. I'm more than curious as to why.

Yet another of the original suspicions I and others shared with both OIG and GAO officials was apparently never investigated by *anyone*, not by the OIG, not by the GAO, and certainly not the Department of Justice; Connelly's suspected relationship with young informants and underage boys in the community.

* * *

One revealing thing about all of the cover-up efforts is the apparent assumption that I would simply go along with the plan, not "ever tell anybody about this," and make no extraordinary efforts to expose what I had witnessed. That may have been a reflection of the prevailing agency culture and the expectation that all NPS employees are so devoted to not only the NPS mission, but the agency itself, that they would never risk embarrassing the organization or its managers by exposing deficiencies. Few others seemed to have a problem with what was occurring. The victims of this incredible misconduct were, themselves, perceived as "bad guys," drug dealers, or worse yet, political opponents of the NPS. I was the odd man out. So how many employees simply kept their mouths shut out of blind loyalty and obedience, or fear? Worse yet, how many actually viewed this type of conduct as acceptable within the unspoken tenets of "NPS law enforcement," the ranger image, and the NPS culture? Then and now, that culture has included its own unwritten "code of silence"; as intimidating, effective, and often ruthlessly enforced as that found in any big city police department or other organization in need of serious reform. That unfortunate reality raises even more troubling questions about how long this sort of thing had really been going on, and how many more incidents like this had actually occurred but not been reported.

By exceeding expectations about the lengths to which I would go to report these matters – to do what we're told we are supposed to do – I was elevated to the same level as Chuck Cushman, the person most hated by the National Park Service. I was guilty by association, however inadvertent and tenuous that "association" might be. But as one of the Park Service's own – a member of the so-called "NPS family" – what I had done was even worse, not only exposing the agency to scrutiny and embarrassment by forcing an investigation (such as it was), but validating at least some of Cushman's claims that the management of the NPS could not be trusted. Doing the right thing had benefitted the wrong cause and certainly the wrong person, and in the NPS, that crossed the line. That wasn't NPS law enforcement; that was law enforcement out of control and turned back around on the NPS, itself. It was more than a violation of the code of silence; it was an act of betrayal and a rejection of NPS family values. And so, by doing what I still believe was the right thing, I became the most vilified and hated *employee* in the NPS.

Endnotes

1. Federal Personnel Manual, 5 CFR 41 and related Merit Personnel Procedures.

2. Herbert R. Gherke (NPS Regional Law Enforcement Supervisor), OIG interview, June 13, 1984, DOI-OIG Case #4VI-090.

3. John Crockett (USPP Captain), OIG interview, June. 29, 1984, DOI-OIG Case #4VI-090.

4. John Crockett (USPP Captain), written statement to OIG, undated, DOI-OIG Case #4VI-090.

5. Joseph Lowry "Bill" Orr (Supervisor, NPS Seasonal Academy, Santa Rosa Junior College, CA), OIG interview, Aug. 15, 1984, DOI-OIG Case #4VI-090.

6. Kathy J. Monroe, OIG interview, Oct. 16, 1984, DOI-OIG Case #4VI-090, "Detailed Summary."

7. DOI-OIG Case #4VI-090, "Synopsis."

8. Steve Rothlein, "Noble Cause Corruption," *Public Agency Training Council E-Newsletter,* 2008.

9. Thomas J. Martinelli, "Unconstitutional Policing, The Ethical Challenges in Dealing With Noble Cause Corruption," *Police Chief Magazine,* Vol. 73, No. 10, Oct. 2006. *Also,* "Dodging the Pitfalls of Noble Cause Corruption and the Intelligence Unit," *Police Chief Magazine,* Vol. 76, No. 10, Oct. 2009.

10. Justice Louis D. Brandeis, dissenting, in *Olmstead v. United States,* 277 U.S. 438 (1928). Also see *Katz v. United States,* 389 U.S. 347 (1969).

11. Peter Fimrite, "Scientists side with Drakes Bay oyster farm," *San Francisco Chronicle,* May 6, 2009.

12. DOI-OIG Case #4VI-090, "Synopsis."

13. Press release, "New For Release", Committee on Interior and Insular Affairs, House of Repre-

sentatives, "Vento Announces GAO Findings in Yosemite Probe," Jan. 15, 1986.

14. Gene Rose, "Report Indicates Yosemite Drug Funds Misused," *Fresno Bee,* Apr. 27, 1986, (front page).

15. McClatchy News Service, "Ranger's Yosemite drug report supported," *Merced Sun-Star,* Apr. 18, 1986, p. 20.

16. The *Fresno Bee* issued corrections on May 7, 1986 ("Binnewies probe results not released"), including a notation that "The April 27 article also incorrectly said that the conversation Binnewies recorded was in a phone call with Cushman. The conversation actually occurred in Binnewies' office."

17. Robert Lindsey, "National Parks Try To Cope With More Crime," *New York Times,* May 11, 1986.

18. John S. Crockett, Jr. (USPP Captain), undated memorandum, DOI-OIG Case #4VI-090.

19. Leland J. Shackelton, written statement to OIG, Feb. 26, 1985, DOI-OIG Case #4VI-090.

CHAPTER NINETEEN

Unjust Rewards

In just about any other agency, the findings and conclusions documented by the OIG about Shackelton and his associates would probably have resulted in serious discipline, if not outright termination; but
not in the National Park Service.

Lee Shackelton remained in his position at Yosemite National Park
as Chief Law Enforcement Officer for five more years after my departure.
When the dust finally settled in the second half of 1986, he was invited to
present a summary of the Yosemite Drug Investigation to members of the
NPS directorate. Regional Director Chapman subsequently presented
Shackelton with the following letter of commendation:[1]

> I congratulate you for your recent excellent presentation to the Di-
> rector and other key National Park Service personnel concerning
> the result of the Yosemite Drug Investigation. Your presentation
> was extremely well organized, comprehensive, and articulate.
>
> You have helped those of us who attended the presentation to
> gain new insight into the truly complex and demanding nature of
> the task undertaken at Yosemite. You, and the other professionals
> who accepted responsibility for the investigation, and carried it
> through, are to be highly commended.
>
> I regret that the closing months of the investigation were com-
> plicated by the need to examine various internal management
> concerns related to the investigation. With that examination now
> behind us, I am delighted that the full accomplishments of the Yo-
> semite law enforcement staff, and its colleagues in the Office of the
> United States Attorney, have come to light.
>
> As we look ahead, the Yosemite Drug Investigation undoubt-
> edly will prove to be a significant point of reference and a learning
> tool for the National Park Service. We may wish otherwise, but the
> problem of law enforcement in parks will grow in difficulty. You
> certainly have proven that, with diligence and experience, Park
> Rangers can be responsive to the problem at the highest levels of
> law enforcement competence.

Not surprisingly, conditions and practices in Yosemite's law enforcement office remained essentially unchanged throughout the remainder
of Shackelton's tenure. Finally, in 1991, after more than twenty years as

Yosemite's chief of law enforcement, Shackelton submitted his retirement papers, reportedly after being confronted with a proposed 30-day suspension for new allegations that he was still driving a government vehicle on government time to his paid part-time job with the State of California, teaching at the seasonal NPS law enforcement academy.[2] Thereafter, Shackelton worked as a private investigator in and around the Yosemite area, at one point answering the call for assistance from his long-time friend, Scott Connelly. That assignment was accepted when the park prosecutor's own history of dubious personal activities caught up with him in another jurisdiction, and he experienced serious legal problems of his own. Shackelton died of a heart attack on November 7, 2009. In the tributes made by friends and colleagues, he was widely lauded for helping to set the standard for how the NPS runs its law enforcement program, to this day.

M. (Marshall) "Scott" Connelly remained in his ranger position at Yosemite National Park, serving as park prosecutor for another thirteen years. He was finally arrested in 1998 by the Fresno, CA Police Department, after a young teenage boy reported that "he was walking in northeast Fresno when Connelly grabbed him, forced him into his pickup, and tied him up."[3] Connelly was subsequently linked to three other victims in Fresno, in similar incidents going back several years. Prosecutors alleged that Connelly "preys upon young boys on the fringe, plies them with alcohol and pays them for sex."[4] NPS sources reported that "It looks like Connelly was involved with other adults who would 'pass around' kids to each other."[5] Other NPS sources reluctantly acknowledged that "Our prosecutor thought it was okay to have sex with teenagers."[6] But none of that should have come as any surprise to NPS officials, given Connelly's reputation within the Yosemite community, and especially in light of the accounts about Connelly that I and others had shared with investigators from the OIG and GAO more than a dozen years earlier. As a defense, Connelly's attorney argued that the sex acts with teenagers (three of them under the age of 16) that his client had video-taped were "consensual." Shackelton wrote a letter of support, asking the court to show leniency to Connelly, claiming that he had "served the [NPS] Law Enforcement Department faithfully," with "annual job performance evaluations … consistently at the highest level allowed in the personnel system, [with] many commendations and awards for that level of excellence." Connelly was charged with fourteen counts, ranging from kidnapping to lewd and lascivious acts and oral copulation with juveniles in that community. He subsequently pled guilty in state court to four felony counts; one for each of the four identified victims.[7,8] He was never investigated for or charged with any crimes committed in Yosemite National Park.

SATURDAY
August 1, 1998

50 ¢

CENTRAL CALIFORNIA'S LEADING NEWSPAPER FOR 75 YEARS

The Fresno Bee

Police hold Yosemite ranger on molestation charge[s]

alleged attacks on two teen
oys occurred in Fresno.

BY PABLO LOPEZ
THE FRESNO BEE

A Yosemite National Park ranger liv-
ig in Fresno was arrested Friday on
spicion of molesting two teen-age
ys, including one he allegedly kid-
apped and tied up.

Fresno police detectives arrested Mar-
sell Scott Connelly, 53, and searched

his home in the 6600 block of North
Raisina Street about 2 p.m.

Connelly — who goes by Scott Connelly — is a veteran ranger who works
as a legal officer, prosecuting misdemeanor crimes that occur in the park.

The alleged attacks against the boys,
ages 15 and 16, occurred a year apart —
one in 1997 and one earlier this month,
said Lt. Jerry Davis.

In the attack said to have occurred a
year ago, Connelly allegedly lured a boy
into his pickup, took him to his house
and molested him, Davis said.

"The victim reported the crime some-
time later but was not able to give detectives enough information about his
attacker or where he lived," the lieuten-
ant said.

In July, another boy came forward
and told detectives that he was walking
in northeast Fresno when Connelly
grabbed him, forced him into his pickup
and tied him up, Davis said.

Connelly then took the boy to his
Raisina Street home and molested him,
Davis said.

"The victim was able to escape and

give us enough information to tie the
two cases together," Davis said. "We
then got a warrant to arrest him."

Davis and Sgt. Tim McFadden declined to comment on what was seized
from Connelly's home, which is near
First Street and Barstow Avenue, saying
the investigation was continuing and
that there could be more victims.

A neighbor said Connelly had lived at
the Raisina address for at least 10 years.

He was booked into Fresno County
Jail Friday on charges of kidnapping
with the intent to commit a sexual as-

sault, child molestation and aïde
child molestation.

Bail was set at $700,000.

Connelly has worked at Yosemi
ly is a paralegal assigned to the
office at Yosemite Village.

Park spokesman Al Naab said C
His duties include filing crit
charges against people who co
crimes in Yosemite, authorities sai

"He has been suspended pendin
resolution of this case," Naab said.

(*Fresno Bee*, August 1, 1998).

Robert O. "Bob" Binnewies resigned from the NPS in 1986. He was
replaced at Yosemite by the same official who, as chief ranger in the 1970s,
had served as the agency's paid technical consultant to MCA during filming of the TV show, *Sierra*.[9] Binnewies moved east to become Assistant
Commissioner in New York's Department of Environmental Conservation, and then Executive Director of the Palisade Interstate Park Commission. He is the author of *Palisades, 100,000 Acres in 100 Years* (Fordham
University Press, 2001), and more recently, *Your Yosemite. A Threatened
Public Treasure* (White Cloud Press, 2015).

In his most recent book, Binnewies offers his own account of the
bugging incident and of my congressional testimony, making clear that
he still blames me for his downfall and for the embarrassment and trauma that both he and his family subsequently experienced. But in making
his case, Binnewies omits all references to documented violations and,
more significantly, makes selective use of only the most favorable and
ultimately disproven press releases and news accounts, in his effort to
challenge my motives and credibility, and argue for his own innocence.
In so doing, Binnewies reveals his continuing commitment to the same
pattern of deception and cover-up that is so much a part of the legacy of
the Yosemite Mafia. His account also highlights the lasting damage from
NPS efforts to fabricate its own image, obscure the facts, and manipulate
the historical record, as demonstrated by the extent to which even Binnewies remains seriously misinformed about the actual series of events
that led to his removal.

Nevertheless, without realizing it, in his 2015 account Binnewies
does shed some new light on the story, contradicting not only his own
written statement provided to the OIG in 1986, but also Shackelton's
written account (see pages 194-197). Binnewies reveals, for the first time,
that the chief law enforcement officer had been consulted and was very
much aware of the surreptitious purpose behind the request to use the
eavesdropping equipment.

221

In chapter thirteen ("Mr. Rent-A-Riot"), Binnewies writes,

> Prior to the meeting, a park ranger [Loach] who I held in the highest regard (and still do) suggested that a tape recording be made of the discussion with Cushman so that an accurate after-the-fact transcript of the proceedings would be in hand; translation, we did not trust Cushman. I realize that I should have either declined this suggestion or, if a tape was to be made, asked in advance for Cushman's permission. I did neither. Instead, without giving the suggestion the thought it deserved, I contacted Yosemite's senior law enforcement officer [Shackelton] who assured me that such a recording would be legal…

Binnewies continues his discussion of the bugging in chapter fourteen ("Not So Great"), writing,

> A park ranger named Paul Berkowitz, who I did not know at the time of the recording, had handled the tape equipment. Subsequently, in succeeding years, he had become dissatisfied with the law enforcement activities in Yosemite, so much so that he felt compelled to express his concerns in "whistle blower" style in letters to NPS Director William Penn Mott and members of Congress. This was follow-up to a chance he grasped in October 1985, to testify at a Congressional sub-committee fact-finding hearing held in the park. The hearing was intended to invite comment on general park management issues, including law enforcement activities. At that hearing Berkowitz made dramatic allegations of possible misuse of funds and tampering with evidence within the investigative branch of Yosemite's law enforcement structure, singling out his supervisors, Lee Shackelton and Scott Connelly. The chairman of the subcommittee, Congressman Bruce Vento, was so startled that he promptly adjourned the hearing and then called for an investigation by the federal General Accounting Office of the Berkowitz allegations.
>
> Berkowitz may not have been satisfied with the pace of the GAO investigation. For whatever reason, a few weeks after the hearing he fired off his letters, tying my lapse with Cushman to his other severe criticisms of park investigative activities. For me, the result was swift and blunt. When NPS Director Mott learned of the recording incident, he ordered my immediate transfer out of Yosemite. The newspaper headlines were sensational. One example was a *Los Angeles Times* headline proclaiming that, "Yosemite Chief Firing Tied to Ranger Morale, Crime." I was in shock and so was my family.
>
> A few days after I cleaned out my office, a subsequent McClatchy News Service headline, dated January 20, 1986, read, "U.S. Clears Yosemite Drug Probers.": As reported by Gene Rose, "Fed-

eral investigators have cleared Yosemite law enforcement officers of allegations between 1982 and 1984. A General Accounting Office investigation found there was no basis to any of the 11 allegations made in October by Yosemite Ranger Paul Berkowitz, said Representative Bruce Vento, Chairman of the Subcommittee on National Parks and Recreation. The General Accounting Office has spent considerable time looking into Mr. Berkowitz's charges, particularly the five specific charges of possible criminal misconduct. Vento said, 'The GAO found no evidence of criminal conduct, but more importantly no basis to support such allegations.'

For me and most of the park ranger corps in Yosemite, the result of the investigation was welcome, restorative news....[10]

Not surprisingly, there has been considerable support within NPS circles for Binnewies' book and his account of events, as various current and retired employees seize upon his words for comfort and reassurance that all is and always has been well, within the agency. Such is the legacy of the Yosemite Mafia.

James Loach did transfer out of Yosemite shortly after Binnewies was replaced. He obtained a promotion to NPS headquarters in Washington, D.C., working on Congressional affairs and as a staff assistant in the Assistant Secretary's office. He has continued to enjoy a very successful NPS career, rising to his current position as the Associate Regional Director for Operations and Education in the Midwest Region (1992-present).

Mary Sargent enjoyed a successful career, rising to the position of Superintendent at Mojave National Monument and Preserve, and then Lassen Volcanic National Park. She retired in 2007.

Arthur J. "Butch" Abell Jr. continued as Yosemite's Administrative Officer for several more years. He transferred to the NPS Southwest Regional Office in Santa Fe, New Mexico in 1989, where he worked as a management analyst until his retirement in 1993. He died in 2007.

Howard H. Chapman retired from his position as Western Regional Director in 1987. In a gesture that increased his stature within the environmental community, he tendered his resignation in protest over the policies of the Reagan Administration and Interior Secretary Donald Hodel. Chapman came under scrutiny after testifying before House and Senate subcommittees. He had "gone public" to protest "Interior Department policies that emphasize increased public use of the nation's parks rather than protection of the natural environment." Chapman's own above-average performance appraisal, issued by Director Mott, was subsequently reduced by the Secretary's office to "below average." In a 1987 interview, Chapman told the *Los Angeles Times*, "The secretary is not on the side of the Park Service." Addressing his decision to retire, he stated "I'm doing this on my own," and that "sooner or later" Hodel would have found some way to remove him. Finally, the article quoted Chapman as saying, "Maybe I can be more effective on the outside," indicating that he was considering speaking out in opposition to the Reagan Administration's national park policies.[11] Interestingly, NPS officials have since speculated that the conflicts with Interior officials stemmed directly from disputes with "Chuck Cushman's group" over inholdings in Yosemite National Park.[12] Chapman died in 2005 from complications of Parkinson's disease, in Mt. Vernon, WA.

Bruce Vento served a total of 24 years in the House of Representatives. For much of that time he presided as chairman over the Natural Resources Subcommittee on National Parks, Forests, and Public Lands. In 1988, just two years after revelations about the Yosemite bugging had finally surfaced, Vento advocated for giving the NPS even greater autonomy and freedom from DOI oversight. He declared the NPS to be "one of the most respected professional organizations in the national government."[13] Vento retired in 2000, after being diagnosed with lung cancer. He died that same year. The non-profit National Park Trust established its Bruce F. Vento Public Service Award in his honor, bestowed annually upon elected and other officials with a demonstrated record of support for national parks.

Tony Coelho served a total of six terms in the House, retiring in 1989, in the wake of reports that he'd received a loan from a savings and loan executive to purchase junk bonds. He was not charged with any crime. He subsequently occupied executive positions with various investment firms, while remaining active in politics. In 1999, he was appointed chairman of Al Gore's presidential campaign, seeing that effort through the Democratic primary. Coelho retired as campaign manager before the Democratic convention and general election, for medical reasons. One of the principle sponsors of the Americans With Disabilities Act, he remains active in the academic community, lecturing on matters related to disability law.

Richard Lehman remained in the House of Representatives until 1995, serving as a member of the powerful Energy and Commerce Committee and the Natural Resources Committee. He still lives in California, where he is a partner in a Sacramento-based lobbying firm.

Charles "Chuck" Cushman continues to serve as the Executive Director of the American Land Rights Association (formerly the National Inholders Association), based in Battleground, Washington. He still owns his cabin in the Wawona District of Yosemite National Park.

* * *

I spent a total of six years in my assignment at Whiskeytown National Recreation Area. With a supportive and honest superintendent and a great group of talented young rangers, I was able to develop a remarkably professional and effective law enforcement program, implementing many reforms and innovations – including proper position classification for my entire staff – that would set the stage for pay and benefit reforms, service-wide.[14] I simultaneously immersed myself in the therapeutic process of lecturing and writing as a regular contributor to trade and professional journals such as *S.W.A.T.* and *Police* magazines. I wrote separately about the history of law enforcement in the NPS. I was also able to speak out publicly on topics related to police ethics and conduct through essays that appeared in various magazines and professional journals. Aided by the advent of the internet and email communications, many of these articles and essays received wide circulation within and beyond the NPS, elevating my own profile and visibility to levels beyond those I had attained through my actions at Yosemite.

In 1992, in a brief window of opportunity, I was recruited by a colleague and supporter from my days back at Lake Mead, for an assignment in Washington, D.C. as the Assistant Special Agent-in-Charge of the developing NPS special agent program.[15] My efforts focused on internal investigations, coordinating the purchase of rifles and new semi-automatic pistols for the Ranger Force, securing better pay and retirement benefits for NPS law enforcement officers, and the revision of NPS law enforcement policies.[16]

Among the more interesting experiences for me was the response I received to a proposal to amend national policies with a declaration of priorities for NPS law enforcement personnel, listing the defense of Constitutional principles and rights at the top of the list, followed by the protection of human life, and thereafter the NPS mission and park resources. I was openly ridiculed by the workgroup chairman (the NPS deputy chief ranger), while many others, including several influential park superintendents and even chief rangers, argued that the NPS mission belonged ahead of the Constitution. My proposal was soundly rejected, revealing for me the extent to which many NPS officials truly do not understand the legal responsibilities associated with federal service.

Still, many successes were actually realized, frequently as a result of evidence and arguments based upon my research and my writing about the history of NPS law enforcement. It was a productive but contentious time and experience, as I got a first-hand glimpse into agency politics "inside the Beltway." The very fact that I was even tolerated in that environment signaled at least a glimmer of hope for change in the way the NPS operated. That hope, however, would be short-lived. With a change in administration and the elimination of my D.C. position as part of the "reinvention" and "downsizing of government," I found myself reassigned to a supervisory field agent position, based at Grand Canyon National Park.[17] But that was OK, because it provided the opportunity to once again move "back west" in the middle of the magnificent scenery of northern Arizona and the Four Corners where, more than anyplace else, I wanted to live and work. I spent the next twelve years to the end of my career in 2007, as a supervisory special agent based at the Grand Canyon and finally transitioning into an assignment on the Navajo Indian Reservation focusing on Indian Country crimes.

But the NPS is still the NPS, and I would come to learn that the situation in Yosemite was not an anomaly. The corruption I saw there was not an isolated condition, as I witnessed similar operations run by equally unscrupulous characters at other NPS sites across the country – from the Grand Canyon to Yellowstone to Mount Rainier; from the Northeast Regional Office to the Southeast Regional Office, and even Washington, D.C. – all empowered and emboldened by a decentralized system and approach to law enforcement devoid of meaningful oversight or accountability. With the benefit of maturity and hindsight, that impression has only been reinforced over the years, as I have been able to reflect on the disturbing practices exhibited by far too many of my own superiors and supervisors.

All told (including Connelly), at least three of them were eventually investigated and prosecuted by other agencies, and ultimately convicted of their own crimes. I had personally reported two of them to my own supervisors and to the OIG; but not a single investigation or prosecution was pursued by the NPS. Several more supervisors could easily have been prosecuted, had a more effective system of checks, balances, and oversight been in place. Many of those people, like Shackelton, were the power-players of their day; members of a fraternity (e.g., the Yosemite Mafia) widely viewed as the unassailable leaders of the NPS law enforcement program. Far too many of those same characters have been able to use their positions and their power to intimidate both naïve NPS managers and enemies, alike, and influence the manner in which NPS law enforcement programs have been run and developed over time. In combination with its benign public image and its ability to cultivate powerful political allies, this helps to explain how the NPS has been even more successful in resisting needed changes and meaningful reforms than monolithic organizations like the New York Police Department. And in spite of my own brief acceptance into the agency's inner circles of the Washington offices, and many accomplishments related to advances in equipment, training, position classification, pay and benefits, very little has really changed in the way the agency operates or behaves. No lessons have been learned and certainly no reforms have been implemented to prevent a recurrence of these types of events.

As newly appointed DOI Inspector General Earl Devaney observed in 2003, while addressing a congressional subcommittee,

> Mr. Chairman and members of the committee, I have served in
> Federal government for a little over 32 years. I have never seen an

organization more unwilling to accept constructive criticism or embrace new ideas than the National Park Service. Their culture is to fight fiercely to protect the status quo and reject any idea that is not their own. Their strategy to enforce the status quo is to take any new idea, such as law enforcement reform, and study it to death. Thus, any IG recommendation or, for that matter, Secretarial directive, falls victim to yet another Park Service work group charged by their National Leadership Council to defend the status quo from those of us who just do not understand the complexities of being a ranger.[18]

Endnotes

1. Howard H. Chapman to Leland J. Shackelton, letter of commendation, Aug. 12, 1986 (WR-RP).

2. J.R. Tomasovic, interview with the author, Dec. 9, 2008.

3. Pablo Lopez, "Police Hold Yosemite Ranger on Molestation Charges," *Fresno Bee*, Aug. 1, 1998.

4. "Ranger Videotaped Sex Acts, Prosecutor says," *Fresno Bee*, Aug. 13, 1998.

5. Don Coelho, internal NPS email, Aug. 24, 1998.

6. Jeff Sullivan, internal NPS email, Aug. 13, 1998.

7. Jerry Beir, "Ex-Ranger pleads guilty in unlawful-sex case," *Fresno Bee*, Sep. 24 1998.

8. State of California v. Marshal Scott Connelly, Consolidated Fresno Judicial District Case #F98911279-8/D.A. #98S0729. Connelly was convicted for violation of California Penal Code (CPC) 288 (c)(1) "lewd/lascivious acts with minor of the age 14 or 15 yrs.; CPC 664/288 (c)(1) "attempted lewd/lascivious acts with minor age 14 or 15 yrs."; CPC 288 (b)(2) "oral copulation with minor age 16 yrs."; CPC 288 a(b)(1) "oral copulation with minor under 18 yrs."

9. John M. "Jack" Morehead served as Yosemite chief ranger from 1971 to 1974, and then as superintendent from 1986 to 1989.

10. Robert O. Binnewies, *Your Yosemite: A Threatened Public Treasure* (Ashland, OR: White Cloud Press, 2015), p. 256-259, 277-278.

11. Ronald B. Taylor, "Park Service Official At Odds With Hodel Over Public Use, Quits," *Los Angeles Times*, Apr. 21, 1987.

12. Philip Shabecoff, "U.S. Park Service Roiled by Change," *New York Times*, Dec. 20, 1986; Philip Shabecoff, "Washington Talks: Would Freedom Help the National Park Service?" *New York Times*, May 27, 1988.

13. Philip Shabecoff, "Washington Talks: Would Freedom Help the National Park Service?" *New York Times*, May 27, 1988.

14. Law enforcement rangers at Whiskeytown NRA were the first to be uniformly classified into a recognized Office of Personnel Management law enforcement series, GS-1811 (criminal investigator).

15. Bob Marriott, the park service's first special agent-in-charge.

16. Chip Moore, "National Park Service Adopts a Sig Family," *Sigarms Quarterly*, Vol. 7, Spring 1995, 20-23.

17. http://govinfo.library.unt.edu/npr/whoweare/historyofnpr.html

18. Earl Devaney (DOI Inspector General), testimony before the Senate Committee on Finance, U.S. Senate ("U.S. Borders: Safe or Sieve"), Jan. 30, 2003.

CHAPTER TWENTY

The Price of a Legacy

The passage of time obscured recollection about what really happened in Yosemite in the 1980s. Certainly, the NPS made no effort to correct the record, much less learn from or even discuss the agency culture and organizational deficiencies that allowed those events to occur. Instead, the NPS once again succeeded in obscuring the facts and fooling the public, the press, and even the majority of NPS employees working for the agency, both then and now.

Evidence of that success is revealed in the perplexed writing of environmental author Tim Palmer, who curiously noted in his 1988 book, *The Sierra Nevada:*

> Many theories attempt to explain why Superintendent Bob Binnewies was transferred from Yosemite... [1]

Agency success in burying and distorting this story for literally decades was highlighted again, in 2011. In October of that year, yet another noted author, Michael Frome, echoed that same question while blogging on the Google Group, *Parkland Watch.*[2]

The group was discussing the recent on-line (YouTube) release of the 1986 documentary, *Law of Nature: Park Rangers in Yosemite Valley,* the same documentary in which Binnewies and I were interviewed separately about our different views on NPS law enforcement.[3] Near the end of the film the narrator notes Binnewies' sudden removal as park superintendent, while the news headline from the *Los Angeles Times* with a photo of Binnewies is flashed on the screen, offering the official NPS explanation, "Yosemite Chief's Firing Tied to Ranger Morale, Crime."[4]

That unsatisfactory account apparently led Dr. Frome to ask, twenty-five years later:

> Why do you think Bob Binneweis [sic] was fired as Yosemite superintendent?

None of the other bloggers, comprised largely of NPS retirees (including several who worked in Yosemite at the time) was able (or willing) to answer his question; at least not in a public forum.[5] And just two years ago

(2015) yet another author – a founding member of the Yosemite Mafia – confidentially expressed his festering resentment over what he seemed to believe about me and my role in exposing what had occurred in Yosemite thirty years earlier, rhetorically complaining to a colleague, "I would be interested in learning what he says on how he got the Supt. of Yosemite, Bob Binnewies placed out to pasture and essentially fired; it was a shame."[6]

But to this day, the very same group of vocal NPS supporters and employees (including other members of the Yosemite Mafia) who express bewilderment and bitterness over Binnewies' removal as superintendent of Yosemite, continue to bemoan and complain whenever Chuck Cushman and his organization "rears his ugly head."[7] Beyond that, many of these same people reveal antagonistic and even spiteful (as opposed to professional) motivations behind their own official interactions with Cushman and his group, voicing contempt, while vicariously rubbing salt into old wounds, as they gleefully recall their own contributions to the conflict. As one retired ranger – another original member of the Yosemite Mafia – recently bragged, on-line,

> While I was the Wawona District Ranger in Yosemite I had the pleasure of burning Cushman's family home which the NPS had purchased. The house was old and we burned it as a fire training exercise. I have always wanted to shake his [Cushman's] hand and hold on tight while I told him that.[8]

By its own account, in its *Administrative History of Cuyahoga Valley National Recreation Area,* the NPS, through its own policies and the conduct of its managers, was the driving force behind the rise of the Sagebrush Rebellion and the Wise Use Movement.[9] That assessment is undoubtedly overstated. Many factors contributed the rise of those movements, including private and corporate commercial interests reliant on the exploitation of public resources, federal management of western grazing lands, and – yes – a good measure of fundamental anti-federal ideology.[10] But in its arrogant treatment of him and his father (a genuinely loyal NPS employee) and the deliberately inconsistent application and enforcement of the law, the NPS most certainly has almost single-handedly "created" people like Chuck Cushman and groups like the National Inholders Association. The Wawona District of Yosemite National Park could arguably be labeled the birthplace of Cushman's National Inholders Association – now the American Land Rights Association – as the single most powerful force opposing expansion of the National Park System.

Since the inception of the National (Park) Inholders Association, Cushman and his supporters have successfully opposed park establishment or expansion efforts in dozens upon dozens of areas across the country. From Big Sur in California, to Little River in Alabama; from the Columbia Gorge in Oregon and Washington, to the North Woods in Maine, New Hampshire, Vermont, and New York, Cushman estimates that he and his group have prevented as much as 50 million acres of land from being converted into protected federal reservations.[11]

At these sites and elsewhere, and even in the halls of Congress, Cushman has been a relentless source of aggravation to NPS officials who, he maintains, cannot be trusted to effectively manage parks and, more significantly, to deal honestly and fairly with inholders. He has successfully lobbied to keep millions if not billions of dollars in federal funds from being authorized for the Land and Water Conservation Fund, otherwise used to acquire new lands for parks and other federal reservations.

People can debate the accuracy of those figures. Even more fundamentally, they can argue over whether Cushman's level of success is a good thing or a bad thing. But anyone interested in conservation, natural resource preservation, national parks, and public lands management should be interested in studying the motives behind those efforts and the reasons Cushman has been so successful since his own early experiences with the NPS, undeterred even by attempts to discredit him through an illegal bugging.

However much the NPS may resist and resent people like Cushman, the leadership of the NPS cannot credibly challenge him, his agenda, or his tactics, until they deprive him of the argument that the NPS cannot be trusted. Government officials need to conduct themselves and be held to a higher standard. The failure to act professionally, even in the face of "coercive" and "underhanded" tactics, only feeds the anti-NPS agenda; angering and alienating many who might otherwise be friends and allies of the agency. In truth, among the organizations and individuals who have reached that same conclusion are stalwart advocates for environmental and park protection, which have experienced their own rude awakenings in their interactions with NPS officials.[12] Regrettably, that now includes a sizeable portion of the environmental community in Marin County, California, which remains sharply divided in the heated argument over management of Point Reyes National Seashore.[13]

By almost any standard, the NPS and the citizens of the United States have paid dearly for the historic Yosemite cabin that Cushman's father, ranger Dwight Cushman, was pressured into selling to the NPS so many years ago. That cost has grown over the years through a series of interest payments resulting from incidents like the 1983 Yosemite bugging that took place in the superintendent's office, and subsequent efforts at the highest levels of the NPS to protect the participants and cover up those and other unfortunate but historically significant events.

* * *

My own relationship with Chuck Cushman is cordial and friendly. But in spite of what some people may claim or want to believe, Cushman and I are not close personal friends or political allies. I did not know him before these events took place. I have met him only once, and we have spoken only infrequently since, principally in conducting research for this book. But while those conversations have always been civil, friendly, and helpful, I certainly do not agree with most of the things Cushman supports or with many of his tactics.

To this day Cushman maintains that he is not so much anti-environment, anti-park, or even anti-wilderness, as he is anti-government abuse. But more than just inholders, Cushman now represents the interests of off-road vehicle enthusiasts, developers, loggers, miners, hunters, ranchers, and others staunchly opposed to government restrictions on the use of public lands, including some individuals and groups who have, most certainly, independently crossed the legal line in their strident opposition to the NPS mission and authority.[14]

In contrast, I like the idea that public lands are wide-open, undeveloped, and protected by the federal government for *all* Americans, and not just local communities and commercial interests. In spite or perhaps *because* of what I've seen, I still trust the federal government more than I do state and local agencies to protect those wild and historic places.

As far back as 1885, Congress struggled with the challenge of how to administer and protect Yellowstone National Park, all the while (and still, today) refusing to make adequate appropriations for the civilian park administration and, particularly, the promulgation and enforcement of criminal laws. Serious consideration was given to turning the park over to Wyoming when that territory became a state (1890). But that same strategy had been tried in California through the Yosemite Grant, where "the State's attempt to preserve and protect the park areas ended ... in abject failure."[15] In the interim, it was determined that the Wyoming Territorial government lacked jurisdiction to independently take any enforcement action within the park. That left the park "without any form of effective legal government."[16] Seeking a solution, the Secretary of the Interior dispatched special agent W. Hallet Phillips to the park to evaluate conditions and submit recommendations for how the park should be administered in the future. Following an on-site visit and extensive legal evaluation, Phillips submitted his report to the Secretary and, eventually, to Congress. Speaking specifically about the legal machinery necessary to administer and protect the park, he closed his report with a recommendation to strengthen park rules, increase the law enforcement staffing, and appoint two U.S. Commissioners (i.e., judges) to hear the park's criminal cases, stressing that "in a national park, the laws and regulations should be enforced by a national tribunal."[17] Today, 120 years later, and after more than three decades on my own working in law enforcement both within and outside of the National Park Service, with much of that time spent studying these very issues, I remain convinced that Phillips' analysis and recommendation was correct.

As inconsistent and frequently deficient as NPS law enforcement is, especially for a single agency, variance in the quality of state and local law enforcement across the country can be even greater. In spite of the push for improvements that occurred in the 1970s and thereafter, the state of law enforcement in the U.S. is still not what it should or could be. I have personally witnessed alarming levels of variance and inconsistency in the literally hundreds of state and local agencies I've worked and interacted with over my 33-year career. Some departments have been highly sophisticated and professional, with well-trained and disciplined personnel throughout. But others, including several situated right at the doorstep to major national parks, have proven to be pervasively corrupt and dangerous, lacking in compliance with even the most minimal education, training, and other standards.[18] Concerns over issues like these are compounded by the conflicting priorities faced by state and local agencies, where laws and policies frequently show deference to the exploitation of resources in order to generate revenues for both state and local coffers and businesses communities, over the genuine protection and preservation of natural and cultural resources. Constitutional oaths notwithstanding, local officials. including county sheriffs and chiefs of police. are usually elected or appointed to represent their local communities, not national interests. This can be a concern not just for national parks, but for other public lands, as well, where local and national interests may conflict.[19] I have far too often witnessed local law enforcement officials betraying their own oath of office by shamelessly pandering to extreme elements in their communities who have, themselves, attempted to defy federal court orders as well as federal laws and regulations legitimately enacted to protect and preserve public lands.[20] As national icons and federally owned destination sites for millions of national and even international tourists, our parks should not be subjected to that kind of inconsistency or disparate pressure from local interests. At least in the NPS, for a variety of reasons, with proper funding and under the right leadership, there is the real potential to turn things around and create a uniformly excellent law enforcement program; one that could serve as a model of professionalism for other agencies to emulate. If our national parks are truly a part of a national park *system*, then they should all be uniformly managed, protected, and policed to a single high standard. That's all the more reason to push for improvements, including greater integrity and consistency in how the NPS operates.

But more than that, history has shown that much of wild and historic America, including most of the sites we now treasure as national parks, would long ago have been monopolized, developed, or destroyed by greedy individuals and commercial interests, if left to the discretion of state and local officials over whom those interests exercise such enormous influence.[21] Those interests and types of relationships fueled much of the fraud that accompanied America's westward expansion and settlement, ultimately leading to changes in those settlement laws and policies, and establishment of the first national parks, forest preserves, and other protected federal lands.

> The question then arises whether the people ... will permit one of the richest and most attractive portions of the Territory to be set apart for the exclusive benefit and behoof of a few ... aristocrats, or whether the Government itself shall keep its title to the park, pass stringent laws relative to fish and game, and so have this broad and lovely domain, forever kept as a National "Institution," of a general benefit to the people ... ?[22]

Most of our national parks and other public lands would never have received real protection were it not for action taken at the federal level through agencies like the NPS, however imperfect and poorly managed they may sometimes be.

Consequently, where Cushman is widely associated with the Sagebrush Rebellion, I view myself more along the lines of what author Ken Wright describes as a Sagebrush Patriot.[23] I view vast areas of undeveloped, undisturbed wild lands and historic places as valuable in their own right, without the need for convoluted scientific, legal, or economic arguments to justify their existence and their protection. That's not to say that there are not valid arguments to be made. But more than that – perhaps more honestly – I just *like* it that places like that still exist and are federally owned and protected, particularly in the American West where I grew up and choose to live. I like it that I, along with other Americans, share in the ownership of places like that across the nation, however distant they may be from my own home. I view those areas and their native wildlife as part of our great American heritage, and I resent it when selfish groups and individuals abuse the privilege of access to those lands, or try to strip me of my own proprietary interest in those places and things. I want public lands to remain public, protected, and sustainably accessible to all Americans. That is a simple and honest statement of *values* that I'm willing to discuss with others, including those who may have a different perspective. For that matter, I also support the selective expansion of the National Park System, even through the careful and considered assertion of eminent domain. I generally support the designation of wilderness areas, and the protection and re-introduction of threatened and endangered species through the Endangered Species Act. Cushman and I undoubtedly disagree on many of these things – especially these last points – and we are unlikely allies on most issues related to public lands management.

But we have been able to maintain a respectful relationship and, on occasion, even support one another in a common effort. That is not simply because I stood up for his rights many, many years ago, and because he helped me escape what, in the process, had become a nightmare. Chuck Cushman and I are able to engage in friendly debate and respectfully dialogue with one another because he knows that I genuinely understand why he does not trust the National Park Service.

Endnotes

1. Tim Palmer, *The Sierra Nevada – A Mountain Journey* (Washington, D.C.: Island Press, 1988) 276 (Epilogue).

2. Among Frome's many books are *Conscience of a Conservationist* – 1989; *Regreening the National Parks* – 1992; *Battle for the Wilderness* – 1997; *Green Ink* – 1998; *Greenspeak* – 2002; etc.

3. *Law of Nature: Park Rangers in Yosemite Valley,* 1986, John Philbin – "Philbin Philms,"

4. "Yosemite Chief's Firing Tied to Ranger Morale, Crime," *Los Angeles Times,* Jan. 29, 1986.

5. GoogleGroups, *Parklandwatch,* http://groups.google.com/group/parklandsupdate/browse_thread/thread/451b62482fef73d4/f4fbec40b0a74edd?lnk=gst&q=The+Law+of+Nature#. Ironically, Frome had apparently forgotten that he'd answered his own question years earlier, in his 1992 book, *Regreening the National Parks* (Tucson, AZ: University of Arizona Press,1992) p. 193. Frome died in 2016.

6. Email dated March 31, 2015 (confidential source).

7. Rick Smith, "Cushman rears his ugly head again," Parklandwatch (Google Groups), Jan. 30, 2012 (reference Steve Scauzillo, "Park's comment time extended: Opponents call plan a federal land grab," Jan. 30, 2012); Rick Smith, "Cushman rears his ugly head again," Parklandwatch (Google Groups), Aug. 18, 2015 (reference Ron Arnold, "Property Owners Stand Up To National Park Bullying," *Daily Caller,* Aug. 18, 2015).

8. Roger Siglin, contributing to on-line exchange/blog about Chuck Cushman, posted on Parklandwatch (Google Groups), "Just to tickle your old memories," Jan. 14, 2015.

9. National Park Service, *The Administrative History of Cuyahoga Valley National Recreation Area,* Chapter 11.

10. *See* Phil Roberts, *Cody's Cave,* (Laramie, WY: Skyline West Press, 2012), "Federal Management v. Local Control" (chapter one).

11. Chuck Cushman, telephone conversation with the author, June 7, 2012.

12. *See, for example,* Carsten Lien, *Olympic Battleground* (San Francisco, CA: Sierra Club Books, 1991).

13. Laura A. Watt, *The Paradox of Preservation: Wilderness and Working Landscapes at Point Reyes National Seashore,* under contract with the University of California Press, anticipated publication in 2015.

14. E.g., *see* http://www.landrights.org/ak/wrst "McCarthy Creek Access Crisis," and related links. *Also,* Tom Kizzia, *Pilgrim's Wilderness: A True Story of Faith and Madness on the Alaska Frontier* (New York, NY: Crown Publishers, 2013). *Also see,* "Declaration of Hunter Sharp," Nov. 12, 2003, Case No. A03-0257-CV (RRB), U. S. District Court for the District of Alaska (viewable at http://www.landrights.org/ak/wrst/Hale-v-Norton.03-11-12.sharp.htm); "National Park Service War in the Wrangells," posting on website for the American Land Rights Association at

http://www.landrights.org/ak/wrst/cast.htm.

15. H. Duane Hampton, *How the U.S. Cavalry Saved Our National Parks* (Bloomington, IN: Indiana University Press, 1971) p. 18.

16. H. Duane Hampton, *How the U.S. Cavalry Saved Our National Parks* (Bloomington, IN: Indiana University Press, 1971) p.74.

17. H. Duane Hampton, *How the U.S. Cavalry Saved Our National Parks* (Bloomington, IN: Indiana University Press, 1971) 72-74 (W.H. Phillips to H.L. Muldrow, Act. Sec. Int., Sept. 21, 1885, NA, Dept. Int., P&M, 1885-1886, File 4072. In Response to a Senate Resolution, Jan. 12, 1886, the Acting Secretary forwarded the Phillips report to the Senate, where, on Feb. 1, 1886, it was referred to the Committee on Territories and ordered to be printed as *Senate Exec. Doc.* 51, 49th Cong., 1st Sess. (SN 2333), pp.1-29).

18. E.g., *see* Mariposa County, "Corrupt County – The Law of Sheriff Paige," *20/20* ABC News magazine (1991), https://www.youtube.com/watch?v=OvG6Y1w_Le4. *Also,* Clair Johnson, "State investigators seek criminal prosecution of West Yellowstone police chief," *Billings Gazette,* Apr. 30, 2014; Carly Flandro, "Unwritten Law of Small Towns," *Bozeman Daily Chronicle,* Jan. 16, 2011. *Also,* Christopher N. Osher, "Colorado laws allow rogue officers to stay in law enforcement," *Denver Post,* July 12, 2015; Christopher N. Osher, "How Colorado laws give fired police officers from other states a second chance here," *Denver Post,* Oct. 11, 2015; Christopher N. Osher, interview with Ryan Warner, "Why Fired Cops Get Second Chances in Colorado," *Colorado Public Radio,* Nov. 2, 2015.

19. See, *Crime in Federal Recreation Areas:A Serious Problem Needing Congressional and Agency Action,* Feb. 9, 1978, p. 11-13.

20. Article VI of the U.S. Constitution: "... all executive and judicial Officers, both of the United States and of the several States, shall be bound by Oath or Affirmation, to support this Constitution ..."; E.g., Ryan Lenz and Evelyn Schlatter, "Western 'patriots' Clash with Feds on Land-Use," *Southern Poverty Law Center Intelligence Report,* Summer 2011, Issue No. 142.; John M. Glionna, "Federal agency, local lawman dispute actions in Cliven Bundy case," *Los Angeles Times,* July 7, 2014; Les Zaitz, "Grant County sheriff viewed as 'security leak' as state seeks investigation," *The Oregonian,* Feb. 18, 2016.

21. E.g., *see* Amanda Marcotte, "Political Sleight of Hand," *Salon,* July 4, 2016 (http://www.salon.com/2016/07/04/its_political_sleight_of_hand_for_their_next_trick_republican_magicians_will_make_your_federal_land_disappear/)

22. James H. Pickering, *This Blue Hollow: Estes Park, the Early Years, 1859-1915,* (Boulder, CO: University Press of Colorado, 1999), 33-51, quoting *Denver Tribune,* August 26, 1874.

23. Ken Wright, *Why I'm Against It All* (Durango, CO.: Raven's Eye Press, 2003), 158-161.

CHAPTER TWENTY-ONE

Lessons Not Learned (The Legacy Lives On)

I t's amusing to recall my youthful observations about the beleaguered landscape in Northwest Indiana, and my surprise at the "culture of corruption" that existed there. I thought I would escape all that when I transferred to Yosemite National Park. I was naïve and more than a little idealistic.

Far from the dream assignment I had anticipated, the entire Yosemite experience was something closer to a nightmare, offering an even more intimate glimpse into government and police corruption than I had ever witnessed in Northwest Indiana. In a grim irony, one of the major differences between the two was the more insidious nature of what was going on in Yosemite, shrouded by the magnificent setting and the wholesome ranger image of the NPS. And there, instead of the Chicago Mob or "Outfit," the corrupting influence came from at least one member of Congress and members of what is still affectionately known within the NPS as the Yosemite Mafia. That loose-knit group that came together in the 1970s, remains an acknowledged presence in the agency. It has even been identified and described in academic works, such as a paper written in 1999, by Boise State University professor of political science, John Freemuth, Ph.D.:

> NPS is not a monolith, and questions of who decides agency policy must also be looked at from an internal perspective. There is surprisingly little information available on the internal culture of the NPS. What does seem apparent, however, is that there are a number of 'world views' within the agency. One example, told to me anecdotally, is the so-called Yosemite Mafia, employees with formative experiences in law enforcement gained at Yosemite who are now in positions of influence throughout the agency.[1]

As its name implies, the Yosemite Mafia is comprised of families and close friends who, over the years, have dominated the NPS law enforcement program through their own "clear line of succession." Even today, the same familiar family names can be found scattered among positions of power and influence, as the children of original members have been groomed and pre-positioned for their ascendancy within the agency. Meanwhile, even retired members retain significant influence over agency policies and practices, through their recurring roles as contracted instructors and consultants, or as board members of non-profit support organizations. Within this group there have, no doubt, been a variety of attitudes and approaches to law enforcement and ethics, generally, exhibited over the years and generations. However real and influential it may be, the Yosemite Mafia is still, after all, only an informal fraternity of current and former NPS employees. Many members have served with honor and integrity. But it is troubling to note just how many of those individuals have demonstrated an unhealthy tolerance and even empathy for their many powerful brethren who have crossed the line by engaging in serious acts of misconduct, up to and including felonies and other genuine acts of corruption.

In many ways, *that* is the real legacy of the Yosemite Mafia – where it all begins, by *enabling* abuse and misconduct by looking the other way, turning a blind eye, ignoring what they know or suspect, not reporting, destroying or throwing away evidence, covering up, or just forgiving serious and habitual violators because they are "good guys," friends, popular rangers, fun to be with, 2nd, 3rd, or even 4th generation NPS, or just loyal "green-blooded" employees. The beneficiaries of this troubling form of "professional courtesy" – select individuals who are effectively shielded from accountability – can be found scattered throughout the NPS to this day. Almost every veteran NPS employee, if candid, can identify someone they know who has managed to retain their grade, their position (and perhaps their law enforcement commission), and even been promoted, in defiance of all sense of reason and administrative norms. This approach to accountability and discipline cannot even be said to employ a "double standard," because it's not *that* consistent. It all depends on where you work, who you are and who you know; not what you did. Over the decades, this type of favored treatment and exemption from the normal rules of conduct and consequences has come to be accepted as a fact of life in the NPS, sometimes represented as agency support for its employees. But support for employees does not (should not) equate to the absence of accountability. The net result is a diminished respect and regard throughout the workforce for the rules and regulations that actually do exist, and an overall lowering of expectations for de facto (as opposed to official) standards of conduct and performance. If and when finally forced to do *something* by disclosures from other agencies, the press, or the courts, what action that *is* taken by the NPS is usually pursued with great reluctance, typically in the form of a convenient transfer or retirement, accompanied by quiet whispers between friends and colleagues, acknowledging that they knew there was a problem, all along (but did nothing about it).

This unfortunate condition helps explain why the NPS consistently ranks among the bottom third of federal agencies in surveys assessing employee job satisfaction and, particularly, respect for agency leadership.[2]

While there is a measure of truth in Freemuth's assessment that "the NPS is not a monolith," there is also, most certainly, a distinct, identifiable agency culture and a unique NPS-way of doing most things (e.g., "NPS law enforcement"). Certain common characteristics, good and bad, permeate the agency, affecting virtually all program areas. Among the arguably desirable characteristics is a deep sense of loyalty to the agency and a passion for its mission. Most NPS employees view themselves as members of an elite family, rather than mere bureaucrats and civil servants. However, those attributes can manifest negatively when priorities become confused and loyalty to the agency and its leaders conflicts with fulfillment of the statutory mission and other legal requirements. Outsiders are not expected to understand this. A cult-like mentality can be observed within the NPS, as organizational and personal loyalty frequently trumps knowledge, skill, or ability as a basis for advancement, serving to promote and perpetuate that same mentality over time. NPS employee organizations exist to promote this fraternal-like order, with membership and participation in obligatory gestures of homage, wining, dining, networking and self-promotion a virtual prerequisite for advancement in the agency. This mode of selecting leaders is increasingly apparent the higher up one goes in the agency food chain. Ironically, there are probably fewer enforced standards or prerequisites needed to qualify for a position as a park superintendent than there are for any other position in the agency, with no comprehensive superintendent "academy" or other officer-candidate-like school to attend, or even mandatory certifications to maintain. And while there certainly are many genuinely competent managers in the NPS, it is simultaneously stunning to witness the number of managers, up to and including superintendents and regional directors, who in spite of the perception of expertise and authority associated with their titles, have absolutely no credible background or training in the broad-based park operations or even basic legal standards for which they are responsible, relying instead upon political alliances to secure and retain their positions.

Where the NPS goes to extraordinary lengths to maintain an outwardly uniform appearance (the "green and grey"), little if any effort is expended on real program integrity and enforcement of uniform standards for performance and conduct. Those latter aspects are, instead, left to the discretion of local managers. This is accomplished through the agency's deliberately decentralized mode of operation and the absence of meaningful systems for program oversight. Collectively, these traits serve to resist outside pressures to change and impede organizational reforms. While there is most certainly an agency hierarchy, it does not always translate into – or coincide with – a coherent and disciplined chain-of-command. As I have observed in other discussions, in many respects "The NPS functions more as a loose confederation of independent parks, regions, and managers than as a unified federal agency under the meaningful direction of an agency head."[3] It is in this regard that Freemuth comes closest to the mark in his assessment that "NPS is not a monolith, and questions of who decides agency policy must also be looked at from an internal perspective ... there are a number of 'world views' within the agency." Parks, regions, programs, and their respective managers function with alarming levels of power and autonomy, and little if any real oversight.

Contrary to public perception, most Washington-level officials such as associate directors and national division chiefs (including the NPS chief ranger) have no line authority over local operations, and are therefore unable to exercise oversight or to intervene even when local or regional decisions may have adverse national, precedent-setting implications. From recruitment and hiring, to distribution of funds and accounts, local managers retain excessive levels of control over a wide range of critical programs, with the ability to manipulate the manner in which those programs function. Policies, regulations, and even administrative statutes are frequently viewed as mere guidelines. Instead, decisions made by managers and others are often based upon passions, loyalties, or raw political expedience.

Not surprisingly, this leads to an inconsistent and bewildering approach to parks management. The system is aggravating not only for employees, but for local constituents as well, who are frequently left with the impression that many park superintendents are more politicians than impartial bureaucrats or managers; that the right hand frequently does not know what the left hand is doing; and that the NPS is incapable of speaking with one voice, especially over time. Instead, each new superintendent or regional director is able to establish a new and often different set of local policies and priorities, while simultaneously abandoning or ignoring the priorities set by his or her predecessor, along with any promises or agreements previously reached with members of the local community, employees and outside stakeholders alike. The widespread acceptance of this management approach more than hints at the enormous damage that can be done by a single superintendent not only to community relations and public trust, but to park resources, as well.[4]

Perpetuation and even cultivation of this management model as an integral part of the NPS culture opens the door for serious abuse in all program areas, creating a vacuum to be filled by strong-willed or charismatic leaders in search of power and authority (big fish in little ponds), and by influential cliques and alliances like (but not limited to) the Yosemite Mafia. At the very same time, employees in the NPS who rigorously try to abide by policies, regulations, and other legal requirements or professional standards, encounter all manner of obstacles and are frequently viewed and labeled as obstructionists and troublemakers instead of "team players."

This troubling condition was identified, but not remedied, more than thirty years ago. In his seminal 1984 book, *America's National Parks and Their Keepers*, Ron Foresta observed that

> This confusion is not merely a matter of academic interest; rather, it is a serious practical concern. Criticisms of the agency's behavior indicate that there is basic uncertainty about its decisions. For example, one of its students told the author, "Many of the Service's problems would be solved if only it would say 'yes' and 'no' with some sort of predictability." Administrators in other federal agencies and environmental activists also perceive this inconsistency and blame it for the Service's unsettled and erratic relationship with its supporters.[5]

Foresta speculates that this condition developed during the Nixon administration under NPS director Ron Walker (1972-1975), when

> more autonomy went to agency subunits. Once routines of autonomous operation and interaction were established below leadership level, especially in the regional offices and in units responsible for congressional liaison, it was very difficult for directors to reassert their authority ... while regional directors and the superintendents of major parks established independent power bases through their dealings with local congressmen.

That, according to Foresta, caused the NPS to experience "a loss of steering capacity."[6]

* * *

One of the great ironies about the NPS is the role it plays in the preservation of America's history at numerous national historic sites by archiving documents, conducting research, and telling ("interpreting") its story to the public so that we may learn the lessons of history. This includes intense discussions about many of our nation's darker and more disturbing episodes. Yet the NPS, itself, has repeatedly demonstrated incredible resistance to accurately documenting and talking about its own history.

The concerted effort to craft the image of the NPS and to misrepresent the historical record of crime and other problems in parks was acknowledged in the 1992 CNN documentary, *Parks in Peril*. Reporters found that "The Park Service has put too many of its limited dollars up front, catering to the visitors, creating an illusion that all is well." That observation was followed with comments from a prominent NPS superintendent who tacitly acknowledged long-standing NPS efforts to manipulate its own public image, stating, "You want to create an experience for these people [visitors]. You want them to acknowledge that the parks are special. But by creating that magic you want, you do remove them from reality."[7]

But even more than crime, violence, and the need for law enforcement, the NPS has been particularly resistant to documenting and acknowledging agency history when it comes to the misconduct of its own managers and other employees, once again creating a "magical" image that is removed from reality.

Even while scandals are actually occurring and have been propelled into the public eye, the NPS successfully employs a strategy of "ignore it, it'll go away." Managers and their spokespersons skillfully dodge legitimate inquiries from the press, by refusing comment beyond their crafted statements and accounts because "This is an ongoing legal matter and as such we cannot discuss any details publicly," and thereafter still refusing comment on the same topic because by then, of course, it is "an old matter that we consider closed." All of this is predictably followed by the standard catch-phrase, "The National Park Service is committed to ensuring integrity and professionalism among its employees and will continue to take appropriate action when incidents, or accusations, of misconduct arise."[8] Regrettably, the action most commonly taken "when incidents, or accusations of misconduct arise" is to circle the wagons and call in government attorneys from the solicitor's office, who are there not to seek justice or to uncover the truth, but to defend the actions of miscreant managers and other employees against damages arising from civil claims that might otherwise be borne by the agency.[9] The knowledge that they will have access to free legal representation, regardless of their misconduct or poor judgment, only reinforces tendencies toward arrogance displayed by many managers, confident in the knowledge that most people, including aggrieved members of the NPS workforce, cannot afford the legal fees associated with a protracted action against the government. Meanwhile, employees who would love to speak up are stripped of a voice or the opportunity to tell what they know, through official gag orders and legitimate fears of reprisal.[10] So even if, as the saying goes, there truly are at least two sides to every story, the NPS frequently succeeds in making sure that only its version of the story is ever really heard. Consequently, over time, the truth never comes out, agency wrongs are never righted, no one is held accountable, the matter is forgotten, and the only account of events is tainted with agency spin and obfuscation.

This tendency toward cherry-picking, spinning, or altogether ig-noring historical accounts has not gone completely unnoticed. Com-menting on a 2012 study that documented weaknesses and inconsis-tencies in NPS support for historic preservation, retired NPS historian and author Richard West Sellars observed, "The NPS is indeed tone-deaf whenever it wants to be.... so much depends on timing and per-sonalities ... not so much on laws, regulations, and management poli-cies."[11] But the NPS can be far more than tone-deaf, and resistance to accurately preserving the historical record has been more than passive, as some managers have resorted to full-blown censorship by actually prohibiting park bookstores from carrying works that present docu-mented accounts of NPS misconduct and other incidents that are em-barrassing for the agency.[12]

This approach stands in contrast to the position recently taken by the Federal Bureau of Investigation regarding its own history of abuses, such as the surveillance and persecution of lawful political dissidents and pro-testers. Those abuses included the illegal eavesdropping on private con-versations of citizens such as civil rights leader Martin Luther King, Jr., in an attempt to gather potentially damaging information that could be used against him. Acknowledging that history, in 2013, FBI director James Comey established a new policy calling for classroom ethics training in his agency to be augmented with the requirement that "all new agents and analysts ... visit the national memorial to late civil rights leader Martin Luther King Jr. as a reminder not to repeat the abuses of the U.S. investi-gative bureau's past." In a speech to agency employees, Comey explained the new policy, declaring, "It will serve as a different kind of lesson – one more personal to the bureau – of the dangers of becoming untethered to oversight and accountability."[13]

More recently, in 2016, the president of the International Association of Chiefs of Police (IACP), Terrance M. Cunningham, addressed the or-ganization's annual convention with a similar message, observing,

> The history of the law enforcement profession is replete with ex-amples of bravery, self-sacrifice, and service to the community. At its core, policing is a noble profession made up of women and men who have sworn to place themselves between the innocent and those who seek to do them harm.... At the same time, it is also clear that the history of policing has also had darker periods.... This dark side of our shared history has created multigenerational – almost inherited – mistrust between many communities of color and their law enforcement agencies.... While we obviously cannot change the past, it is clear that we must change the future.... The first step in this process is for law enforcement and the IACP to acknowledge and apologize for the actions of the past ...[14]

Expanding on his message in an interview with *Police One* on-line magazine, Cunningham acknowledged that "not everyone will embrace the message we are carrying forth. However in no way does recognizing historical injustice discredit or take away from the nobility and valor of the [law enforcement] profession today." He added, however, that "Acknowledging what brought us to this current point, I believe, will form a deeper sense of trust, respect, and empathy among communities and law enforcement agencies."[15]

But no such acknowledgements are made by, and no such lessons are taught to the employees of the NPS. Instead, the agency continues to present its own form of sterilized, revisionist history, romanticized and largely void of accounts about disturbing historical events. Even oral histories undertaken for the agency reflect a concerted effort to exclude participation by "troublemakers" and others who might offer an unflattering or dissenting view.[16] That, in turn, perpetuates the cycle and fuels the passions of people who could accurately be described as history-deniers within the agency, who have chosen to "see no evil," as if blinders were an optional part of the iconic green and grey NPS uniform.

The failure to talk about these incidents or learn the lessons they have to offer, leaves far too many employees uninformed and unprepared to confront the legal, political, and ethical challenges that will be forced upon them when they, too, experience their own "rude awakening" in the face of misconduct in the workplace, and reprisal for attempting to reporting it.

When viewed from a historical perspective with access to inside information, one can see the same patterns of misconduct occurring over decades; from at least the 1970s to the present. This is true not just for minor infractions, but for serious violations; and not just by lower-level employees who might claim they didn't know any better, but also by senior managers who have learned not in the classroom, but through experience and observation, that for the politically and socially connected, there are no real consequences for serious misconduct and there is no consistent system of accountability in the agency. Even formal recommendations for administrative action contained in official incident reviews and reports (e.g., the Ken Patrick murder), are more often than not ignored; lost to history. These incidents are not studied and findings of accompanying reviews and reports are not retained or consolidated for application to reforms.

* * *

Though incidents of serious misconduct and acts of reprisal against whistleblowers were a fact of life in the NPS for as long as I was in the agency, it's no longer quite so easy to keep things quiet. Consequently, embarrassing incidents that are now exposed through the internet and the improved capabilities of the contemporary media are conveniently painted as anomalies or the result of recent leadership and organizational changes that took place in just the past decade or two; purportedly shifting away from "traditional NPS values" and an otherwise long tradition of integrity in NPS leadership found not more than a generation ago. That is a serious misdiagnosis of the problem, suggesting that the current condition is new rather than old, acute rather than chronic, and localized rather than systemic. That, in turn, keeps the door open for a continuing pattern of managerial malpractice. Looking to the leadership that created or embraced the culture and the conditions that I witnessed throughout most of my career is not likely to lead to a cure for what truly ails the NPS today.

For me, proof of a continuing tolerance for serious misconduct within the NPS, its management, and its law enforcement program, materialized in 2004, when the agency launched and aggressively pursued its "Hubbell Trading Post Investigation." I assumed responsibility for that investigation in 2006, after the case had already been underway for more than a year and half, and after the NPS had spent nearly a million dollars targeting an old-time Indian trader on the Navajo Reservation, falsely accused of stealing government funds. My investigation – the very last of my career – once again revealed a pattern of serious misconduct extending into the highest levels of the agency, confirming that nothing had been learned and nothing had really changed in the NPS since the scandal in Yosemite, a quarter-century before. Issues included false allegations and statements made in official reports and affidavits, key witnesses not interviewed and important witness statements not documented, the illegal search and subsequent illegal seizure of millions of dollars in property, the concealment of exculpatory evidence, and later the concerted effort by not just the Park Service, but also the OIG and even federal prosecutors, to cover up that same and other misconduct. While the characters, circumstances, and crimes were different from those I saw in Yosemite, there was a disturbingly similar pattern in the nature and dynamics of agency misconduct. Present, once again, were shoddy law enforcement practices and a federal prosecutor complicit in a "sloppily run" investigation, misuse of government funds and funds provided by a cooperating association, inappropriate management influence and pandering to powerful political interests, and ultimately another self-inflicted wound to the reputation of the NPS and fulfillment of its statutory mission. Absent, once again, was any form of accountability whatsoever for those who had created and contributed to the disturbing series of events. That investigation is chronicled separately in another book titled *The Case of the Indian Trader.* That story picks up where this story leaves off, filling in the gaps of the interim years with still more examples of high-level misconduct and corruption, and expanding on the NPS culture with an entire chapter devoted to the subject and the broader picture of how the NPS operates and continues to manage its law enforcement program to this day.

A synopsis of the events that occurred in *this* story – in Yosemite during the 1980s – is actually presented as background material in chapter five of *The Case of the Indian Trader*. Response from within NPS circles yielded a wide range of comments that reveal a great deal about the culture of the agency. One NPS retiree said:

> It seems there are a lot of people who leave NPS who are not happy with the agency, but I keep telling myself, they would probably not be happy anywhere"[17]

Another former NPS employee wrote:

> Paul Berkowitz had a hard time dealing with people at many locations, in numerous jobs. This might have indicated the real problem was his, not the people he worked for, or with....
>
> I perceived, sorry if I'm wrong, that Paul is a frustrated LAPD officer or detective, maybe FBI criminal investigator, who found himself in an agency he should have left after six months. He spends a lot of time on a culture (NPS) he apparently didn't like from the beginning.

Most telling is the observation that same blogger made about the events and people I encountered in Yosemite:

> I knew those "Yosemite mafia" folks he just can't get over, and didn't find them that bad.[18]

* * *

Through its success in obscuring the real history of misconduct within the agency, the NPS has succeeded in reframing the discussion now taking place about problems that *have* risen to the surface in the media. Those include the scandal at the Chesapeake and Ohio Canal National Historic Park where, without any administrative repercussions, senior officials perjured themselves in their efforts to prosecute a whistleblower; and at Lassen Volcanic National Park where a federal district court found that both the superintendent and chief ranger had destroyed evidence and obstructed investigation into the death of a young boy.[19]

In December of 2013, the Office of Special Counsel found that the new superintendent at Mesa Verde National Park in Colorado had acted in reprisal against two seasonal rangers (a retired married couple) for their previous whistle-blowing activities. The superintendent rescinded a job offer that had already been extended to the couple, when he learned about their role in reporting the previous park superintendent for suspected travel fraud and conflicts of interest in awarding a multi-million dollar contract related to development of the park's new visitor center.[20]

Even more recently, in May of 2014, watchdog group Public Employees for Environmental Responsibility (PEER) helped to expose and force an eventual (albeit long-overdue) investigation into "the largest official mass destruction of Indian pre-historic burial sites in modern history." In a press release subtitled "No Officials Punished in 10-Year Building Spree Defacing Effigy Mounds Monument," it was revealed that the park superintendent at Effigy Mounts National Monument (Iowa) had continually violated numerous environmental and historic preservation laws as part of her "$3 million 'empire building' with some 78 illegal structures, including boardwalks, ORV trails and other structures doing 'significant adverse damage' to irreplaceable archaeological artifacts.... Yet, despite knowledge of these actions for years, the Park Service said nothing and did little.... Multiple whistleblower reports to the [Midwest] Regional Office were ignored..."[21] Subsequently, in a 2015 article titled "National Park Service Buries Report on Effigy Mounds Scandal," the Associated Press reported that "The U.S. Attorney's Office ... declined to charge [the superintendent] and [the] monument maintenance chief ... with violating the Archaeological Resources Protection Act in 2012 after concluding the agency's 'weak and inappropriate initial response' undermined a criminal case." The article also described NPS efforts to conceal "a blistering internal report" prepared by an NPS special agent, by initially claiming that no such report existed.[22]

The NPS did subsequently release its own "after action review" of events at Effigy Mounds. In addition to the illegal ten-year building spree (2001-2011), that report acknowledged an entirely separate incident involving the *prior* superintendent (1971-1994), who, it was learned, in 1990 had directed an employee to help him steal two boxes filled with the remains of more than 40 native Americans that had been stored in the park's curatorial facility. A 2014 investigation revealed that the retired superintendent then kept the remains in his garage for more than twenty years, where several of the human bones were found "broken or fragmented beyond recognition."[23]

The purpose of the after-action review was "to determine root causes of the incidents that took place at Effigy Mounds National Monument ... that led to impacts to cultural resources and strained relations with American Indians, and to recommend positive actions to improve National Park Service practices going forward." The report offers details not only about failures in leadership at the monument, but also failures in operational oversight provided by the Midwest Regional Office. But one casual statement in the review also reveals a great deal about the agency's own failure to learn about NPS history and past incidents of misconduct and failures in leadership, service-wide. In discussing their collective reaction to their own findings, the authors of the report acknowledge that "everyone is astonished that the incidents at Effigy Mounds National Monument could have happened over the course of so many years" They then ask "Are similar incidents happening at another park?"[24]

* * *

2016 marked the Centennial of the National Park Service (1916-2016). That milestone was celebrated at parks across the country, in the media, and even on the National Mall.[25] But the 2016 celebration was marred by an unprecedented number of highly publicized disclosures about ethical lapses and failures of leadership in the NPS. Those disclosures prompted *High Country News* executive editor and publisher Paul Larmer to pen an article titled "For the Park Service, an uncomfortable birthday."[26] Other national coverage included an article discussing a half-dozen cases involving NPS managers caught up in scandals for which they received little if any punishment. That article, appearing in E&E's *Greenwire* series on the NPS Centennial, was aptly titled "Park Service leaders break rules but skate by."[27]

Most prominent in the national news were the results of a 2014-2016 OIG investigation confirming a 15-year pattern of sexual harassment, discrimination, and even assault perpetrated by boatmen river-rangers at Grand Canyon National Park, targeting female employees assigned to conduct scientific research and other work on the Colorado River. The investigation was initiated only after a group of thirteen current and former park employees co-signed a complaint letter sent to the Secretary of the Interior. The OIG's resulting January 2016 report, titled "Investigative Report of Misconduct at the Grand Canyon River District," documented failure at every level of the agency – local, regional, and national – to address the known problem, with "evidence of a long-term pattern of sexual harassment and hostile work environment," including cases where "incidents were reported to GRCA [and regional] supervisors and managers, but were not properly investigated."[28] According to the publicly released version of their report (which identifies victim-"employees" as well as "boatmen" and "supervisors" by numbers rather than names), the OIG:

> interviewed 19 current and former NPS and commercial contractor employees who reported that River District employees had behaved inappropriately toward them during river trips. These individuals stated that the four current and former River District

employees had touched them inappropriately, made inappropriate sexual comments, propositioned them for sex, or otherwise behaved inappropriately during river trips. For example:

- Employee 1 described an incident in which Boatman 2 took a photograph under her dress during a 2005 river trip.

- Employee 2 described being repeatedly propositioned for sex by Boatman 1 during river trips.

- A former seasonal employee (Employee 3) reported that Boatman 1 repeatedly propositioned her for sex, that Boatman 3 was rude, and that Supervisor 1 had yelled at her....

- Another former employee, Employee 4, said that during a 2005 river trip, Boatman 3 behaved in a threatening manner toward her – yelling at her while holding an axe – while he was intoxicated.

- Employee 5 said that Boatman 1 inappropriately touched her back and buttocks during a 2013 river trip ...

- Eight of the 19 employees added that the men would behave in a hostile manner if their advances toward women were rejected or if women reported sexual harassment. For example, three former employees ... said that after Boatman 3's sexual advances were rejected, he would arbitrarily take them to different project sites than the ones they needed to work at, or he would refuse to take them to project sites altogether, which meant that they could not accomplish their assigned tasks for the trip.

- Employee 4 also stated that during one 2006 river trip, Boatman 3 refused to provide food for female GRCA employees after they rejected his sexual advances.

Several GRCA employees said that they witnessed abusive treatment of employees by Supervisor 1. One described him as a "classic bully" who "trains [other employees] through intimidation" and said that he has once seen him make a female NPS employee cry. Another said he had seen Supervisor 1 spit beer on a woman's head during a river trip.

Another River District Employee, Employee 10, described Boatman 2 as "aggressive" about trying to get women to have sex with him. He stated that Boatman 2, Boatman 3, and Supervisor 1 all tried to "get laid as much as possible" during river trips and that there was "some sort of wager ... or challenge between the three of them ... to see who would get laid the most."

The OIG report went to equal lengths to document the extent to which victim-employees had been afraid to report their experiences, and how both park and regional managers had failed to properly investigate incidents or take appropriate disciplinary action in response to numerous incidents that *had* been reported and that they *did* know about. But what the report did not identify was the OIG's own failure to address the issue when they had a chance, at least as far back as 2004.

Sexual discrimination and abuse in the workplace has been a well-known problem at the Grand Canyon since at least the 1970s. In the summer of 1971, when I worked there as a student volunteer, I was told stories about "wife swapping" between four or five married couples. Supervisory rangers on the south rim openly bragged about their sexual conquests with subordinates and female seasonal employees.

Years later, in August of 1986, a number of women independently came forward with complaints about a Grand Canyon ranger who had been caught "peeping" through their residential windows to watch them undress.[29] That ranger was "counseled" and later transferred several times to other park units, at each of which he was successively caught (and even arrested) for voyeurism, but never fired. He eventually reached the position of deputy superintendent at a national lakeshore in Indiana, where, in 1998, he was again arrested by local authorities, all the while retaining his position until his retirement in 2015.[30]

In 1999, several female rangers came together to file a formal EEO complaint alleging sexual discrimination and hostile working conditions at the Grand Canyon, in violation of Title VII of the Civil Rights Act of 1964. That complaint led to a federal lawsuit and finally, in 2001, an out-of-court settlement.[31] But when a new superintendent was assigned to the park, he refused to honor that agreement, claiming that since he had not been a party to the negotiations and settlement, he did not feel obligated to abide by it. He said if the women wanted the agreement enforced, they should file another lawsuit, if they thought they could afford it.

When I returned to work at the Grand Canyon as a supervisory special agent around that same period, I found that little if anything had really changed in the 20 years since my time there as a seasonal employee. Most apparent was the alcohol-fueled party atmosphere that existed on many official river trips, including those attended by the various park superintendents and their guest VIPSs. When it came to employee conduct on the river trips, a hands-off attitude seemed to be embraced by supervisors as well as senior park managers, characterized by the oft-cited motto, "what goes on the river, stays on the river."

Consequently, following a series of preliminary notifications, on July 30, 2004, I sent a memorandum to a senior official with the OIG, captioned "2004 Update; 18 USC 2244 (b), Abusive Sexual Contact in the GRCA [Grand Canyon] Workplace. Seeking outside intervention, I began the memo with the following admonition:

As you know, an alarming number of incidents of abusive sexual contact have been exposed this past year (2004) within the NPS workforce at Grand Canyon National Park (GRCA). I make particular mention of the term "exposed," because investigations and other inquiries that have been conducted (both official and unofficial) reveal that a number of these reported/detected incidents more than likely represent known recurring conduct by these same individuals, not previously acted upon.

The memo continued for five pages, outlining a series of documented incidents of workplace sexual abuse and assault – including incidents occurring on the river, involving NPS boatmen – identifying employee-suspects by name, and alerting the OIG to efforts by the park's superintendent and chief ranger to obstruct investigation by my own office.

My memo to the OIG closed with the following explanation:

I am sending you this letter for several specific reasons:

1. To document the alarming pattern of incidents occurring at GRCA involving NPS employees engaged in acts of [alleged] abusive sexual conduct both in the workplace as well as off-duty; and to question whether there exists some underlying tone or condition, set by current park management, that serves to tolerate and/or contribute to this type of behavior.

2. To draw your attention to the pattern of obstruction of investigations into these same, and similar incidents.

3. To once again point out the legitimate sense of hopelessness and fear of reprisal that GRCA employees feel, resulting in a reluctance to report misconduct.

4. To again highlight the inconsistent manner in which internal investigations are being requested and conducted at GRCA (as well as Service-wide), depending upon one's standing within the community and one's relationship(s) with key officials who are able to influence and/or prevent investigations conducted in response to these and other types of complaints and/or incidents.

Stressing the need for the OIG to undertake its own independent investigation, particularly with respect to river operations, I reiterated that such an investigation would need to include

exploration of whether this alleged incident represents a larger pattern of behavior (generally characterized as a "party atmosphere," that typically includes lewd behavior and excessive alcohol consumption) on "administrative" river trips that has long been, and continues to be, openly tolerated by senior management of the park (aka, "what goes on, on the river, stay s on the river"). Exploration of this broader issue as a contributing factor in the [supervisory river ranger's] case, would necessarily require a number of aggressive interviews with the park's most senior officials, including Division Chiefs and officials from the Superintendent's office, and could clearly not be effectively undertaken by the NPS, itself.[32]

Two years later, on June 4, 2006, I sent a second letter to the OIG, observing that nothing had improved with respect to sexual harassment and abusive sexual contact in the Grand Canyon workplace. Stressing, again, management's own role in contributing to the hostile working environment, and its dismissive and even obstructive approach to employee complaints, I reiterated the need for the OIG to intervene and conduct an independent investigation.[33]

Obviously, neither of these reports resulted in the needed investigation or any other form of intervention. In fact, one of the employees specifically named as a suspect in my 2004 memorandum was the very same supervisory river ranger (Supervisor 1) who *was* later identified as a ring-leader and principle offender by the OIG in their eventual 2016 report documenting sexual harassment within the Grand Canyon river unit.

But the highly publicized 2016 disclosures surrounding the scandal at the Grand Canyon did have a ripple effect, motivating courageous employees at other parks, including Yosemite, Yellowstone, and Canaveral National Seashore to speak up and complain, en masse, about hostile and abusive conditions. Those disclosures, in turn, led to hearings convened by the U.S. House Committee on Oversight and Government Reform, along with calls for the removal of several prominent park, regional, and even Washington-level managers. Those hearings, with powerful testimony presented by two current NPS employees, resulted in even more negative publicity for the NPS, with national news headlines from major outlets such as NBC News, Fox News, the *New York Post*, and *New York Magazine*, reading (respectively), "Sexual Harassment Rampant at National Parks, Official Say"; "Sexual harassment common in national parks, panel told"; "National parks are a hotbed of sexual harassment"; and even "The National Park Service is Full of Predatory Pervs."[34] Consequently, before the year was out, the superintendents at the Grand Canyon, Canaveral, and Yosemite – each hand-picked by the NPS director – had all been forced out, not so much for their failures in leadership, but by political pressure resulting from embarrassing national news reports about those failures in leadership that had been known and tolerated in the agency for a very long time.[35]

If this wasn't enough, that same centennial year (2016) the two-term director and career employee of the NPS, Jon Jarvis, was implicated in his own personal scandal after he deliberately bypassed agency ethics rules to have a book he had written while in office and on his government computer (*Guidebook to American Values and our National Parks*), published by the cooperating association known as Eastern National. The discussions between Jarvis and Eastern National were found to have occurred "around the time" that "Jarvis signed renewals for both of Eastern National's cooperating association agreements." Government ethics guidelines specifically state that employees who want to do outside work with any entity seeking to do business with the Interior Department must first gain approval from the Ethics Office, regardless of whether there is payment involved. Jarvis failed to comply with this directive, resulting in a request from the Department of the Interior for an investigation conducted by the Office of the Inspector General.[36]

When questioned by the OIG, Jarvis first claimed that Eastern National had initially approached him to write the book. He even provided emails to the OIG that made it appear as though that was the case. But other emails uncovered later in the investigation revealed that "it was in fact Jarvis who approached ... Eastern National's Chief Executive Officer to see if [he] would be interested in publishing it." The OIG also found that "Jarvis approved Eastern National's use of the [NPS] arrowhead logo on the book cover," and that "Jarvis stated he knew he risked '[getting] in trouble' by not seeking advice on his book from the Ethics Office. He felt, however, that if he had involved the Ethics Office and other DOI officials, the book would probably never have been published due to what he viewed as a lengthy approval process and some content that he believed was controversial." Explaining his actions, Jarvis told the OIG,

> [Looking back], Would I have done the same thing? Probably ... I think I knew going into this there was a certain amount of risk. I've never been afraid of a risk ... I've gotten my ass in trouble many, many times in the Park Service ... by not necessarily getting permission ... I've always pushed the envelope ... And I felt that this values analysis ... could be a very, very powerful tool to not only connect to the next generation but to resonate across political spectrums ... And it could be a little bit of something I could give back to the Park Service ... to the [National Park] Foundation, sort of set the bar in place that I feel needs to be for our second century ... And I felt, again, that if I wrote this on the job, subject to all of the review, [all] of the input ... all of the machinations that goes on in here, the Department, Communications, the Solicitor's Office ... [it] wouldn't happen ... So I took the risk knowingly, I guess.

If the tone expressed by Jarvis sounds familiar, it may be because of the similarity it bears to the attitude the OIG found in Yosemite National Park thirty-two years earlier, in 1984, when they observed that along with bending the rules, "Lee Shackelton's philosophy was 'it is easier to take punishment than to ask permission.'"[37] Much easier, indeed.

Now, as punishment for *his* actions, Jarvis received a "formal letter of reprimand" from the Secretary of the Interior, and was ordered to attend monthly ethics training (i.e., watch training videos). He was also "relieved of his responsibility to manage the NPS ethics program."[38]

In their report, the OIG cited many violations of policy that had occurred when Jarvis made his deal with Eastern National. But once again, in a manner reminiscent of their reports about Yosemite in the 1980s, the OIG omitted reference to potential criminal violations. Most conspicuously, the OIG made absolutely no citation or reference to 18 USC 1001, "false statements," relating to Jarvis's claim that it had been Eastern National that approached him to write and publish the book, rather than the other way around.

Nevertheless, news about the OIG's investigation into Jarvis's actions and his resulting "punishment" did generate considerable discussion within the NPS. Many people were quite critical. But at least as many others were supportive of the powerful director and the actions he had taken in pursuit of his own "noble cause."

Commenting on the story, as covered in *National Parks Traveler* online magazine, one NPS retiree wrote:

> I totally understand what he did and why. It's a good book and a positive heartfelt action by a dedicated man. I wouldn't have retired if there were more senior staff like Director Jarvis.[39]

Still another wrote:

> It's too bad a man who dedicated his life to public service gets a slap on the hand for something so minor so late in his career. I am sure he had something he thought was important to say in support of our National Parks, and that's why he wrote the book. Good for him![40]

And most telling of all:

> Director Jarvis is no more the criminal than any other NPS employee who tries to find a way to serve the resources and people they are committed to serve. No doubt there was someone near him who has an axe to grind and found a way to get him. In to-

day's political environment and social norms employees looking for ways to hurt those in leadership will file formal complaints and charges when they don't agree with a manager's decisions. There is little left of respect for the person, their knowledge, skills and devotion. Jarvis has devoted over 40 years of his life to the NPS and we must believe his intentions were and continue to be the very best for the NPS. Three cheers for this man who is NPS tried and true![41]

Enough said. The legacy lives on.

Endnotes

1. John Freemuth (Department of Political Science, Boise State University), *The National Park Service's Management Policy in the 21st Century,* The George Wright FORUM, 1999. *Also see,* Arthur H. Westing (Robert Paehlke, editor), "The National Park Policy Environment," *Conservation and Environmentalism: An Encyclopedia* (New York, NY: Garland Publishing, Inc., 1995).

2. *The Best Places to Work in the Federal Government,* "Agency Report (National Park Service)," 2014, http://bestplacestowork.org/BPTW/rankings/detail/IN10.

3. Paul Berkowitz, *The Case of the Indian Trader: Billy Malone and the National Park Service Investigation at Hubbell Trading Post,* (Albuquerque, NM: University of New Mexico Press, 2011) 71.

4. For example, see Public Employees for Environmental Responsibility, press release of May 12, 2014, "Park Service Circles Wagons On Indian Burial Mounds Debacle; No Officials Punished in 10-Year Building Spree Defacing Effigy Mounds Monument."

5. Ronald A. Foresta, *America's National Parks and Their Keepers* (Wash., D.C.: Resources for the Future, Inc., 1984), 2.

6. Ronald A. Foresta, *America's National Parks and Their Keepers* (Wash., D.C.: Resources for the Future, Inc., 1984), 89-90. Interestingly, this period coincides with the years in which the Yosemite Mafia was "formed."

7. CNN, *Parks in Peril,* 1992, interview with Yosemite superintendent Mike Finley.

8. Dave Barna (NPS Public Affairs Officer), interview with *National Parks Traveler,* (refusing comment on then the Hubbell Trading Post Investigation), May 2, 2011. Dave Barna, interview, refusing comment on the Hubbell Trading Post Investigation, *E&E News,* July 27, 2011.

9. Claims awarded that exceed established thresholds are deferred to the treasury.

10. *See* Public Employees for Environmental Responsibility, "Park Service Forbids Off-Duty Staff From Writing About Work Issues Without Approval," Sep. 23, 2002, referencing NPS Intermountain Region Memorandum, from Intermountain Regional Director to All Employees, "Employee Ethical Responsibilities and Conduct," Sep. 16, 2002.

11. Kurt Repanshek, "Review of National Park Service's Approach to History Points to Weak Support for That Mission," *National Parks Traveler* (on-line news), Mar. 26, 2012. Dr. Sellars is the author of *Preserving Nature in the National Parks: A History* (New Haven: Yale University Press, 1997).

12. P.J. Ryan, "A View From the Overlook: Forbidden Books," *National Parks Traveler* (Apr. 3, 2013).

13. David Ingram, *Reuters News Agency,* "FBI orders new agents to see Martin Luther King memorial," Oct. 28, 2013.

14. Chief Terrence M. Cunningham (Wellesley, MA P.D.), speaking at the 2016 annual convention of the International Association of Chiefs of Police, San Diego, CA, Oct. 17, 2016.

15. Heather R. Cotter, interview with IACP President and Wellesley Police Department Chief Terrence Cunningham, *Police One* on-line magazine, Oct. 24, 2016.

16. Dwayne Collier, multiple emails to/from Robert Sutton, NPS/ANPR oral history coordinator, Apr. 28, 2014.

17. John Cissell, posting on Parklandwatch (Google Groups), May 22, 2011, http://groups.google.com/group/parklandsupdate/browse_thread/thread/ab40102b61e6b019/c434a9bf-f214e0c6?lnk=gst&q=The+case+of+the+indian+trader#c434a9bff214e0c6.

18. Doug Troutman, posting on Parklandwatch (Google Groups), May 22, 2011, http://groups.google.com/group/parklandsupdate/browse_thread/thread/ab40102b61e6b019/c434a9bf-f214e0c6?lnk=gst&q=Doug+Troutman+Paul+Berkowitz#c434a9bff214e0c6.

19. Rob Danno, *Worth Fighting For: A Park Ranger's Unexpected Battle Against Federal Bureaucrats and Washington Redskins Owner Dan Snyder,* (Shepherdstown, VA: Honor Code Publishing, L.L.C., 2012). *Thomas Botell, et al. v. USA*, U.S. District Court, Eastern District of California, Case #2:11-cv-1545 GEB GEH, document #91, June 8, 2011. Denny Walsh, "Judge Rules Negligence in Boy's Lassen Park Death," *Sacramento Bee*, May 15, 2013; Denny Walsh, "Feds settle with family whose son died in park," *Sacramento Bee*, Feb. 19, 2014.

20. Office of Special Counsel press release, Dec. 11, 2013, "OSC Settles Retaliation Case for Park Rangers." Also see, Kurt Repanshek, *National Parks Traveler*, "Seasonal Rangers Who Said They Lost Their Jobs For Blowing The Whistle Win Their Case," Dec. 16, 2013; Schundler.net family website ("The Dark Side of the NPS"), http://www.schundler.net/.

21. Public Employees for Environmental Responsibility, press release of May 12, 2014, "Park Service Circles Wagons On Indian Burial Mounds Debacle; No Officials Punished in 10-Year Building Spree Defacing Effigy Mounds Monument."

22. Ryan J. Foley, "National Park Service Buries Report on Effigy Mounds Scandal," *Associated Press*, Aug. 3, 2015.

23. National Park Service Investigative Services Branch, "Former Effigy Mounds Superintendent admits to stealing human remains," news release date Jan. 4, 2016.

24. National Park Service, *Strengthening Cultural Resources Stewardship in the National Park Service – Effigy Mounds National Monument After Action Review, April 2016*, p. 6 & 11.

25. https://www.nps.gov/subjects/centennial/index.htm.

26. Paul Larmer, "For the Park Service, and uncomfortable birthday," *High Country News*, Aug. 22, 2016.

27. Corbin Hiar, "Park Service leaders break rules but skate by," *Greenwire (E&E News)*, June 7, 2016.

28. DOI-OIG, "Investigative Report of Misconduct at the Grand Canyon River District," Jan. 12, 2016; Lyndsey Gilpin, "Investigations show broad harassment history in Park Service," *High Country News*, May 4, 2016; Phil Taylor, "Agency is failing to punish ethical lapses," *E&E News*, May 25, 2016; Dave Boyer, "National Park Service under fire for mismanagement, climate of sexual harassment," *The Washington Times*, June 19, 2016; Felicia Fonseca, "A federal investigation has found that National Park Service river trips turned the Grand Canyon into a hostile workplace for women," *U.S. News and World Report*, Jan. 12, 2016; Story Hinckley, "Grand Canyon National Park: History of sexual assault?", *Christian Science Monitor*, Feb. 18, 2016; Lisa Rein, "New Grand Canyon park chief of sexual assault: 'Some of our colleagues have suffered immeasurable harm,'" *The Washington Post*, Jul. 25, 2016; Kathryn Joyce, "Out here no one can hear you scream," *Huffington Post* (undated); Davis S. Lewis, "Scandal at Yellowstone – National Park Service Centennial Blackened by Disturbing Allegations." *The Montana Pioneer*, Sep. 7, 2016.

29. Written statement of Beth Betts, submitted 2001 to DOI-OIG, documenting 1986 "peeping tom" incident involving Gary Traynham.

30. Harrisonburg Police Department, Case #87-08-12-1822; Harrisonburg Police Department,

Case #87-1463; Shenandoah National Park, Case/Incident #('87) 701516; Shenandoah National Park Case #('87) 701518; Transmittal memorandum from John P. Alderman, AUSA, to Mary Thurman, Deputy Clerk, U.S. District Court for the Western District of Virginia, "*United States v. Gary M. Traynham*"; Ken Kosky, "Locker room peeping case goes to trial," *Porter County Times* (?), July 3, 2000; Grand Canyon National Park Case #01-03576; etc.

31. *Beverly Perry, Jennifer Sypher, and Sherrie Collins v. Bruce Babbitt* (*Secretary of the Interior*, filed Jan. 2000 in USDC for the District of Arizona (No. CIV '00 0092 PHX RCB), alleging violation of title VII of the Civil Rights Act of 1964, as amended, 42 USC Sec. 2000, et seq. This civil action was preceded by formal administrative complaints filed with the NPS in April of 1999.

32. Paul Berkowitz to DOI-OIG Stephen A. Hardgrove, "2004 Update, 18 USC 2244(b), Abusive Sexual Contact in the GRCA Workplace," July 30, 2004.

33. Paul Berkowitz to DOI-OIG Stephen A. Hardgrove, "Whistleblower Complaint/Report Update, regarding 18 USC 2244(b), Abusive Sexual Contact in the GRCA workplace," June 4, 2006.

34. Voluntary testimony was presented by NPS employees Brian Healy and Kelly Martin. News coverage included that by *NBC News*, "Sexual Harassment Rampant at National Parks, Officials say," Sep. 23, 2016 (http://www.msn.com/en-us/news/us/sexual-harassment-rampant-at-national-parks-officials-say/ar-BBwvK9V?OCID=ansmsnnews11); *Fox News*/Associated Press, "Sexual harassment common at national parks, panel told," Sep. 22, 2016 (http://www.foxnews.com/politics/2016/09/22/sexual-harassment-common-at-national-parks-panel-told.html); *New York Post*/A.P., "National parks are a hotbed of sexual harassment," Sep. 23, 2016 (http://nypost.com/2016/09/23/national-parks-are-a-hotbed-of-sexual-harassment/); and Adam K. Raymond, "The U.S. National Park Service Is Full Of Predatory Pervs," *New York Magazine*, Sep. 23, 2016.

35. Kirby-Lynn Shedlowski (NPS/GRCA Public Affairs Officer), "Superintendent Dave Uberuaga Announces Retirement," *Grand Canyon News Release*, May 17, 2016; Dinah Voyles Pulver, "Canaveral seashore chief reassigned following investigations," *The Daytona Beach News Journal*, Sep. 24 & 25, 2016; Don Neubacher (NPS superintendent at Yosemite National Park) to All Employees, "Retirement of Yosemite Superintendent Don Neubacher," Sep. 28, 2016.

36. DOI-OIG, "Investigative Report of Jonathan Jarvis," posted to the web Feb. 25, 2016.

37. Herbert R. Gherke (NPS Regional Law Enforcement Supervisor), OIG interview, June 13, 1984, DOI-OIG Case #4VI-090.

38. Michael Connor, Deputy Secretary, memorandum to Mary L. Kendall, Deputy Inspector General, "Response to Office of the Inspector General Report of Investigation Regarding Jonathan Jarvis (Case No. OI-PI-15-0609-I)."

39. "Left after 34 years service," posting on *National Parks Traveler*, "OIG: National Park Service Director Skirted Ethics Office in Writing Book, Reprimanded," article by Kurt Repanshek, Feb. 25, 2016.

40. Sally Gale, Feb. 26, 2016, posting on *National Parks Traveler*, "OIG: National Park Service Director Skirted Ethics Office in Writing Book, Reprimanded," article by Kurt Repanshek, Feb. 25, 2016.

41. "Alex," Feb. 26, 2016, posting on *National Parks Traveler*, "OIG: National Park Service Director Skirted Ethics Office in Writing Book, Reprimanded," article by Kurt Repanshek, Feb. 25, 2016.

CHAPTER TWENTY-TWO

A New Legacy
(A Call to Action)

My time in Yosemite was most certainly a life-changing experience, my own rude awakening. That experience left me with a healthy dose of skepticism and a distinct lack of reverence for officials who abandon their oath of office in favor of their egos and their quest for power. My own skepticism and irreverence has been mistakenly perceived by some as cynicism, but those people are wrong. I am not a cynic. I did not give up on my dreams. I remain an unapologetic idealist. It is my idealism that accounts for the decisions I've made and the seemingly crazy things I've done ("career suicide") to reject and report what I saw and experienced in Yosemite, and thereafter. It is my idealism that reinforces my belief that institutions and agencies like the NPS can change and get better.

I offer no apologies for the decisions I made and the things I did throughout the entire ordeal in Yosemite. If I have any regret at all, it is only that I was not more forceful in my efforts to expose what occurred, and less concerned with protecting the reputation of my supervisors and the image of the NPS. A handful of unscrupulous politicians and corrupt NPS officials effectively got away with their crimes and their cover-up. But neither the public nor the parks have been well served by the Park Service's continuing ability to hide behind its image and conceal its bad behavior and organizational deficiencies.

And that brings me back full circle to a point made earlier. The events documented in this book, when juxtaposed against the events documented in *The Case of the Indian Trader,* span a period of more than thirty years. But these events – each of these true accounts – are merely bookends demarcating the beginning and end of my career as a criminal investigator with the NPS. The middle years, while not quite so tumultuous, were nevertheless filled with an equally disturbing array of encounters with unscrupulous supervisors working within an organization corrupted by the absence of meaningful oversight, and an unacceptable level of tolerance for misconduct, especially within the ranks of its managers.

That pattern suggests that the NPS has a corruption problem. It is not systemic corruption, per se', so much as a systemic lack of accountability, allowing corruption that does exist to go unaddressed over the long-term.

And though it is not the unabashed and sometimes violent corruption that has plagued the governments and agencies in and around Chicago and Northwest Indiana, or Frank Serpico's New York Police Department, it is still quite real, frustrating and compromising the legitimate efforts of many honest, hard-working employees who are trying to play by the rules and do the right thing. It is a sub-culture of corruption borne not so much out of greed, as it is out of a misplaced set of values and priorities (e.g., over what is "America's best idea"), and an obsession with the agency image at the expense of real professionalism.

While not addressing the embedded, multi-generational nature of the problem, a similar observation about the NPS was offered by Public Employees for Environmental Responsibility (PEER, est. 1996) in a 2014 news release captioned "Accountability & the Park Service – Like Oil and Water."

> "The current leadership of the Park Service cultivates a culture of corruption where even gross management misconduct is overlooked in return for loyalty," stated PEER Executive Director Jeff Ruch, pointing to a string of cases where flagrant violations were not acted upon until they reached the public's attention. "By contrast, the Park Service has no tolerance for whistleblowers and will rabidly pursue the pettiest of violations to punish perceived dissidents."[1]

Evidence of that culture can be observed throughout the NPS, to varying degrees at different times in the various parks, regions, and programs across the country. Those fluctuations occur based almost entirely on the personality and character of the local manager, who independently sets the standards and the tone for behavior throughout his or her domain, with near complete autonomy.

Nationally, however, because of the heightened potential for abuse, this culture has had its most damaging and reverberating impact on the agency's law enforcement program – or more accurately, its "protection" program, where an historic commitment to the ranger image has systematically delayed or altogether impeded efforts to professionalize.

That is not to say that things have not improved over the years. Basic training that NPS commissioned rangers now receive at the Federal Law Enforcement Training Center is every bit as good, if not better, than that presented in most state or local police academies. Most rangers are now properly classified, adequately compensated, and adequately equipped to carry out their law enforcement duties. Since the mid-1990s the agency has had its own small cadre of special agents, responsible for investigating major crimes that occur in parks. Written policies are in place to guide rangers and managers in the proper exercise of law enforcement authorities. But in spite of all these trappings and at least the appearance of improvements – including periodic background investigations (but still no psychological screening) and the agency's own internal affairs unit known as the Office of Professional Responsibility – the single most critical component of a true "profession" is still missing from the agency. The agency still lacks the *discipline* and the *will* to employ an effective system for accountability and adherence to professional standards. Critical policies that should be rigorously applied as tools to achieve genuine program integrity are, at best, inconsistently enforced. Many managers still view such policies more as flexible guidelines to be conveniently ignored, or worse, to be just as conveniently applied for use as administrative weapons when needed for political purposes, including acts of reprisal. Law enforcement is still not recognized or managed in the NPS as a legitimate profession, and that says a great deal about the agency, overall.

* * *

Though it does not get enough attention in the popular media today, behind the scenes in the law enforcement community, most good cops – the real professionals and real leaders (including a lot of frustrated NPS rangers and special agents) – hate dirty cops even more than they hate common crooks. Dirty cops, dirty departments, and even "merely incompetent" cops, make it harder and more dangerous for good cops and good departments to do their job; eroding public trust and fostering resistance to our legitimate efforts, often with immediate and deadly consequences. I have participated in conversations about this with colleagues at the federal, state, and local level, throughout my own law enforcement career. It is unfortunate, however, that most of these conversations do, indeed, occur only "behind the scenes." That suggests that police administrators still have a lot more to do to create an environment where good cops are comfortable taking a stand and confronting bad cops and bad practices when and where they see them. While long overdue, this is a subject that appears to finally be receiving appropriate attention, at least in part as a result of the ease with which questionable police behavior is increasingly documented on smart phones and shared on the internet and with the media.

But in the same way that good cops are justly angered whenever a bad cop brings shame to the law enforcement profession, and as renewed attention is being directed to the need for law enforcement to better "police" itself, environmentalists and all those who love our national parks should be angered and moved to action whenever an NPS (or other agency) manager – through arrogance, deception, underhanded tactics, or other forms of misconduct, with or without "noble cause" – provides fuel for those who would see those parks and other public lands afforded a diminished level of protection. Lip-service and policies notwithstanding, this is something I have *not* heard discussed within the NPS. Perhaps that's because the consequences of misconduct in the environmental community are not so readily apparent, but are seen only with the benefit of hindsight and *full* access to the complete historical record. Only then does it become apparent that the failure to acknowledge and confront misconduct, whether openly or internally, and to hold employees accountable, is a *disservice,* not only to our treasured parks and the cause of resource protection, but also to the vast majority of NPS employees; good people placed in untenable work situations, while simultaneously exposed to the indiscriminate backlash of suspicion and scorn from those who are affected by unaddressed agency misconduct.

In truth, most of the problems that exist in the NPS could be fixed if the agency could move beyond its obsession over image, and simply focus on integrity and achieving true excellence in all of its programs. If the NPS could get past its own prejudices and misconceptions about cops versus rangers, and were to ever really understand, embrace, and promote law enforcement, along with other programs in the agency, as a genuine profession – with all of the special demands and safeguards that implies – it might well find that its long-held anxiety about the image it projects to the public would be readily resolved on its own. Stated more bluntly, the NPS needs to clean up its act and stop supporting supervisors, managers, and other employees who do stupid things – legal or not – in the name of a cherished image and their own "noble cause," but who, in reality, only piss people off and bring shame to the agency. That change in approach might also go a long way toward silencing agency critics (like Cushman) or at least diminishing their own legitimacy in opposition to the NPS and its mission.

* * *

In 2011, I was interviewed by *Indian Country Today* magazine for an article subtitled "A Whistleblower Speaks." When asked why I had stayed with the NPS as long as I did. I offered the following explanation:

> I love our national parks and genuinely believe they serve a great national purpose by preserving our natural and cultural resources and heritage. I was drawn to the agency by the same idealism that infects most NPS employees. But over time my relationship with the NPS became far more complicated. I love the NPS for what it is supposed to be – for its idealistic mission, its frequently magnificent work settings, its many great employees and the incredibly diverse and unique challenges it offers to someone interested in professional law enforcement, or any other profession, for that matter.

I love it for what it could be. But I hate the manner in which many incredibly talented, hard-working and honest employees are repeatedly beaten down, abused, dismissed and maligned as malcontents or troublemakers. Meanwhile the agency seems to simultaneously tolerate and often even reward incompetence, misconduct, or just overinflated egos. The tolerated presence of a powerful and influential minority of incompetent and unscrupulous employees in the workforce has held the agency back. The NPS has failed to achieve its full potential, largely through the inconsistent application of laws and policy and an uncanny ability to deflect or ignore legitimate criticism and to resist reforms.

As much as anything else, I stayed with the NPS because I'm idealistic and I'm stubborn ... my early experiences in Yosemite National Park in the 1980s had a profound effect on me. That was a rude awakening, to find out that in spite of its public image, there are some genuinely bad and unscrupulous people in the NPS in positions of significant power, undermining the ideals of the agency and abusing and taking advantage of the authority they've achieved. In the wake of my efforts to expose illegal bugging, extortion, blackmail, the falsification of reports and destruction of evidence in Yosemite's law enforcement office, the NPS (aided by certain members of Congress and even the OIG) embarked on such an effective cover-up effort, comprised of outright lies and simultaneous character assassination, that arguably I didn't have anywhere else to go. Realistically I had only two choices; to flat-out quit law enforcement and find another career, which is what they wanted me to do, or stubbornly stick it out and stand my ground. I chose the latter. I decided to stay in law enforcement and try to make a difference in how the NPS operates.[2]

I still think that sums it up pretty well.

National parks may not be America's *best* idea, but I do believe they are one of America's *better* ideas, and are worth preserving and protecting for future generations. And in spite of its flaws, the NPS does fulfill its mission, serving hundreds of millions of people every year who are able to enjoy America's iconic scenery and treasured natural and cultural resources, largely unimpaired. That still happens because of the federal laws and regulations that are in place to protect those resources, and because of the thousands of dedicated NPS employees – often maligned as "faceless bureaucrats" – who honorably live up to their Constitutional oath and give their all in the performance their duties every day, out of the limelight.

But there is much that can be done to improve the NPS and make it a better agency. Structural reforms are critically needed to enhance oversight, increase accountability, and assure consistency in how parks and NPS programs are run. But even more than that, and before anything else, the NPS needs a different kind of leadership; honest, credible, intolerant of misconduct and incompetence, and courageous enough to shake things up; true to the NPS mission, but neither wedded nor beholden to a stagnant NPS culture.[3] People with those qualities have long worked in the NPS, but they have seldom been recognized or rewarded with advancement to positions where they can affect the type of cultural and structural change that is needed. But with those kinds of people properly positioned throughout the top levels of the agency, significant reforms could be achieved in relatively short order. Even if agency critics do not agree with NPS goals or decisions, they should then no longer be able to argue that the NPS and its leaders cannot be trusted. As the NPS embarks on its second century as steward of our national parks, and on the heels of an embarrassing centennial year, now is the perfect time to set about that task.

But to reach that goal and avoid the repetition of past mistakes, the NPS needs to confront its own history and the reality of what actually goes on inside the agency – what actually has gone on inside the agency for a very long time. If the FBI and the IACP can do that, then the NPS certainly can, too. Finally sharing this account as a private citizen, these many years later, is part of my ongoing effort to make that happen.

Endnotes

1. Public Employees for Environmental Responsibility, "Accountability & the Park Service – Like Oil and Water: Canaveral Seashore Probe Finds Fraud, Nepotism, and Mismanagement, But No Action," (news release) Oct. 8, 2014 (http://www.peer.org/news/news-releases/2014/10/08/accountability-and-the-park-service-like-oil-and-water/).

2. Melvin Jordan, "National Park Service Gone Rogue: A Whistleblower Speaks," *Indian Country Today*, Nov. 3, 2011 (interview with Paul Berkowitz).

3. That NPS culture has previously been described as "100 years of tradition, unimpeded by progress."

Appendix:

Testimony of Paul Berkowitz, presented before the House Subcommittee on Parks, Forests, and Public Lands, October 15, 1985, Yosemite, California[1]

My name is Paul Berkowitz. I am a National Park Service Ranger stationed here in Yosemite National Park. My testimony is presented as that of a citizen and a concerned member of Yosemite's law enforcement community.

I feel considerable anxiety about testifying here today, as I am certain I will be subjected to reprisal, just as I have already been subjected to reprisal and harassment for having previously attempted to address these same issues to National Park Service management. I also harbor fears for my career as well as personal and family safety. A number of people very highly placed in the Park Service as well as the local federal criminal justice system will be implicated by this testimony. However I view this opportunity to speak to you as a last resort directed at drawing attention to what I believe is grossly unethical, unprofessional, and perhaps criminal conduct on the part of some members of NPS upper management as well as senior law enforcement officials within Yosemite National Park.

---

1. It's fascinating to look through this document, more than thirty years later, and evaluate my frame of mind back then. It may not be the most well written or eloquent piece, but I think the pressure and the passion of the period still comes through. Even now, as I read and transpose my testimony, I remain convinced that I was right on almost every point, and said most of the things that needed to be said, whether anyone was listening or not.

Some of the points I raised in my testimony were addressed over subsequent years. During the time I was assigned to the Washington, D.C. office, between 1992 and 1995, we succeeded in re-writing the basic position description for so-called "law enforcement rangers," increasing pay to a livable wage by locking-in the journeyman level to GS-9. At the same time, we won the hard-fought battle to obtain what is referred to as "6-c" law enforcement retirement for uniformed, commissioned rangers. Even before then, a handful of us succeeded in securing proper civil service classification for the Service's criminal investigators, or Special Agents, as they are now known. In spite of those successes, there is still a lot of work to be done to professionalize the NPS law enforcement program. .

The first issue I'd like to address is that of the federal criminal justice system in Fresno which serves the Yosemite community. I am concerned about what I perceive as a growing trend among Yosemite area defendants to successfully avoid aggressive prosecution by simply declining our local magistrate's jurisdiction and having their cases transferred to District Court in Fresno. There, cases are all too often dismissed or bargained down simply because the U.S. Attorney and courts are overloaded with more traditional federal crimes, or because the structure of the federal criminal justice system in Fresno is not designed to serve the needs of an exclusively federal residential and resort community with mundane street crime. I don't question a defendant's right to have cases heard in Fresno. But I do propose that we should insist on a structure in the court and prosecutor's office which ensures that victims of crime and all citizens in Yosemite are afforded full consideration and justice comparable to that provided by courts in most normal communities, and that consideration and justice be afforded without routine dismissals or bargains being rendered out of expedience rather than for true lack of prosecutorial merit.

The next point I wish to address is considerably more sensitive, and is the issue which I believe NPS management has, for nearly the last two-and-a-half years, attempted to hide and keep from view.

In February of 1982 I transferred to Yosemite to work as a criminal investigator in what was then known as the Law Enforcement Office. Early on, within a year of my arrival, I was detailed to full-time involvement in what has been referred to as the Curry Case; an investigation directed at illegal drug use in Yosemite and the Yosemite Park and Curry Company's alleged role in protecting area drug dealers and users. This investigation was conducted under the direct supervision of the two law enforcement specialists, Lee Shackelton and Scott Connelly, with regional supervision and fiscal monitoring provided by the Regional U.S. Park Police Captain in San Francisco. In the course of my involvement in this investigation I became aware of what I perceived as a recurring pattern of unprofessional investigative procedure and, in many instances, outright unethical and perhaps criminal conduct on the part of the two lead investigators. In an effort to address this conduct and to remove myself from a position of potential culpability through passive complicity, I attempted to go through supervisory channels to make report of this matter. General allegations which I would make included:

- Obstruction of justice
- Suppression of exculpatory evidence
- Tampering with physical evidence
- Falsifying and embellishing criminal reports

- Misrepresentation and possible perjury before the Grand Jury
- Misuse of government imprest funds
- Violation of OPM [Office of Personnel Management] and NPS policies and guidelines
- Routine unauthorized use of government vehicles
- Acceptance of supplemental second salaries for work performed on government time
- Falsification of overtime pay requests
- Falsification of government imprest vouchers

Some of the specific points which were cited in support of these allegations included:

1. That imprest "buy" and "information" funds were improperly being used to actually supplement the regular incomes of salaried GS-5 officers and informants.

2. That informants with criminal backgrounds were being recruited [and] at government expense sent through a law enforcement academy, and then placed on regular government salary with a law enforcement commission so that they could operate without constraints normally placed upon informants, and could technically be represented as federal officers in testimony before the Grand Jury and criminal courts.

3. That informants with criminal backgrounds were recruited, placed on normal government salary, and without a law enforcement commission allowed to operate independently, making uncontrolled drug buys; and that their activities were represented to the Grand Jury and criminal courts as those of commissioned officers.

4. That acquisition of exculpatory evidence was routinely discouraged, and once acquired was often destroyed.

5. That OPM and NPS personnel and law enforcement policies and guidelines were routinely ignored.

6. That independently received reports of criminal conduct on the part of informants and/or so-called officers were routinely not investigated for fear that court credibility would be diminished. In one instance, one "officer" was routinely required to submit urine samples as a means of controlling his own drug use. Those urine samples were subsequently destroyed and never tested.

7. That in an effort to resolve a threatened personal lawsuit against him, the lead investigator gave orders to retroactively falsify

overtime pay for an employee [retained] as a professional informant who was filing that suit.

Additionally, specific violations of federal criminal statutes were cited, and in all instances supporting physical, documentary, and testimonial evidence was cited in support of these allegations.

As early as June or July, and again on August 11, 1983 I initiated telephone contact with the Regional U.S. Park Police [USPP] Captain in San Francisco to make report of these matters. I outlined my concerns and cited specific examples of possible illegal conduct which concerned me, with emphasis on misuse of the special imprest fund which had been established to buy drugs and information.

The response I received from the USPP Captain was that there was nothing he could do; but with a caution to make sure I did not participate in any illegal acts. This is the same response I received in two separate phone conversations with this individual.

On September 1, 1983 I personally met here in Yosemite with the Regional USPP Captain to make a third report of suspected conduct in the Law Enforcement Office as a part of the special investigation. I presented documentary evidence in support of my allegations. The USPP Captain expressed deep concern over these allegations and acknowledged there appeared to be a problem, but went on to claim that there was nothing he could do, and he again cautioned me not to participate in any illegal activities.

On March 7, 198[4], after having observed this conduct continuing without intercedence [sic] from the regional office, I established telephone contact with the U.S. Department of [the] Interior Office of Enforcement and Security. I spoke with a ranking official in that office, detailed my allegations, and requested his assistance by placing me in contact with an investigator worthy of trust from the Office of the Inspector General [OIG]. This individual acknowledged that my allegations were extremely serious and promised to establish contact with the OIG on my behalf, and arrange for investigators to get in touch with me.

In May of 1984 after having heard nothing from the OIG, I re-contacted the Office of Enforcement and Security. I was advised that my request for involvement of the OIG had been reconsidered and that, instead, the matter had referred back to Washington-level NPS management. I objected to this maneuver, citing previous lack of response from the regional office. But, expressing my desire to pursue the matter at the lowest possible effective level, I agreed to be patient and await the NPS response.

On May 16, 1984, at 4:30 p.m., I was called in to meet with Yosemite's personnel officer. In this meeting I was advised that the Office of the Inspector General had, in fact, entered into an investigation of the Law Enforcement Office. The personnel officer stated she had been requested to elicit information from me concerning my allegations. She stated that this information would be turned directly over to investigators for the OIG, who would be in the park to meet with me the week of June 4, 1984.

Stipulating that this was only because of the promised arrival of the OIG, I agreed to outline in very general terms the allegations I was directing toward operations of the Law Enforcement Office.

On June 4, 1984 I learned from a co-worker who had been in contact with the Regional USPP Captain that investigators from the OIG would, in fact, not be coming to Yosemite. I phoned the park personnel office to confirm this change in fact. That afternoon, enraged, I placed a phone call to the hotline of the U.S. Department of [the] Interior Office of the Inspector General.

On June 5, 1984 I made contact with a Sacramento-based agent of the OIG. I identified myself, explained my allegations, and detailed the ordeal which had brought [me] ultimately to contact his office. I expressed my dismay that agents from his agency had failed to show up in Yosemite as I had been promised. He responded saying he didn't know what I was talking about.

Over the next day or two, after extensive inquiry with the Washington-office, the agent from the OIG confirmed that the OIG had never been contacted by the NPS or anyone else in the Department of [the] Interior with regard to my allegations of misconduct in Yosemite's Law Enforcement Office.

I subsequently learned in a meeting which took place on October 23, 1984 with this same OIG agent, that the direction to lie to me by having the park personnel officer approach me to elicit information under the guise of representing the OIG, took place under the direction of one of the Associate Regional Directors in the Western Regional Office.

On June 15 and 16, 1984, fully ten months after making my first reports to the NPS regional office, I met in secret at my home with two agents from the OIG. There, I provided them with details of my allegations as well as documents to support the charges and a list of suggested witnesses they could contact to further support my claims. From this point on, for the next six months, I engaged in no less than 22 separate meetings and/or phone conversations with agents from the OIG for the purpose of assisting them with this investigation. These include meetings with an agent from the U.S. Secret Service who was appraised [sic] of abuse of the imprest funds and payroll procedures. The bulk of these contacts were for the purpose of providing information to the OIG. They had requested that, where possible, I and another individual secure and/ or make copies of pertinent documents to which we had lawful access, which were then turned over to the OIG in support of the investigation.

However, some contacts were made for the purpose of requesting guidance from the OIG on how to proceed in the park, in light of the secrecy of their presence. At this point in time the NPS did not, in fact, know that the OIG had actually entered in to this investigation.

In the interim period the NPS did finally initiate an inquiry into this matter. Another captain from the USPP, John Crockett, was assigned to conduct interviews in the park in this regard.

On June 23, 1984 I met with Captain Crockett in my home. There, in a taped interview, in response to questioning, [I] advised that I had already reported the matter to the OIG, and preferred at this point to restrict my information to that office. This, then, was the first time the NPS actually learned that the OIG had become involved in the matter.

From approximately that point to the present I have been subject to repeated incidents of harassment. My wife, who also worked in the Law Enforcement Office, was physically confronted by the two primarily implicated parties; ordered by them to turn over her office keys; and ordered out of the office with the understanding that she could not return to work; this, under the pretense that she presented a security risk. I was on one occasion, by pre-arrangement with the OIG, to meet with the park's administrative officer. During this meeting, wherein I was to turn over evidence for him to seal and secure, he deviated entirely from procedures stipulated by the OIG. When I protested, citing instructions both he and I had received from the OIG, he stated that the OIG had no authority to conduct investigations in Yosemite without permission of the superintendent. He further threatened that I had better turn the evidence over to him anyway or he would have a dozen rangers hold me down and break into my house, if necessary, to get what he wanted. He added that it was my responsibility to obey all orders I was given by superiors, even if those orders were illegal.

There have been numerous other incidents wherein my reputation has been attacked by management, and/or my involvement in reporting this matter has been used as a basis for denying me training and employment opportunities.

[It] has now been over two years and two months since I first attempted to report misconduct in [the] Law Enforcement Office. It has now been one year and four months since the OIG began its investigation into this matter. And only now, after repeated inquiries to your office, Mr. Coelho, and to the offices of your colleagues, is the OIG's report making its way down the chain to Yosemite to await a response and corrective action.

I have not seen the OIG's report, so I have no way of knowing whether it actually addresses all the issues that were initially raised. I will wait until I have that opportunity before I comment on its completeness, objectivity, and treatment of my allegations and related conclusions. The treatment of the specific allegations is, at this point, a secondary concern. What now disturbs me most is the outrageous reluctance and resistance on the part of management which met my efforts to report and [to] have reviewed what I felt was entirely unprofessional and unethical conduct on the part of other government officials within that same agency and department. It appears to me that this lack of responsiveness to matters of internal misconduct goes far too high up the management ladder, and impeaches any credibility of claims of professionalism. I have been advised by officials of the Federal Criminal Investigator's Association that the delay in the OIG's response to this matter was at least a contributing factor in the recent dismissal of the Director of the Office of the Inspector General. If this claim is true, and any of my allegations are founded, then you as our elected representatives should be as outraged as I am. And you should take immediate steps to rectify these matters.

And that brings me to my final point.

The National Park Service has a long and proud history of public service and dedication to the protection of our public lands. Unfortunately, among its own ranks of people who work in this field, it is known for having an equally long history of resistance to the adoption of an effective, modern, and professional law enforcement program.

In discussing the passage of the National Park Service General Authorities Bill, Congress went on record as believing that law enforcement in the parks should be performed by NPS rangers (and not by the U.S. Park Police). This was stated in a statutory effort to perpetuate the long-standing tradition of the Ranger as the guardian of our public lands and the people who visit them. I believe this concept is a good one, and fully endorse its application. However, once again, I believe the Park Service has failed to come to terms with the full burden imposed upon them to carry out this mission. The parks are no longer the safe wilderness haven that they may have been twenty or thirty years ago. The crime rates experienced here are fully comparable to those found in virtually any other community with a similar day-to-day population. The crooks have come to the parks. This proposition is supported by the very fact that there was ever a need to pass the General Authorities Act. And it is further supported by the fact that there was ever a need to undertake a massive drug investigation in Yosemite. But I believe it is equally apparent, based upon my testimony here today, that something is not yet quite right, and that NPS management has not yet fully come to terms with what is required of them to fulfill their law enforcement and public safety mission.

I recognize that by speaking publicly here today, and by alerting you to the matters on which I have just given testimony, that the impact and credibility of Yosemite's special drug investigation may be seriously compromised. That is unfortunate. But in professional law enforcement, the ends do not justify the means. With a different posture on the part of NPS management, this compromise could have been avoided. With a different posture on the part of NPS management, I'm sure I wouldn't feel compelled to speak here today, at all.

The different posture I'm alluding to would be one of full and aggressive support for truly professional law enforcement as a bona' fide part of the field of ranger services. And incorporated into this posture must be an attendant aggressive commitment to a professional law enforcement ethic. I believe it is the lack of a commitment to this professional law enforcement ethic that gave rise to and has allowed the perpetuation of what I allege is misconduct on the part of some of Yosemite's senior law enforcement officials.

Steps must be undertaken to ensure that individuals who enter into a career as an NPS ranger do not view law enforcement as a mere collateral duty. We must ensure that this law enforcement responsibility is taken with deadly seriousness, and with the understanding that aggressive law enforcement is an integral part of the wider public safety mission with which the rangers are charged. As a part of this, we must ensure that our rangers as well as our managers are truly committed to a program whereby whenever conceivably possible, all laws are enforced, all the time, and for all people to the same levels of compliance. We must more fully assure that our rangers and Park Service managers do not enforce laws with preference based upon the "old buddy" system, and that similarly they do not enforce laws with excessive enthusiasm against personal enemies.

Specific steps which I believe must be undertaken include the creation of a new or modified federal civil service classification series for rangers which fully recognizes law enforcement and other emergency services such as SAR [search and rescue] and EMS [emergency medical services] as a legitimate and full-time professional endeavor. This series must carry with it attendant professional salary scale and enhanced 20-25 year retirement benefits such as afforded to virtually every other federal law enforcement officer in the country. Failure to include these professional benefits will result in the continuation of what is already a high attrition rate from the ranks of the rangers, as they flee to other agencies which more fully recognize and reward their professional law enforcement and public safety skills. By way of contrast, I cite the present OPM standards and definitions of a park ranger, which do not even recognize law enforcement and related public safety skills as warranting pay and grade beyond the meager GS-5 level.

I believe the suggestions I have made, along with a general scrutiny of our NPS management approach to law enforcement, would be a giant step forward in the direction of bringing true professionalism to NPS law enforcement operations. Additionally, by the creation of a truly valid

"Public Safety Ranger" series into existence, it would open up avenues for dedicated and professional law enforcement rangers to enter into the management ranks where their contributions could again be realized as the completion of a valid career ladder.

In closing, I'd like to make one final comment. Yosemite National Park and the National Park Service as a whole has in its field rangers some of the most dedicated and motivated employees in the entire federal workforce. They consistently demonstrate that they are among the most highly trained and highly skilled law enforcement and public safety officials to be found anywhere. As a group, we are immensely proud of the work we do. All I ask is that you make it possible for us to be equally proud of the agency for which we work.

The expertise is there. The longing for professionalism is there. All that is needed is your firm guidance to bring us to that end.

Index

A

Abell, Arthur "Butch" 143, 174, 223
Acadia National Park 15, 32, 107
Adam-12 79
Adams, Ansel 48, 56
Administrative History of Cuyahoga Valley National Recreation Area 159, 229, 234
Albright, Horace viii, 12, 17, 18, 40
American Land Rights Association (ALRA) 150-151, 224, 229, 234
"America's best idea" 3, 201, 258, 261
America's National Parks and Their Keepers 240, 254
Andrus, Cecil D. 153
Antiquities Act 31-32, 35
Archaeological Resources Protection Act (ARPA) 246
Arnold, Ron 46, 154, 234
Asheville Times 16
Assimilative Crimes Act 124-125
Audio Intelligence Device (AID) 120, 196-197
Audubon Society 61, 129, 199

B

Beal, Merrill 27, 34
Berkowitz, Paul D. v-ix, 6, 18, 35, 40, 82, 108, 110, 138-140, 142, 159, 161-177, 181, 182, 186-191, 195-196, 201-202, 211-213, 215, 222-223, 245, 254-256, 262-263
Berta, Richard 187-194, 197, 201, 205
Binnewies, Robert "Bob" 127-128, 147, 156, 160, 168, 170, 176, 179, 181-182, 184-199, 201-202, 206, 209, 211-212, 214-215, 218, 221-223, 227-229
Blake, Bill 144, 179, 190, 200
Blaze of Glory Society (BOGS) 98
body wire 1, 117, 120-123, 127-128, 196, 202, 208-209

Bonaparte, Charles J. 25
Boulder County Sheriff's Department 61, 67, 70, 112, 114, 145
Brady v. Maryland 111, 117
Brandeis, Louis D. 208-209, 217
Brick, Philip 46, 56
Bureau of Land Management (BLM) 22, 35
Burton, John L. 50, 54, 57, 153
Burton, Phillip 54, 153

C

Calhoun, Gil 88
California Chronicle 74
California Magazine 154, 155, 159
Cannon, Lou 153
Cape Codder, The 97
Cape Cod National Seashore 41-42, 97
Cape Hatteras National Seashore 103, 109
Carey, James 14, 107
Carlsbad Caverns 32
Case of the Indian Trader, The 82, 244-245, 254, 257
Cato Institute 46
Cawley, R. McGreggor ("Greg") 46, 56
Channel Islands National Seashore 163
Chapman, Howard H. 85, 94, 100, 107-109, 146, 156, 173, 184-186, 219, 223-224, 227
Chesapeake and Ohio National Historic Site 245
CHiPS 79
Chittenden, Hiram 27, 34
Christensen, Carl 95, 96, 108
Clark County Police and Sheriff's Academy 88, 107
Clark, Galen 74-75
Coconino Sun 14
Coelho, Tony 142, 156, 180-182, 185-187, 192, 224, 227, 268
Colby, William 78
Comey, James 242
concessions and concessionaires 45, 76, 78-82, 114, 157, 159
Connelly, Marshall "Scott" 1, 114-117,

272

127-128, 131, 133, 144, 156, 162-164, 175-176, 179, 185, 187-188, 191, 194-198, 202, 214, 216, 220, 222, 226-227, 264

Conness, John 74

Constitution (US) 3, 7, 19-20, 33, 44, 58, 73, 75, 111, 118, 123, 160, 192, 201-202, 208-210, 214, 217, 225, 232, 235, 261

Crater Lake National Park 19, 28

Crockett, John 131, 137-141, 173, 179, 207, 215, 217-218, 268

Cunningham, Terrance M. 242-243, 254-255

Curry Company 45, 80, 114-155, 117, 131, 133, 144, 156, 157, 214, 264

Curtin, John 78

Curtis, Ralph 137, 169, 188-189, 191

Cushman, Charles "Chuck" 125, 147-154, 159-160, 168, 176, 179, 180, 182, 189-191, 193-199, 201-202, 206, 212, 214-215, 217-218, 222, 224, 229-231, 233-234, 260

Cushman, Dwight 147, 148, 230

Cuyahoga Valley National Recreation Area 41, 47, 67, 153, 159, 229, 234

D

Daily News (Port Angeles) 154

Danigan, Danny P. 193, 202

Davis, Eliot 15

DeLashmutt, Harry 132-135, 137-139, 142, 162, 172, 173

Delaware Water Gap National Recreation Area 43

Denali (Mt. McKinley) 28

Denver Tribune 24, 235

Department of the Interior (DOI) 17, 22, 29, 31, 35, 52, 57-58, 87, 93-94, 97, 103, 107, 109-110, 118, 125, 130, 132-136, 138, 141, 145, 159, 171, 186, 194, 202, 205, 212-215, 217-218, 224, 226-227, 252, 255-256

Department of the Treasury 21, 33-34, 39

Devaney, Earl 226-227

Dickenson, Russell E. 184, 185

DOI-Office of the Inspector General (OIG) 87, 107, 109, 114, 118, 125, 134-137, 139, 141, 143, 145-146, 151, 156, 159-161, 163, 171-172, 174, 176, 179, 181, 183-184, 186-187, 189, 191-194, 197-198, 201-202, 205-221, 226-227, 244, 247-256, 261, 266-269

Douglas, Paul 64

Duel for the Dunes: Land Use Conflict on the Shores of Lake Michigan 151, 159

Dunraven, Earl of see Wyndham-Quinn

E

E&E News 247, 254-255

eavesdropping (bugging) viii, 1, 120-130, 137, 147, 155-156, 160-162, 167-170, 174-176, 179, 182-202, 210, 212, 214-215, 221-222, 224, 230, 242, 261

Effigy Mounds National Monument 246-247, 255

Enemies – A History of the FBI 24-25

Escobedo v. Illinois 111, 117

exclusive federal jurisdiction 20-21, 27, 93, 98, 114, 124-125, 141

F

Federal Bureau of Investigation (FBI) 15, 24-25, 34, 71, 95, 106, 108, 118, 175, 242, 245, 254, 262

Federal Land Policy Management Act (FLPMA) 22

Federal Law Enforcement Training Center (FLETC) 109, 114, 170, 191, 258

Feinstein, Diane 53-54, 58

Forest Reserve Act 30-31, 35

Foresta, Ron 41-42, 240, 254

Foust, Ray 201

Franklin, Kay 55, 151, 159

Fraternal Order of Police 18, 100, 109-110

fraud (land fraud) 19, 22-25, 30, 233

Freedom of Information Act (FOIA) 151-152, 161, 177, 191

Freemuth, John 236, 238-239, 254

Fresno Bee 145, 159, 178-179, 183-184, 186, 198, 202, 205, 211-212, 218, 221, 227

Frome, Michael 228, 234

Frontline 47, 56

G

Gaylor, Jack 30, 35

General Accounting Office (GAO) [Government Accountability Office, 2004] 160-182, 184-186, 189-192, 198, 205, 210-213, 216, 218, 220, 222-223

General Land Office (GLO) 21, 22, 31, 35

Gideon v. Wainwright 111, 117

Glacier National Park 28

Glen Canyon National Recreation Area 80

Golden Gate National Recreation Area 51, 57

Grand Canyon National Park viii, 14, 17, 19, 32, 35, 42, 61, 90, 225-226, 247, 249-251, 255, 256

Grand Teton National Park 15, 32, 42, 61, 108

Grazing Service, U.S 22

Great Smoky Mountains National Park 16, 36-37, 40

Greeley Tribune 24

Guidebook to American Values and our National Parks 252

H

Halleck, Charles A. 65

Hardy, Ed 156-159

Harrison Daily Times 16

Hartzog, George B. 153

Harvard Environmental Law Review 45, 56

Hearst, William Randolph 78

Helvarg, David 152, 159

Hess, Karl Jr. 46

High Country News 48, 56, 247, 255

Hinson, Norm 113-114, 132, 143-145, 185, 207, 215

Hodel, Donald 223, 227

Holland, Robert Perkins 37-39

Hollinrake, John Paul 193, 202

Homestead Act 22-23, 30-31, 35

Hot Springs National Park 14, 26

Hot Springs Reservation 26, 29

House Committee on Interior and Insular Affairs 57, 65, 93, 146

House Subcommittee on National Parks, Forests, and Public Lands 57, 146, 153, 156, 176-177, 179, 181, 194, 215, 222-224, 263

Hubbell Trading Post Investigation 82, 244-245, 254, 257

Hutchings, J.M. 33, 74-76, 81

Hutchison, Andy iii, 56, 95-96, 107-109, 119, 170, 191, 197

I

Independent Journal. 84

Indiana Dunes National Lakeshore v, 41, 45, 56, 61-63, 65-69, 72-75, 112, 114, 141, 147, 151, 153

Indian Country Today 260, 262

inholdings and inholders 1, 31, 35, 42-46, 49, 68, 74-75, 128, 137, 144, 147-153, 181, 196, 198, 201, 224, 229-231

International Association of Chiefs of Police 87, 242, 254-255, 262

J

Jackson, Andrew 25

Jarvis, Jon 57, 252-254, 256

Jensen, Jens 52

Johnson, Lyndon 41, 56, 57, 66, 125, 235

Johnson, Robert Underwood 77

Johnson Oyster Company 47-58, 210, 217

K

Kastenmeier, Robert 181

Katahdin Times, The 155

Kentucky National Park Commission 37

Kiesling, Mark 71, 73

King, Martin Luther Jr. 242, 254

Kings Canyon 28
Kleppe v. New Mexico 21, 33
Kreis, Wes iii, 89, 95-96, 107-108
Kumorek, Jeffrey 71

L

Lacey Act 28, 34
Lake Mead National Recreation Area 16, 61, 88, 90, 91, 103
Lambert, John F. Jr. 40, 45, 56
Land and Water Conservation Fund (LWCF) 41
Laney, Jim 156, 190, 196
LaPorte, Frankie 71
Lauzon, Bert 14
Law of Nature: Park Rangers in Yosemite Valley 18, 202, 228, 234
Le Conte, Joseph 75-76
Lehman, Richard 156-157, 180, 182, 224
Lennox, Dave 130-132, 138-139, 141, 172
Lewiston Daily Sun 15
Light v. United States 21, 33
Lincoln, Abraham 74
Lindsay, John 111
Loach, James "Jim" 144, 147, 154-156, 159, 176, 185, 189-191, 194-198, 200, 202, 214, 222-223
Los Angeles Times 182, 186, 222-223, 227-228, 234, 235
Louisiana Purchase 25
Low, Frederick F. 33, 41, 55, 75, 81
Lunsford, Steve 135-137, 140, 142-143, 146, 161-163, 168-171, 174-176, 184, 187-189, 191, 205-206, 216

M

Mammoth Cave National Park 36-37, 39-40
Mapp v. Ohio 111, 117
Mariposa Gazette 74, 83, 183, 186
Martinelli, Thomas J. 208, 210, 217
Mather, Stephen 62, 63
McClaughery, John 153
McCloskey, Paul "Pete" 53, 57
Merced Sun-Star 158, 186, 211-213, 218

Mesa Verde 28, 245
Mesterharm, James 71
Miller, George 157
Mills, William H. 77, 78
Miranda v. Arizona 111, 118
Mitchell, John H. 25, 103, 109
Montalbano, Dave 107, 109, 170
Moomaw, Jack 104, 110
Morrow, Duncan 184
Mott, William 146, 182, 184-186, 222-223
Mount Rainier 19, 28, 94, 108, 226
Muir, John 75, 76, 77, 78
Music Corporation of America (MCA) 79-81, 158-159, 180, 221

N

Natchez Trace Parkway 88-89, 103, 109
National Academy of Sciences 45, 53-54, 56, 58
National Environmental Policy Act 58, 150, 210
National Inholders Association 46, 128, 137, 147, 150-153, 196, 198, 201, 224, 229
National Parks Conservation Association 55
National Park Service (NPS) iii, vii-ix, 3-7, 11-18, 27, 29-30, 36-37, 39, 41-45, 47-49, 52-57, 61-64, 67-70, 79-82, 84-85, 87-110, 113, 115-116, 130, 132-137, 141-156, 158-159, 164, 166, 170-172, 176, 179-180, 182, 184-186, 192, 194-195, 197-202, 205- 211, 213-217, 219-233, 236-248, 250-270
National Park System Advisory Board 147, 152, 153, 159, 198
National Parks Traveler 82, 253-256
Newsweek 43, 48, 56, 58
New York Magazine 251, 256
New York Post 251, 256
New York Times 118-119, 213, 218, 227
Nixon, Richard 41, 80, 112, 240
Noble Cause Corruption v, vii, 205, 208-210, 217

Northwest Ordinances 19, 33
Nugent, Jim 24
NYPD 111

O

Office of the Inspector General (OIG) *see* DOI-Office of the Inspector General
Office of Personnel Management (OPM) 132, 143, 265, 270
Office of Special Counsel 245, 255
Ohlfs, Jeff 11, 14, 17
Olmstead v. United States 208, 217
Omnibus Crime Control and Safe Streets Act of 1968 122
Olympic National Park 19, 28, 32, 234
Orsi, Richard 56, 76-77, 82

P

Palisades, 100,000 Acres in 100 Years 221
Palmer, Tim 80, 82, 125, 129, 228, 234
Pardee, George C. 77
Parker, Homer "Dick" 38
Parks in Peril 241, 254
Pashayan, Charles "Chip" 180-181, 201
Patrick, Ken 84-87, 91, 93-94, 96, 98- 99, 102, 106-109, 243
Pelican Island 31
Phillips, W. Hallet 122, 125, 231-232, 235
Pickering, James 28, 34, 235
Point Reyes National Seashore 47, 49-51, 56,-58, 84, 88, 107, 210, 230, 234
Police Magazine 225
Pribilof Islands 26, 34
Property Clause 21, 33, 75
professionalism (defined) 112-113
Public Broadcasting System (PBS) 47, 56
Public Employees for Environmental Responsibility (PEER) 202, 246, 254-255, 258, 262

R

Ranger Image Task Force 94-96, 100, 108
Rasker, Ray 46
Reagan, Ronald 73, 147, 153, 159, 184, 223, 224

Recollections of a Rocky Mountain Ranger 104, 110
Reed, Nathaniel P. 65, 118
Rethinking Urban Parks: Public Space and Cultural Diversity 41
Reynolds, J.T. ix, 5, 107
Richardson, James G. 81
Ridge, Joseph M. 37
Rocky Mountain National Park 23, 29, 104
Roosevelt, Theodore 24, 25, 31-32, 35, 78
Rose, Gene 145, 179, 186, 202, 205, 211, 218, 222
Rothlein, Steve 208, 217
Roush, Jon 46, 64, 65
Ryan, P.J. 3

S

sagebrush rebellion 33, 154, 229, 233
San Francisco Chronicle 57, 84, 158-159, 182, 186, 217
Sargent, Mary 81, 135-136, 142, 171, 216, 223
Schaeffer, Norma 151, 159
Sellars, Richard West 242, 254
Sequoia National Park 17, 19, 28, 34, 56, 77
Serpico, Frank 111, 118, 258
Setting Priorities for Land Conservation 45, 55, 56
Shackelton, Leland "Lee" 18, 113-116, 121, 125, 131-133, 137, 144, 156, 162, 165-167, 169-170, 173, 175-176, 179, 185, 188, 191, 194, 196-198, 202, 206-209, 212, 214-216, 218-220, 221-222, 226-227, 253, 264
Sheehan, Bess 64, 202
Shenandoah National Park 36-37, 40, 82, 256
Sierra Club 50, 53, 56-57, 61, 76-78, 152, 159, 234
Sierra Nevada; A Mountain Journey, The 80, 82, 228
Sierra (TV show) 79, 81, 221
Sleeping Bear Dunes National Lakeshore 67, 153

Smith, Dave 137, 140, 188-189
Solicitor (Office of the) 50, 52, 57-58, 241, 252
Stegner, Wallace 3, 4
Student Conservation Association 61, 148
Sunset Limited: The Southern Pacific Railroad and the Development of the American West 1850-1930 76, 82
Supremacy Clause (to the Constitution) 21
S.W.A.T. Magazine 225

T

Taylor Grazing Act 22
Terry v. Ohio 111, 118
This Blue Hollow: Estes Park, the Early Years, 1859-1915 28, 34, 235
Timber Culture Act 22, 31
Times of Northwest Indiana, The 71
Townsley, Forest 12-14, 17, 92, 108-109
Tunney, John 50, 57

U

U.S. Cavalry 28-30, 34, 37, 235
U.S. Forest Service and national forests 26, 28, 30-31, 35, 42, 82, 93, 233
U.S. Park Police (USPP) 55, 108, 130, 141, 217-218, 266-268
U.S. Secret Service 25, 114, 117, 119, 137, 173, 188, 191, 215, 267
U.S. v. Grimaud 21, 33
U.S. v. Hall 125

V

Vento, Bruce 153, 156, 158, 160, 174-176, 178-182, 184-186, 190, 194, 198, 210-211, 218, 222-224
Visclosky, Pete 73, 181

W

Walker, Ron 42, 80, 240
War Against the Greens, The 152
Washington Monthly 157, 159
Washington Post 153, 255
Watkins, Carleton 74

Watt, James 58, 151-152, 234
Wawona 45, 81, 125, 144, 147-150, 180, 189-190, 195-196, 198, 224, 229
Webb, Del 80, 82, 107
Weiner, Tim 24, 34
Wells, Vernon 36, 40
Wendt, William "Bill" 131-132, 141, 187, 201
Whalen, Bill 44, 108, 128, 150
Whiskeytown National Recreation Area 201, 224
White, James 208, 210
White, Lowell 25, 69, 132, 153, 171, 208, 209, 210, 214, 221, 227
Wilderness Act 46, 58
Wilderness Society 46
Williamson, John H. 25
Wilson, William G. 85-87, 99, 105, 107, 109
Wolf in the Garden: The Land Rights Movement and the New Environmental Debate, A 46, 56
Woodring, Sam 12, 14, 17, 92
Wornum, Michael 51, 57
Wyndham-Quinn, William Thomas (Fourth Earl of Dunraven) 23, 24

Y

Yates, Sid 125, 150, 181
Yellowstone National Park 12, 14, 17, 26-29, 34, 42, 82, 97-98, 226, 231, 235, 251, 255
Yellowstone National Park, The (book) 27
Yosemite Grant 26, 74, 75, 77, 78, 231
Yosemite Mafia ii, vii, ix, 92, 113, 114, 199, 221, 223, 226, 229, 236, 237, 239, 254
Yosemite National Park xx vii, 12-14, 18-19, 26, 29-30, 34-35, 42, 45, 48, 56, 72, 74-76, 77, 78, 79, 81-84, 87-88, 91-93, 106, 113-118, 124, 125, 127-129, 131-132, 135-137, 143-149, 152, 156-159, 164, 170, 177-179, 183-187, 190, 198-202, 205, 209, 211, 213, 214, 219, 220-231, 234-239, 244-245, 251, 253-254, 256-257, 261, 263-271

Yosemite Natural History Association
    (YNHA) 206
Yosemite Park and Curry Company 114,
    156, 157, 158, 182, 208
Yosemite Riot ix, 82, 83, 87, 88, 91, 92,
    93, 201
Yount, Harry 28, 34, 109
Your Yosemite. A Threatened Public Treasure
    221

Z

Zumwalt, Daniel K. 77